Fishing
Georgia

Kevin Dallmier

FALCON®

HELENA, MONTANA

A **FALCON** GUIDE ®

Falcon® Publishing is continually expanding its list of recreational guidebooks. All books include detailed descriptions, accurate maps, and all the information necessary for enjoyable trips. You can order extra copies of this book and get information and prices for other Falcon® guidebooks by writing Falcon, P.O. Box 1718, Helena, MT 59624 or calling toll-free 1-800-582-2665. Also, please ask for a free copy of our current catalog. Visit our website at www.Falcon.com or contact us by e-mail at falcon@falcon.com.

Front and back cover photos by Soc Clay.

All inside photos by Kevin Dallmier. Illustrations by Chris Armstrong.

Library of Congress Cataloging-in-Publication Data

Dallmier, Kevin, 1968-
    Fishing Georgia / Kevin Dallmier
        p.   cm.
    ISBN 1-56044-777-X
    1. Fishing—Georgia—Guidebooks. 2. Georgia—Guidebooks.
    I. Title.
    SH 485 .D36 2000
    799.1'09758—dc21

CAUTION

Outdoor recreational activities are by their very nature potentially hazardous. All participants in such activities must assume the responsibility for their own actions and safety. The information contained in this guidebook cannot replace sound judgment and good decision-making skills, which help reduce risk exposure, nor does the scope of this book allow for disclosure of all the potential hazards and risks involved in such activities.

Learn as much as possible about the outdoor recreational activities in which you participate, prepare for the unexpected, and be cautious. The reward will be a safer and more enjoyable experience.

 Text pages printed on recycled paper.

Contents

Map Legend

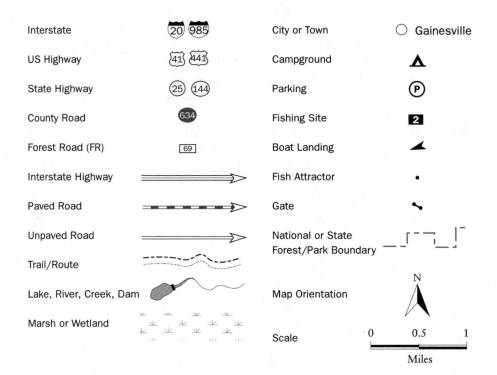

Interstate	20 985	City or Town	○ Gainesville
US Highway	41 441	Campground	▲
State Highway	25 144	Parking	Ⓟ
County Road	634	Fishing Site	2
Forest Road (FR)	69	Boat Landing	◣
Interstate Highway	⟹	Fish Attractor	•
Paved Road	⟹	Gate	⌐
Unpaved Road	⟹	National or State Forest/Park Boundary	
Trail/Route			
Lake, River, Creek, Dam		Map Orientation	N
Marsh or Wetland		Scale	0 0.5 1 Miles

Overview Map

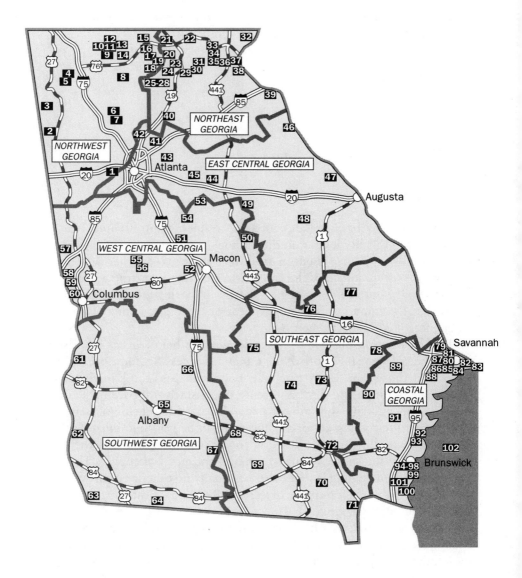

For Lisa, who patiently tends the home fires while I am off indulging my passion, and Kali, who I hope someday will continue in her father's footsteps and be fascinated by Mother Nature and all her creations, big and small.

Preface

The contents of this book are the cumulative result of many lifetimes of angling. Not only does this book contain the author's personal knowledge, but also a wealth of information passed on from one angler to another with the sole purpose of helping someone else catch fish. Far from being the notorious liars they are made out to be, most anglers delight in sharing their knowledge in the hopes that by doing so, they might vicariously live someone else's angling experiences in addition to their own.

The information provided here is designed to help readers increase their angling knowledge and improve their angling success. In addition, the author hopes that those who learn from this book will pass the knowledge on to others. Many times, the thrill and sense of satisfaction of seeing a friend or family member catch fish is almost as good as catching them yourself.

The first great thing about angling is it can be very humbling. Just when you begin to swell with pride thinking you have it all figured out, the fish will show you why the sport is called "fishing" and not "catching." The second great thing about angling is that there is virtually no other pastime where even if you fail at the implicit purpose of the activity, which is catching fish, it is still so utterly fun and relaxing.

Anglers who think they know it all are fooling themselves and probably are often made a fool of by the fish. There is always room for more information about other fish species, different fishing techniques, and new locations to try. Georgia's aquatic resources are so extensive and varied that nobody can possibly learn everything there is to know about fishing in Georgia. Therefore, this book really contains just a sample of what Georgia has to offer the angler. However, a person who dedicates a lifetime to trying to learn everything about fishing Georgia will find that it was indeed a lifetime well spent.

Introduction

GEORGIA—FROM THE MOUNTAINS TO THE COAST, SOMETHING FOR EVERY ANGLER

Encompassing about 59,441 square miles of forests, broad coastal plains, and the southern terminus of the Blue Ridge Mountains, Georgia is the largest state east of the Mississippi River. The state has been blessed with abundant and diverse aquatic resources including more than 4,000 miles of trout streams, 12,000 miles of warm-water streams, 500,000 acres of impoundments, and 100 miles of Atlantic Ocean coastline.

Georgia waters are home to many popular sport fish and the largemouth bass is at the top of the list. Although the largemouth may reign as king of Georgia sport fish, the crown is not undisputed. Striped bass, rainbow trout, bluegill, and channel catfish, to name a few, are all species that have a dedicated cadre of anglers who faithfully pursue them in hopes of catching a trophy specimen.

Georgia has a well-deserved reputation for excellent fishing. After all, the world-record largemouth bass was caught here from Montgomery Lake, a small backwater slough off the Ocmulgee River, more than 60 years ago. And it appears that the record will stand for many more years. Anglers love to fish Georgia for many reasons including the natural beauty of the state and the temperate climate, but mostly for the unrivaled fishing of the Peach State.

Although often overlooked because of the vast opportunities for fresh-water fishing, Georgia's coast offers fine saltwater angling. Spotted seatrout, king mackerel, flounder, sheepshead, red drum, and many other species are available in Georgia's Atlantic waters. Georgia's coast is relatively undeveloped, and must look nearly the same today as it did in 1733 when General James Oglethorpe colonized the state as a settlement for poor and religiously persecuted Englishmen.

Georgia's aquatic resources are rich in abundance, diversity, and history. From mountain trout streams to blackwater coastal rivers, from huge hydro-power reservoirs to small backwater sloughs, from intensively managed state Public Fishing Areas to pristine wilderness streams, Georgia offers something for every angler.

Georgia Weather

Essential to successfully dealing with Georgia's weather is being prepared for a range of possibilities. Weather plays a significant role in the success or failure of a fishing trip. Weather affects fish behavior and the angler's degree of comfort.

Elevations range from sea level to 4,784 feet, and Georgia spans approximately 4.5 degrees of latitude, so the weather in Georgia can be wildly different depending on your location in the state. It is not uncommon for the coast and south Georgia to experience a balmy winter day while snow falls in the north Georgia mountains.

1

Georgia is the meeting ground for tropical weather systems originating from the Gulf of Mexico and cooler weather systems originating in the Great Plains and Midwest. When warm meets cool, precipitation usually results. On average, Georgia receives more than 50 inches of rainfall annually, with the mountains averaging more than 75 inches. Violent weather often appears with little warning. If storms are approaching, get off the water and take shelter. If you are trapped in an open area, lay as flat as possible to avoid becoming the highest point and increasing the likelihood of a deadly lightning strike. In wooded areas, take shelter on low ground and avoid dead limbs and trees that could fall and cause injury or death.

Especially in the heat of summer, approaching fronts often cause fish to go on a feeding spree. Under these conditions, the fishing may be so good that leaving is hard, but use good common sense and get off the water before conditions become dangerous.

Spring cold fronts are the bane of all anglers. Although fish are usually active immediately before the front's passage, the high pressure, cooler temperatures, and cloudless skies that follow often cause fish to be inactive and hold tightly to cover. To be successful under these conditions, persistence and presentation are the keys. You must make sure your bait is getting right in front of the fish's nose and stays there long enough to coax the fish into striking. Cold-front fish are not going to chase bait; it has to be in their face and easy to catch. Before the actual passage of the front there is often a strong north or west wind. Anglers can use the wind to their advantage. A strong wind that has been consistently blowing from the same direction will push the baitfish onto windward shores and points. Where the baitfish go, predators are soon to follow. Although fishing in the wind can make casting, presentation, and boat control more difficult, the rewards can be tremendous. On any lake, especially Georgia's large reservoirs, high winds can cause dangerous waves. Make sure your craft and seamanship is up to the task of handling rough waters.

Spring weather requires dressing in layers. A trip that begins with a frosty morning boat ride can turn out to be unseasonably warm by the end of the day. By dressing in light layers topped off with a windbreaker, anglers can quickly adjust their clothing to match the conditions.

Georgia's summer heat and humidity are oppressive and can quickly lead to heat exhaustion or heat stroke. To guard against harmful ultraviolet rays and prevent sunburn, anglers should keep themselves covered in lightweight clothing or sun block. Many anglers have discovered that fishing at night offers relief from the daytime heat and crowds and is also better fishing. In the summer, fish are active all night and will strike with gusto.

When the water starts to cool in the fall, fish begin to feed aggressively to build up their energy reserves to help them make it through the coming winter. Although often overlooked by anglers, autumn is perhaps the best time of year to fish. Moderate temperatures, stable weather, steady water levels, and the desire to fatten up for winter all cause fish to move shallow from their deep summer haunts and feed aggressively.

Although Georgia winters can bring snow and subfreezing temperatures, they are usually short-lived. A hardy angler can fish year-round in Georgia. Especially for crappie, the cold weather can mean the best fishing of the year. Cold-weather fish are lethargic but concentrated. Most fish will be found at the first good deep-water holding area out from their normal shallow haunts. Channel ledges often provide this type of winter structure. Once fish are located, a slow, careful presentation is best. Since the cold temperatures slow the fish's metabolism, they do not need to feed as often, but they do still feed. A careful presentation right in front of a fish's nose will result in strikes. During winter, anglers should downsize their baits and use light line. Because of the generally clear water, wintertime fish require a subtle presentation of a small bait.

Clothing

Nothing will take the fun out of a fishing trip faster than being miserably hot or freezing cold, no matter how good the fish are biting. The best way to dress for a fishing trip in any season is to wear light layers of clothing that can easily be taken off or put on as needed.

During cool weather, the first layer should be a set of quality thermal underwear that will provide warmth and wick perspiration away from the body. On top of the thermal underwear should go as many layers of clothing as the day's worst case scenario might require. Since most body heat is lost through the head, a knit cap that provides complete coverage is critical. Although gloves make handling your tackle difficult, sometimes conditions demand their use. I prefer to wear knit wool "fishing gloves" that have open fingers down to the first knuckle. These gloves allow you to tie knots and perform other detailed work without completely removing the gloves. In addition, the wool retains its insulating properties even when the gloves are wet.

Often the most important piece of clothing to have along on a winter fishing trip is a quality rain suit. Obviously, a rain suit will help keep you dry if it rains, but more commonly it can offer protection from the wind. A stiff north wind blowing over water will set your teeth chattering like nothing else can.

Hypothermia, brought on by the core body temperature reaching dangerously low levels, can be a real threat to the unprepared angler, especially if a sudden rainstorm or unexpected plunge into the water soaks you to the bone. Wool is a material that continues to provide insulation even when wet. Always carry a spare set of dry clothing, especially if fishing from a boat. To be of any value though, the clothing must be easily available in an emergency. All the dry clothing in the world will not help you if it's stored in the vehicle back at the launch ramp or trailhead.

Although summer conditions do not have as much life-threatening potential as winter conditions, some thought should still be given on what to wear on any given day. Lightweight cotton long-sleeved shirts and pants protect the body from the sun's damaging rays while allowing perspiration to rapidly evaporate providing a cooling effect. If shorts and short-sleeved shirts are preferred, be sure to use plenty of sun block on any exposed skin to protect against damaging ultraviolet rays. A wide-brimmed, light-colored cotton hat is much more effective than a baseball-style cap at keeping the sun off the neck and face. Finally, the trusty rain suit should still accompany you on summer trips. Although the first few drops of rain may feel refreshing on a hot day, after a few minutes of steady downpour, the protection offered by the rain suit will be greatly appreciated.

Rounding out the clothing worn by the well-equipped angler is a quality pair of polarized sunglasses. Polarized sunglasses cut the glare reflected off the water, thus reducing headaches and fatigue, and enabling the angler to better see fish, stumps, rock piles, and other objects under the surface. Nonpolarized sunglasses darken without reducing glare. Also, invest in a quality pair of sunglasses from a reputab™le manufacturer. Cheap sunglasses have poor quality lenses and can cause headaches during extended wear. If you wear glasses, invest in a pair of prescription polarized sunglasses and you will find that they become the most indispensable item of your angling equipment.

Protection from the Sun

Research has shown that long-term exposure to the sun's ultraviolet rays poses a serious health risk. Anglers are especially prone to overexposure since they not only receive direct rays, but also those reflected off the water. Any skin not covered by clothing and exposed to the sun should receive applications of sun block periodically throughout the day. Consider SPF 15 sun block at a minimum. Do not forget the lips; apply lip balm with at least a 30 SPF rating.

Water Safety

Boating in Georgia is very safe, but unfortunately accidents do happen. Accidents are usually caused by lack of common sense and poor judgment. Georgia law dictates that all vessels be equipped with a wearable personal flotation device (PFD) for each person on board. In addition, one Type IV throwable flotation device must be on board every boat. All flotation devices must be readily accessible, in good and serviceable condition, legibly marked with the U.S. Coast Guard approved number, and of appropriate size for the occupants.

Many boating fatalities could have been prevented if the victims were wearing PFDs. Although the law does not require adults to wear PFDs, Georgia law does require that children under age 10 must wear an appropriate-sized PFD when the vessel is underway, unless the child is within a fully enclosed, roofed cabin. Regardless of age, PFDs are just a good idea and the life saved may be your own.

So that all can safely enjoy our waterways, boaters should always follow the U.S. Coast Guard watercraft "rules of the road." As more people discover the pleasures of boating, Georgia waterways are becoming more crowded. It is imperative that all boaters know the rules for safe operation of their craft and follow them religiously.

The most important decision a boater can make is not to operate a boat under the influence of alcohol. Booze and boating do not mix! Even one drink coupled with the fatiguing effects of sun, glare, and constant motion on the water can lead to poor decision-making abilities and slow reactions. Safely operating a boat requires all the concentration a person can muster and fast reaction times, especially in rough or crowded conditions. Please do not endanger lives by drinking and boating.

Another threat to anglers is fast or rising water. Areas below dams are subject to very sudden increases in current and water level. Always heed any warning signs and audible alerts of rising waters. Do not fish in an area that would make a retreat to higher ground slow and difficult.

When wading swift, slippery streams, felt-bottomed wading boots and a wading staff will provide good traction and extra stability. Wear a wading belt to prevent your waders from filling with water during a spill. Wearing a PFD is never a bad idea, even while wading, and is required by law on some Georgia rivers and streams.

Georgia Wildlife

Georgia wildlife poses little threat to humans. Using common sense, an individual can spend a lifetime outdoors in Georgia and never have a problem.

Six species of poisonous snakes are present in Georgia. The eastern coral snake, cottonmouth (water moccasin), copperhead, eastern diamondback rattlesnake, timber rattlesnake (commonly called the canebrake rattlesnake in parts of Georgia), and the pygmy rattlesnake are all found in certain areas of Georgia and some are distributed statewide. Every Georgia county is home to at least one poisonous snake species. Snakes are much more scared of you than you are of them, and as long as they are not startled and an escape route is available, they will likely slither out of your way. The cottonmouth, however, is very defensive and will more quickly take offense to sharing the outdoors with you than do many other snakes. Cottonmouths are found only in certain parts of the state, and every snake in or near the water is not necessarily a water moccasin. Various species of nonpoisonous water snakes (*Neurodea* sp.) are very common across the state, but pose no serious threat to anglers. Like the cottonmouth, though, water snakes are defensive about their territory and will strike at anyone annoying or harassing them.

The best way to avoid being bitten by a snake is not to put your hands or feet anywhere you cannot see, especially around rocks, piles of old timber, etc. If you do have the misfortune of being bitten by a snake, it is best to forget the old "cut and suck" method, tourniquets, and any folklore you may have heard about treating a snake bite. The best treatment for a snakebite in most cases is right in your pocket—a set of car keys. If bitten, seek medical attention as quickly as possible, but do not panic. Unless you are on foot in a very remote location, there should be plenty of time to receive medical attention before any truly debilitating symptoms begin to occur. Keep in mind a fair percentage of snakebites are "dry" and do not result in venom actually being injected; however, to be on the safe side, always seek medical attention.

Other than poisonous snakes, the only other Georgia wildlife that could cause a serious threat would be big-game species like black bears and white-tailed deer. As with snakes, bears and deer will likely be long gone before you even realize they were nearby. If you treat these animals with respect for the wildness they represent, there should be no problem. Most attacks are a result of people feeding wild animals and assuming they have become docile pets, when in fact they are still wild creatures that will do whatever necessary to defend themselves when threatened. To prevent bears raiding a camp, all food should be kept in airtight containers and in a separate location from the campsite.

Encountering a rabid animal in the wild is unlikely, but it is a possibility. Small mammals such as raccoons, skunks, and bats are most likely to carry rabies, but any animal, domestic or wild, is a risk. Common sense is the rule. If you see an animal that is acting unnaturally or is not afraid of you, keep a wide distance. Do not handle or closely approach animals that seem sick or injured.

By using common sense, there is nothing to fear from Georgia's wildlife. In fact, if you quietly observe from a safe distance, you will find all of Georgia's wildlife to be benign creatures who simply want to go about their daily business of survival, and observing them will add much to your enjoyment of Georgia's outdoors.

Insect Pests

Because of Georgia's temperate climate, there are only a few months that the angler will be totally free of the scourge of some pesky, irritating insect. The cooler months do offer some relief, but on all but the coldest days there are always a few insects around to irritate you.

A whole variety of flying, biting pests are waiting to draw the blood of an unprepared angler. Mosquitoes, deer flies, black flies, and sand gnats are some of the worst offenders. All these insects will inflict a bite that is either painful, itches, or both. Wearing long pants, a long sleeve shirt, and a cap coupled with an application of an insect repellent containing diethyl toluamide (DEET) will go a long way toward keeping most flying insects at bay.

The members of the mite family commonly known as "chiggers" or "red bugs" will make the careless angler wish he or she had never ventured away from the pavement. Chiggers are almost invisible to the naked eye and are found in low-lying grassy areas around the edges of ponds, streams, and other damp places. Chiggers burrow into the skin and produce excretions that cause a large welt to form. The welt will itch intensely for days. At the time of exposure, you will not even know you are being bitten. Twelve hours later though, the urge to scratch the welts until they bleed is almost irresistible.

The problem with chiggers is that on a one-on-one basis, the itch would be bearable. Unfortunately, chiggers love company and if you escape an exposure to chiggers with less than a dozen bites, consider yourself lucky. Chiggers prefer to burrow into the skin in areas where there is a constriction like the sock cuff, the waistband, and other more private areas.

An aerosol repellent containing DEET applied around the socks, pant cuffs, and shirt cuffs will help keep chiggers away. The best prevention is trying to avoid walking through damp grassy areas if possible. Sometimes taking a few extra steps on higher ground en route to your destination is well worth it for preventing the maddening itch of chiggers.

Many tick species are found in Georgia, including those that are carriers for Lyme disease. Several steps can be taken to reduce the chances of a tick bite. As with chiggers, the best prevention is to avoid the areas ticks favor. Ticks hitch a ride on a host and begin to burrow their mouthparts into the skin for a meal of the host's blood. Staying on well-cleared trails and in open areas will reduce exposure. DEET has been proven somewhat effective at deterring ticks, but repellent containing permanone is much more effective and should be considered in heavily tick-infested areas. Permanone should only be applied to clothing, not bare skin. It is up to you to weigh the risks of prevention versus the risks of attack, and make your own decision about what steps are reasonable for each situation.

Wearing light-colored clothing with the pants tucked into the socks will make spotting ticks before they get a chance to attach much easier. Anytime you have been outdoors in Georgia, especially in the summer, always thoroughly check yourself for ticks periodically during the day and when returning home. The longer a tick is attached, the greater the chance for transmission of disease.

Other insects you are likely to encounter are bees, wasps, yellow jackets, and hornets. Of these, hornets are the most aggressive and deliver the most painful sting. Anglers should be especially wary of hornets. Hornets build a large gray cone-shaped "paper" nest in trees or shrubs, often around or overhanging water. Especially when wading streams with overgrown banks, keep a careful eye out for hornet nests and give them a wide berth lest you disturb them and feel their wrath. Boat anglers should also be wary when casting toward overgrown banks. Approaching the bank to retrieve an errant plug that overshot its mark may bring a lot more than you expected if a hornet's nest is nearby. Any individual who is allergic to stings from bees, wasps, etc. should always carry the appropriate medication with them when venturing outdoors. It may save your life.

Not only does fishing from a boat or wading allow better presentations to the fish, being in or on the water puts you out of range of all the creepy-crawly insect pests. Even many winged pests prefer to stay in the shady areas near the shore instead of out over open water. To the unprepared, insects can turn a good fishing trip into a miserable one. A few preventive measures can keep insect pests at a tolerable level.

Take a Kid Fishing

A love and appreciation of the outdoors is one of the best gifts an adult can give a child. It is a gift that will last them a lifetime. When taking a boy or girl fishing, remember that the prime goal is to have fun, whether or not that actually involves catching any fish. Fishing for bream, bullheads, or some other abundant fish species is a great way to start a child off on the right foot. Kids want action and they want it now. Save the bass and trout fishing for when the child has mastered the basic skills of fishing and has learned patience and persistence.

When taking a child fishing, always remember comfort is very important. Take appropriate clothing, sun block, plenty of food and drinks, and let the child do as he or she will. Do not be surprised if after 10 unproductive minutes the child is ready to move on to chasing dragonflies along the shoreline. When a fish is eventually caught, the child's full attention will be gained again, and he or she will likely be ready for another go at catching a fish all by himself or herself. If you take a kid fishing, the purpose of the trip should be for the child to catch fish, not the adult. Many adults become so distracted by catching fish themselves that the child's needs go virtually unnoticed. However, once you have your first good experience with kids' fishing, you may find you get more enjoyment from watching a child catch a fish than if you had caught it yourself.

Kids' fishing should be kept simple at first. Little fingers are not suited for tasks like tying complicated knots, thumbing a baitcasting reel, or executing a perfect roll cast with a fly rod. A simple spin-casting or spinning outfit, a bobber, a few hooks, some pinch-on weights, and bait are all a child needs to have a wonderful fishing trip. However, do not buy a budding angler low-quality gear. Poorly designed and constructed fishing gear is difficult to use and may frustrate the child to the point that he or she becomes turned off by the sport. However, a child does not need the latest, greatest gear with all the bells and whistles. Instead, he or she needs solid, functional equipment that will serve him or her well during many youthful forays into the great outdoors.

Teaching children to fish is a gift that will provide them with a lifetime of pleasure.

Respect Your Catch

There is absolutely nothing wrong with harvesting your catch within the limits set by laws and regulations. However, many anglers derive great satisfaction from rewarding a fish's valiant struggle by granting the fish its life and returning it to the water to fight again another day.

Whether or not to harvest your catch is a personal decision. There are several factors to keep in mind as you make your decisions on a case by case basis. In some instances, harvest is an effective tool used by fisheries managers to improve the fish population. Other times, especially on heavily fished water or in very infertile streams and lakes, if every angler harvested every fish caught regardless of size, the fishing would likely decline. Another factor to keep in mind is that fish mortality is often compensatory. It is a fact of nature that a certain percentage of a population is going to die every year, whatever the reason. Often, the percentage of the population harvested by anglers never exceeds the percentage that dies naturally of old age or disease. With compensatory mortality, until angler harvest exceeds natural mortality, the effect of harvest on the population is minimal. Angler harvest simply makes use of fish that would otherwise die a natural death and go to waste.

If you decide to harvest some fish, respect your catch. An individual who harvests fish simply to show them off to friends and neighbors and then throws the fish away is considered unethical by most anglers. If you harvest fish, know what you are going to do with them before leaving the lake. A stringer of fish hauled around all evening looking for someone willing to take them is not going to be of much value as table fare. For best eating, fish should be immediately placed on ice and cleaned and dressed as quickly as possible. If a fish dinner is planned in the next few days, the fish can be kept in water in the refrigerator; otherwise, completely submerge the fish in water and immediately place in the freezer. Fish frozen in water will taste best if thawed and prepared within 6 months.

If you do decide to practice catch-and-release, handle the fish carefully to increase its chances of survival. Do not touch the fish with dry hands; doing so will disturb the fish's protective slime coat that helps prevent infection from parasites and diseases. Slip the fish gently back into the water, do not toss it 10 feet in the air and halfway across the pond. If the fish has swallowed the hook, simply cut the line. Trying to disgorge a swallowed hook will cause more damage than simply cutting the line and letting stomach acids dissolve the hook away. Avoid touching the fish's gills. The gills are very delicate tissue and easily damaged. A fish bleeding from the gills has a very slim chance of survival and should be harvested if legal to do so.

Be an ethical angler and respect your catch. Even in the face of humankind's negligence, Mother Nature does a wonderful job, so respect what she has given us to enjoy.

Georgia Fishing Regulations

Georgia fishing regulations have been kept as simple as possible while still meeting the fisheries management goals of the Georgia Wildlife Resources

Division. The standard fishing regulations apply to all public waters across the state with just a few site-specific exceptions, including the eight state-managed Public Fishing Areas, which have a different set of standard regulations. Anglers unfamiliar with fishing Georgia need to study the annual *Georgia Sport Fishing Regulations* pamphlet to learn what the regulations are, and whether the body of water they wish to fish is an exception to the standard regulations.

Trout anglers in particular need to study the regulations carefully. Some trout streams are open to fishing year-round, while others are seasonal streams only open during the designated trout season. Compounding this, often a stream will be designated trout water for only a part of its length. Many Georgia trout streams are marginal trout habitat, and at lower elevations are classified as warm-water streams falling under the standard fishing regulations. Georgia trout streams with special restrictions such as "artificial lures only" are very few and the regulations are typically posted at access points in addition to being clearly stated in the regulation pamphlet.

The law requires all Georgia resident anglers between 16 and 65 years of age purchase a Georgia fishing license to fish in either salt water or freshwater. Senior (65+) Lifetime and Honorary (those with qualifying disabilities) Licenses are available at no charge simply by applying and showing proof of one's age or disability. All resident anglers between the ages of 16 and 65 are required to possess a Georgia trout stamp when fishing designated trout water unless they hold an Honorary License. In addition, anglers fishing Georgia's state-operated Public Fishing Areas are required (with one exception) to possess a Georgia Wildlife Management Area stamp. The stamp is not required of anglers holding a Senior Lifetime, Honorary, or one-day license. In what may seem an apparent contradiction, anglers fishing on Georgia Wildlife Management Areas are not required to possess the stamp (with one exception). Residents can purchase an all-inclusive "sportsman's license" that includes all the licenses and stamps needed to hunt and fish in Georgia.

For nonresidents, several license options are available including one-day, seven-day, and annual licenses. All nonresident anglers 16 years of age or older are required to possess a valid nonresident license and appropriate stamps. Nonresident anglers less than 16 years of age, who are not fishing for trout, are not required to possess a license. However, a valid license and trout stamp are required regardless of age or disability for all nonresident anglers to fish for or possess trout, or to fish in designated trout waters.

For both resident and nonresident anglers wishing to test the waters of Georgia fishing, a very reasonably priced one-day license is available. One-day license holders are not required to purchase a Wildlife Management Area stamp to fish any Public Fishing Area, but a trout stamp is still required to fish for trout, possess trout, or fish in any designated trout water.

Anglers have several choices on how to purchase their fishing license and any required stamps. About 1,200 license dealers are found statewide at major retailers, bait shops, and other businesses catering to anglers. Anglers can also purchase licenses by telephone (800-748-6887) or over the Internet at www.ganet.org/dnr/wild/.

Fish Consumption Advisories

The Georgia Department of Natural Resources conducts an ongoing survey of the quality of fish in Georgia with emphasis placed on large reservoirs and rivers, and smaller bodies of water popular with anglers, or near suspected or known pollution sources. The quality of fish caught in Georgia is generally very good.

Fish tissue samples are tested for 43 metals and chemicals, and of these, only a few have been detected at problem levels. Polychlorinated biphenyls (PCBs), chlordane, and mercury are the only contaminants that have been detected from a few bodies of water in Georgia at levels sufficient to cause concern. Georgia provides anglers with suggested guidelines for eating fish in the annual *Georgia Sport Fishing Regulations* pamphlet. The guidelines take a tiered approach to fish consumption (i.e., "No restrictions," "One meal per week," etc.), and it is important to note they are based on regular consumption of contaminated fish over a 30-year period. The contaminants that have been found in fish in Georgia accumulate in the human body over time. It would take many months or even years of eating contaminated fish to affect your health. However, pregnant women, nursing mothers, and children less than 6 years of age may want to take extra precautions. These groups are especially susceptible to the effects of some contaminants.

It is up to you to evaluate the risks versus benefits of eating fish on a case by case basis. However, several steps can be taken in the selecting, cleaning, and preparation of fish for the table that will greatly reduce the amount of contaminants in the consumed tissue.

Eat smaller fish that are still within legal size limits. Older, larger fish have been exposed for a longer period and have had more time to accumulate contaminants in their flesh.

Vary the kind of fish you eat. Contaminants build up in top predators (largemouth bass, striped bass) and bottom feeders (catfish, carp) quicker than they do in panfish (bluegill, crappie).

How the fish is cleaned and cooked can sometimes reduce contaminant levels by as much as 50 percent. Some contaminants concentrate in the fatty tissue and by removing the skin and trimming the back, side, and belly fat off the fillet, contaminants can be substantially reduced.

Cook the fish so the fat drips away. Broiling, baking, or grilling the fish in a way that allows fat to drip away will reduce some contaminants. Deep-fat frying will remove some contaminants, but the oil should be discarded once the fish is cooked. Pan frying does very little to remove contaminants.

The Georgia Department of Natural Resources issues the consumption guidelines not to discourage people from eating fish, but to give anglers the information they need to decide which fish to harvest and eat.

Boat Ramps

The Georgia Department of Natural Resources maintains many fine boat ramps all around the state. In addition, many other boat ramps are operated by federal agencies, county and city governments, and private marinas. The Georgia DNR publishes a guide, *Public Boat Ramps in Georgia,* that is available by contacting any Wildlife Resources Division Fisheries Section office. *The Angler's Guide to Georgia Saltwater Fishing Access Sites,* published by the Coastal Resources Division of DNR, is an excellent guide to fishing Georgia's coast and includes many boat ramps. Also, boat ramps and other notable sites such as campgrounds are shown in DeLorme's Georgia Atlas and Gazetteer. Finally, most commercial lake maps include information on boat ramps and other access points.

Campgrounds

No matter if your preference is for primitive or all the comforts of home, Georgia has many beautiful and well-maintained campgrounds. Many Georgia campgrounds, on or near prime fishing destinations, are operated by government agencies and are available to the public at very reasonable fees. The site maps included in this book include some campgrounds found near each site. Anglers interested in camping should refer to the site description, the site map, and the appendix to find campgrounds and obtain more information on rules and regulations and what is available.

Private Property and Public Access

In Georgia, fishing on someone else's property without permission is unlawful, and fishing rights are often privately held on nonnavigable streams. Wading in or floating upon nonnavigable streams flowing through private property does not exempt anglers from the need to obtain the landowner's permission.

Many trout streams flow through private land, but public access is some-times possible on road right-of-ways. Keep in mind, however, that just because your feet may be on the public side of the property line, the law does not grant you the right to cast to a privately owned section of the stream. Many streams have areas where the land is held for use by the public. Permission is not required to fish in the Chattahoochee or Oconee National Forests, Georgia DNR Public Fishing Areas and Wildlife Management Areas, or Georgia State Parks.

Case law is constantly redefining waterways considered navigable and there-fore public, and those that are nonnavigable and privately held. If in doubt, the safest bet is to ask permission. The occasional refusal is worth the peace of mind of knowing you are within the law, and it is after all a landowner's right to grant or refuse trespass onto their property. If granted access to private property, be sure to take care of it better than if it were your own. Always close gates behind you and carry out more trash than you carried in. By doing so, gaining permission will be easier for the next angler.

Georgia River Systems

Ten major drainage systems and seven physiographic provinces give Georgia a wide variety of fish habitats. The major drainage systems of Georgia are the Tennessee, Alabama, Savannah, Altamaha, Apalachicola, Ogeechee, Satilla,

Suwannee, Ochlockonee, and the Saint Mary's. These river systems channel Georgia's water to either the Atlantic Ocean or the Gulf of Mexico.

An angler can use a working knowledge of river systems to their advantage when pursuing a particular species. For example, smallmouth bass are present in Georgia but generally are not found outside the streams and lakes contained in the Tennessee drainage. Dedicated smallmouth anglers searching for little-known bronzeback streams would do well to focus their efforts on Tennessee drainage streams and ignore the Alabama drainage. Although only a high ridge may separate the two streams, a Tennessee drainage stream will have smallmouth and the Alabama drainage stream will not.

Another example would be the relatively unknown Suwannee bass, a member of the black bass family. The range of the Suwannee bass is very small and is limited to the Suwannee and Ochlockonee drainages in extreme southeast Georgia and north Florida.

Live Bait

Georgia has many natural baits and most of them are easy to collect. The venerable earthworm has probably caught more fish than all other baits combined. Especially for a child, fishing just would not be fishing without a trip to the garden or flower bed to dig up a supply of earthworms for bait. Nightcrawlers also make good bait, either whole or in pieces; hunting for nightcrawlers makes great sport.

Live gizzard shad, threadfin shad, and blueback herring make great bait for large predators such as striped bass and flathead catfish. All these baitfish can be collected with a cast net. Georgia law allows the use of certain-sized minnow seines to capture live bait as long as any game fish or American eels captured are immediately released. However, minnows as bait or minnow seines cannot be used in designated trout water.

When using live fish as bait, it is very important to ensure that their use does not lead to the introduction of a species into a body of water where it is not already found. Moving live fish, aquatic plants, or mussels from one body of water to another can cause irreversible damage to the ecological balance of the lake, pond, river, or stream. To be on the safe side, always collect your live bait in the same body of water you will be fishing, therefore ensuring you will not contribute to the growing problem of species introductions.

Other good live baits are catalpa worms, which can be simply plucked off catalpa trees in the summer; crickets and grasshoppers, which can be collected with an insect net in grassy areas; dragonfly nymphs, which can be found under rocks in streams; and the list goes on and on. Let ingenuity be your guide. Very few live baits will not catch some sort of fish. Of course, if you prefer to let someone else do the collecting, common live baits are available at bait shops, marinas, and convenience stores catering to the angler.

Moon Phases

When fish bite best in relation to the moon phase is a constant source of debate among anglers. Some prefer to fish the dark of the moon, and some like a full moon. The only thing many anglers will agree on is that most fish spawn during the full moon.

Fishing the Spawn

The impact of spawning activities on fishing success varies depending on the fish species involved. Some fish, bluegill for example, become very aggressive during the spawn and are concentrated in shallow-water spawning colonies. Other fish, such as largemouth bass, don't feed while spawning, but can sometimes be coaxed into striking a lure to remove the perceived threat to their nest. Other fish like white bass are no more or less aggressive during the spawn, but are more easily found as they migrate out of the reservoir and into the tributary rivers.

Every angler must decide whether or not to intentionally take advantage of the spawn. Some anglers have very strong feelings against trying for spawning fish, and others see it as an opportunity to put the odds more in the angler's favor. Fishing during the spawn is unlikely to negatively affect fish populations any more than fishing at other times. When a fish is harvested, the loss of reproductive potential is the same whether the fish was taken during the spawn or two months before the spawn. Fortunately, fish are very prolific and reproduction soon makes up for any fish that anglers harvest.

Tides

Understanding tides and how they influence fish will greatly improve your success with Georgia's inshore marine species like spotted seatrout and red drum. Tide stages and times are information a good angler will be sure to find out before hitting the water.

On the Georgia coast, the daily difference between high tide and low tide is about 7 feet, although the difference can range from as little as 6 feet to more than 9 feet. Extreme times have a strong influence on the fishing. Unlike most weather though, anglers can predict the tidal conditions for any future day and time by simply using a yearly tide chart (see the appendix for sources of this information). Strong tides result in strong currents. The stronger the current, the more silt it stirs up and decreases water clarity. With decreased visibility, fish have a harder time finding the bait or lure and fishing success suffers.

To better understand tides, it is important to relate them to moon phases. During a new moon, the moon exerts increased gravitational pull and the tides are higher, resulting in turbid water. Fishing is usually poor during this moon phase. During the moon's first quarter, the high tide heights will only be in the 6- to 7-foot range, and the water will be clearer. This is a good time to go fishing. The effects of a full moon on the tides are similar to those of the new moon. For about three days on either side of the full moon, tides will be high and the water turbid. Try to avoid fishing during these big tides.

The 6- to 7-foot high tides that accompany the last quarter moon phase, or waning phase, are called neap tides. This is a great time to be on the water.

The currents caused by the ebb and flood of the tide have a lot to do with finding fish—both bait species and those pursued by the angler. If any constant exists in angling, it is that where the bait goes, the predators will not be far away. Every time you find bait, there will not always be a school of predators with them; but every time you find a school of predators, there will be some bait around. When fishing inshore, be mobile and move around until you find action. A spot that produces nothing on your first visit may be a feeding frenzy a couple of hours later when the tide has changed. Many fishing holes are good only at a certain tide stage. What is hot on the ebb tide is probably not during the flood tide.

Look for rips and water flowing over a bar or point, especially if there is a shell bottom. Some of the best times to fish these areas are during the last three hours of the ebb tide and the first three hours of the flood tide. During high flood and high ebb tides, try fishing around marsh islands and points. Fishing directly over shell mounds and off the tips of marsh islands can be productive during high tide, but during dead low tide nowhere is going to be good. Take a break and get ready for the action that is sure to pick back up when the water starts moving again.

Good anglers strive to learn everything possible about the watery world their quarry inhabits. Learn the tide, try to relate it to your fishing success or lack of it. In time your saltwater angling success will improve.

Log Your Trips

Unlike most paperwork, maintaining a fishing log is a thoroughly enjoyable way to spend a few minutes of your time. Not only will a detailed log enable you to spot general trends, it may be just the jog your memory needs to find that seldom-fished honey hole again. Basic information that should be included with every entry includes: type and number of fish taken, air and water temperature, weather conditions both during and immediately before the trip, wind direction and speed, moon phase, most productive lures or patterns, a simple sketch of any new fishing areas discovered, and anything else you think may be important. Do not overlook Mother Nature's signals either. The stage of development of local flora and fauna can be a consistent indicator of when conditions are the same in following years. For example, one old saying goes "when the dogwoods are blooming, the crappie are biting." This adage does not mean that crappie only bite when dogwoods are blooming. What it means is that the same conditions that signal dogwoods to bloom also signal crappie to move shallow and spawn, which is when they are most easily caught.

Periodically review your log and try to spot trends or eliminate unproductive patterns you may slip into out of habit. On days when inclement weather does not make fishing an attractive proposition, reviewing your log will help pass the time with recollections of balmy spring afternoons and crisp fall sunrises, and might even improve your angling skills.

Escaping the Crowds

Fishing and boating are popular pastimes all across Georgia. Especially on spring and summer weekends, it can seem like there are more anglers than fish. Crowded conditions and heavy fishing pressure not only make the fish skittish and reluctant to strike, but for many anglers they detract from the quality of the fishing trip.

Although some anglers accept crowded water as a fact of life, other anglers quietly go about escaping the crowds and often experience better fishing for their efforts. A little research with maps may help you find out-of-the-way and overlooked waters that receive very little fishing pressure. Even on popular lakes, rivers, and streams, anglers can escape the crowds by literally going the extra mile. Examples can be seen on any popular stream. Just look at the bank nearest the parking areas; it is usually worn slick from all of the foot traffic. Although a trail may lead to more distant sections of the stream, it usually peters out after only a few hundred feet, or at most the next good pool. Go beyond and blaze your own trail.

There is a direct correlation between how much fishing pressure a particular place receives and how much work the angler must invest in getting there. A mile of bushwhacking through briars and brambles or picking your way through long stretches of slippery rocks may result in scratches and bruised shins, but the rewards can be tremendous. Virtually unfished water is often available within shouting distance of where 90 percent of the anglers do their fishing.

Boat anglers can use their extra mobility to their advantage in several ways. On rivers and larger streams, anglers can use a small boat to float from one access point to another. Although the areas around the access points may be heavily fished by bank anglers, the areas between likely receive limited angling pressure. Even on large reservoirs, many boat anglers will not invest the time or effort to reach anywhere they cannot directly motor to. Often the backs of coves and sloughs will have a feeder creek reachable only by poling or even dragging the boat over a shallow mudflat before reaching the deeper water of the creek channel. These small overlooked creeks can offer truly tremendous fishing, though they may be barely wider than the boat.

Watch Your Step, But Talk All You Like

For generations, budding anglers have been told not to talk so much lest they scare the fish away. This old wives' tale has very little merit. Fish cannot hear anything that goes on above the water's surface. However, fish can sense even the minutest activities in their watery world. Although a fish does not hear in the same way mammals do, they can detect even the slightest disturbance in or near the water by sensing the vibrations.

This ability to sense vibrations imperceptible to humans is what keeps a fish alive and allows it to find its prey even in the murky depths. Water is an excellent transmitter of vibration. When fishing from the bank or wading, take care to walk very softly and avoid causing any more disturbance than necessary. Since dry ground does not transmit vibration nearly as well as water, staying well back from the water's edge will allow you to move into position to make a cast without warning the fish of your presence. If fishing from a boat, try to avoid shuffling your feet or sliding tackle boxes and other gear around in the boat. The boat's hull will transmit vibrations directly to the water. Carpet or rubber matting placed on the boat's flooring will do a great deal to deaden any vibrations coming from the boat.

Although a fish's sense of sight is not as keen as its ability to detect vibration, fish can see above the water for a short distance, especially when the surface is calm and unbroken by wave action. Much detail is lost in the transition from water to air, but movement is still easily detected. Especially when bank fishing or wading small streams, wear clothes of muted colors that blend into the background and keep sudden movements to an absolute minimum.

Finally, when fishing from a boat, wading, or walking the bank, always keep your shadow behind you whenever possible. To a fish, a sudden shadow overhead only means one thing, and that is danger, usually a predator intent on a fish supper.

Tread Lightly

It is the responsibility of all of us who love the outdoors to leave it in better shape than we found it, or at the very least, leave no trace of our passing through. With the increasing number of people discovering the joys of outdoor recreation, wise use of the resource is becoming ever more important. Several basic guidelines should be followed to help ensure the resource is still around for our children and their children to enjoy. All these can be summed up with the simple phrase "tread lightly," but a few deserve extra emphasis.

The most obvious thing people can do to clean up our natural resources is to carry out more than you carry in. The amount of litter deposited through sheer laziness and carelessness is truly a disgrace. Litter detracts from the pleasure of those who come after you, costs resource management agencies dollars and personnel time that could be better used for other activities, and can even be harmful to wildlife. Always place your trash in provided receptacles, or better yet carry it out with you and dispose of it properly yourself.

Anglers harvesting their catch face the extra challenge of disposing fish entrails in a responsible manner. Where allowed or possible, securely bag up and dispose of fish entrails in provided receptacles. If this is not an option, bury the entrails deep enough to discourage scavengers and smooth over the hole so it will quickly again become part of the forest floor.

Human waste, food scraps, and other biodegradables that cannot practically be carried out should also be buried in the same manner. It they are provided, treat comfort stations as if they were your own home. Leaving a disgusting mess is an insult to those who come after you, and a slap in the face to people who are working hard to keep the facilities as clean and inviting as possible.

Other things that can be done to tread lightly should be obvious with just a little thought. For instance, when camping in primitive areas, use established campsites, or if you do use an undisturbed area, leave it as you found it. Replace any rocks pulled up into a fire ring, smooth any disturbed ground, and dispose of waste properly.

Boating anglers should make sure everything is secured before motoring to another location, to prevent trash from being blown out of the boat and into the water. The same thing goes at the launch ramp. Before trailering your boat home, remove all trash and place it in provided receptacles. If trash receptacles are not available, stow the trash so it will not blow out on the highway and then properly dispose of it at home.

Whenever possible, stay on established trails. Trails are susceptible to erosion, especially those descending steep slopes in a straight line. Established trails usually change elevation in a series of switchbacks across the face of the slope, reducing the potential for erosion. Erosion and sedimentation are insidious dangers facing our aquatic resources. Silt fills in streams and lakes leading to changes in the habitat and eventually a change in the species composition as more sensitive species die out. While it is true that poor use of machinery and changing land use patterns are the primary causes of erosion and sedimentation, it is a cumulative problem. We anglers cannot overlook our own activities as partly to blame, especially in remote areas.

Attend to Details

Often, the difference between a passable angler and a good angler is the attention each pays to details. The time it is certain an overlooked detail will catch up with you is when a big fish is on the end of the line. Things to keep in mind are many, but never overlook a few of the most important ones. Always keep hook needles sharp. Constantly run the last few feet of line through your fingers to checks for nicks and abrasion and retie if even the slightest roughness is felt. Check your reel's drag at the start of each fishing trip; it has a tendency to tighten up when not used for a time. Replace the line on your reels often, especially if they are constantly exposed to ultraviolet light during storage.

Plan each cast before you make it, taking into account all factors. The goal is to make the most natural presentation possible to a place where you believe there should be a fish. Things to consider include current, wind, sunlight, and others. Only experience will teach an angler these things to the point that angling becomes almost a subconscious pursuit with all of the variables factored without any conscious thought. A good angler, though, will use the time freed up by the subconscious taking care of the basics to consciously search for and analyze more subtle details. Does the shoreline ahead change from mud to gravel? These transition areas often hold fish. Does the steep bank ahead indicate a sharp drop-off underwater? Areas with sudden depth changes are often excellent fishing. Pay close attention to the natural world around you, and not only will your angling success likely improve, your satisfaction with putting the pieces together and solving the puzzle by catching a fish will increase also.

HOW TO USE THIS GUIDE

The **Species** section provides information on the most popular game fish species in Georgia. Included for each species is basic life history information and how to identify the species. The more you understand the basic biology and habits of a particular species, the greater your angling success will be. The information in this section is by no means complete, but should serve as a good starting point for learning more about your favorite fish species.

The species section also provides a list of techniques commonly used to fish for each species. The list is a starting point, not a hard and fast judgment on what angling methods are most effective for any given species. Many times giving the fish "a different look" will prove to be successful, especially in heavily fished waters. Also, the techniques listed are hardly all-inclusive, but are a sampling of a few favorite methods of fishing Georgia.

A **Best bet** section appears at the end of each species listing. Each site listed has been selected because it is a popular and consistent producer of a particular species. For species not widely distributed, the best bet section lists those waters where the species is present in large enough numbers to provide the angler a reasonable chance of success.

Sites

Each site listing contains the following basic information: The key species found in this particular body of water, a short overview of the site, the best way to fish it, the best time to fish, and *DeLorme's Georgia Atlas and Gazetteer* (GA~G) reference. (DeLorme's GA~G available in stores throughout the state or by contacting DeLorme Mapping, P.O. Box 298, Yarmouth, ME 04096; 207-846-7000; www.delorme.com.)

Note the following example:

2 Coosa River at Mayo's Bar Lock and Dam

Key species: striped bass, white bass, crappie.
Overview: Mayo's Bar Lock and Dam is a popular early-season destination for anglers after white bass and crappie as these species make their annual spring spawning migration up the river.
Best way to fish: bank, boat.
Best time to fish: March through July.

After reading the listing, you can see popular species on the Coosa River at Mayo's Bar Lock and Dam are striped bass, white bass, and crappie. It is easily accessible by both bank and boat anglers, and the best time to go is March through July.

The **Description** contains general information about the site and will include special features, interesting historical information, and other local attractions.

For each site, a section called **The fishing** is provided to pass on information to help you have a successful and rewarding fishing trip. Best times to fish for certain species will be given in addition to some suggestions on where and how to start. As any angler knows, however, weather plays a very strong role in determining what fish will be doing, and the information contained here is only a suggestion based on normal conditions. For example, the early arrival of summer will cause fish to move deeper than they usually would be that time of year. Use the suggestions as a starting point, but do not be afraid to head out on your own if the suggested approach is not productive. The more you strike out on your own, the more familiar you will become with Georgia fish and fishing, and the more versatile and successful an angler you will eventually become.

The **GA~G grid** tells you where to find the site in the *DeLorme Georgia Atlas and Gazetteer.* Note that the GA~G references are often approximate. Not all sites fall on the confluence lines of the numbers and letters given. Some sites are so large they cover more than one GA~G map grid, and may spill over onto a different map page. In these cases, the GA~G reference will be the approximate center of the site or will be simply the page number(s) with no corresponding grid references.

The **General information** tells you anything special you need to know about the site and any special rules and regulations. Any special cautions regarding hazards found at the site will also be included in this section. Also included are small tidbits of information that might be useful to the visiting angler, including an idea on how far you must travel for food, lodging, and supplies.

The **Nearest camping** tells you where to find camping opportunities close to your fishing site. Preference was given to public campgrounds for this listing, although some privately owned campgrounds were included if a public campground is not available in easy driving distance.

The **Directions** are given from the nearest major highway, population center, or other landmark. A **site map** is provided to help find the area and support the text. For very large sites with multiple access points, for instance large reservoirs and rivers, the map will provide a selection of access points that cover the whole site. The directions to these sites are more general and will put you in the immediate area. From there, you can use the site map with the GA~G or other map to reach the specific access point that interests you. For sites with good public access, only public facilities are shown. Private facilities are shown only when publicly owned access is absent or limited.

The **locator maps** are broken down into regions and are designed to show the relationship of nearby sites to each other and to major roads and population centers. The locator maps should be used with other reference material like the GA~G or other maps. The state map shows all sites on a statewide basis.

For more information will refer the reader to the appendix for sources of more information regarding the site.

Georgia's State Record Freshwater Fish

Species	Weight	Location	Date
Bass, Hybrid	25 lbs. 8 oz.	Lake Chatuge	05/01/95
Bass, Largemouth	22 lbs. 4 oz.	Montgomery Lake	06/02/32
Bass, Redeye	3 lbs. 5 oz.	Tugaloo River	02/27/99
Bass, Shoal	8 lbs. 3 oz.	Flint River	10/23/77
Bass, Smallmouth	7 lbs. 2 oz.	Lake Chatuge	03/28/73
Bass, Spotted	8 lbs. 0.5 oz.	Lake Sidney Lanier	05/20/85
Bass, Striped	63 lbs. 0 oz.	Oconee River	05/30/67
Bass, Suwannee	3 lbs. 9 oz.	Ochlockonee River	10/06/84
Bass, White	5 lbs. 1 oz.	Lake Sidney Lanier	06/16/71
Bowfin	16 lbs. 0 oz.	Stephen Foster State Park	05/25/76
Bullhead, Brown	5 lbs. 8 oz.	O.F. Veal pond	05/22/78
Catfish, Blue	62 lbs. 0 oz.	Clarks Hill Reservoir	09/12/79
Catfish, Channel	44 lbs. 12 oz.	Altamaha River	05/18/72
Catfish, Flathead	67 lbs. 8 oz.	Altamaha River	05/24/00
Catfish, White	8 lbs. 10 oz.	Savannah River	06/10/96
Common Carp	35 lbs. 12 oz.	Lake Jackson	1972
Crappie, Black (tie)	4 lbs. 4 oz.	Acree's Lake	06/01/71
Crappie, Black (tie)	4 lbs. 4 oz.	Lake Spivey	3/75
Crappie, White	5 lbs. 0 oz.	Bibb Co. pond	04/10/84
Gar, Longnose	28 lbs. 6 oz.	Flint River	01/28/95
Muskellunge	38 lbs. 0 oz.	Blue Ridge Lake	6/57
Perch, Yellow	2 lbs. 8 oz.	Lake Burton	02/23/80
Pickerel, Chain	9 lbs. 6 oz.	Homerville	2/61
Pickerel, Redfin	2 lbs. 10 oz.	Lewis' pond	07/07/82
Pike, Northern	18 lbs. 2 oz.	Lake Rabun	06/27/82
Sauger	4 lbs. 3 oz.	Clarks Hill Reservoir	04/05/86
Shad, American	8 lbs. 3 oz.	Savannah River	04/05/86
Shad, Hickory	1 lbs. 15 oz.	Ogeechee River	04/02/95
Sunfish, Bluegill	3 lbs. 5 oz.	Shamrock Lake	07/03/77
Sunfish, Flier	1 lb. 4 oz.	Lowndes Co.pond	02/26/96
Sunfish, Green	1 lb. 1 oz.	Gordon Co. pond	05/17/98
Sunfish, Redbreast	1 lb. 11 oz.	Coweta Co. pond	04/16/98
Sunfish, Redear	4 lbs. 2 oz.	Richmond Co. pond	06/06/95
Sunfish, Warmouth	2 lbs. 0 oz.	Private pond	05/04/74
Trout, Brook	5 lbs. 10 oz.	Waters Creek	03/29/86
Trout, Brown	18 lbs. 2 oz.	Rock Creek	05/06/67
Trout, Rainbow	15 lbs. 0 oz.	White Co. pond	04/18/85
Walleye	11 lbs. 6 oz.	Richard B. Russell Lake	09/11/95

Georgia's State Record Saltwater Fish

Species	Weight	Location	Date
Amberjack	92 lbs. 1 oz.	J Reef	6/75
Barracuda	46 lbs. 8 oz.	Savannah Snapper Banks	7/93
Black Sea Bass	5 lbs. 11 oz.	Navy Tower R2	4/94
Bluefish	17 lbs. 12 oz.	G Reef	4/80
Cobia	88 lbs. 12 oz.	A Buoy	5/85
Croaker	5 lbs. 12 oz.	Lanier Bridge	3/77
Dolphinfish	67 lbs. 6 oz.	East of Navy Tower R8	5/97
Drum, Black	86 lbs. 8 oz.	Cumberland Sound	4/98
Drum, Red	47 lbs. 7 oz.	KC Reef	11/86
Flounder	15 lbs. 10 oz.	Jekyll Pier	11/90
Grouper, Gag	34 lbs. 8 oz.	67 mi. E of St. Simons Island	4/86
Jack Crevalle	36 lbs. 0 oz.	Wassaw Sound	6/96
Ladyfish	5 lbs. 0 oz.	Cumberland Island	8/78
Mackerel, King	63 lbs. 8 oz.	Brunswick Snapper Banks	8/90
Mackerel, Spanish	8 lbs. 4 oz.	5 mi. E of Buoy YS	5/91
Marlin, Blue	491 lbs. 8 oz.	Gulfstream, off Brunswick	6/85
Marlin, White	49 lbs. 12 oz.	Gulfstream E of St. Catherines	6/86
Striped Mullet	9 lbs. 3 oz.	Darien River	12/94
Florida Pompano	4 lbs. 15 oz.	Christmas Creek	11/98
Sailfish	65 lbs. 0 oz.	NOAA Buoy	6/81
Scamp	26 lbs. 0 oz.	East of R2 Tower	11/95
Spotted Seatrout	9 lbs. 7oz.	Christmas Creek	7/76
Shark, Black Tip	131 lbs. 0 oz.	Wassaw Channel	5/78
Shark, Bull	455 lbs. 0 oz.	STS Buoy	7/78
Shark, Dusky	272 lbs. 8 oz.	STS Buoy	10/78
Shark, Hammerhead	770 lbs. 0 oz.	Little Cumberland	8/73
Shark, Lemon	375 lbs. 0 oz.	St. Andrew Sound	7/74
Shark, Mako	228 lbs. 8 oz.	Off Savannah	5/75
Shark, Nurse	244 lbs. 0 oz.	Sapelo Channel	8/81
Shark, Sandbar	158 lbs. 8 oz.	Jekyll Pier	4/79
Shark, Sand Tiger	290 lbs. 0 oz.	Ossabaw Island	5/77
Shark, Thresher	116 lbs. 0 oz.	C Reef	3/76
Shark, Tiger	794 lbs. 0 oz.	STS Buoy	9/75
Sheepshead	13 lbs. 8 oz.	KC Reef	4/94
Red Snapper	37 lbs. 8 oz.	Savannah Snapper Banks	9/88
Snook	10 lbs. 2 oz.	Kings Creek	3/90
Spadefish	11 lbs. 12 oz.	G Reef	5/81
Swordfish	86 lbs. 0 oz.	Gulfstream, E of Savannah	5/80
Tarpon	161 lbs. 0 oz.	Buttermilk Sound	7/95
Little Tunny	20 lbs. 0 oz.	East of St. Catherines	7/73
Triggerfish	11 lbs. 5 oz.	Savannah Snapper Banks	11/87

Georgia's State Record Saltwater Fish (continued)

Species	Weight	Location	Date
Tripletail	28 lbs. 7 oz.	South Brunswick River	7/93
Tuna, Blackfin	29 lbs. 8 oz.	Gray's Reef	5/94
Tuna, Yellowfin	249 lbs. 2 oz.	Gulfstream	5/80
Wahoo	106 lbs. 8 oz.	ESE of R2W Tower	5/96
Weakfish	6 lbs. 8 oz.	Troupe Creek	3/76
Whiting	2 lbs. 12 oz.	Mackay River	2/75

An angler checks to see if he has won striped bass bragging rights for the day on the Coosa River.

GEORGIA'S ANGLER AWARD PROGRAM

Catching a big fish is a notable achievement, and requires exceptional angling skill and luck. Every year, the Georgia Wildlife Resources Division recognizes those skilled anglers who have caught a trophy fish in Georgia. The fish does not have to be a new state record to qualify, and both resident and nonresident anglers may apply. To qualify, the following basic conditions must be met: the fish was caught by legal sport fishing in Georgia; the fish was weighed on certified scales in the presence of two witnesses (immediate family not allowed); the fish must meet the minimum weight requirement for that species; the fish is positively identified by a fisheries biologist or technician; and a clear side view photo of the fish is included with the application. Angler Award applications and further information are available from all Fisheries Section offices.

Minimum Weights Eligible for a Georgia Angler Award

Game Fish	Minimum Weight
Largemouth Bass	10 lbs.
Shoal Bass	4.5 lbs.
Spotted Bass	4 lbs.
Smallmouth Bass	3.5 lbs.
Suwannee Bass	2.5 lbs.
Redeye Bass	1.5 lbs.
Striped Bass	30 lbs.
Hybrid Bass	10 lbs.
White Bass	3.5 lbs.
Bluegill	1.5 lbs.
Redear Sunfish (Shellcracker)	1.5 lbs.
Redbreast Sunfish	1 lb.
Rock Bass	1 lb.
Warmouth	1 lb.
Shadow Bass	1 lb.
Flier	0.5 lb.
Spotted Sunfish	0.5 lb.
Walleye	5 lbs.
Sauger	2 lbs.
Chain Pickerel	4 lbs.
Redfin Pickerel	1 lb.
Brown Trout	5 lbs.
Brook Trout	2 lbs.
Rainbow Trout	6 lbs.
Black Crappie	2.5 lbs.
White Crappie	2.5 lbs.
Channel Catfish	12 lbs.
Flathead Catfish	20 lbs.
American Shad	5 lbs.
Hickory Shad	1.5 lbs.

Non-Game Fish	Minimum Weight
White Catfish	3 lbs.
Brown Bullhead	2 lbs.
Yellow Bullhead	2 lbs.
Spotted, Flat, and Snail Bullhead	2 lbs.
Carp	20 lbs.
Bowfin	10 lbs.
Longnose Gar	11 lbs.
Spotted and Florida Gar	5 lbs.
Yellow Perch	1.5 lbs.

Fish Species of Georgia

BROWN TROUT

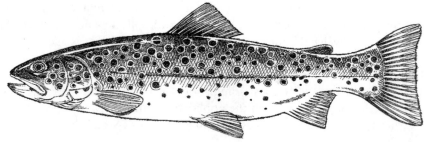

A native of Europe, the brown trout, *Salmo trutta,* was introduced to the United States as early as 1883, and arrived in Georgia by the 1930s.

Though many Georgia trout streams contain brown trout, either through stocking or natural reproduction, they usually play second fiddle to rainbow trout in terms of numbers. What they lack in numbers, however, they make up in size. The largest fish found in a stream are often brown trout. The Georgia record brown was caught in 1967 from Rock Creek and weighed 18 pounds, 2 ounces. Most brown trout caught will be 9 to 11 inches. Stream-reared fish weighing 5 pounds or more are not unheard of, and when fishing the Chattahoochee tailwaters below Lake Sidney Lanier, all bets are off and fish exceeding 10 pounds are possible.

Brown trout are aptly named. The body has an overall golden brown hue with many black spots, encircled with a light-colored ring. Red spots may be present, especially on mature fish.

The brown trout spawns in the fall and early winter. As humanity made its mark on the land, the resulting erosion and sedimentation decreased the habitat suitable for trout spawning. While this is not the only factor preventing natural trout reproduction in some Georgia trout streams, it is a significant one.

Although rainbow trout are more tolerant than browns of the marginal temperatures found in many Georgia trout streams, brown trout are less affected by competition from other warm-water species. Brown trout depend on insects for food when young, but once they have progressed beyond the juvenile stage switch to a diet predominantly made up of crayfish, spring lizards, and other fish. This strategy does not ensure there are a lot of brown trout, but it does suggest that the ones who manage to survive are likely to be large fish. Consequently, many trophy trout caught from Georgia streams are brown trout.

Another brown trout characteristic that gives it trophy potential is the fish are no pushovers when it comes to angling. Brown trout, especially large adults, are wary and it is the careful and stealthy angler who will experience the most success. Trophy fish living in Georgia's infertile streams did not get that way by eating the first Muddler Minnow that comes crashing down over their heads.

As they age and grow in size, brown trout will begin to find deep pools to their liking and will wait out the daylight hours resting in the depths before venturing out in the darkness to find something good to eat.

The first part of a solid game plan that may result in a trophy brown is finding the right place and being there at the right time. A good bet would be a deep pool, the more remote the better. Do not overlook small tributary streams. Very small water can hold a very big trout. If night-fishing is allowed on the stream, try it. Big fish start to stir at dusk and go out in search of supper. If fishing a stream where night-fishing is not allowed, fish as early in the morning or as late in the evening as the law allows.

Brown trout are a great sport fish and can provide fine fishing for either numbers of fish or the trophy of a lifetime. Consistently catching brown trout is probably the most difficult challenge a Georgia trout angler can undertake, but is definitely a pursuit that offers tremendous rewards.

Techniques

Casting: Although some lures only come in sizes suitable for black bass angling, many are now available in sizes that perfectly match the forage found in trout streams. Ultralight spinning tackle and the lightest line you are comfortable using is the most effective way to present them. Probably the two most popular lures for brown trout in Georgia are a small Rapala or an in-line spinner, such as a Rooster Tail or Panther Martin.

When casting artificials, slowly work your way up the stream. Cast the lure upstream of good holding areas and retrieve it with the current. Big brown trout can be found in amazingly small waters, so casting must be sharp to put the lure where it needs to be to make the most natural presentation possible.

Bait fishing: Big brown trout like to eat crayfish, spring lizards, nightcrawlers, and minnows. Minnows are not allowed as bait in Georgia trout streams, but do not overlook crayfish or lizards for big trout. Using such big bait will not result in many strikes, but they will be big strikes. A juicy worm will draw strikes from all sizes of brown trout and is the most consistent bait available. For stocked trout, try canned corn, marshmallows, crickets, or worms. All of these baits are best fished on an ultralight spinning outfit. Use a light wire hook and pinch on just enough weight to keep the bait bouncing along the bottom. Always use the lightest line possible.

Flycasting: Fly fishing is a great way to catch trout, but the problem for Georgia flycasters is that most Georgia trout streams are small, overgrown, and not well-suited to flycasting. Other than tailwater fishing below dams, the best places to catch a big brown are remote stretches of small streams where the casting is confined. Stick with a general attractor pattern. Hatches are usually sparse, so matching the hatch is not that important. When dry-fly fishing, choose something visible so both you and the fish can track it on the broken surface of most Georgia trout streams. To catch the biggest brown trout in the creek, go with a fly that mimics a crayfish, sculpin, or other large forage common to the stream.

Best bets for Georgia brown trout: Conasauga River, Site 13; Jacks River, Site 14; Waters Creek, Site 26; Dukes Creek, Site 30; Chattooga River, Site 32; Chattahoochee River National Recreation Area, Site 41.

BROOK TROUT

The Eastern brook trout, *Salvelinus fontinalis,* is not a true trout but is a member of the char family. When the first European settlers arrived in north Georgia, this colorful little species was abundant in the high-altitude headwater streams. The introduction of rainbow trout and brown trout in the early twentieth century spelled the demise of brook trout as the dominant salmonid in Georgia. Rainbows and browns have found the hills of Southern Appalachia to their liking, and have replaced the brook trout as the dominant species in much of the brookies' natural range. In today's Georgia, brookies are typically found only in remote headwater streams above 2,200 feet. Brook trout are often found upstream of barrier falls that prevent rainbows and browns from moving in and displacing the brookies. Despite the problems faced by the brook trout, sound management by State and Federal agencies has preserved a fishable population of Georgia's only native salmonid.

Although most of Georgia's brookies are native fish that live in remote areas, a few streams do receive occasional stockings of brook trout. The current Georgia record brook trout was caught from one of these streams. The gargantuan brookie weighed 5 pounds, 10 ounces, and was taken in 1986 from Waters Creek, a stream intensively managed for trophy trout. Under normal conditions, a brook trout of even a pound would be considered a trophy, and a 6-inch brookie is the norm.

Techniques

Casting: A 4-foot ultralight rod and a tiny spinning reel spooled with 2-pound or 4-pound test monofilament is just the ticket for the tight quarters in the small mountain streams brookies call home. Brook trout are aggressive feeders and will take small spinners like Mepps, Panther Martins, and Rooster Tails.

Living their lives in the thin water of tiny mountain streams makes brookies very skittish. Flip the spinner upstream of the brookies' lair and retrieve it slow and steady while allowing the current to wash it under rocks and into other good holding areas. Although not as acrobatic as rainbow trout, brookies put up a vigorous fight with strong runs.

Bait fishing: Brookies will readily take worms, crickets, grasshoppers, hellgrammites, and any other natural bait. Present the bait using ultralight spinning tackle and use only enough weight to keep the bait lightly ticking the bottom as the current carries it along.

Flycasting: The overhead tangle of rhododendron, mountain laurel, and other plants lining the creeks make fly fishing an exercise in frustration on most brook trout streams, even for the expert flycaster. There are some exceptions. Generally the larger streams that receive periodic stockings, have sections large enough to fish with a fly rod, although roll casts will still generally be the rule. Any fly pattern that is a fair imitation of the natural forage will catch fish. Nymphs and other subsurface flies are favored for brook trout, although they will hit dry flies during a hatch. When packing for a first-time trip to a mountain stream, a wise angler will include a small spinning outfit to ensure all the bases are covered if the stream proves unsuitable for fly fishing.

Best bets for Georgia brook trout: small headwater streams at high elevations.

RAINBOW TROUT

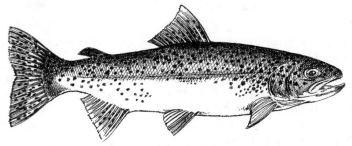

Rainbow trout, *Oncorhynchus mykiss,* are the most common trout in Georgia. Rainbows are native to the northwestern United States, but have been widely introduced throughout the country and have found many of their new homes to their liking, including the trout streams of north Georgia. Self-sustaining rainbow trout populations are present in some north Georgia streams, while others require periodic stocking to maintain a viable fishery.

Rainbows spawn from early winter through spring depending on the genetic strain of the fish and local conditions.

Rainbows have a bluish green back and dark spots on their sides. In mature fish, a vivid red stripe runs from the gills to the tail, hence the name. In hatchery-reared fish only recently stocked, the stripe will sometimes be almost indiscernible or a very light pink.

The current state record rainbow trout weighed 15 pounds and was caught in 1985 from a private pond in White County in north Georgia. Gargantuan rainbows are often from private ponds and are intensively fed commercial fish food and face little fishing pressure. The Chattahoochee River tailwater below Lake Sidney Lanier has produced rainbows within a couple of pounds of the record and so have a few specially-managed public trout streams. Nevertheless, the average rainbow caught will be 9 to 10 inches in stocked streams and even smaller in streams with natural reproduction and no stocking. Fish that have survived and grown into the 15-inch range are a challenge to find and fool, but the task is not insurmountable.

Techniques

Casting: Small in-line spinners like Rooster Tails and Panther Martins are perennial favorites. Small floating minnow-imitators like Rapalas and Rebels are also effective. Several manufacturers have a line of tiny plugs that imitate a crayfish, hellgrammite, or other small bottom-dwelling stream creature. All these can be effective at times and may fool the biggest fish in the pool.

Light tackle is especially important when using small artificials. To perform properly and have good action, many of these lures need to be fished on light line (around 4-pound test). Anything much heavier will dampen the lure's action and limit the number of strikes. Most Georgia trout streams do not require very long casts. In fact, sometimes an underhand "flip" will do, but it must be accurate and place the lure in the water under the rhododendron and mountain laurel bushes, not in the bush 3 feet above the water's surface.

Bait fishing: A great majority of the trout caught every year in Georgia fall prey to canned corn, marshmallows, the venerable earthworm, crickets, or even factory-concocted "trout candy." For the most fun and to get the most strikes, match the tackle to the fish being sought. Use small hooks, as little weight as is necessary, and if one is needed, as small a bobber as is necessary to keep the bait at the desired depth. Light spinning or spin-casting tackle is the way to go, both to give the fish a chance to exhibit their maximum fighting abilities, and to make the fishing easier on the angler. Small trout streams are no place for a long rod and a reel holding 150 yards of line. Fishing larger rivers and tailwaters may call for slightly heavier tackle, but the idea should still be to keep it as light as possible.

Flycasting: Most streams are small and overgrown, making flycasting a nightmare if not impossible. The streams are infertile with very few large trout and hatches are usually sparse. Most water is fast and a fly selection should be based on choosing a fly that both the angler and the fish can see in the turbulence. A 5- or 6-weight outfit is just about right for most Georgia trout streams.

Dry flies, wet flies, nymphs, and streamers all will catch fish. What is more important in dry flies than an exact match is something buoyant enough to stay afloat as long as it needs to and is visible on the troubled waters of most Georgia trout streams. As a starting point, some patterns that have proven successful are Adams, Humpys, and the Royal Wulff. Wet flies one may want to consider include the Adams pattern again, and the Royal Coachman. Good nymphs are anything that resembles a caddis fly or stone fly, and in the streamer category, the Muddler Minnow is a pattern that is hard to beat anywhere you go.

Best bets for Georgia rainbow trout: Holly Creek, Site 9; Cooper Creek, Site 20; Chattahoochee River National Recreation Area, Site 41; many other streams in northwest and northeast Georgia.

LARGEMOUTH BASS

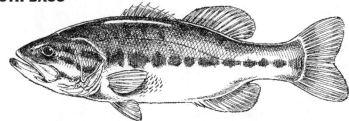

The largemouth bass, *Micropterus salmoides,* is the king of Georgia's sport fish. A 22.25-pound largemouth bass, the current world record, was caught in 1932 from Montgomery Lake, a backwater slough off the Ocmulgee River in southeast Georgia. Although a few catches have come close in recent years, no one has yet unseated Georgia as the home of the world-record largemouth bass.

The popularity of largemouth bass stems from their aggressive nature, explosive strikes, and strong fighting abilities.

In Georgia, largemouth bass spawn anytime from mid-February to May. Largemouths prefer to build their nests on fine gravel bottoms, but almost any type of bottom may be used if it is firm and free of silt that would smother the eggs.

Georgia largemouth bass grow big because of a long growing season and fertile waters. They are voracious predators and will eat anything they can fit in their cavernous mouths.

The largemouth bass is the primary target of tournament fishing in Georgia. Thousands of anglers hit the water every summer weekend to pit their bass-fishing prowess against both the fish and their fellow competitors. Tournament bass fishing is a fast paced version of a relaxing sport, but tournaments are not limited solely to expert anglers. A neophyte wanting to learn how to catch largemouth bass would be hard pressed to find a better method of "on the water training" than participating in a few tournaments.

Caught up in the pursuit of their elusive quarry, die-hard bass anglers have a tendency to overcomplicate the sport. Although zipping around a huge lake in a high-powered boat equipped with all of the latest lures, equipment, and electronic fish finders has its aficionados, anglers fishing with simple tackle can still catch largemouth bass in just about any body of water in Georgia.

Although the practice of catch-and-release angling in tournament bass fishing has increased acceptance of catch-and-release among recreational anglers, largemouth bass in Georgia are very prolific and one should not feel bad about harvesting fish as allowed by law. Creel and length limits are designed to allow a sustainable harvest that will not adversely affect the population. In fact, harvest is a management tool used by fisheries' biologists to manipulate a bass population to provide the best fishing.

Techniques

Spin fishing: A medium-weight outfit spooled with 8-pound monofilament will fit the bill for most situations. Spinning tackle is best suited for open water, but can be used effectively in thick cover with heavier line. Properly used, spinning tackle allows for long casts and is easily mastered. By using the index finger to feather the line coming off the spool during the cast, an experienced angler can gain near the control offered by the tougher-to-master baitcasting reel.

All popular bass lures can be used with spinning tackle, but it excells at fishing lures retrieved in a slow, erratic manner. Examples would be a Texas-rigged plastic worm, jig-and-pig, or topwater plug.

Spinning tackle is also very useful for "skipping" lures under docks and over-hanging brush. A small slip-sinker pegged with a toothpick to keep it from sliding up the line will give the lure enough momentum to skip far under the dock.

Baitcasting tackle: Baitcasting tackle offers the ultimate in control and is the most popular tackle with serious Georgia bass anglers. A baitcasting reel on a medium-heavy 6-foot graphite rod with 12-pound test monofilament will meet the needs of most bass fishing situations. Serious largemouth bass anglers prefer to carry several rods, each rigged with a different lure. With more than one rod available, an angler can fish down a shoreline and have several options available without having to constantly change lures. Also, having several outfits allows the angler to tailor the rod and reel to the lure. Lightweight and topwater lures cast better and have more action with medium action rods. Heavier lures like a jig-and-pig that are generally fished in deep water or heavy cover do better on a medium-heavy or heavy-action rod. Baitcasting rods up to 7 feet are often used for deep-water fishing. The extra length helps take up slack during the hookset and compensates for the inherent stretch in monofilament.

A fast-ratio baitcasting reel allows an angler to quickly fish a shoreline in rapid-fire fashion. A slower-ratio reel will aid in fishing large deep-diving crankbaits on deep points and ledges. The large bills on deep-diving lures provide a lot of water resistance, and the lower gear ratio provides more cranking power. Baitcasting reels are much better than spinning reels at overcoming strong resistance, and are less tiring for the angler to use for hours at a time.

Bait fishing: Anglers catch countless largemouth bass every year in Georgia using worms, nightcrawlers, crickets, and minnows.

Anglers after trophy bass prefer large baitfish like shad or golden shiners. Shad or shiners are usually fished under a float around heavy cover. The bait will swim up under the cover into areas where presenting an artificial lure would be nearly impossible. When using shad or shiners, fresh and lively bait is essential. Bait should be kept in cool water in an aerated baitwell. Keep casts short, and lob the bait as gently as possible.

Flycasting: Fly fishing for largemouth bass in Georgia is generally limited to small ponds and lakes. Very few anglers use fly-fishing equipment on large reservoirs and rivers. Large poppers, deer-hair bugs, or streamers fished on an 8-weight outfit near lilypads, stumps, and other structure will catch largemouth bass. To help the line turn over during the cast, use a weight-forward or bass-bug taper fly line.

Best bets for Georgia largemouth bass: Lake Richard B. Russell, Site 46; Clarks Hill Lake, Site 47; Lake Sinclair, Site 50; West Point Lake, Site 57; Lake Seminole, Site 63; Altamaha River, Sites 73, 90, 91; many others.

SMALLMOUTH BASS

Despite its national popularity, smallmouth bass, *Micropterus dolomieu,* rank far down the list of prized Georgia bass. The number of anglers pursuing smallmouth in Georgia is not a reflection on the fish themselves, rather on their limited range. Smallmouth are native only to the streams, lakes, and rivers of the Tennessee drainage in north Georgia. Attempts to establish self-sustaining populations of smallmouth in other drainages through stocking have proved fruitless. Stocked smallmouth have never been able to supplant redeye bass as the dominant coolwater stream bass in north Georgia.

The opportunistic feeding habits of smallmouths are similar to other stream bass, but smallmouths do show a decided preference for crayfish. In streams, smallmouth will be found on rocky shoals holding in slack water areas waiting for the current to provide a meal. In lakes, smallmouth can be found nearly anywhere, but they do relate to rocks. Smallmouth lakes are generally deep and clear, and smallmouths stay deep during daylight hours for most of the year. With the setting of the sun, however, smallmouths will migrate onto shallow rocky points and bars and begin feeding. Nighttime is the best period for catching smallmouths, even during the cooler months.

Identification of smallmouth bass is made easy by their limited range, and because they lack several distinctive characteristics of redeye bass, notably the white edging of the tail and the brick-red fins. Redeye bass are the species with which a smallmouth could most easily be confused. Largemouth and spotted bass also share the range of the smallmouth, but both lack the generally brown coloration and the distinct vertical dark bars on the side of the body.

While Georgia's smallmouth lakes will never rival the fabled trophy lakes of Kentucky and Tennessee, trophy fish are available to the lucky and skillful angler. The Georgia record smallmouth weighed 7 pounds, 2 ounces, and was caught from Lake Chatuge in 1973.

Techniques

Casting: Although fearsome fighters, smallmouths do not require heavy gear. The lakes where smallmouths occur in Georgia are generally deep, clear, and free of obstructions. Since most fish will be caught in open water, a light spinning outfit spooled with 6-pound or 8-pound test monofilament will suffice. Many anglers prefer baitcasting equipment and with today's advanced reels, casting the light lures used for smallmouth on baitcasting tackle is no longer the problem it once was. However, especially for stream smallmouths, spinning tackle gets the nod from most anglers. Due to the smallmouth's affinity for clear-water lakes and streams, anglers should stick to the lightest line possible.

Popular lures for smallmouth in Georgia include small crankbaits, spoons, minnow-imitators, and jigs. All have their place, but the venerable lead-head jig tipped with a plastic grub is the most versatile and effective smallmouth bait there is. Given smallmouths' love for crayfish, the color of the crayfish in the body of water being fished should be kept in mind during lure selection.

When casting for smallmouths the key is rocks. When fishing a lake, use a depth finder to search for rock piles on points and bars.

In streams, finding fish is much easier. Smallmouths hold in areas that provide relief from the current but are prime feeding stations. An example would be a large boulder in the middle of a fast run. The cast must be placed so the current will carry the bait right into the smallmouth's lair in a lifelike manner. Maintain just enough tension on the line to feel the strike without impeding the natural look of the lure. Light jigs and soft-plastic jerk baits like Slug-Gos are excellent for this type of fishing. When smallmouths are actively cruising and feeding, a floating minnow-imitator like a Rapala is a great lure for tempting a hungry smallmouth.

Other good techniques for reservoir smallmouth include working crankbaits over shallow points at night. During the nighttime hours, smallmouths will move shallow to feed, even in the winter months.

In the dead of winter, smallmouths will hold deep and can be tempted into striking with a vertical presentation of a jigging spoon.

Bait fishing: Smallmouth, including trophy fish, are regularly caught on live bait. Some anglers like to sweeten their artificial baits with a minnow, leech, or pinch of nightcrawler. Good live baits to try for smallmouths include minnows, crayfish, and spring lizards (salamanders). Use a hook suited to the size of the bait and just enough weight to keep it at the desired depth.

Flycasting: Fly fishing for smallmouths in Georgia is mostly limited to larger creeks and rivers where there is room to cast. Any large fly that imitates forage found in the stream stands a good chance of being eaten. Fly fishers equipped with sinking lines could have good success on reservoir smallmouth.

Trolling: Trolling for smallmouths in reservoirs can be very effective, but is not as common as casting artificials or live bait. Troll crankbaits and other diving plugs around points and islands. Some experimentation will be required to learn what depth is the most effective on any given day.

Best bets for Georgia smallmouth bass: Blue Ridge Lake, Site 16; Lake Nottely, Site 21; Lake Chatuge, Site 22.

SPOTTED BASS

The spotted bass, *Micropterus punctulatus,* is one of the six black bass species found in Georgia. Spotted bass, commonly called "spots," are second only to largemouth bass in their importance to Georgia bass fishing.

To those unfamiliar with them, at first glance spotted bass are almost indistinguishable from largemouth bass. A closer look at a few telltale characteristics makes identification easy. Spotted bass usually have a sandpaper-like tooth patch on the tongue that largemouths lack. Also, the rear of the jaw does not extend behind the eye as it does in largemouths, and the spiny and soft dorsal fins are connected with a shallow notch not reaching all the way to the body. Spotted bass are common in central and north Georgia in the Coosa, Chattahoochee, and Savannah river systems. Some northeast Georgia lakes in the Tennessee drainage now harbor spotted bass, likely due to unauthorized stockings. Illegal introduction of spotted bass, probably by well-intentioned but misguided anglers, has resulted in the decline of Georgia's limited smallmouth bass resource. Spotted bass have a competitive edge over smallmouth bass, and when spots are introduced, a precipitous decline in smallmouths usually follows.

The state record spotted bass was 8 pounds, 0.5 ounce, caught from Lake Sidney Lanier in 1985. The average Georgia spotted bass weighs about a pound and anything more than 4 pounds is considered a trophy.

Reservoirs that seem to favor spotted bass can be generally characterized as deep and clear. Spots also do extremely well in rivers. In still water, spots are a more open-water fish than largemouth, and are commonly found in deeper offshore areas as opposed to the shoreline habitats preferred by largemouths. In moving water, spots can be found nearly anywhere, and will tolerate more current than slack-water loving largemouths.

In reservoirs try deep points, humps, and ledges, especially those that offer stumps or other cover. In rivers, immediately below a shoal, outside bends, and creek mouths are always productive.

Spotted bass can be extremely finicky eaters at times. Especially in reservoir situations, anglers after spotted bass will downsize their baits and fish them slowly.

Techniques

Casting: The smaller lures commonly used for spotted bass are better handled with a light- to medium-action spinning outfit, but many anglers feel that baitcasting tackle is stronger and gives better control. Recent advances in baitcasting reels allow them to handle 6- and even 4-pound test line, so the choice is a matter of preference. Line size is again a matter of preference, but the key is to use quality low-diameter line in the lightest weight practical for conditions. Spotted bass can be line-shy, and using heavy line in clear water is not going to produce as many strikes as thinner, less visible line.

Good lures for spotted bass include plastic worms and grubs, jigs, and crankbaits. The finesse worm is probably one of the most popular and effective spotted bass lures around. These diminutive plastic worms are often the bait of choice for anglers specifically targeting spotted bass. Most anglers prefer these lures in natural hues with perhaps just a touch of color on the tail. One of the best places to fish using soft-plastic baits for reservoir spotted bass is woody cover on deep structure. Slowly work the bait along bottom until a brush pile or stump is felt, and then gently shake the worm while keeping it in contact with the brush. This type of fishing requires a soft touch, and the ability to detect almost indiscernible strikes.

River and stream fishing for spots is a little different. The current does not allow fish a long time for examination and an eventual decision. Faster-moving lures like spinners and crankbaits are very effective at covering a lot of water and drawing strikes. Baitcasting tackle is probably best in this situation since once mastered, it is capable of extremely accurate casts, and is strong enough to turn a big fish in fast current.

Bait fishing: Live bait is not commonly used for spotted bass. A few anglers prefer to fish with spring lizards, crayfish, or large minnows in the same manner as artificials. Fish the bait slowly along the bottom over deep structure.

Flycasting: Fly fishing for spotted bass offers some overlooked possibilities. Although fly fishing for reservoir spotted bass is not practical, rivers offer some real possibilities. Most good spotted bass rivers are large enough to allow for easy casting. Working a streamer or popping bug through feeding zones below shoals or along outside bends is a fun way to fish for spotted bass. Although overlooked by most bass anglers, fly tackle offers the opportunity to efficiently make repeated presentations to a good area without wasting time retrieving the lure through unproductive water to make another cast. Spotted bass are strong fighters, and rivers are usually filled with snags, so anglers who choose to go this route need to make sure their equipment is up to the task.

Best bets for Georgia spotted bass: Allatoona Lake, Site 7; Carters Lake, Site 8; Lake Burton, Site 33; Lake Sidney Lanier, Site 40; others.

REDEYE BASS

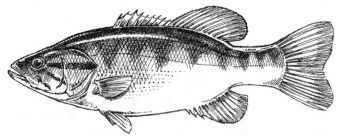

The redeye bass, *Micropterus coosae,* also known as the Coosa Bass, is a unique member of the black bass family whose natural range is limited to areas of the southeastern United States and much of north Georgia. It is most common in the upper Coosa, Chattahoochee, and Savannah river systems but does not do well in reservoirs.

Like other stream bass, redeye do not grow large. Most will be less than 12 inches, and one that measures in pounds should be considered a trophy. Some disagreement exists among scientists and angling record-keeping organizations as to whether the redeye bass is a totally different species than the shoal bass. Since the shoal bass was finally scientifically described, named, and recognized as a species in 1999, the International Game Fish Association and the National Freshwater Fishing Hall of Fame did not historically consider redeye bass and shoal bass to be separate species. Therefore, the larger-growing shoal bass holds most records. The state of Georgia, however, does recognize different records for the two species and the current redeye bass state record fish is 3 pounds, 3 ounces, caught from the Tugaloo River in 1990.

Identifying a redeye bass is fairly easy. The patch of sandpaper-like teeth on its tongue separates it from a largemouth bass. Smallmouth, spotted, and shoal bass lack the white edging on the tail and brick-red fin coloration. The redeye's range does not overlap with the range of the Suwannee bass. These traits together with the namesake bright red eye (also exhibited by shoal bass and sometimes smallmouth and spotted bass) are diagnostic.

Redeye are aggressive, opportunistic feeders. Although their diet mostly consists of insects, crayfish, and other small fish, anything that catches their attention and appears edible is likely to be struck. Redeye like to hang out where a riffle tails out into a deep pool. Read the water to figure out where the best feeding stations are. A good feeding station is where a boulder or log breaks the current. Redeye will hold in the slack water downstream of the structure and dart out to nab prey items swept along by the current. The biggest fish will usually be holding at the best feeding stations and smaller fish are relegated to cruising the fast water of the riffle looking for prey. Do not overlook deep holes as prime redeye territory, although the head or tail of the pool usually holds the most fish.

Wading small coolwater streams for redeye with an ultralight spinning outfit and a handful of small surface plugs is great summertime sport.

Techniques

Casting: An ultralight spinning outfit spooled with 6-pound monofilament is everything needed for redeye bass. Rods should be less than 5 feet because of the close quarters on many redeye streams. Although redeye will strike nearly any artificial lure, the most exciting and effective way to fish for them is to use small topwater lures like chuggers and floating minnow-imitators. Small Rebel Pop-Rs and Rapalas are perfect.

Bait fishing: Redeye can be caught on all types of live bait, but redeye are so aggressive that live bait is often unnecessary, and an angler would do well to stick with artificials.

Flycasting: Redeye are easily caught with a fly rod. However, the overhanging canopy of rhododendron and mountain laurel common on redeye streams can make casting an exercise in frustration, if not impossible. Popping bugs, dry flies, and small streamers are all good flies for redeye bass.

Best bets for Georgia redeye bass: Stamps Creek, Site 6; Conasauga River, Site 13; Jacks River, Site 14; Chattooga National Wild and Scenic River, Site 32; Lake Hartwell, Site 39.

SHOAL BASS

As described under the redeye bass section, some confusion existed over whether the redeye and shoal bass, *Micropterus cataractae* are two separate species or simply variants of one black bass species.

Shoal bass are creatures of moving water, and are native to the Flint and Chattahoochee river systems in Georgia. They are also found in the Ocmulgee River. The Georgia record shoal bass was caught from the Flint River in 1977 and weighed 8 pounds, 3 ounces. However, the average fish will be less than 12 inches long and weigh less than a pound.

Shoalies occasionally are caught from the headwaters of reservoirs impounding rivers in their range, but these occurrences are not common.

Distinguishing shoal bass from redeye bass can be difficult, and their ranges overlap. Shoal bass lack the sandpaper-like tooth patch usually found on redeye and spotted bass. In addition, shoalies lack the white fin margins exhibited by redeye bass. Shoal bass are easily distinguished from largemouth bass since their jaw does not extend past the rear edge of the eye as in largemouth bass. The ranges of the shoal bass, smallmouth, and Suwannee bass do not overlap.

Techniques

Casting: A light spinning outfit spooled with 6-pound test monofilament is perfect for shoal bass. Although shoal bass will strike nearly any artificial lure, the most exciting and effective way to fish for them is with small topwater lures like chuggers and floating minnow-imitators. Do not overlook small spinners like Rooster Tails and Roadrunners as effective lures for fishing shallow shoals.

Bait fishing: Shoal bass are caught on all types of live bait. Rock worms (hellgrammites) are a favorite. The bait should be presented as naturally as possible with very little weight and a small light-wire hook.

Flycasting: Shoal bass are great fun for the flycaster, and wading the shallow stretches of the rivers the shoalie calls home is a great way to polish your casting skill before venturing to the closer quarters of small mountain trout streams. Popping bugs, Wooly Worms, and streamers are all good bets for shoal bass.

Best bets for Georgia shoal bass: Upper Flint River, Site 55.

SUWANNEE BASS

The most exotic member of the black bass family in Georgia is the Suwannee bass, *Micropterus notius*. The Suwannee bass is generally restricted to the rivers and creeks of the Suwannee River drainage of north Florida and deep southern Georgia. The only major exception is the Ochlockonee River in southwest Georgia.

As with other stream-loving members of the bass family, the Suwannee bass does not grow as large as its slack-water-favoring cousins. The average fish is 10 inches long and weighs less than a pound. The Georgia record Suwannee bass was caught in 1984 from the Ochlockonee River and weighed 3 pounds, 9 ounces.

The Suwannee bass has a few traits that make it extremely well-suited for its habitat. Suwannee bass are tolerant of the infertile, highly acidic, tannic "black water" flowing through the creeks and rivers the Suwannee calls home.

Identification is made easier because the largemouth bass is the only other black bass that shares the Suwannee's limited range. A Suwannee's coloration is similar to a largemouth's except Suwannee bass are more brown compared to the largemouth's greenish color scheme. Suwannee bass often have a bright blue coloration on the bottom rear area of the body. In addition, the Suwannee's jaw only extends to below the eye compared to the largemouth's jaw that extends well behind the eye.

Suwannee bass spawn from April through June, in areas with a substrate of sand or fine gravel.

Techniques

Casting: An ultralight spinning reel filled with 6-pound test line mounted on a 4.5-foot ultralight spinning rod will allow the diminutive Suwannee to exhibit its fighting abilities to the fullest. Several lure companies produce a line of tiny crankbaits and topwater baits that are perfect for fishing for wary stream bass. Lures that imitate crayfish and small minnows are the most effective. Suwannee bass rarely strike plastic worms.

Bait fishing: Live bait can be presented with ultralight tackle in a way that makes it appear very natural and appealing to the fish. Use an ultralight spinning outfit, small wire hook, and as little weight as necessary. An earthworm hooked once or twice through the middle with the ends left to wiggle seductively and drifted through a riffle into the pool below will draw jarring strikes. Small live crayfish can be hooked in the tail and slowly retrieved along the bottom of deep holes.

Flycasting: A 6-weight outfit with a floating line is perfect for catching Suwannee bass. Any fly that imitates forage found in the creek or river will draw strikes. Finding room to make a backcast may be a problem in some waters.

Best bets for Georgia Suwannee bass: Ochlockonee River, Site 64.

BLUEGILL

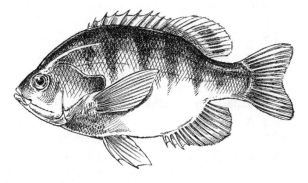

The bluegill sunfish, *Lepomis macrochirus,* is the most common sport fish in Georgia. Although not considered one of Georgia's exalted game fish like the largemouth bass or striped bass, few Georgia anglers have not spent some time catching these scrappy members of the sunfish family. The bluegill is the fish that most anglers cut their teeth on.

The typical bluegill will weigh less than half a pound, but some monsters do exist. The Georgia record bluegill weighed 3 pounds, 5 ounces, and was caught from Shamrock Lake in 1977.

Bluegill begin to spawn the first full moon after the water temperature has warmed above 70 degrees. Spawning will continue throughout the summer based on the lunar cycle, but the first spawn of the spring is usually the largest. Bluegill spawn in colonies, commonly called "bream beds" in Georgia; and often simply looking in shallow water along the shore will reveal a collection of the plate-sized, light depressions.

Fishing a bream bed is a Georgia tradition, and bluegill need to be fished to prevent overpopulation.

Bluegill are fine eating and their abundance and willingness to bite have been the makings of many a Georgia fish fry. The flesh is tender and has a delicate, clean taste. Bluegill can be prepared and cooked many ways; simply headed, gutted, scaled, and then rolled in corn meal and fried whole is a Deep South favorite.

Techniques

Casting: Due to their wide bodies and scrappy nature, bluegill put up quite a struggle on light tackle. A 4.5-foot ultralight spinning rod and a small spinning reel spooled with 4-pound test monofilament is perfect. Bluegill readily hit both live bait and artificials. Small jigs and tiny crankbaits will catch fish, but the best artificial for catching bluegill is a small Beetle Spin or a similar model safety-pin spinner. Bluegill have a hard time resisting the erratic wobbling action of Beetle Spins. In-line spinners like Rooster Tails and Panther Martins are also effective, but are not as snagless when used in the brushy and weedy habitats bluegill prefer. Bluegill like a slow, steady retrieve and will go up or down to strike a bait.

Bait fishing: Bluegill will bite nearly anything. Favorites include crickets, earthworms, and pinches of a nightcrawler, but other live baits including minnows, hellgrammites, leeches, and grasshoppers will also work. A No. 6 long shank Aberdeen hook is best for live bait. Fish live bait under a small bobber or retrieve it slowly along the bottom with the aid of a small split shot sinker. Bluegill are nibblers and will quickly steal the inattentive angler's bait. If using a bobber, use the smallest one possible. Not only will the small bobber show light strikes better, it provides less resistance for the fish to feel while taking the bait. Many bluegill anglers favor the more sensitive stick bobber.

Flycasting: Fly fishing for bluegill is great sport. A 6-weight rod with a weight-forward floating line is perfect. Especially when they are on the spawning beds, bluegill will rise to the top to slurp small poppers, sponge-bodied spiders, and dry flies. Wet flies are also effective. The Black Ant is fine pattern for catching bluegill, although almost any pattern will catch fish since bluegill are not choosy. Especially in clear water, bedding bluegill are spooky. You should be careful not to spook fish off the beds with a clumsy approach.

Other methods: Some anglers prefer to fish for bluegill with a light and springy telescoping fiberglass pole up to 14-feet long. These specialized rods are known as bream poles. Bream poles typically have no reel and no line guides other than the tip. A length of monofilament line a few feet shorter than the pole is tied to the tip of the pole, and a hook or small lead-head jig is tied on the other end of the line, sometimes with a dime-sized bobber a foot or two above the bait. When using a bream pole, no cast is made. The long pole is used to swing the bait into likely places. When the angler detects a strike, a brisk lift of the pole will both hook the fish and bring it to the angler. Bream poles are very good at fishing heavy cover since the bait can be presented vertically into tangles of roots and limbs or holes in thick mats of aquatic vegetation. Bream poles are also very efficient since no time is wasted retrieving the bait through unproductive water. After presenting the bait in one spot, a simple lift and drop of the pole will place the bait in another location.

Best bets for Georgia bluegill: Any Georgia Wildlife Resources Division Public Fishing Area.

REDEAR SUNFISH

Redear sunfish, *Lepomis microlophus,* is one of the most popular species in Georgia. Redear, commonly called shellcracker, are favorites with anglers because they are one of the largest sunfish species in Georgia, are pugnacious fighters, and taste delicious.

The Georgia record redear sunfish weighed an amazing 4 pounds, 2 ounces, and was caught from a private pond in Richmond County in 1995. The average Georgia shellcracker will weigh about half a pound.

Shellcrackers can be distinguished from other sunfish species by their short, stiff earflap edged in red or orange, especially noticeable in large adults. Shellcrackers have a deep and slab-sided body, and their mouth is smaller than most other sunfish species.

Redear sunfish prefer still water, and even in rivers and creeks will seek out protected areas out of the main current. The redear sunfish feeds primarily on small snails and other mollusks. The throat is equipped with a set of teeth allowing the fish to crush the shell of its prey to get to the meat inside, hence the name. Although snails are preferred prey, like most sunfish, shellcrackers are opportunistic feeders and will attempt to eat nearly anything that appeals to them as food and they can get in their mouth. Other prey includes worms, crickets, and small minnows.

Redear are one of the first sunfish to spawn in early spring, and generally are on the beds before bluegill. The beds appear as shallow dish-like depressions in the bottom and are clustered into a colony, with the edges of the beds nearly touching.

At times other than the spawn, big shellcrackers will be found in deeper water around aquatic vegetation or other cover. Smaller fish will be around shoreline weeds and brush. Good fishing can still be had during these times, but finding a concentration of fish is much more difficult than during the spawn.

Techniques

Casting: Although live bait is undoubtedly the best for shellcrackers, a small Beetle Spin worked along the bottom will draw strikes, as will a sixteenth-ounce lead head paired with a small plastic grub. Sweetening the lure with a tiny pinch of worm may make all the difference in the world and result in a heavier stringer at the end of the day. Ultralight spinning tackle is best suited to casting the little lures used for sunfish, and gives the fish a chance to show its fighting skills.

Bait fishing: A light spinning or spin-casting outfit and a handful of hooks, small weights, and perhaps a bobber is everything needed to catch redear sunfish. A No. 6 long-shank Aberdeen hook is a favorite since it is small enough to ensure the fish will take the hook along with the bait, is light enough to bend and come loose if snagged, and the long shank makes unhooking fish easier. Probably the best bait for redear sunfish is a small earthworm, commonly called a red wiggler.

Flycasting: Fly fishing gear can be very effective for redear sunfish. Although they will not come to the top to smash popping bugs with the same abandon as bluegill, a wet fly can be very productive, especially during the spawn. Patterns like the Black Ant worked slowly near the bottom are productive.

Best bets for Georgia redear sunfish: Any Georgia Wildlife Resources Division Public Fishing Area.

REDBREAST SUNFISH

The redbreast sunfish, *Lepomis auritus,* or red belly, is found in most Georgia rivers and creeks, and is usually the most common sunfish species encountered, especially on Georgia's coastal rivers like the Satilla and the Ogeechee. The Georgia record redbreast sunfish is a 1 pound, 11 ounces, specimen caught from a private pond in Coweta County in 1998. The average Georgia redbreast sunfish will run 5 to 6 inches.

The best spots to find redbreasts are around heavy cover in outside river bends. The combination of cover and deep water found in the bends creates a combination redbreasts find hard to refuse. Unfortunately for the redbreast sunfish, flathead catfish prefer the same type of habitat. These large predators, not native to Georgia's coastal rivers, have severely impacted the redbreast population in some rivers.

Redbreast sunfish can be identified by their long and narrow earflap, large mouth, and a bright coloration words cannot do justice to, especially for breeding males. The term "roosters" is sometimes used to describe large male redbreasts all trimmed out in their finest colors to attract a mate. Redbreasts spawn in early spring, and like other sunfish fan out a dish-shaped depression in which to lay their eggs. The nest is defended until the eggs have hatched and the young are on their own.

Techniques

Casting: An outfit spooled with 6-pound monofilament works well for redbreasts. If you plan to fish heavy cover, 8-pound test line might be in order and will enable you to straighten out the hook and pull free when snagged.

Small spinners like Beetle Spins and Rooster Tails are hard to beat. Cast the spinners around heavy cover where there is some current. Outside bends are good places to try. Redbreast sunfish will also smash small topwater lures.

Bait fishing: The most popular live baits for redbreast sunfish are worms and crickets.

The standard No. 6 Aberdeen long-shanked hook will work fine. A few hooks along with several small split shot weights and a bobber or two will put you in business. Bumping the bait along the bottom without a bobber will catch fish, but sometimes is not practical because of snags.

Flycasting: Fly fishing is one of the best tactics for this scrappy sunfish. Redbreast sunfish will throw caution to the wind and aggressively smash popping bugs. Fly fishing gear also allows several quick presentations to the same small area without have to retrieve the lure through unproductive midchannel water.

Other methods: A fly rod or long limber bream pole can be used to dabble live bait or artificials around blowdowns and other shoreline cover. Some anglers have perfected a method of using a fly rod or bream pole, a fixed length of line slightly shorter than the pole, and a popping bug to "shoot" the lure into likely places. Taking care not to hook yourself, grasp the popping bug between two fingers of one hand, point the pole at the target with the other hand, pull back on the line to load the rod, and when the lure is released it will fly right to the target. With a little practice, this technique can result in accurate rapid-fire presentations to tight places that only an extremely skilled caster could reach, if it were possible at all.

Best bets for Georgia redbreast sunfish: Ochlockonee River, Site 64; Saint Marys River, Site 71; Satilla River, Site 72; Altamaha River, Sites 73, 90, 91; Fort Stewart Military Reservation, Site 89.

CRAPPIE

(WHITE)

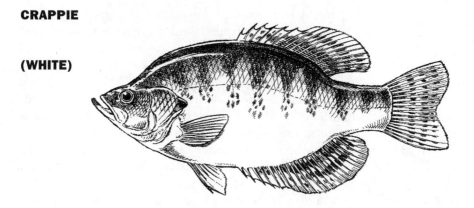

There are two crappie species in Georgia, but to anglers, they are as one. Both species are often found side by side. Both crappies have deep, compressed bodies and large paper-like mouths. The color is olive with emerald and purple highlights on top fading into silvery-white sides and belly. White crappie, *Pomoxis annularis,* have dark spots sometimes arranged into faint vertical bars, while the dark spots of the black crappie, *Pomoxis nigromaculatus,* are arranged in an irregular pattern that gives them a calico appearance and serves as excellent camouflage. The easiest way to distinguish the two species is that white crappie have six dorsal spines, and black crappie have seven or eight dorsal spines.

(BLACK)

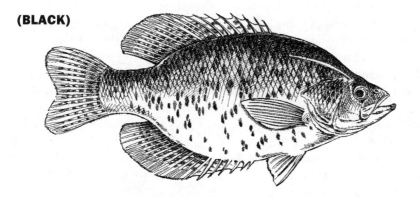

Crappies do well in Georgia and are one of the most important sport fish in the state. Georgia offers some excellent crappie fishing, and they are very popular with anglers because of the fine sport they offer and their delicious flavor when prepared for the table. The state record white crappie weighed 5 pounds and was caught from a Bibb County pond in 1984. The state record black crappie is a tie between two 4.25-pounders, one caught in 1971 and one in 1975, both from small lakes.

Most anglers would be hard-pressed to correctly distinguish between white and black crappie, and unless you think you have caught a record fish, there really is no reason to try. Interestingly, scientific research has suggested in some bodies of water the hybridization rate is so high that a good percentage of the crappie caught are actually hybrids of the two species. Hybrids of any two species are usually faster-growing and more aggressive, which may explain why hybrid crappie show up more frequently in the creel.

Anglers interested in good crappie fishing should focus their efforts on reservoirs and rivers; smaller bodies of water may have crappie present, but they probably will be stunted due to overpopulation.

Crappie are one of the first fish to spawn in early spring, and fishing the crappie spawn usually kicks off the angling year for many fishing enthusiasts. Anglers have developed all sorts of ways to figure out when the crappie are spawning based on what other living things are doing. For example, one saying is "when the dogwood trees are blooming, the crappie are spawning."

During the spring spawn, crappie move shallow around woody cover and are easily found and caught using a variety of techniques. After the spawn, crappie move deep and spend the warmer months in deeper water, often suspending over offshore structure. Once early winter arrives, crappie begin to closely reltate to offshore structure like channel ledges and provide fine fishing for anglers willing to brave the elements. After a little work to find the fish, an angler can experience some of the best crappie fishing of the year during the winter. This period also produces some of the biggest crappie of the year.

Although not the strongest-fighting fish that swims, their abundance, willingness to strike, and delicate taste make crappie a fine game fish. There are many good crappie fishing holes in Georgia, and a lot of different ways to catch them, making crappie one of the most popular sport fish in the Peach State.

Techniques

Casting: Light spinning or spin-casting gear is well-suited for crappie fishing. Six-pound test monofilament will work well, although 4-pound or 8-pound may be more suitable in certain circumstances. Lighter line will result in more strikes, but heavier line will result in fewer hooks lost to snags.

If you prefer artificials, small lead-head jigs are the way to go. A sixteenth-ounce jig with a small plastic grub or tube body is an excellent lure for crappie. Work the lure slowly with a lift and drop retrieve around woody cover. If fish are suspended in deep water, count the lure down to the desired depth and give it a slow steady retrieve. Small spinners can also be effective crappie lures.

Bait fishing: A small minnow fished on a No. 1 light wire hook suspended under a small bobber probably catches more crappie in Georgia every year than any other technique. The float should be small enough to be easily pulled under so the fish on the other end does not feel resistance and drop the bait.

A bait-fishing method for catching inactive crappie in very deep water is to bump the bottom. Once a large stump, channel bend, or other piece of deep cover or structure is found, a rig consisting of a bell sinker tied directly to the end of the line and a No. 1 Aberdeen hook on a dropper tied 12 inches above the weight is used to put the bait right in front of the crappie's nose and keep it there. No casting or retrieve is involved. Position the boat directly over the target, free-spool the rig to the desired depth, and then use the trolling motor to maintain position and "hover" over the target. This method excels at catching huge crappie during cold weather.

Flycasting: Crappie are not typically pursued with fly fishing gear in Georgia. When the crappie are shallow, some fish can be caught on small streamers, but more productive techniques are available.

Trolling: Crappie are one of the few fish species in Georgia routinely targeted by trolling. Especially in the winter, when crappie are concentrated over offshore structure, using an electric trolling motor to slowly troll a spread of small crappie jigs is a killer technique. Crappie fishing with numerous rods is sometimes called "spider rigging." A pair of skilled anglers with a well-designed setup may troll 10 or more rods at once. Not much specialized equipment is needed for this style of trolling other than some simple rod holders. However, some bodies of water have regulations dictating how many rods can be used at any one time, so be sure to check the regulations before your trip.

Other methods: Crappie holding in thick cover in shallow water are best caught using a long limber pole typically called a bream pole. These poles sometimes have a small reel built in or attached to them, but the reel is only used to store line, not cast or retrieve. A small minnow or jig is used as bait. The angler lets out a length of line slightly shorter than the pole, and uses the long pole to reach out and drop the bait right in the middle of the cover. When a fish strikes, a quick lift of the pole hooks the fish and brings it straight up out of its snag-infested lair. This type of fishing is especially effective in early spring when the crappie have moved into shallow cover to spawn. The water is usually stained or muddy from spring rains, which allows for a close approach without spooking the fish.

Best bets for Georgia crappie: Coosa River at Mayo's Lock and Dam, Site 2; Allatoona Lake, Site 7; Lake Oconee, Site 49; Lake Sinclair, Site 50; Lake Blackshear, Site 66.

STRIPED BASS

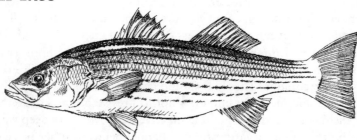

The striped bass, *Morone saxatilis,* commonly called striper or rockfish, is without question one of the hardest fighting fish that swims in Georgia waters.

Although primarily a saltwater fish, stripers have found some Georgia freshwater reservoirs and rivers to be to their liking. Stripers are rarely able to spawn successfully in landlocked systems, however, and their numbers must be maintained by periodic stocking. The striper's voracious appetite makes it a favorite with reservoir fisheries managers. Striper stocking in reservoirs is a forage management tool that benefits anglers in two ways.

Baitfish, like shad and herring, tend to overpopulate resulting in high numbers of large adults and almost no reproduction. The large adults are too big for other predators like black bass and crappie to eat. Stocking stripers ensures sufficient predatory pressure is available to keep baitfish populations dynamic. Stripers are well-suited for this duty for several reasons. They are voracious eaters, they grow to large sizes and thus are able to eat larger baitfish, and they prefer the same type of pelagic, or open-water habitat, as do shad and herring. The predatory pressure stripers put on baitfish populations helps prevent overpopulation. By helping keep the baitfish populations in check, all fish species benefit.

The second benefit from stripers is not only are they a great tool for manipulating forage populations, they are a great sport fish themselves. Stripers exemplify brute force, and nothing else, at least in freshwater, can compare.

Striped bass are true bass, versus the black bass species like largemouth and smallmouth bass, which actually belong to the sunfish family. Stripers have a compressed, deep body giving them the familiar bass-like shape. Stripers are dark olive to blue-gray above, fading into a silvery-white side and belly. There are six to nine prominent dark stripes running the length of the fish. The stripes are usually unbroken.

The state record striped bass weighed 63.0 pounds and was caught from the Oconee River in 1967. In saltwater, stripers have been known to achieve even heavier weights. The average striped bass caught in freshwater will weigh between 5 and 10 pounds, but specimens up to 40 pounds are fairly common.

Unfortunately, Georgia's saltwater population of stripers has also faced barriers preventing successful reproduction. The Savannah River striped bass population underwent a serious decline after alteration of flow patterns in the Savannah River. Because of this, there is a year-round closed season on striped bass in the Savannah River and its tributaries below New Savannah Bluff Lock and Dam. Perhaps at some future time this once great fishery can be reopened to harvest, but while recovery is still taking place, it will remain closed.

Luckily for Georgia anglers, the Savannah River is not the only place in Georgia to catch striped bass. Many Georgia reservoirs and other coastal rivers have good fishing for striped bass. Look for stripers to be holding in the coolest water available during the hot summer months, either in the depths or where there are springs or another source of cool water. Stripers find the cold water of winter to their liking, and the cooler months can offer the best striper fishing of the year.

Stripers can be frustrating fish. Sometimes absolutely nothing will coax a strike, and other times the strikes come fast and furious.

As a final caution, stripers are big, strong fish with sharp spines and razor-like gill plates. Get careless handling one, and they will do unpleasant things to you, your equipment, or both.

Techniques

Stripers are amazingly strong, and successfully landing even an average-size fish requires good tackle. Heavy spinning or baitcasting outfits are the order of the day for stripers. If the reel has a smooth drag and is set properly, typical heavy-duty bass fishing tackle can be used for reservoir stripers. Since stripers are open-water fish and are usually caught from places with few snags, a big fish can be landed even on tackle that seems light compared to the size of the quarry. However, since stripers are not exceptionally line shy, use line heavy enough to give yourself a chance of landing the fish. Twelve-pound test monofilament ought to be considered the absolute minimum, and 20-pound line greatly increases the odds of completing the battle in the angler's favor.

A good depth finder is an invaluable aid for finding stripers. Stripers are constantly on the move looking for baitfish, but a search of likely places such as humps, deep points, and channels should eventually reveal the right combination of structure and bait.

Saltwater fishing for stripers is much the same game as catching them in freshwater. The key is to find the right combination of bait and structure, and the stripers should be there. Tides add another variable to the equation. Feeding usually occurs when the tide is moving, either in or out. Dead low or high tides are not the best time to fish.

Casting: One of the most exciting ways to fish for stripers is to find an area where a school of stripers have pushed baitfish to the top and are actively feeding. These feeding frenzies, commonly called jumps, usually occur early or late in the day over offshore structures. When the surface is calm, the commotion caused by baitfish frantic to escape, and stripers equally frantic to catch them, can be spotted from quite a distance. Wheeling and diving gulls are also a good sign a striper jump is in progress. When this condition occurs, head toward the area as fast as possible since the action is often short-lived. Take care to shut the boat off and drift in for the final approach since the fish are easily spooked. Any lure closely imitating a baitfish will work, but heavy lures can be cast farther and prevent having to approach the school too closely. Large topwater plugs are excellent for this type of fishing and seeing a big striper smash a topwater plug will set any angler's pulse to racing.

If you cannot get into a jump, fish bucktail jigs, a jigging spoon, or large topwater plugs in areas you believe hold fish. Points and humps are always good. Try the surface baits during low light conditions, and go with the bucktail jig or jigging spoons later in the day.

Bait fishing: Bait fishing is the most consistent method of catching stripers. Two tactics are used, and the choice depends on how active the fish are and what depth they are holding. Both methods require live bait like shad, herring, trout, or small sunfish. The choices are to down-line or free-line.

Down-lining means making a vertical presentation using a weight to hold the bait at the desired depth. Slide a heavy egg sinker on the main line and then tie on a heavy-duty barrel swivel. Then add a 3-foot leader and finish the rig with a live-bait hook tied on the end of the leader. This rig is usually fished vertically for suspended fish.

With free-lining, no weight is used and the bait can swim wherever it chooses. A hook is simply tied on the end of the line and baited with a lively baitfish. A small balloon is sometimes tied to the line as a strike indicator and to keep the bait from going too deep.

The key to any bait fishing is to make sure the bait is lively and swimming strong. Most anglers prefer to carefully hook the bait through the nose to allow the best swimming action. Change baits frequently. A fresh bait often means the difference between no action and catching fish. If live bait is not working, try a piece of cut bait. The scent trail from the cut bait may be what it takes for a fish to find the bait.

Flycasting: Fly fishing for stripers is not common in Georgia, although some anglers are willing to settle for fewer fish just for the chance of hooking a big striper on a fly rod. Catching a striper on fly fishing gear requires a reel with a good drag and plenty of backing. Fly fishing for stripers is best suited for below shoals and other river feeding stations, but some reservoir anglers have success by being patient and making repeated presentations to a good area hoping to coax a striper up for a strike. Large streamers that imitate a baitfish are the best choice.

Trolling: Trolling is a common method of catching stripers. Once structure and baitfish are found, trolling around the area with either artificials or live bait can be very productive. The use of an "umbrella rig" has become popular for trolling for stripers in recent years. An umbrella rig is a heavy wire spreader that allows five baits to be worked on short leaders off one main line. The baits of choice are usually bucktail jigs. Other anglers prefer to troll diving plugs or a single bucktail. Down-lining and free-lining can also be used when trolling. Set out the baits and use the trolling motor to slowly move the boat back and forth across a productive area.

Best bets for Georgia striped bass: Coosa River at Mayo's Lock and Dam, Site 2; Allatoona Lake, Site 7; Lake Nottely, Site 21; Lake Sidney Lanier, Site 40.

HYBRID STRIPED BASS

The hybrid striped bass is a cross between the striped bass, *Morone saxatilis,* and the white bass, *Morone chrysops.* Georgia Wildlife Resources Division hatcheries produce millions of these fish every year. The fish are stocked into the reservoirs at about an inch in length. Hybrids can tolerate warmer water temperatures than striped bass, and thus do extremely well in reservoirs where the habitat is marginal for stripers. Hybrids grow larger than white bass, but do not even come close to obtaining the huge sizes of their striped bass cousins. Nevertheless, hybrids are aggressive feeders and are usually much easier to catch than striped bass, making them one of Georgia's most popular sport fish. The Georgia record hybrid striped bass was caught in 1995 from Lake Chatuge and weighed 25.5 pounds.

Techniques

Casting: The same gear normally used for largemouth bass fishing will work well for hybrids. Anglers should outfit themselves with a medium-heavy to heavy rod and reel spooled with plenty of line. Twelve-pound test monofilament should be the minimum when chasing hybrids.

The most common method of casting to hybrids is fishing the jumps. Especially in the summer, hybrids will push schools of baitfish to the top and go on a brief but frantic feeding spree. Jumps usually occur during the low light conditions of dawn or dusk, and are often out in the middle of the lake over a deep channel or submerged island. Anglers should scan the water in likely areas for the disturbance caused by a school of wild predators chasing frantically fleeing baitfish. Jumps are short-lived, so approach as quickly as possible taking care to shut off the outboard short of the school of fish. Motoring right into the school will spook them and put them down.

Any topwater bait that imitates a shad is a good bet for fishing jumps, as are spoons, crankbaits, and lead-head jigs. One of the more effective methods is to use a popping cork and jig. A popping cork is a large bobber that is concave on one end and tapers to a point on the other end. The tapered end has an eye, and this is where a 24-inch dropper line is tied. A quarter-ounce jig rigged with a 3-inch curly-tailed plastic grub tied onto the dropper line completes the rig. Retrieving the popping cork with short jerks of the rod will create a commotion that imitates the actions of a wounded baitfish. As the hybrid investigates the possible feeding opportunity, the jig on the dropper line dances seductively in front of its nose. Hybrid strikes are ferocious, and leave no doubt in your mind what is happening.

If hybrids are not actively feeding, search for them with a depth finder around offshore structure like channels, points, and humps. Look for strong fish signals suspended below a school of baitfish. Even when not actively feeding, hybrids will always be near a school of baitfish. Once fish are found, make a vertical presentation at the depth the fish are at using a heavy jigging spoon.

Fish the jigging spoon by sharply snapping the rod tip upward and then using the rod to follow the lure back down with a controlled amount of slack in the line. If there is no slack while the spoon falls, there will be very little of the fluttering action that imitates a dying baitfish. Most strikes come as the spoon is falling, and with the necessary slack in the line, an angler often sees rather than feels the strike.

Bait fishing: Fishing live bait is a very good technique for hybrids. Commonly used baits include shad, herring, large shiners, small sunfish, and in some areas of the state, rainbow trout. Free-lining refers to allowing the bait to swim freely with only enough tension maintained to feel the strike. Down-lining is similar except that a heavy egg sinker is used 3 feet in front of the bait to keep it at the desired depth. A barrel swivel is used to keep the sinker from sliding all the way to the bait and to prevent line twist. Live bait can also be fished below a float. Small balloons about the size of a lemon are commonly used as a float in this method of fishing. The balloon is inflated and tied on the line at the desired depth. Under most conditions, lively bait is the key to catching hybrids. Using a heavy-duty short shank 1/0 or 2/0 hook, hook the bait through one nostril and out the upper lip to avoid killing the bait or impeding its action. If the bait is not active and swimming strong, replace it. However, in muddy water conditions, cut bait can sometimes be more effective. The scent and blood trail produced by a piece of cut bait can help hybrids find the bait when visibility is low. Some anglers even borrow a catfishing trick and use chicken livers as bait. The blood from the livers produces a scent trail for the hungry hybrids to follow.

Flycasting: Fly fishing is not a common method for catching hybrids. However, fly fishers can catch surfacing hybrids using large streamers that closely imitate the predominant forage, usually small shad.

Trolling: Trolling is an effective method of catching hybrids. Using a depth finder to quickly scan a prospective area for fish is an advantage to those who have the equipment available, but trolling blind over likely areas near channels, points, and humps will eventually put you into a school of fish. Without a depth finder, experiment to find out the depth the fish are holding. Effective lures for trolling include crankbaits and jigs. The depth the bait will run is dependant on the size of the bait, speed it is trolled, and how much line is out. Once the first fish is caught, try to duplicate what was taking place and repeatedly troll over the same area.

Best bets for Georgia hybrid striped bass: Most large reservoirs.

WHITE BASS

The white bass, *Morone chrysops,* is a close relative of the striped bass. White bass were native or have been introduced throughout much of Georgia in medium to large rivers and in reservoirs, and are usually abundant wherever they are found.

Although closely related to the striped bass, white bass do not grow to near the size of their larger cousins. The average white bass in Georgia will weigh 0.75 pound. The Georgia record white bass was caught in 1971 from Lake Sidney Lanier and weighed 5 pounds, 1 ounce.

White bass can be caught in great numbers in the early spring when they begin to make their upstream spawning migration. During the spawn, the best place to find white bass is near the bank in flowing water. Creek mouths are also prime places to find schools of white bass during the spawn.

White bass are aggressive feeders and are often the saving grace for a fishing trip when nothing else is willing to bite. Especially during the dog days of summer, many a fruitless day of fishing on Georgia's reservoirs has been saved by picking up an ultralight spinning outfit and casting to jumps of surfacing schools of white bass.

In reservoirs, white bass will usually be found near schools of baitfish, except during the spawning migration. Points, humps, and channels are always good places to hold shad and white bass. Using a depth finder, anglers can often find schools of white bass simply by idling over likely areas looking for the telltale cloud of shad.

In rivers, white bass prefer sandy bars and banks during the warm months. In fact, in some regions of the United States, white bass are commonly known as sand bass because of their affinity for sandy bottoms. If the bite suddenly stops when fishing a river sandbar, try moving the boat farther out into the river and fishing the deeper portions of the sandbar. White bass will often repeatedly move in and out on a piece of structure throughout the day. When fishing slows, often a change in the depth you are fishing will reacquire the school of fish.

Techniques

Casting: An ultralight spinning outfit spooled with 6-pound test monofilament will work for any white bass fishing situation that an angler might encounter. An eighth-ounce lead-head jig with a plastic grub body will catch any white bass that swims, but small spinners and crankbaits are also effective. Reaching bottom in strong current may require a heavier jig. White bass are usually not picky about details, but on rare days even the color of the jig head can mean the difference between a great day and no strikes.

Bait fishing: Minnows, small shad, and other baitfish are used to catch white bass. Minnows can be hooked through the head with a jig and fished in the same manner as a plastic grub. A minnow and bobber combination can be used anytime white bass are shallow enough to make fishing with a bobber practical.

Flycasting: Few anglers flycast for white bass, but those who do will experience some great sport. White bass are especially prone to being caught on fly gear when they are shallow to spawn and when they are near the surface during a jump.

Best bets for Georgia white bass: Coosa River at Mayo's Lock and Dam, Site 2; Lake Sidney Lanier, Site 40; Lake Oconee, Site 49; Bartletts Ferry Lake, Site 58.

WALLEYE

Despite its huge popularity in more northern climes, the walleye, *Stizostedion vitreum,* is not really a sought-after game fish in Georgia. Part of this lack of interest is undoubtedly because only a few fishable walleye populations exist, all in the northern portion of the state. Since north Georgia is included in the walleye's natural range, there are a few bodies of water where walleye populations maintain themselves at a fishable level without stocking. In other bodies of water, stocking has taken place in an attempt to "jump start" a low-level natural population up to the level where it can support good fishing. Some north Georgia rivers also support small populations of native walleye, but catches are rare.

Northern transplants are sometimes startled to discover there are walleye in Georgia, and cannot understand why the species is almost totally ignored by most Georgia anglers. With the influx of experienced walleye anglers into the state, walleye techniques will likely start to become part of every angler's bag of tricks.

Walleye are slender yellowish or olive-brown fish with a large mouth full of prominent, needle-sharp teeth. The Georgia record walleye is a 11 pounds, 6 ounces, specimen caught in 1995 from Lake Richard B. Russell. The average walleye caught in Georgia will weigh a couple of pounds.

Walleye spawn in late winter or early spring and often migrate up tributary rivers to find their desired spawning habitat. Fish become concentrated during the spawning migration, and the spawn is one of the best times to fish for this tasty member of the perch family.

Techniques

Casting: The best tackle to use for walleye is largely a matter of personal preference. Spinning tackle is the most common, but spin-casting or even light baitcasting gear will work. Casting crankbaits or a jig-and-grub combo over rocky points and bars is a productive technique. As their large eyes might suggest, walleye are primarily nocturnal feeders and will bite aggressively throughout the nighttime hours. Many anglers prefer to fish at night for walleye, even in the dead of winter. During the darkness, walleye move up from their deep daytime haunts onto shallow points and bars and feed aggressively.

Bait fishing: A nightcrawler or minnow still-fished or retrieved slowly along the bottom in the right places will catch Georgia walleye. Keep terminal tackle as light as possible to give the bait the most natural action possible.

Trolling: Trolling crankbaits or jigs over points and bars covers a lot of water and will catch fish, especially during the hours of darkness.

Best Bets for Georgia walleye: Carters Lake, Site 8; Blue Ridge Lake, Site 16; Lake Chatuge, Site 22; Lake Rabun, Site 35; Lake Sidney Lanier, Site 40.

FLATHEAD CATFISH

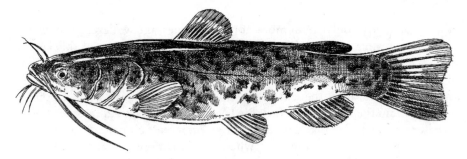

A large flathead is the bully on the block that other fish fear. Because of its preference for live bait and its large size, the flathead catfish, *Pylodictis olivaris,* is usually at the top of the food chain wherever it is found. In recent years their range has expanded via illegal introductions into Atlantic Slope drainages like the Altamaha, and in some areas have seriously impacted native fish species like redbreast sunfish and bullheads.

The flathead catfish is a creature of large streams, rivers, and reservoirs. Flatheads use a variety of habitats, but in moving water are rarely found in areas of high gradient or intermittent flow. In reservoirs, flatheads usually associate with submerged channels. The flathead catfish is a solitary species and usually any one logjam or other piece of cover will only yield a few adult flatheads. Flatheads feed actively at night and will spend the daylight hours loafing in a favorite deep hole before venturing shallow to feed.

Flatheads are a slender catfish with a broad flat head. The back and sides are a pale yellow to light brown mottled with dark brown or black, with the belly a pale yellow or cream-white. The upper lobe of the rounded or slightly notched tail is often tipped in white. Flatheads can be distinguished from other Georgia catfish species by the white-tipped tail, and a lower jaw that extends slightly beyond the upper jaw giving the fish the facial appearance of a truculent child.

Flathead spawning is similar to other catfishes. A shallow depression is excavated in a natural cavity, a hollow log for example, or near some other submerged object.

Many anglers feel that unlike other catfish species, a large flathead is just as tasty and tender as a small one. A big flathead will yield a lot of meat, delicious battered and deep-fried.

Flathead catfish are one of the largest-growing Georgia sport fish and are often overlooked by anglers, especially in reservoirs. The Georgia record flathead catfish weighed 67.8 pounds and was caught in 2000 from the Altamaha River.

Techniques

Casting: Anglers after other species sometimes accidentally catch a flathead on artificial lures, but it is not a common occurrence.

Bait fishing: Fishing with live bait on very heavy tackle is the best and really the only way to go for catching monster flatheads. Light saltwater tackle may even need to be considered. If you plan on tangling with a monster flathead, 25-pound line is the minimum.

A sunfish or shad makes good bait, and is usually fished on bottom. A standard fish-finder rig consisting of a sliding sinker, a heavy swivel trailed by a 3-foot leader of heavy monofilament, and a large sturdy hook on the end is a simple yet productive rig. The current dictates how much lead is required to keep the bait in place. The bait should be hooked in a way to keep it as lively as possible and not impede its action. Cast the rig out into a likely place like a logjam in a deep channel bend, a feeding flat at the head of a deep pool, or on the edge of a submerged channel, and wait the fish out. Flathead bites may not be many, but they may produce the largest fish you have ever caught.

Best bets for Georgia flathead catfish: Altamaha River, Sites 73, 90, 91.

CHANNEL CATFISH

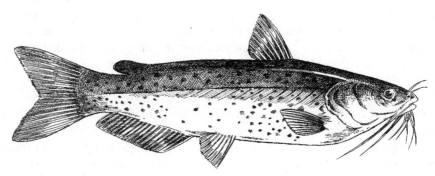

The channel catfish, *Ictalurus punctatus,* is one of the bread-and-butter fish species of Georgia anglers. Nearly every angler in Georgia has enjoyed fishing for these whiskered denizens of the deep at one time or another. Channel catfish are widely distributed throughout the state, are usually easy to catch, pull like a mule, and are great eating. A meal of deep-fried catfish fillets and hush puppies is a Dixie tradition.

As their name suggests, channel catfish have an affinity for rivers and moving water. However, they are very adaptable and have been widely stocked into lakes and ponds all over Georgia.

Channel catfish are not fussy eaters and will chow down with gusto on a smorgasbord of baits, both live and dead. Anglers hunting monster channel cats will generally stick with live fish as bait, but those hunting eating-size cats prefer to use stink bait. Channel catfish feed mostly by scent and taste, which explains the popularity of baits that leave a strong scent trail for the catfish to follow to the hook. Every catfish angler has their favorite stink bait, often a home-concocted combination of the vilest, smelliest substances imaginable. Nearly anything will work for bait. Some channel cat aficionados swear by a chunk of soap, preferably the old-fashioned lye soap variety! Channel cats are nibblers and will often tentatively mouth a bait for some time before finally taking it completely.

Channel catfish can be identified by their deeply forked tail and small dark spots on the body, although the spots are often very faint or absent in large specimens. Large channel catfish sometimes are confused with blue catfish. However, the anal fin of the channel catfish is rounded versus the straight-edged anal fin on blue catfish.

Although channel catfish have been known to grow to the 100-pound range, the Georgia record channel catfish weighed 44.75 pounds and was caught in 1972 from the Altamaha River.

Techniques

Bait fishing: Anglers seeking trophy catfish prefer live baits like small sunfish or shad. Large channel cats are more predatory than their smaller brethren, and a lively sunfish fished just off bottom in a deep river hole can produce some monster fish. Horsing huge channel cats out of their snag-infested lairs requires heavy tackle. A heavy baitcasting or spinning outfit spooled with 20-pound test line should be considered the minimum. Hook the live bait with a heavy 4/0 or larger hook allowing it to swim freely. Use enough weight to keep the bait on the bottom and when a strike occurs, allow the fish ample time to completely take the bait before setting the hook. Reels with a free spool bait-clicker are excellent for this type of fishing.

For the average-sized channel catfish, or "fiddlers," stink baits and smaller live baits like nightcrawlers get the nod. Fish these baits on bottom. Use a slip-sinker ahead of a small split shot weight pinched on the line 12 inches ahead of the hook. This rig will allow the catfish to take the bait without feeling resistance from the weight. When using pasty or nearly liquid stink baits, many anglers prefer a specialized hook that consists of a treble hook attached to a small piece of sponge or ribbed plastic. These hooks are designed to hold the bait on the hook and slowly release it into the water. Whatever type hook is used, the bait should be well secured to prevent a crafty catfish from nibbling away without ever being detected.

Best bets for Georgia channel catfish: All Georgia Wildlife Resources Division Public Fishing Areas, medium to large rivers, and major reservoirs.

SPOTTED SEATROUT

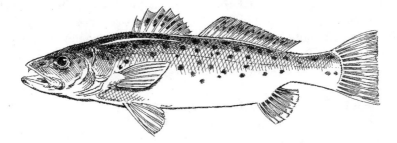

Spotted seatrout, *Cynoscion nebulosus,* are the most sought-after marine sport fish in Georgia. Spotted seatrout (also known as speckled trout) are members of the drum (Sciaenidae) family. The drum family is so named because its members can make a noise using their air bladder that sounds very similar to the beating of a drum. Spotted seatrout are common along Georgia's coast, and can be found from Massachusetts south to the waters of the Yucatan Peninsula.

Studies have shown that spotted seatrout prefer to live out their lives in the same estuary where they were born. Spotted seatrout prefer fringe areas along banks, points, jetties, and bars. In the spring and summer, the urge to spawn sends them to the beaches. With the coming of autumn and the subsequent drop in water temperature, spotted seatrout move into the lower sounds to take advantage of abundant prey. With the coming of winter, the fish migrate farther up the estuary into rivers and creeks. During harsh winter weather, spotted seatrout will often move into the deepest holes and channels.

Spotted seatrout exhibit strong schooling behavior and are opportunistic feeders whose preferred diet varies. Juvenile fish primarily feed on zooplankton and other small crustaceans. Larger fish prey on shrimp and small fish. Spotted seatrout larger than 18 inches feed almost exclusively on other fish.

The Georgia record spotted seatrout weighed 9 pounds, 7 ounces, and was caught in 1976 from Christmas Creek. Spotted seatrout average 1 to 2 pounds, although gator trout weighing more than 5 pounds are occasionally caught.

Techniques

Casting: Live shrimp are considered the best all-around bait for spotted seatrout. However, artificials can be just as effective, and sometimes even better than live bait, especially from November through March when water temperatures are cooler. Any lure that imitates a shrimp or small fish will work. A plastic shrimp body threaded on a lead-head jig is perfect for spotted seatrout, and crankbaits can also be effective. When using artificials, retrieve the lure as slowly as possible while keeping the lure near bottom. Preferred tackle for fishing artificials is a light spinning or casting outfit spooled with 10-pound test line.

Bait fishing: The most commonly used method for spotted seatrout is drifting a live shrimp under a standard deep floating rig. When using a float rig, a medium-sized spinning or baitcasting reel filled with 10-pound test line together with an 8-foot rod fits the bill. Shrimp is the most popular bait, but live finger-sized mullet, mud minnows, or menhaden (pogies) also work well. Spotted seatrout are typically midwater feeders, so adjust your rig so the bait is presented well off the bottom. For larger fish, live-line a small mullet or other bait fish.

Flycasting: Fly fishing gear is not commonly used for spotted seatrout, but can be effective. Spotted seatrout are opportunistic feeders, and will strike any fly that imitates prey. An 8-weight rod and a reel with plenty of backing will handle any spotted seatrout and the heavier gear and backing may be appreciated if a large flounder or red drum strikes the fly.

Best bets for Georgia spotted seatrout: All along the Georgia coast.

KING MACKEREL

King mackerel (or kingfish), *Scomberomorus cavalla,* are related to tuna and are a popular sport fish off the Georgia coast. Big king mackerel are sometimes called smoker kings, perhaps because they are strong enough to smoke a hundred yards of line off a reel in the blink of an eye.

These fish are highly migratory and live their entire lives in the open waters of the Atlantic Ocean and Gulf of Mexico. Water temperature governs the migration patterns of mackerel. As the water warms in the spring, fish will begin to move up the Atlantic coast and make the return trip in the fall. Kingfish have a strong schooling instinct and seeing a school of smoker kings tear into bait on the surface is a sight to behold. Since they are an open-water fish, the details of their life history are not completely known. Kingfish spawn in midsummer well offshore, and are aggressive feeders on small fish and squid.

Kingfish have a long, streamlined body and a tapered head. The back is an iridescent bluish green with silvery sides. King mackerel resemble Spanish mackerel, but kingfish have no black pigment on the front of the dorsal fin. Yellow spots are sometimes visible on the sides of young king mackerel, but as the fish grow the spots fade away. On a king mackerel, the lateral line starts high and drops sharply below the second dorsal fin.

The first step to finding and catching king mackerel is finding the bait. Kings will never be far from their food source. Look for surface activity to find schools of menhaden (pogies) or small Spanish mackerel. Do not overlook schools of groundfish such as spot, croaker, and weakfish as an attraction that king mackerel, especially big smoker kings, find hard to resist. A good depth finder will help find forage and structure. The key to finding catchable fish is water clarity. Mackerel are sight feeders and will be in places where they can easily spot and track their target.

Fishing for kingfish is primarily an offshore game. However, from May through August, anglers catch kings around nearshore tidelines, shipping channels, and reefs. During this time, the nearshore waters are especially rich with forage, and the kings move in to take advantage of the easy pickings. A tideline transition from dirty water to clear water near an inlet is always a good place to try.

The chances of catching a good king mackerel from shore are not that great, but in saltwater fishing, anything can happen. A few fish may occasionally move in close to the beach and give anglers on piers and in the surf a shot at catching a smoker king.

King mackerel more than 20 pounds are common. The Georgia record king mackerel weighed in at 63.5 pounds and was caught in 1990 from the Brunswick Snapper Banks. Chasing smoker kings is popular with tournament anglers, and lucky anglers win thousands of dollars in money and prizes every year.

Techniques

Casting: Casting plugs or live bait is not the most productive way to fish for kings, but can be the most exciting. When actively feeding fish are found, casting to the boils will produce fish, but stumbling upon this usually short-lived situation is a hit and miss proposition. Any lure that imitates a baitfish will draw strikes, and a stout spinning or casting outfit spooled with lots of 20-pound test monofilament will suffice for tackle. Because of their sharp teeth, king mackerel will cut off a bait if a heavy leader is not used. The reel should have a high line capacity, and the drag should be silky smooth. When they feel the hook, kings will quickly run off a lot of line, and following them with the boat may be necessary to prevent being spooled.

Bait fishing: Most bait fishing for king mackerel is done by trolling. In some situations, live-lining bait may work, but trolling is the favorite presentation.

Trolling: Trolling is the preferred method for catching king mackerel. Most boats will fish four lines with a three-person crew; one to handle the boat, one to handle the rod, and the third to clear the decks for action and land the fish. Usually two lines are trolled on top, one short and one long, and the other two lines are fished deeper using downriggers. Castnetting a baitwell full of menhaden is preferred, but purchasing frozen bait will do in a pinch. When targeting smoker kings, go with bigger bait such as mullet or Spanish mackerel. Correctly rigging baits for trolling takes some skill and specialized knowledge. The basic idea is to troll the bait behind a wire or monofilament leader connected to the main line by a heavy swivel. Both spinning and casting gear will work for trolling live bait. The reels should hold at least 300 yards of 20-pound monofilament and have smooth adjustable drags.

Although trolling natural baits at idle speed is the most common method of fishing for kings, fast-trolling artificials at around 5 knots will work on days when bait is hard to come by. Lures to consider for trolling are spoons, plugs, or anything that resembles a baitfish.

Flycasting: Fly fishing for king mackerel is a little like casting for them. It is great fun when you can get it to work, but trolling will cover more ground and produce a lot more strikes. If you do manage to get in a situation where a king is possible on a fly, be sure to have an outfit that will handle strong, fast, long runs. Flies should resemble baitfish the fish are feeding on.

Best bets for Georgia king mackerel: Offshore or around any tidal inlet.

SPANISH MACKEREL

Spanish mackerel, *Scomberomorus maculatus,* are very closely related to their larger and more famous cousins, king mackerel. Like kings, Spanish mackerel are a highly migratory species and travel up and down the coast depending on water temperatures. They usually show up in Georgia sometime in April.

Spanish mackerel travel in huge schools looking for baitfish. One thing to keep in mind is the fish school based on size, so the first few fish caught will give you an idea of what to expect from that particular school.

Spanish mackerel have a long, streamlined body and a tapered head. The back is greenish shading to silvery sides. Golden yellow spots are present on the sides above and below the lateral line. Two traits that distinguish a Spanish mackerel from a king are that Spanish have a black blotch at the front of the dorsal fin, and the lateral line gently curves down from head to tail.

The key to finding Spanish mackerel is finding bait, be it shrimp or baitfish. A good way to find fish is to keep an eye on the birds. If you see birds wheeling and diving, chances are they are working a school of bait. Lacking birds, look for a large patch of disturbed water. If mackerel are around, they will be below the baitfish. Traditional places to begin your search are around capes and inlets, beaches with distinct sloughs, and cuts in the sandbars.

Like kingfish, Spanish mackerel are sight feeders and prefer clean water. Spanish mackerel offer more opportunities for the surf or pier angler since they can be found nearly anywhere from just off the beach to well offshore. Each beach or pier has a set of certain tide and wind conditions that will clear up the water and bring the Spanish mackerel in close along with the bait.

Since mackerel are so migratory, finding them in one place one time does not mean they will always be there for a repeat performance. It is common to find huge schools of Spanish mackerel at a spot one day, and then absolutely nothing the next day.

Although closely related to king mackerel, Spanish mackerel do not grow nearly as large. The average fish will weigh a couple of pounds. The Georgia record Spanish mackerel weighed in at 8.25 pounds and was caught in 1991 in the Buoy YS vicinity.

Techniques

Casting: Locating a school and casting artificials is a great way to enjoy a fast and furious Spanish mackerel bite. Any plug that imitates the size of the bait the mackerel are feeding will work, but Spanish mackerel seem to especially like bright colors. Any medium-weight spinning or casting outfit spooled with 8- to 12-pound monofilament will work. Spanish mackerel have a mouthful of sharp teeth, so a leader of something like 20-pound monofilament is required if you want to land many fish. Instead of casting into the middle of the school of bait where your lure can get lost, work the edges with an erratic, darting retrieve.

For surf fishing, go with a 7- to 11-foot light-action rod that can propel a lure way out into the surf. Spoons are a favorite with surf anglers since they cast like a bullet out to where the fish are feeding. Use whatever type of reel you are most comfortable with, but it should have a fast retrieve ratio since Spanish mackerel like a fast-moving bait.

Bait fishing: If you like using the real thing, once you have found the fish, free-line a small menhaden and wait for the bite.

Trolling: Fast trolling covers ground in a hurry, and is good for those days when the fish are shy about revealing their whereabouts. Spanish mackerel are schoolers; if you catch one fish, be sure to give the area a few more passes before moving on. Since Spanish mackerel can usually be found in close, even anglers with smaller boats can join in on the action. Spoons are good for trolling and can be fished near the surface with a trolling weight or deeper using planers and downriggers. Spanish like baits that move briskly along, so try to keep the speed around 5 to 6 knots.

Flycasting: Spanish mackerel offer good opportunities for the fly fisher. Find a school of feeding mackerel, and go to work. Work the edges of the school with flies that imitate the bait. Since Spanish mackerel do not get all that big, a lighter outfit can be used. Keep in mind, though, that there might be a smoker king or other large saltwater game fish either running with (or feeding on) the school of Spanish mackerel. Use whatever weight outfit you are comfortable with, but be sure to have plenty of backing on the reel.

Best bets for Georgia Spanish mackerel: All along Georgia's coast and offshore.

SHEEPSHEAD

Sheepshead, *Archosargus probatocephalus,* are members of the porgy family of saltwater fishes. Sheepshead can be caught both inshore and from offshore structure like wrecks and reefs. A glamour species they are not, but sheepshead provide consistent fishing for both shorebound and boat anglers.

The body is silvery, with five to seven distinct vertical black bands on the sides. The bold black stripes give the sheepshead the nickname of "convict fish." The sheepshead's teeth are flat and protruding, and with a little imagination, one can see how the fish could resemble the face of a sheep.

Sheepshead will average 2 to 4 pounds inshore, with larger specimens more than 10 pounds readily available offshore. The Georgia record sheepshead weighed 13.5 pounds and was caught in 1994 from KC Reef.

The best time for inshore fishing around oyster bars, seawalls, and bridges is from early spring until fall. May and June are probably the best months for inshore fishing. Sheepshead gather to spawn in late winter over debris, artificial reefs, and around navigation markers.

The sheepshead's impressive dental equipment gives it the ability to grind nearly anything to dust to get at the succulent morsels inside. Fish for sheepshead anywhere there is an accumulation of barnacles or over oyster bars.

The sheepshead's method of feeding makes it a challenge to catch. The fish will daintily pick up a fiddler crab, crack it to pieces, suck out the good parts, and spit out the shell. The problem with hooking the fish is feeling the bite. By the time the angler feels it, both the shell and the hook are no longer in the fish's mouth. There is a saying that goes "to catch sheepshead, you gotta strike before they bite."

Since they are such light biters and can strip the bait off the hook with nary a twitch of the rod tip, an angler needs to do a few things to even up the playing field. Make sure your hook is very sharp. Constantly retouch the hook point with a small file. Just one encounter with a sheepshead's teeth is enough to dull the hook. When fishing around bridges, docks, or pilings, use a garden rake or a flat-blade shovel to scrape barnacles off the structure. A sudden shower of food creating a chum line will often attract fish and excite them into feeding, hopefully to include your bait.

The sheepshead's firm, white flesh is excellent table fare and can be prepared nearly any way you choose. A favorite method is to fillet the fish leaving the scales and skin on, and then to grill them (scale side down) with plenty of melted butter and lemon juice.

Techniques

Sheepshead do not require special tackle. A casting or spinning outfit equipped with 12-pound test monofilament will suffice for most inshore fishing. Use an 18-inch leader of 20-pound monofilament to prevent breakoffs around the barnacle-encrusted structure sheepshead love. When fishing offshore, use slightly heavier tackle. Any outfit that can handle 20-pound test line will suffice, and 40-pound material should be used for a leader.

Give some care to rod selection. Since sheepshead are such light biters, a limber tip is needed to detect strikes. On the other hand, they are strong fish and live around structure with all sorts of sharp projections, so you need to quickly get them away from the structure, which requires a rod with plenty of backbone.

Casting: Sheepshead are not regularly pursued with artificial lures. Natural bait is much more productive. For the angler limited to artificials, very slowly fishing a lead-head jig around piers, pilings, and other structure would probably be the best choice.

Bait fishing: Sheepshead fishing is best done vertically. The more line out, the more difficult it will be to detect a strike. A simple fish-finder rig consisting of an egg sinker ahead of a swivel and followed by the leader and hook is all you need. Some anglers prefer to forego the fish-finder rig in favor of a simple lead-head jig. Whatever you use, keep the weight as light as possible to better detect strikes. Hooks should be kept small and sharp. A 1/0 to 3/0 Kahle hook is a good choice.

Not a particularly finicky feeder, sheepshead will take shrimp, sea worms, sand fleas, oysters, tiny minnows, or cut bait, and many feel the best bait is a small fiddler crab. A short stroll through the marsh flats should produce plenty of bait.

Lower the rig to the bottom next to the structure, lift it up a few inches, and wait for the bite. A slight tap is all you can hope to feel when the fish takes. Wait until the line develops that certain heaviness that all good sheepshead anglers can detect, and set the hook. Try different depths until you find the fish. Also, keep moving. For reasons known only to them, sheepshead will stack up around one piling and the pilings only a few feet away will be devoid of fish.

Unlike most inshore angling, the tide is not terribly important for catching sheepshead. When the tide is moving, fishing the upcurrent side will help keep the bait near structure. Fishing can be good at slack tide too.

Flycasting: Sheepshead are not a common a target for flycasters on the flats, but extra high tides and strong onshore winds will push water farther up into the marsh drawing sheepshead into these areas to take advantage of the feeding bonanza in the newly-flooded grass. The best flats are those near deep creeks and inlets that normally are good sheepshead producers anyway. Clear water will help spot fish as will a cap and a good pair of polarized sunglasses.

Almost any light saltwater outfit can handle sheepshead. Casts will likely be short, and a 10-pound-test tippet and a crab fly completes the outfit. When a fish is spotted, drop the fly in front of its nose, and make the fly quiver. Sheepshead are not used to having to chasing their prey, and they will ignore anything moving too fast. Concentration is required to detect the strike and make a successful hookset.

Best bets for Georgia sheepshead: All along Georgia's coast and offshore.

FLOUNDER

Two species of these odd fish are common to Georgia waters, the summer flounder, *Paralichthys dentatus,* and the southern flounder, *Paralichthys lethostigma.* Southern flounder can be distinguished by light spots on dark fins, and summer flounder are the opposite, with dark spots on light fins. Separating the two species is not critical from an angling standpoint, and Georgia anglers should have no trouble distinguishing an adult flounder from anything else that swims in Georgia waters. If you catch a fish that resembles a doormat in shape and has two eyes on one side of its head, and no eyes on the other, you have caught a flounder.

Granted, flounder are not the most glamorous of Georgia's sport fish, and no one could claim they are attractive. What they lack in the looks or glamour department though, they make up for by their availability and the fact they are great eating. Flounder are not as combative as some saltwater species but are still able to use their wide bodies to put up quite a fight. Flounder can be caught from depths of a few inches to many fathoms, making them one of Georgia's most ubiquitous saltwater game fish.

Prime locations for flounder are tidal creeks, bays, sounds, and inlets. During spring, look for the best action to be in shallow bays and creeks where the water warms the quickest. In hot weather, expect the fish to be in deeper, cooler waters. For example, channels, the lower sections of creeks, and open inlet and bay waters. Of course, tides also play a role. At high tide, fish follow the tide up onto the flats, and as the water retreats, so do the fish.

Flounder do not grow to huge sizes. The average fish caught inshore will weigh 1 to 4 pounds. Heading offshore will generally put you on the bigger fish; however, the Georgia record flounder weighed 15 pounds, 10 ounces, and was caught in 1990 from the Jekyll Pier.

Techniques

A medium-weight spinning or baitcasting outfit works well for flounder. Line size can range from 6- to 20-pound monofilament depending on your rig and the size of fish you think you might encounter. A short, heavy leader is not a bad idea since flounder do have sharp teeth, and the type of habitat they prefer is usually full of shells and other sharp objects.

Casting: Since flounder are not really a schooling fish, casting is not that efficient for finding and catching fish. If you find an area that has plenty of flounder, slowly retrieve a jig tipped with a plastic tail resembling a shrimp or small fish. Remember to keep the jig on bottom and retrieve it with a slow stop-and-go action for best results.

Bait fishing: As described above, flounder are generally solitary fish. If you find a place where the fish are concentrated, try dragging a weighted shrimp or small fish slowly along the bottom.

Flycasting: Fly fishing is not a common method of catching flounder, but there is no reason it would not catch a few fish when conditions are right. When fish are shallow, slowly stripping a shrimp or fish-imitator along bottom should produce strikes.

Trolling: Fishing on the move, either under power or by drifting, is the most productive method for catching a limit of flounder. A simple bottom rig and some bait are all that is needed to catch flounder this way. Pre-rigged flatfish setups are available in most coastal tackle shops. Anglers can rig their own by tying a bell sinker to the end of the main line and then adding one or two leaders using three-way swivels 6 to 18 inches above the weight. The weight needed depends on the speed the boat will be moving due to wind and tide. The idea is to use enough weight to keep the bait moving right along the bottom, but no more. Detecting the difference between a strike and the weight ticking the bottom can sometimes be difficult.

Flounder are not picky eaters. A finger mullet or silverside is a good choice, as are strips of squid or even the belly flesh of other flounder. For bigger fish, use a strip up to 8 inches long and taper the cut to give the strip some action as it moves through the water.

Other methods: Another method of taking flounder is by nighttime gigging. A head lamp, old clothes and sneakers, a sturdy gig, and a sharp eye are everything needed for this exciting sport. Pick a still night with no breeze to ripple the water. Use a small boat or wade the shallows looking for the telltale outline of a half-buried flounder. One well-aimed jab with the gig will be the start of a fine supper.

Best bets for Georgia flounder: Inshore or nearshore anywhere along Georgia's coast.

RED DRUM

The red drum, *Sciaenops ocellatus,* is also known as redfish, spottail, or channel bass. By any name they are a challenging sport fish and excellent eating.

Red drum spawning occurs from late summer through fall near major river inlets like the Savannah and Altamaha. Red drum spend the first three to four years of their lives in the tidal creeks and rivers of the estuaries. The fertile estuarine habitat provides the food and shelter necessary for the fish to survive to adulthood. Preferred foods of immature red drum are shrimp, crabs, and fish. Once red drum reach maturity at 27 to 30 inches in length, they leave the estuaries and join the adult spawning population in the nearshore Atlantic Ocean waters.

The Georgia record red drum was caught in 1986 from KC Reef and weighed 47 pounds, 7 ounces.

Techniques

For immature (less than 15 pounds) red drum, the techniques are the same as listed for spotted seatrout. To catch large adult red drum, an angler must head offshore and fish wrecks or reefs. Seasonally in the spring and fall, red drum can be found in the heavy surf near inlets. Surf fishing requires specialized equipment for making long casts and handling the heavy rigs necessary for fishing rough surf. Most anglers use 30-pound test line at a minimum, a 7/0 or larger hook, 4 ounces or more of lead, and a fresh-cut mullet or blue crab for bait. Since Georgia regulations only allow harvest of red drum between 14 and 27 inches in length, some anglers have found that using a 12/0 to 14/0 circle hook not only increases hooking percentage, but makes releasing large fish unharmed much easier since the circle hook makes it less likely the fish swallows the hook along with the bait.

Best bets for Georgia red drum: All along the Georgia coast.

OTHER SPECIES

Georgia waters contain many different fish species with sporting qualities. However, some of these species are not widely distributed throughout the state or have only a limited following of anglers. Sometimes though, going against popular opinion has its rewards, and many of these species are virtually untapped resources.

BLUE CATFISH

The blue catfish is one of the largest-growing catfish in Georgia; the state record is 62 pounds. The fish's range is limited in Georgia. Although it is not the only water in the state where blue catfish are found, the Coosa River in northwest Georgia is probably the best place to catch a monster blue cat. Fish for blue cats using a shad, either live or as cut bait, fished on the bottom in deep holes in bends and below islands. With their deeply forked tail, blue catfish look very much like a channel cat, but lack the spots on the body. Distinguishing large blue cats from big channel cats can be difficult; however one distinguishing feature of blue catfish that is easy to spot is that the outer margin of the long anal fin is straight, not rounded as in other catfish species.

WHITE CATFISH

This medium-sized catfish species is found throughout most of Georgia. White catfish resemble both channel and blue catfish, but lack the channel's spots and the blue cat's straight anal fin. The tail of the white catfish is not as deeply forked as that of the blue or channel catfish. The Georgia record white catfish weighed in at 8 pounds, 10 ounces. White catfish are usually common wherever they are found. Like most catfish, they are not particularly discerning about what they eat and can be caught on virtually any bait fished on bottom.

BULLHEADS

Bullheads are junior members of the catfish family. At least one species of bullhead can be found in virtually every warm-water stream, river, or lake in the state. The Georgia record brown bullhead weighed in at 5.5 pounds, and the average bullhead caught will be much smaller. Bullheads are ready biters and are a great fish for kids. Fishing a gob of earthworms on the bottom is almost a guarantee of some action from bullheads nearly anywhere you may choose to fish. Generally speaking, bullheads look like the other catfish species described in detail above, but with a square or slightly-notched tail. Coloration varies with the species, but is usually some shade of brown or yellow, often in a mottled camouflage-like pattern.

COMMON CARP

The common carp is a native of Asia brought to the United States in the 1800s. Unfortunately, the carp did not find the same favor with American anglers it enjoys in Asia and Europe. Although despised by many anglers as trash fish, carp are very strong fighters and have received a bum rap. Its fighting abilities and size make it a worthy opponent. Hooking a big carp is an experience not soon forgotten. The Georgia record carp weighed 35.75 pounds.

Carp are an adaptable and tolerant species and they can be found in almost any type of warm-water habitat. The carp's ability to thrive in marginal waters makes it a fish that offers angling opportunities where no others exist. Carp are members of the minnow family and resemble nothing less than an overgrown thick-bodied minnow with a sucker-like mouth. The coloration is usually brownish orange. Doughballs, canned corn, or worms fished on a small hook near bottom will produce strikes.

PICKEREL

Two species of pickerel are found in Georgia, the chain pickerel and the redfin (grass) pickerel. Both species are found throughout the state, although they are most common on the coastal plain below the Fall Line. Pickerel are commonly known as jacks or jackfish. Pickerel are close relatives of northern pike, and as one might expect for fish so closely related, possess the same elongated cylindrical shape, duckbill-like snout, and impressive dental equipment. Jacks are found in lakes, swamps, and quiet areas of streams or smaller rivers. Pickerel usually hang near aquatic vegetation that they use as a hiding place waiting for their next meal to swim by. They are explosive strikers and put up a frantic fight, especially alongside the boat. Pickerel will strike all manner of lures or live bait—usually the brighter and gaudier, the better. The razor-like teeth of pickerel require the use of a heavy monofilament or light wire leader if you hope to have any chance of landing the fish and retrieving your lure. Although closely related, pickerel do not grow nearly as large as northern pike. The Georgia record chain pickerel weighed 9 pounds, 6 ounces, and the largest Georgia redfin pickerel weighed in at 2 pounds, 10 ounces.

BOWFIN

The primitive-looking bowfin goes by many names including grinnel, mudfish, grindle, and dogfish. The bowfin looks primitive because it is. This species is the only surviving member of a family of fishes common in the fossil record, but with the one exception, all are extinct. Bowfin are easy to identify because they have an extremely long dorsal fin and the tail is rounded instead of the familiar forked shape. Bowfin are not found in all of Georgia's river drainages, but are common in some areas of the state. The Okefenokee Swamp is a good place to catch bowfin. In fact, the state record fish weighing 16 pounds was caught there. Bowfin readily strike lures, and most catches are accidental by anglers after largemouth bass. Bowfin are strong fighters, are considered by most to be inedible, and have a mouth full of teeth and strong jaws that will reduce your favorite spinnerbait to something resembling a paperclip. While not high on many anglers' lists, bowfin can provide an interesting note to a day's fishing when a big one strikes. You may think you have the next world-record bass on the line, only to discover you have hooked a mudfish.

YELLOW PERCH

Yellow perch are found in several river drainages in Georgia, including the Savannah, Tennessee, Coosa, Chattahoochee, and Altamaha. Despite their popularity in more northern climes, yellow perch are not an important sport fish in Georgia. A few mountain lakes have a small cadre of anglers who dedicate themselves to the pursuit of jumbo perch, but for the most part yellow perch do not even approach the popularity of various sunfish species. The Georgia record yellow perch weighed 2.5 pounds.

OTHER SALTWATER SPECIES

Part of the fun of saltwater fishing is you never really know what you are going to get. The list of Georgia saltwater game fish for which records are kept is a long one. Detailed species descriptions have been provided for some more popular and commonly caught saltwater game species, but many great sport species are swimming in Georgia waters. Included in this list are big-game species like blue marlin, sailfish, yellowfin tuna, snook, and tarpon. Many species of sharks can be found off Georgia's coast and provide good fishing. A few other notable species anglers may encounter are barracuda, cobia, jack crevalle, bluefish, dolphin, gag grouper, red snapper, wahoo, weakfish, and whiting. All these species can provide good sport at times.

Northwest Georgia

Northwest Georgia offers a little bit of everything for the angler. Trout streams, highland reservoirs, and several medium-sized rivers all provide good fishing for a variety of species. The ridge and valley topography of the region makes for a very scenic backdrop to almost any fishing trip.

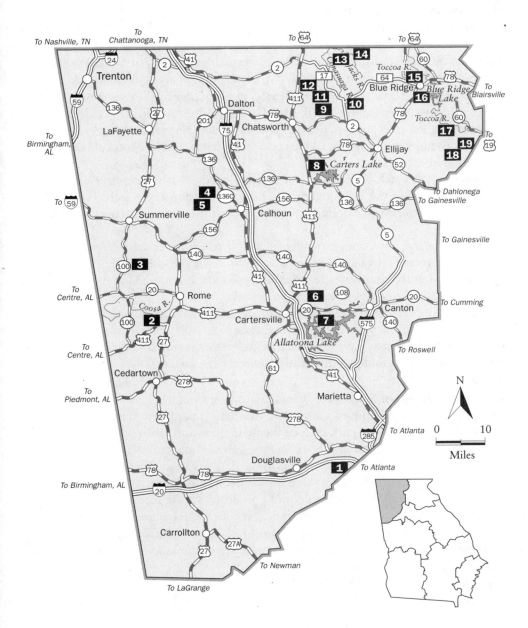

1 George Sparks Reservoir (Sweetwater Creek State Conservation Park)

Key species: largemouth bass, bluegill, redear sunfish, channel catfish.

Overview: George Sparks Reservoir, in Sweetwater Creek State Conservation Park, is a 215-acre lake only minutes from downtown Atlanta.

Best way to fish: shore, boat.

Best time to fish: March through May.

Description: Originally constructed as a water supply for the City of East Point, the state now manages George Sparks Reservoir as part of the 1,986-acre Sweetwater Creek State Conservation Park. The park's proximity to metro Atlanta makes it one of the most heavily used day-use recreation areas in the state.

The fishing: The lake bottom was cleared during construction so very little cover remains other than what is found along the shoreline. Any shoreline cover like fallen trees, riprap, or rock piles is a good place to try for bass and sunfish. The upper end of the lake has the most cover and is a good choice in the springtime.

Anglers can catch channel catfish and bullheads nearly anywhere on the lake. Since most of the fishing pressure is from shoreline anglers, the boating angler has a better chance of finding less-pressured fish away from the popular access points.

In the spring, look for spawning bass and sunfish in the shallows. The backs of protected coves are a good place to start your search. During the hot months, search for deepwater features like points and creek channels to produce the most and biggest fish.

In heavily-pressured waters like George Sparks Reservoir, downsizing your baits and making the most natural presentation possible is sometimes what it takes to catch fish that have seen it all. Extra effort invested in getting away from the crowds should pay dividends in more fish caught.

GA~G grid: 25, B-10

General information: Sweetwater Creek State Conversation Park is a day-use area. There are no camping facilities and camping is not allowed anywhere in the park. Facilities at the park include picnic shelters and tables, playgrounds, fishing piers, a bait shop, and boat rentals. Private boats are allowed on the lake but are limited to electric motors only. The area has 7 miles of hiking trails. The park features a variety of natural and cultural attractions, including the ruins of a Civil War–era textile mill burned by Union forces. Park hours are from 7:00 A.M. to 10:00 P.M. A daily parking fee is required for vehicles. There is no shortage of nearby choices for food, lodging, and supplies.

Nearest camping: Two private campgrounds are within about 5 miles of the park. See the Appendix for contact numbers.

Directions: From Atlanta, take Interstate 20 west to exit 44 at Thornton Road and turn left. Travel 0.25 mile south on Thornton Road and turn right onto

George Sparks Reservoir
(Sweetwater Creek State Conservation Park)

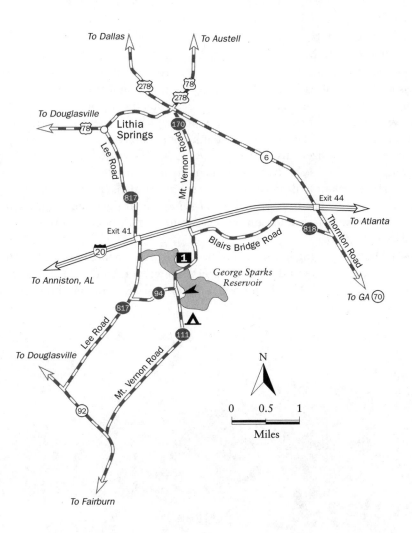

Blairs Bridge Road (CR 818). Travel 2.2 miles to Mt. Vernon Road (CR 111). Turn left and drive 0.5 mile to the park.

For more information: Contact the Wildlife Resources Division Fisheries Section Regional Office in Calhoun or the Superintendent's Office at Sweetwater Creek State Conservation Park.

② Coosa River at Mayo's Bar Lock and Dam

Key species: striped bass, white bass, crappie.

Overview: Mayo's Lock and Dam is a popular early-season destination for anglers after white bass and crappie as these species make their annual spring spawning migration up the river.

Best way to fish: bank, boat.

Best time to fish: March through July.

Description: During the steamboat era, Mayo's Lock and Dam allowed the passage of steamboats carrying passengers and freight up the Coosa River to Rome, Georgia. Although the lock has been inactive for many years, the area has been improved to serve as an access for anglers. Anglers are allowed to fish off the lock structure and from the bank immediately downstream of the lock. A paved boat ramp is also available. At spring flows, the dam is well underwater and provides the combination of structure and flow that fish such as striped bass seek out. Because of the deep water and fast turbulent flow, wading is not an option. The best striped bass fishing is near the dam, but boat anglers should use caution. Eddies and rips can pull a small boat into the turbulence and capsize it.

The fishing: Beginning in early March, anglers catch white bass and crappie by fishing live minnows under bobbers. Fish congregate in the slack area created by the lock. A No.1 Aberdeen hook, a BB split shot, a small bobber, and some

The old lock and dam structure at Mayo's Bar on the Coosa River was completed in 1913.

Coosa River at Mayo's Bar Lock and Dam

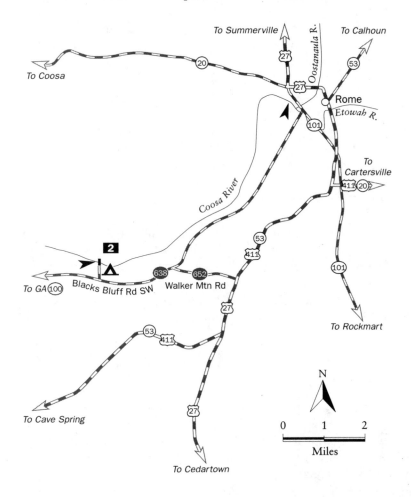

minnows are all you need. Some anglers prefer to cast small lead-head jigs rigged with a plastic grub body and sweetened with a live minnow hooked through the head.

Creek mouths will also hold fish early in the year, especially white bass. Anchor the boat in the main river channel and cast into the mouth of a creek with a jig heavy enough to quickly reach bottom. Rig the jig with a 2-inch plastic grub. In April and May striped bass make their spawning migration up the Coosa River. The dam serves as a holding area for the stripers as they migrate upstream. Fish heavy bucktail jigs or shallow diving plugs in the turbulent water immediately below the dam.

Some anglers fish with live shad on a heavy 3/0 hook 2 to 3 feet below a swivel. Above the swivel use a sliding egg weight of at least 1 ounce. When the fish takes the bait, the line will pass through the weight without allowing the fish to feel any resistance. Let the fish take some line before striking hard. Long, stout rods and heavy line are required to successfully hook and play fish in the strong current.

Summertime is prime for monster blue, flathead, and channel catfish. Fish using live or cut shad in the deep holes. Catch white bass on small jigs fished shallow on bars and sandy banks. Crappie can be difficult to find in the summer, but a few fish are always in the submerged treetops and willing to hit a live minnow.

GA~G grid: 18, D-4

General information: All anglers must meet Georgia licensing requirements. Mayo's Lock and Dam Park provides full-service campsites and bait, tackle, and snacks are available at the general store. Lodging and food are available within 5 miles.

Nearest camping: A full-service campground with electricity and water hook-ups is within Mayo's Lock and Dam Park.

Directions: From Rome, head south on U.S. Highway 27. Continue 3.4 miles south after the intersection of US 27 and US 411. At the stoplight turn right onto Walker Mountain Road (CR 652). Travel west 3.4 miles and turn right on the Mayo's Lock and Dam access road. Continue 0.4 mile to the river.

For more information: Contact the Wildlife Resources Division Fisheries Section Office in Calhoun or Mayo's Lock and Dam Park.

3 Rocky Mountain Recreation and Public Fishing Area

Key species: largemouth bass, bluegill, redear sunfish, channel catfish.

Overview: Operated by the Georgia Wildlife Resources Division, Rocky Mountain Recreation and Public Fishing Area is part of Plant Rocky Mountain, an Oglethorpe Power Corporation pumped-storage hydropower development in northwest Georgia.

Best way to fish: shore, boat.

Best time to fish: March through November.

Description: Although four lakes are on site, two of the lakes are operation pools closed to the public due to extreme water level fluctuations. The two open lakes serve as backup water storage for the generating system, and do not fluctuate on a regular basis.

The two lakes open to the public, Heath Lake and Antioch Lake, are 202 and 357 acres respectively. A road causeway divides Antioch Lake into two sub-impoundments (east and west), but a boat tunnel connects the two halves. Antioch Lake and Heath Lake both offer excellent fishing for largemouth bass, bluegill, redear sunfish, crappie, channel catfish, and bullheads.

The fishing: Largemouth bass and crappie are the first to move shallow in the spring to feed and search for a suitable place to spawn. Crappie spawn around wood, and any submerged timber is likely to hold fish. By late April, the sunfish

Rocky Mountain Recreation and Public Fishing Area

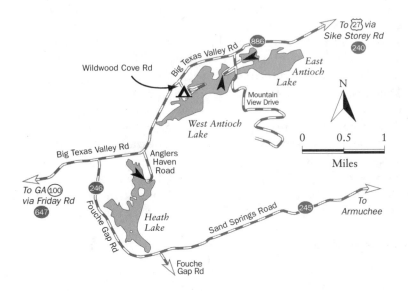

are spawning, with the shellcrackers a few weeks ahead of bluegill. Because the water is relatively shallow, spawning colonies are easily spotted on the north side of Antioch Lake.

Bass anglers should concentrate on fishing shallow shorelines. Try the shallow coves in Antioch Lake and the upper end of Heath Lake. Slowly twitching topwater baits such as Rapalas and Rattlin' Rogues can be productive. On warmer days, do not overlook a buzzbait crawled slowly across the surface for drawing smashing strikes. With the arrival of early summer, bass will take up station on deep structure. Probing the depths with a deep-diving crankbait or Carolina-rigged soft plastic can produce the best fishing of the year.

Many bass anglers overlook autumn, when fish are fattening up in anticipation of winter. A medium-diving crankbait is a good bet during this period because it closely imitates what the bass are feeding on, and covers a lot of water. Winter will find bass deep and lethargic, although they will still strike if a bait is presented in front of their noses. Portions of the south side of Antioch Lake and the east side of Heath Lake drop off very quickly into deep water, and are good places to bass fish in winter. Especially on Heath Lake, the edge of the standing timber can also produce fish. A jig-and-pig combo eased painfully slow along the bottom may produce a winter trophy.

Channel catfish can be caught nearly any time of year. Popular places for catfish include off the causeway crossing Antioch Lake and the fishing jetties near the boat ramps.

GA~G grid: 18, B-4

General information: Rocky Mountain Recreation and Public Fishing Area is a multi-use facility. Along with fishing, there are opportunities for picnicking, hiking, camping, swimming, and hunting. Anglers are not required to possess a Wildlife Management Area stamp to fish at Rocky Mountain. A daily parking fee is charged. No horsepower restrictions are in effect on the lakes, but all boats must be operated at idle speed (no wake). Basic supplies are available from two general stores within 6 miles of the area. Food and lodging are available about 18 miles away in Rome.

Nearest camping: A developed campground is present at the area. Full-service sites with electricity and water and primitive sites are available. The campground has a comfort station with flush toilets and hot showers. Camping is on a first-come, first-served basis; no reservations are taken. Camping is allowed only in designated areas.

Directions: From Rome, go north on U.S. Highway 27 for 10.4 miles. Turn left on Sike Storey Road (CR 240) and go 0.4 mile. Turn left onto Big Texas Valley Road (CR 235) and travel 5.4 miles to the entrance of the area on the left.

For more information: Contact the Area Manager's Office at Rocky Mountain Recreation and Public Fishing Area.

A universally-accessible fishing pier at Rocky Mountain Recreation and Public Fishing Area.

Rocky Mountain at a Glance

	Antioch Lake (West Sub-impoundment)	Antioch Lake (East Sub-impoundment)	Heath Lake
Area (acres)	203	154	202
Maximum depth (ft.)	29	48	24
Average depth (ft.)	14	16	9
% area <10 ft. deep	44%	34%	57%
% area <5 ft. deep	22%	19%	33%
Acres of flooded timber	2	3	58

4 Lake Marvin

Key species: largemouth bass, bluegill, redear sunfish.

Overview: Lake Marvin is owned and operated by the Northwest Georgia Girl Scout Council and is surrounded by Johns Mountain Wildlife Management Area and the Chattahoochee National Forest.

Best way to fish: boat, shore.

Best time to fish: March through June.

Description: Lake Marvin is about 90 acres in size. The lake is part of a Girl Scout Camp, but is open to the public for fishing. Lake Marvin is locally known for fine bream fishing, but the bass fishing can also be good, especially in the early spring. Although Lake Marvin is small, it is picturesque with forested ridges.

The fishing: Redear sunfish, bluegill, and redbreast sunfish are all present and easily enticed with a small worm or cricket. Lake Marvin is also a good place to use a fly rod with sponge spiders or small popping bugs. Flycasting is an excellent way to work a shoreline or bream bed.

Largemouth bass should not be overlooked. The upper end of the lake is shallow and warms quickly, making it a perfect place to try for a trophy-class fish early in the year. A lot of blowdowns are in the lake and they always seem to produce bass for the persistent angler. Good baits to try are plastic worms and spinnerbaits. During the winter and summer months, when bass will be deeper, fish a Texas-rigged plastic worm or a deep-diving crankbait right on the bottom in deeper water.

Crappie are also in Lake Marvin, but they tend to run small. Early in the spring they will concentrate around the blowdowns and other woody cover to spawn. Crappie are easily caught during this time on minnows or small jigs. For the remainder of the year, crappie suspend over deeper water and trolling small jigs is the best method for catching them.

GA~G grid: 13, G-6

General information: The lake is open year-round from 7:00 A.M. to 8:00 P.M.; a daily fee is charged to use the lake. A paved boat ramp is available, and outboard motors are restricted to 10 horsepower or less. Outdoor privies

Lake Marvin • Johns Creek

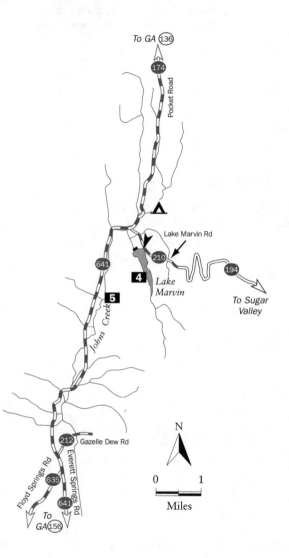

are present near the parking area. Food, lodging, and supplies are available 12 miles away in Calhoun. Johns Creek (Site 5) is a mile away.

Nearest camping: The USDA Forest Service operates the Pocket Campground, which was a CCC Camp in the 1930s. The campground is 2 miles from Lake Marvin. The campground is open seasonally and contains 27 campsites with tent pads, picnic tables, and grills.

Parcels of the Chattahoochee National Forest are found in all directions from Lake Marvin. Primitive camping is allowed on any national forest land unless posted otherwise. There is no public camping at Lake Marvin itself.

Directions: From Interstate 75 in Calhoun, travel west on Georgia Highway 156 until reaching the crossroads of Rosedale (about 14.5 miles). Turn right onto Everett Springs Road (CR 641) and continue 14.2 miles to Lake Marvin Road (CR 210) on the right. Drive 1.2 miles and the access point will be on the right.

For more information: For fishing information, contact the Wildlife Resources Division Fisheries Section Office in Calhoun. For information on the Pocket Campground, contact the USDA Forest Service Armuchee Ranger District.

5 Johns Creek

Key species: rainbow trout, redeye bass.

Overview: Johns Creek flows through the Chattahoochee National Forest and Johns Mountain Wildlife Management Area before eventually joining the Oostanaula River.

Best way to fish: wading, bank.

Best time to fish: April through October.

Description: In its upper reaches, Johns Creek is designated as secondary trout water and receives periodic stockings of catchable-size rainbow trout. Besides rainbows, Johns Creek also has a good population of redeye bass.

Access to the trout water portion of Johns Creek is good since the creek flows directly alongside the road running through the Johns Mountain Wildlife Management Area. The boundaries of the area are well marked. Although the very upper reaches of Johns Creek and its tributaries are on public land, these waters are very small and may dry up completely at times. Anglers would do better to concentrate their efforts on the public portions of the main stem downstream of the Pocket Campground. Beyond the portion of the creek running through public lands, there are several bridge crossings downstream of the management area where anglers can fish the creek from the county road right-of-way.

Since access to the creek is so good, the fishing pressure is heavy, especially early in the spring. However, an angler who is willing to get away from the parking areas will find that most of the pressure is directed toward a few road-side pools. Get away from these areas and you can fish virtually undisturbed, especially after the opening day rush subsides.

The fishing: Like most Georgia trout streams, Johns Creek is difficult going for the flycaster. The creek is relatively narrow with overgrown banks, making backcasting difficult. The best way to approach the creek is with ultralight spinning gear.

Trout anglers preferring natural bait will find that worms, a few kernels of canned corn, or commercially prepared trout bait is an enticing offering to the hatchery-reared trout living in Johns Creek. Several deep pools lend themselves well to this method of still-fishing. Other anglers prefer to fish artificials. Small spinners are a good bet. Fish the spinners through the deep pools and other likely places. Within a few days of being stocked, most of the trout will

Universally-accessible fishing piers and in-stream structures on Johns Creek in Johns Mountain Wildlife Management Area.

have migrated away from the stocking sites. Anglers should wade the creek away from the heavily used access points in search of these less pressured fish.

Redeye bass are regularly caught using the same methods used for trout. Redeye are aggressive feeders and will strike nearly any small plug or spinner. Redeye will also strike explosively at small topwater lures. Slowly twitching a small popper through a still pool will test an angler's nerves waiting for the strike of a small but feisty redeye bass.

Besides trout and redeye bass, you are likely to encounter bluegill, redbreast sunfish, and other small panfish. The same methods used for trout will likely produce some sunfish also.

GA~G grid: 13, G-6

General information: Due to its designation as a seasonal trout stream, Johns Creek is open to fishing from the last Saturday in March through October 31 and night-fishing is prohibited. Anglers must meet Georgia licensing requirements and have a valid Georgia trout stamp to fish the trout water portion of Johns Creek.

Food and lodging are available in Calhoun (20 miles), LaFayette (21 miles), or Rome (24 miles).

Nearest camping: The USDA Forest Service operates the Pocket Campground, which was a CCC Camp in the 1930s. Johns Creek runs through the campground but no fishing is allowed at the campground itself. The campground is

1 mile away from the fishable portion of the creek. The campground is open seasonally and contains 27 campsites with tent pads, picnic tables, and grills. Drinking water and flush toilets are available.

Also, since this site is on national forest land, primitive camping is allowed anywhere unless posted otherwise.

Directions: From Interstate 75 in Calhoun, travel west on Georgia Highway 156 until reaching the crossroads of Rosedale (about 14.5 miles). Turn right onto Everett Springs Road (CR 641) and continue about 10 miles to the Wildlife Management Area.

For more information: Contact the Wildlife Resources Division Fisheries Section Office in Calhoun. For information on the Pocket Campground, contact the USDA Forest Service Armuchee Ranger District.

6 Stamp Creek

Key species: rainbow trout, redeye bass.

Overview: Stamp Creek is a stocked trout stream in Pine Log Wildlife Management Area. Stamp Creek is unusual in two regards: it is a walk-in put-and-take trout stream, and it is open enough for fly fishing.

Best way to fish: bank, wading.

Stamp Creek is a walk-in, put-and-take stocked trout stream, and the open canopy allows for some fly fishing.

Stamp Creek

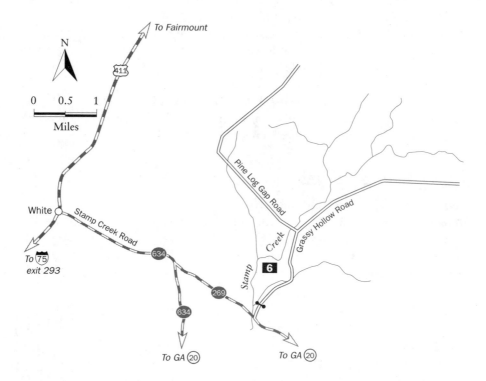

Best time to fish: March through October.

Description: Most of the designated trout water portion of Stamp Creek flows through the 14,913 acre Pine Log Wildlife Management Area. After leaving the management area, Stamp Creek eventually flows into Allatoona Lake (Site 7).

Stamp Creek is periodically stocked with catchable-size rainbow trout. Redeye bass and various sunfish species are also present. A dirt road runs close to the stream in the management area. However, a gate limits the road to nonvehicular traffic for most of the year.

The fishing: Stamp Creek more closely resembles a lowland stream moseying its way along than a rushing mountain trout stream. Although there is no trout reproduction, periodic stocking maintains numbers of catchable fish.

Good places to try are by the check station along the county road, and the section of the stream that parallels Grassy Hollow Road above its intersection with Pine Log Gap Road in the WMA. The pool at the county road does not require any walking and therefore receives the most fishing pressure. To reach the more secluded portions of the stream, walk in on Grassy Hollow Road.

Most of the trout in the creek are not long out of the hatchery and are aggressive feeders. Small spinners, tiny plugs, worms, crickets, and corn will all produce fish on light spinning gear. Flycasters will find that unlike many Georgia trout streams, Stamp Creek is open enough for them to practice their art. Fly selection is not critical. Anything that resembles something good to eat is likely to draw strikes. Redeye bass and various sunfish species are common in the creek and will strike the same lures used for trout.

GA~G grid: 19, C-10

General information: Stamp Creek is a year-round trout stream and thus is open to fishing every day of the year. In addition, night-fishing is allowed on this year-round trout stream. Anglers must meet Georgia licensing requirements and have a valid Georgia trout stamp to fish the trout water portion of Stamp Creek.

Lodging, food, and supplies are 10 miles away in Cartersville.

Nearest camping: The U.S. Army Corps of Engineers (USACE) Upper Stamp Creek Campground on Allatoona Lake is about 7 miles away. The campground has sites with electricity and water, a swimming area, and a launch ramp.

Directions: From Interstate 75 exit 293 at Cartersville, take US Highway 411 2.8 miles north to Stamp Creek Road (CR 634) on the right. Travel 3.5 miles to the check station on left.

For more information: Contact the Wildlife Resources Division Fisheries Section Office in Calhoun. For information on the Upper Stamp Creek Campground, contact the Allatoona Lake Resource Manager's Office.

7 Allatoona Lake

Key species: spotted bass, striped bass, hybrid striped bass, crappie.

Overview: Located only 30 miles from metro Atlanta, Allatoona Lake is one of the most frequently visited USACE lakes in the United States. More than 13 million visitors each year enjoy the angling, camping, and other outdoor opportunities provided by the lake.

Best way to fish: boat, shore.

Best time to fish: February through December.

Description: Allatoona Lake is a 12,010-acre impoundment on the Etowah River. The dam impounds runoff from about 1,100 square miles to alleviate flooding in the lower Etowah Valley and to reduce flood heights at Rome, Georgia. Because a large drainage area feeds a comparatively small reservoir, the lake level can undergo severe fluctuations. Daily increases of 3 to 4 feet are possible following heavy rains. Each fall the lake is drawn down about 17 feet to provide extra flood storage capacity. Allatoona Lake is a multipurpose project providing hydropower, flood control, and recreation.

Preliminary site work began in 1941, but the project was put on hold with the outbreak of World War II. In 1950 the dam was completed. At the time of construction, it was common practice to completely clear the lake basin. The

Allatoona Lake

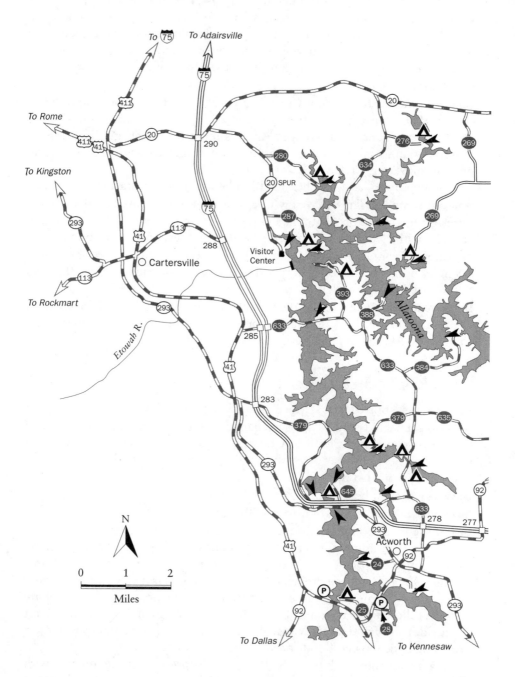

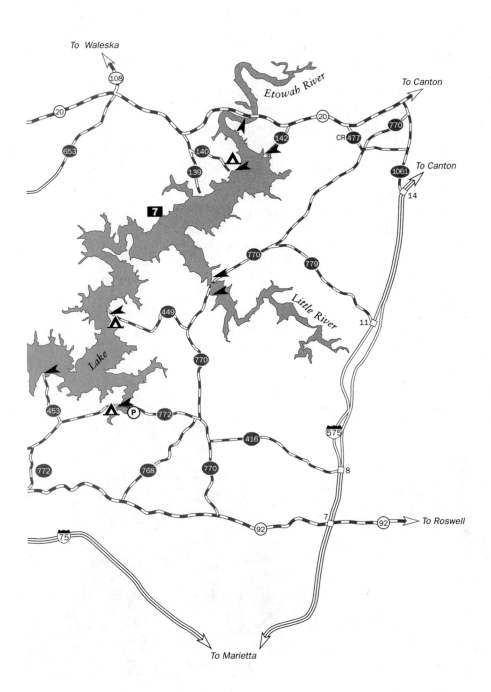

To Waleska

To Canton

Etowah River

To Canton

Little River

Lake

To Roswell

To Marietta

result is a lake with very few stumps or other offshore cover. Successful anglers key on depth breaks and other structural changes that attract fish.

Its proximity to metro Atlanta makes Allatoona Lake a very busy place during the warmer months as pleasure boaters and personal watercraft descend on the lake in force. During these months most Allatoona anglers seek out other less crowded waters or restrict their fishing to very early in the morning or even at night.

The fishing: Allatoona Lake has received the unflattering nickname of "The Dead Sea" with many Georgia anglers. Fish population surveys show that the moniker is not really deserved, but Allatoona Lake is definitely a challenging arena for consistently catching fish. The lack of cover, heavy use, and water level fluctuations make Allatoona Lake a tough nut to crack.

Successful anglers at Allatoona Lake have learned to key on structural breaks to find fish. Points, creek channels, and humps are the types of places to seek out. Most of Allatoona's black bass are spotted bass, but largemouths are also present in good numbers. Generally, largemouths are found in the more shallow, turbid headwaters of the lake, and the spotted bass fishing is better in the deeper waters of the lower end. Any of the popular bass lures can work at times, but the nature of the lake lends itself to fishing deep-diving crankbaits or bumping soft plastics or jigs along the bottom.

Stripers and hybrid striped bass are also popular with Allatoona anglers. These open-water fish are constantly on the move in search of forage, but use humps and

Winter drawdown reveals the piles of brush and tires that have been placed as fish attractors on Allatoona Lake.

other structure as feeding locations during their travels. Trolling is a good method of catching these fish. Another exciting way to catch them is to watch for surface feeding activity early and late in the day during the warmer months.

In the winter months, anglers out for crappie troll offshore structure or fish small minnows or jigs around marina breakwaters. In the summer, fishing at night with floating lights around bridges is popular. The lights attract minnows and other small bait, and predators soon follow.

GA~G grid: 19, 20

General information: Access to Allatoona Lake is excellent for both shoreline and boat anglers. Allatoona has more than 35 access points, most of which have boat ramps. More than 10 public campgrounds are found on the shores of the lake, and there are also several private marinas with launch facilities and sometimes lodging. Some public use areas on the lake charge a daily use fee, so be sure to check area rules and regulations. Angling at Allatoona Lake is managed under standard Georgia creel and length limits. Food, lodging, and supplies are available around the lake in Acworth, Canton, and Cartersville.

Nearest camping: Many fine facilities are found all around the lake. The USACE alone maintains 11 campgrounds with a total of more than 700 campsites. In addition, some state and county recreation areas also offer camping. Camping in nondesignated areas is prohibited.

Directions: Allatoona Lake is about 30 miles north of Atlanta in Bartow, Cherokee, and Cobb counties and is reachable from Interstate 75 (exits 277 to 290) or I-575 (exits 7 to 16).

For more information: Contact the Wildlife Resources Division Fisheries Section Office in Calhoun. Information about the lake and USACE facilities is available from the Allatoona Lake Resource Manager's Office.

8 Carters Lake

Key species: spotted bass, striped bass, walleye.

Overview: With absolutely no private development along its shoreline, Carters Lake is one of the most scenic reservoirs in Georgia. The lake is challenging to fish, but the rewards come in magnum spotted bass and undisturbed vistas.

Best way to fish: boat.

Best time to fish: February through November.

Description: Construction of Carters Lake, a 3,220-acre USACE pumped-storage hydropower and flood control reservoir, was initiated in 1962 and completed in 1977. Although the dam is only 2,053 feet long, it towers to a height of 445 feet above its foundation. The height of the dam makes Carters Lake one of the deepest lakes east of the Mississippi River. Depths of more than 400 feet are present.

Carters Lake impounds the Coosawattee River. Before impoundment, the stretch of river was noted for its remoteness and fantastic whitewater rapids. According to Georgia lore, the James Dickey novel *Deliverance* was

Carters Lake

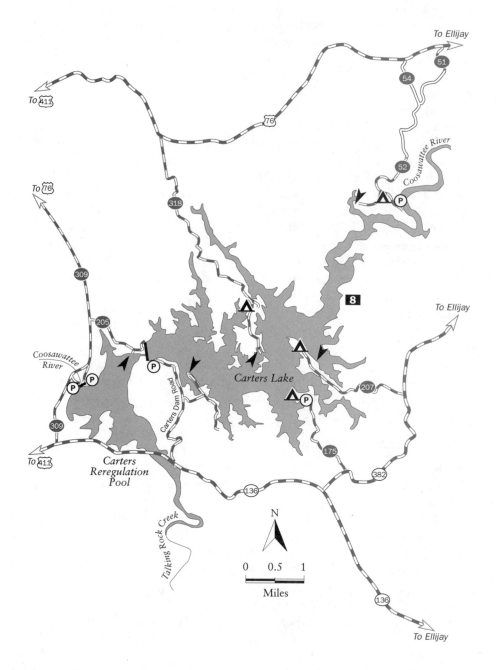

To Ellijay

51

54

To 411

76

To 76

318

Coosawattee River

52

309

205

Coosawattee River

8

To Ellijay

Carters Dam Road

P

P

P

Carters Lake

207

P

Carters
Reregulation
Pool

309

To 411

175

382

Talking Rock Creek

136

N

0   0.5   1

Miles

136

To Ellijay

A view from the top of Carters Dam looking down on the reregulation pool.

inspired by a weekend canoe trip Dickey took on the Coosawattee before impoundment.

Carters Lake is in a constant state of flux; the pumpback operations can cause weekly water level fluctuations of up to 4 feet.

The Carters Lake hydropower system is really two lakes. Water is released from the much larger main reservoir into the shallow reregulation pool at times of peak electricity demand. At times of low demand, the turbines are reversed and the water is pumped back up to the main lake. The effects of power generation are much more severe in the reregulation pool. The water level can vary as much as 10 feet in a 6-hour period and as much as 22 feet weekly. Because of the severe water level fluctuations, recreation on the reregulation pool is limited.

The fishing: Carters Lake has undergone some dramatic changes in its relatively short life. With the illegal introduction of shad, the bluegill fishery declined dramatically. In the years following their introduction, the shad population boomed and the spotted bass took advantage of the abundant prey. After a few years the fish population reached equilibrium; catching a big spotted bass is now a notable event, not a weekly occurrence.

Carters Lake is still a fine fishery, and spotted bass reign supreme. Catching spots in Carters Lake requires some patience and a subtle approach. Finessing small plastic baits through deepwater structure is the norm. Since the lake is relatively clear and the favorite lures are small, lighter tackle is required to consistently fool spots. Favorite places to bass fish are points or other offshore structure, especially if they are sweetened by stumps or brush piles. Deep-diving crankbaits and jigging spoons are also used to comb the bottom in search of fish.

Carters Lake is one of the few lakes in Georgia with a good walleye population, though they are overlooked by most anglers and most walleye are incidental catches. Trolling or casting crankbaits and small jigs over points and deep bars will produce fish.

Striped bass are stocked into Carters Lake to help minimize the abundant shad population. Anglers catch stripers on both live and artificial baits trolled or cast over humps and other offshore structure. The key to finding stripers is to find shad.

The trick to Carters Lake is to think deep. It is common to be sitting over 50 feet of water, and a cast away from five feet of water. Once you find where the fish are holding, maximize the time your bait is at that depth by fishing parallel with the depth break.

GA~G grid: 13, F-10

General information: The USACE maintains four paved boat ramps and a campground on the main lake. A private marina is also present. Access to the reregulation pool is limited to a primitive boat ramp. Bank access is excellent immediately below the reregulation dam on the Coosawattee River. Daily use fees are required at some USACE facilities. Be sure to check area rules and regulations.

Lodging, food, and supplies are about 15 miles away in Chatsworth or Ellijay. Angling at Carters Lake is managed under standard Georgia creel and length limits.

Nearest camping: The USACE maintains several full-service campgrounds on the lake. Primitive, boat-in, and group camping sites are also available.

Directions: Carters Lake can be reached from Georgia Highways 136 and 382 on the south and east side or U.S. Highway 76 on the north side.

For more information: Contact the Wildlife Resources Division Fisheries Section Office in Calhoun. For lake and facility information, contact the Carters Lake Resource Manager's Office.

9 Holly Creek

Key species: rainbow trout.

Overview: Flowing through the Cohutta Wildlife Management Area, this creek provides a good mix of easy access fishing for stocked rainbow trout and the chance at wild trout in its more remote upper reaches.

Best way to fish: wading.

Best time to fish: April through October.

Description: Holly Creek is one of the better trout streams in northwest Georgia. A combination of good public access and heavy stocking on the lower end make that section a favorite with families and those interested in a relaxing trout fishing trip. Farther upstream, as the creek veers away from the road,

Holly Creek • Mountaintown Creek

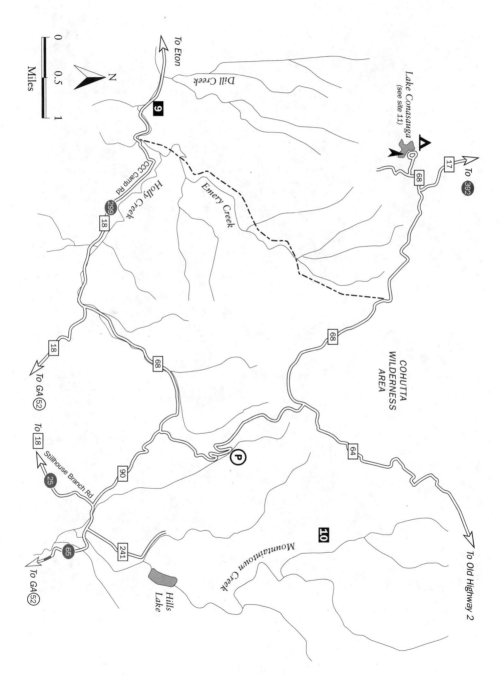

Holly Creek is one of the best trout streams in northwest Georgia.

Holly Creek and its tributaries provide some challenging angling for wild rainbow trout. Typical of most Georgia mountain streams, Holly Creek is a small to medium stream and is better suited to ultralight spinning tackle than fly fishing gear.

The fishing: Most of the fishing pressure on Holly Creek takes place at the popular roadside holes along FR18. Along with rainbow trout, anglers can expect to find redeye bass and other sunfish species. During the trout season, Holly Creek receives periodic stockings of catchable rainbow trout. These fish are fresh out of the hatchery and will fall for small spinners, flies, corn, marshmallows, worms, and virtually anything else that appears edible. The most aggressive fish are caught first, and the survivors are those who display a little more wariness in their approach to feeding. To catch these fish, a natural-looking presentation of a small spinner is a good method.

Even on the stretch of stream that runs alongside the road, getting away from the most obvious access points is worth the trouble. Shortly after being stocked, the fish will begin to disperse. Hitting less pressured holding areas can be very productive.

For more of an angling challenge, fish the upper reaches of Holly Creek or its tributary Emery Creek. A hiking trail leads from FR18 to the confluence of Holly and Emery Creeks, and then follows the path of Emery Creek upstream before connecting with FR 68. Shortly upstream of the confluence, Holly Creek flows through a steep valley. As one might expect, the difficulty of traveling the stream past this point eliminates much of the fishing pressure, and rewards the hard-working angler with virtually untapped waters.

GA~G grid: 13, D-10

General information: Holly Creek does not flow entirely through public lands; there are some private inholdings in this area of the Chattahoochee National Forest. Consult a Chattahoochee National Forest map to find out which stretches of the stream are on private land, and respect the landowner's wishes regarding angler access. Holly Creek is designated as year-round trout water, so fishing can take place all year and anytime of day. All anglers must meet Georgia licensing requirements and a valid Georgia trout stamp is required to fish for any species in the designated trout water portion of the Holly Creek watershed. Refer to the *Georgia Sport Fishing Regulations* pamphlet for more regulations regarding trout fishing in Georgia.

Food, lodging, and supplies are 12 miles away in Chatsworth.

Nearest camping: Primitive camping is allowed around Holly Creek. The nearest developed campground is the USDA Forest Service's Lake Conasauga Campground about 11 miles away.

Directions: From the Chatsworth town square, travel 3.8 miles north on U.S. Highway 411 to the traffic light in Eton. Turn right at the light onto 4th Avenue. Outside Eton, this road is named CCC Camp Road (CR 299/FR18). The paved road eventually gives way to gravel. About 6.5 miles from the turn at US 411, Holly Creek will appear on the left.

For more information: Contact the Wildlife Resources Division Fisheries Section Office in Calhoun. For information about nearby outdoor recreation opportunities and national forest rules and regulations, contact the USDA Forest Service Cohutta Ranger District.

10 Mountaintown Creek

See map on page 91

Key species: rainbow trout, brown trout.

Overview: Mountaintown Creek starts its journey near the boundary of the Cohutta Wilderness Area and eventually joins the Coosawattee River. The upper reach of the stream flows through the Cohutta Wildlife Management Area before reaching private land. Depending on the portion of stream you choose to fish, both stocked or native brown and rainbow trout are possible.

Best way to fish: wading.

Best time to fish: March through November.

Description: Although Mountaintown Creek is designated trout water for its entire length, the upper portion of the stream on the Cohutta Wildlife Management Area offers the most unrestricted public access. A good breaking point when discussing the stream is Mountaintown Creek Watershed Structure #2 (Hills Lake). A short stretch of the stream below the privately held lands around the lake is on public land and popular with anglers. Although this stretch of stream is productive, identifying which portions are public and private can be difficult. Difficult wading conditions and heavily-foliaged banks make fishing anything but the most popular pools difficult.

Upstream of Hills Lake, the stream flows through a solid block of the Chattahoochee National Forest. This portion is more open and better suited to flycasting. Although access to this stretch requires some hiking, the rewards come in uncrowded fishing for stream spawned trout. Wild rainbows up to 12 inches are possible, and the few browns caught will generally run less than 9 inches.

The upper portions of Mountaintown Creek have benefitted from stream structures constructed and placed by the Georgia Wildlife Resources Division working with Trout Unlimited. These structures have transformed some shallow broad stretches of stream to good holding water.

The fishing: On the lower reaches of the stream, where stocking occurs, the usual trout fishing assortment of natural baits and small spinners fished on ultralight spinning tackle will catch fish. When angling for native trout, a little more care is required to catch the wary stream-raised fish, especially the persnickety brown trout.

Traditional match-the-hatch fly fishing is not the way to go on Mountaintown Creek. Hatches of a significant nature are rare, and so the best route is to base fly selection on generalizations instead of trying to exactly match a hatch that may never come. Attractor patterns like the Royal Wulff and Humpys present a general "buggy" look and are always good choices.

If ultralight spinning gear is your tool of choice, small spinners are one of the most effective lures. Experiment with different sizes and colors of spinners to find what is most productive on any given day. Many anglers prefer dark color schemes, but sometimes the most unlikely choice will turn out to be the most productive lure of the day.

Most of the trout caught will be rainbows, but brown trout are also present in lower numbers. The brown trout tend to be more wary and are a challenge to catch. Do not overlook small feeder streams and tiny brooklets as choice locations. These hard-to-fish trickles of water can sometimes produce surprisingly large results.

GA~G grid: 14, C-1

General information: The Mountaintown Creek watershed is designated as year-round trout water. However, some special regulations are in effect on part of the stream. Anglers fishing Mountaintown Creek and its tributaries upstream of Hills Lake are restricted to artificial lures only. Downstream of Hills Lake, standard Georgia trout fishing regulations are in effect. Since Mountaintown Creek is designated trout water, a valid Georgia fishing license and trout stamp are required to fish the stream, no matter the species being pursued. Consult the *Georgia Sport Fishing Regulations* pamphlet for more information on trout fishing regulations and the Mountaintown Creek watershed.

Since portions of Mountaintown Creek are on private property, take extra care to respect landowner rights. Reaching the portions of the creek above Hills Lake requires foot travel either starting on the lower portions of the stream near Hills Lake and hiking up, or starting near the boundary of the Cohutta Wilderness Area and hiking down into the headwaters of the stream. Either way, access to this portion of the stream requires some hard work. Good maps of the area will help determine land ownership and the best routes to reach public-land stretches of the stream.

Food, lodging, and supplies are about 15 miles away in Ellijay and Chatsworth.

Nearest camping: Primitive camping is allowed around Mountaintown Creek. The nearest developed campgrounds are 11 miles away at Fort Mountain State Park and 15 miles away at the USDA Forest Service's Lake Conasauga Campground.

Directions: To reach the lower section of Mountaintown Creek near Hills Lake, travel west from Ellijay on Georgia Highway 52 for about 19 miles. Turn right onto Conasauga Creek Road (FR18) for 1.5 miles. This road is paved but soon changes to gravel. Take a right onto Stillhouse Branch Road (CR 25). After 2 miles you will reach this road's intersection with FR 90. Bear to the right onto FR 90 and go 0.75 mile to the stream. The dirt road on the left (FR 241) just before reaching the stream will take you to the primitive camping areas near the stream.

To hike in from upstream, follow the directions above except continue straight on FR18 past Stillhouse Branch Road (CR 25). At the intersection of FR 18, FR 68, and FR 64 on top of Potatopatch Mountain, bear right onto FR 64. Hiking in off FR 64 will reach to the upper reaches of the Mountaintown Creek watershed.

For more information: Contact the Wildlife Resources Division Fisheries Section Office in Calhoun. For more information about other outdoor recreation opportunities and national forest rules and regulations, contact the USDA Forest Service Cohutta Ranger District. Information on camping at Fort Mountain State Park is available from the Park Superintendent's Office.

11 Lake Conasauga

Key species: largemouth bass, bluegill.

Overview: Situated on Chattahoochee National Forest lands near the summit of Grassy Mountain just west of the Cohutta Wilderness Area, Lake Conasauga is the highest lake in Georgia at 3,150 feet above sea level.

Best way to fish: boat, shore.

Best time to fish: April through October.

Description: At 19 acres, Lake Conasauga is the largest USDA Forest Service lake in northwest Georgia. The Civilian Conservation Corps built the lake during the Great Depression and it was opened to the public in the 1940s. Lake Conasauga is more than 3,000 feet above sea level, which makes it the highest lake in Georgia. With depths down to 30 feet, Lake Conasauga is also deeper than a typical small lake.

Reaching Lake Conasauga requires traveling rough mountain dirt roads, but the lake is worth the journey. The campground and recreation area serve as an excellent base camp for hiking and fishing in the Cohutta Wilderness Area or other surrounding trout streams on USDA Forest Service land.

The fishing: Despite a shorter growing season at the high elevation, an infertile watershed on top of an undeveloped mountain, and a popular campground on the lake, largemouth bass manage to grow to trophy size in Lake Conasauga. In fact, Lake Conasauga has given up many largemouth bass in the 10-pound range.

Lake Conasauga contains a fair amount of woody cover. Some small weed beds are also present. Concentrate on finding deep stumps and other hidden cover for the best bass fishing. Most casual anglers will miss the hidden cover, and it should hold the greatest concentration of fish.

Bluegill and shellcracker provide the most consistent fishing through the year. Beginning in late spring and continuing through the summer, search for a collection of bream beds in shallow water. A small popping bug or sponge spider fished on a light fly outfit is the most sporting way to partake of this hot action. If you prefer live bait, a red wiggler hooked lightly once or twice through the middle with both ends left to writhe seductively is hard for any self-respecting sunfish to pass up. Crickets are also a good choice.

GA~G grid: 13, C-10

General information: Lake Conasauga is perfect for a family trip. Picnic tables and shelters are available. The area also includes a swimming beach and hiking trails. A gravel launch ramp is present and all boats are limited to electric motors only. A daily use fee is required on the area, so be sure to check rules and regulations upon arrival.

Lake Conasauga • Mill Creek

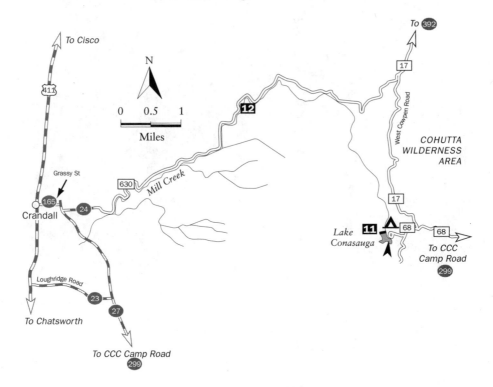

During the season, the gates open at 7:00 A.M. and close at 10:00 P.M. The lake is open to fishing all year, but during the closed season anglers must get to the lake on foot.

If you are planning a trip to Lake Conasauga, call ahead to check the status of fishing in the lake and whether or not the area is open. Besides being open only seasonally, severe weather can block the roads to the area with downed trees or ice.

Since Lake Conasauga has traditionally received periodic stockings of catchable rainbow trout, there are some special regulations related to trout fishing. Anglers can fish for species other than trout without a Georgia trout stamp, but if trout are fished for or possessed, the trout stamp is required. Anglers without a valid trout stamp must immediately release any trout caught. All anglers must meet Georgia licensing requirements. Fishing is allowed year-round and at night.

Food, lodging, and supplies are 17 miles away in Chatsworth.

Nearest camping: A 35-site campground with restrooms and drinking water is on the shores of the lake. Each campsite is equipped with a tent pad and picnic table. Drinking water and flush toilets are available. Lake Conasauga Campground is open from mid-April through late-October.

Lake Conasauga is the highest lake in Georgia.

Directions: To reach Lake Conasauga, travel 6.9 miles north on U.S. Highway 411 from the town square in Chatsworth. Turn right onto Grassy Street in the village of Crandall. Stay on Grassy Street until it crosses the railroad tracks and ends at an intersection. Turn right and then turn left onto FR 630 at the next intersection. FR 630 starts as a paved road but soon changes to gravel. Continue about 7 miles and then turn right on West Cowpen Road (FR 17). Stay on West Cowpen Road until it intersects FR 68. Turn right onto FR 68 and follow the signs to Lake Conasauga.

For more information: Contact the USDA Forest Service Cohutta Ranger District.

12 Mill Creek

See map on page 97

Key species: rainbow trout.

Overview: A fairly small stocked trout stream almost entirely within the bounds of the Chattahoochee National Forest. Access is easy since the creek is paralleled for most of its length by a national forest road.

Best way to fish: wading.

Best time to fish: March through October.

Description: The very upper reaches of Mill Creek are impounded to form Lake Conasauga (see Site 11). Downstream from the lake, the creek runs down Grassy Mountain before losing its trout water designation and running into the Conasauga River west of Chatsworth. The trout-water portion of Mill Creek receives periodic stockings of catchable rainbow trout. Although a national forest road parallels the creek for most of its length, the drop from the road down to the creek is a steep one, which limits the number of places the stocking truck can reach. Most fishing pressure is directed at these obvious access points.

The fishing: Mill Creek has the look of a good trout stream, but actually is somewhat marginal habitat. Redeye bass are common and will make up a good portion of your catch.

Although it is a small stream, Mill Creek is open enough in many places to allow flycasting. Reaching the stream from the road can be a little challenging because of the steep banks. Wading up or down from the few easy access points will escape most other anglers and get you to less-pressured water.

For stocker trout, corn, marshmallows, or store-bought trout candy will all produce strikes. Trout that have been in the creek for a time and regained their wariness will more likely be fooled by worms, crickets, wet or dry flies, or small spinners.

Small spinners are probably the best all-around choice since they will draw aggressive strikes from both trout and redeye bass and can be effectively fished in nearly any type of water.

GA~G grid: 13, C-10

General information: Mill Creek is designated as year-round trout water; fishing can take place all year and anytime of day. A valid Georgia trout stamp and fishing license are required to fish for any species in the designated trout water portion of the Mill Creek watershed. Refer to the *Georgia Sport Fishing Regulations* pamphlet for more regulations regarding trout fishing in Georgia. Food, lodging, and supplies are about 13 miles away in Chatsworth.

Nearest camping: Primitive camping is allowed around Mill Creek. One popular location is near the Hickory Gap section of the stream. The nearest developed camping is at Lake Conasauga Campground.

Directions: To reach Mill Creek, travel 6.9 miles north on U.S. Highway 411 from the town square in Chatsworth. Turn right onto Grassy Street in the village of Crandall. A street sign is at this intersection. Stay on Grassy Street until it crosses the railroad tracks and ends in an intersection. Turn right and then turn left onto FR 630 at the next intersection. FR 630 starts as a paved road but soon changes to gravel. Shortly after the road changes to gravel the creek will start to periodically appear along the right-hand side of the road.

For more information: Contact the Wildlife Resources Division Fisheries Section Office in Calhoun. For more information about Lake Conasauga Campground and national forest rules and regulations, contact the USDA Forest Service Cohutta Ranger District.

13   Conasauga River

Key species: rainbow trout, brown trout, brook trout.

Overview: Considered by some authorities to be one of the top 100 trout streams in the nation, the pristine 15-mile stretch of the Conasauga River is within the Cohutta Wilderness Area.

Best way to fish: wading.

Best time to fish: April through November.

Description: The core of the Conasauga River trout fishery is found on the 37,000 acres of the Cohutta Wilderness Area. Travel in this block of rugged mountain country is restricted to nonmechanical methods of transportation, which in practice means on foot, or in a few designated areas, on horseback. The USDA Forest Service manages the lands of the Cohutta Wilderness Area as a special part of the Chattahoochee National Forest.

Rising near the southern boundary of the wilderness area, the Conasauga River flows northwest into Alaculsy Valley. Along the way, many small tributaries enter the stream, giving it enough flow and width to be considered a small river by the time it leaves the wilderness boundary. Although the designated trout water portion of the river extends beyond the wilderness area, it is marginal trout fishing at best.

Since reaching the river is no small feat, fishing pressure is light. Stream-spawned rainbow trout are plentiful. Some brown trout are also present, and what they lack in numbers they make up for in size. At the highest elevations in the tributaries and main stem itself, even brook trout are a possibility. Since no stocking has occurred in the river in many years, all trout are stream-spawned fish. Although rainbows up to 20 inches and browns weighing more than 5 pounds are possible, most fish caught will be in the 10-inch range.

Because the Conasauga River flows through a valley that has laid undisturbed for many years now, the stream remains clear even during high water. The complete lack of fields, roads, and other human development in the stream's upper basin has allowed the waterway to retain its pristine state. In addition, the restrictions that come with the wilderness designation have limited the recreational use the area would otherwise receive. From the spring through fall, the area is popular with the more hardy variety of hikers and backpackers, but very few of them will be seriously fishing. The Cohutta Wilderness Area is one of the few high quality trout fisheries in Georgia where you can have a reasonable expectation of enjoying your trip in complete solitude.

The Cohutta Mountains are rugged country, and some trails can be exhausting to even the most conditioned trekker. Wading the river usually means navigating slick rocks in sometimes strong current. Trips should be carefully planned and researched beforehand. File a trip plan with a trusted individual to let someone know exactly where you plan to be and when.

The trails vary in difficulty. Some follow old road grades and are relatively easy going, but others are rough with long, straight climbs. The Conasauga River Trail follows the river for most of its length, and is sure to be part of any trip to the Conasauga. The Tearbritches and Chestnut Lead Trails access the midway portions of the river. Both trails are steep, with Tearbritches Trail especially so. The trail is so demanding it is best used as an access trail into the valley with the uphill climb out of the valley taking place on another less demanding trail. Farther downstream, the Hickory Creek Trail gives access to the lower sections of the river in the wilderness area.

Conasauga River • Jacks River

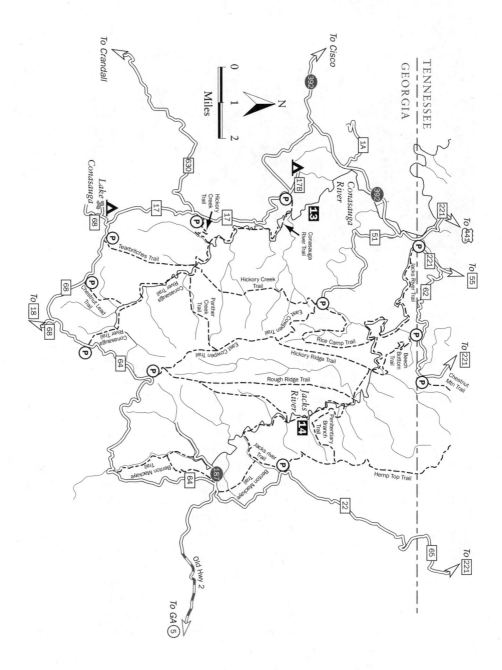

Stream-reared rainbow trout have distinct markings and a pinkish-red stripe..

Although the water may look crystal clear and safe to drink, do not be tempted. Giardiasis, a disease caused by a parasite often present in beavers and deer, is known to occur in the area and can be present no matter how clean the water looks. Boil or purify any water before drinking it.

The fishing: Catching fish in the Conasauga River requires no small degree of stealth and skill. The fish are extremely wary and the first heavy footfall will send them darting for cover. A pool filled with several visible trout does much to pique the angler's interest, but unfortunately if you can see them, they can see you. Camouflage clothing and using all available cover to break up your outline and hide movement is the best way to overcome these tough conditions.

For all except the extreme headwaters, the Conasauga River is open enough for flycasting. Anglers serious about having all the bases covered might want to carry a fly outfit and a short ultralight spinning outfit, but keep in mind even the lightest rod and reel can turn surprisingly heavy well before reaching the trail's end. Travel as light as possible; leave all the superficial gadgets and gizmos at home.

Rainbows will make up most of the catch, but each pool seemingly holds at least one good brown trout. Finding brook trout means bushwacking to the very upper reaches of the stream and small tributaries. Look for tiny brooks that have barrier falls preventing the upstream migration of rainbow and brown trout. On the lower sections of the river, redeye bass start to mix with trout. Good trout fishing can still be had, but redeyes make up a good portion of the catch.

Fly selection should be general attractor patterns since big hatches are rare. A Black Ant or light-colored Elk Hair Caddis in size 16 or smaller would be a good starting point. If spinning gear is preferred, a very small Panther Martin with a gold blade is a local favorite. When nothing else seems to work, a live cricket or worm will sometimes produce results (see the general information section for seasonal natural bait restrictions).

GA~G grid: 14, C-1

General information: The Conasauga River is designated as year-round trout water. All anglers must meet Georgia licensing requirements and possess a valid Georgia trout stamp. Several special regulations apply to the Conasauga River and its tributaries (except the Jacks River, see Site 14). Fishing is allowed 30 minutes before sunrise to 30 minutes after sunset; night-fishing is not allowed. Any type of bait, natural or artificial, may be used during the designated trout season. During the months trout season is closed, fishing is still allowed on the stream but no natural bait is allowed, only artificials may be used. Trout may be harvested following standard Georgia creel limits. Consult the *Georgia Sport Fishing Regulations* pamphlet for more information on the Conasauga River and trout fishing rules and regulations.

Some recreation areas in the Chattahoochee National Forest charge a daily use fee. Be sure to check information boards for rules and regulations on arrival.

Food, lodging, and supplies are 17 miles away in Chatsworth.

Nearest camping: Primitive camping is allowed throughout the Cohutta Wilderness Area. The nearest developed camping is on the western boundary of the wilderness area at the USDA Forest Service's Lake Conasauga Campground.

Directions: To reach the western trailheads, travel 6.9 miles north on U.S. Highway 411 from the town square in Chatsworth. Turn right onto Grassy Street in the village of Crandall. Stay on Grassy Street until it crosses the railroad tracks and ends in an intersection. Turn right and then turn left onto FR 630 at the next intersection. FR 630 starts as a paved road but soon changes to gravel. The road will intersect with FR 17 after about 7 miles. Several trailheads are accessible from FR 17.

To reach the southern trailheads, from the Chatsworth town square travel north 3.8 miles on US 411 to the traffic light in Eton. Turn right at the light onto 4th Avenue. Outside Eton, this road is named CCC Camp Road (CR 299/FR18). The paved road eventually gives way to gravel. About 10.4 miles from the turn at US 411, FR68 will appear on the left. Turn left on FR68 and follow it 7 miles to where it intersects with FR64. Several trailheads are accessible from FR 68 and FR 64.

For more information: Contact the Wildlife Resources Division Fisheries Section Office in Calhoun. For information about the Lake Conasauga Campground and Cohutta Wilderness Area rules and regulations, contact the USDA Forest Service Cohutta Ranger District.

Key species: rainbow trout, brown trout, brook trout.

Overview: The Jacks River is a major headwater tributary to the Conasauga River. The two rivers parallel each other through the Cohutta Wilderness Area and offer excellent angling for wild rainbow, brown, and brook trout.

Best way to fish: wading.

Best time to fish: April through October.

Description: From its headwaters until it joins the Conasauga River near the Georgia–Tennessee border, the Jacks River flows almost entirely through the public lands of the Chattahoochee National Forest and the Cohutta Wilderness Area. One block of private inholdings is near where the South Fork and West Forks join to form the main stem of the Jacks River. With that exception, the river is entirely on public land.

The Jacks River and its valley are very much like the Conasauga River (see Site 13). Although the Jacks River is a tributary to the Conasauga, the Jacks is slightly larger. The Jacks River watershed has escaped development over the years, except for a railroad that was once used to get valuable old-growth chestnut trees out of the valley and to market.

The extreme headwaters of the Jacks River are outside the wilderness area and accessible by road. These streams are very small and overgrown, but they do offer some good fishing for native trout. Most of the fishing takes place within the confines of the wilderness area.

Like the Conasauga, the Jacks River sees a fair amount of use from hikers and backpackers. The 60-foot high Jacks River Falls is a popular attraction, and the immediate area surrounding the falls receives heavy use. Most trail users, though, are interested in angling only as a pleasant diversion, not a primary objective, so serious fishing pressure on the river is light.

The Cohutta Wilderness Area contains more than 90 miles of trails to get to its 37,000 acres. The Jacks River Trail follows the river for most of its length and will be part of any angling done on the river. When hiking the Jacks River Trail, be prepared to get wet. The trail fords the river more than 40 times, with some crossings waist deep even at normal flows. With so many river crossings, high water can pose a problem. The Penitentiary Branch Trail hits the river about midway, and the Beech Bottom Trail accesses the lower third of the river. Penitentiary Branch Trail is steep and difficult. The Beech Bottom Trail is a much more gradual climb, and although it is long, is an easy hike by Cohutta standards.

Take the same precautions for the Jacks River listed in the Conasauga River site description. Plan your trip carefully and let someone know your itinerary. Do not drink the water without treating it first, and secure your valuables and vehicle at the trailheads.

The fishing: The Jacks River rivals the Conasauga in the quality of fishing it offers, and some anglers think the Jacks is even better. Both streams can produce

20 or more fish in a good day and the average size on the Jacks River tends to be larger than on the Conasauga. Rainbows measuring 12 to 14 inches are common, and fish in the 9- to 11-inch range are plentiful. Although brown trout are less plentiful than rainbows, they will be the largest fish in the stream. The Jacks River has produced brown trout weighing up to 9 pounds. Brook trout are a possibility if you don't mind bushwacking up tiny tributaries at high elevations. As with the Conasauga River, the farther downstream you travel on the Jacks, the more redeye bass you will encounter.

Like the Conasauga, Jacks River trout require stealth and a careful presentation especially when the water is low and clear.

In the cramped headwaters upstream of the wilderness area, ultralight spinning gear is the best choice, but the rest of the Jacks River is open enough for flycasting. A favored approach to fishing the Jacks is to concentrate on deep slow pools in the early morning, and then switch to the riffle areas between pools once the sun has burned the mist off the water. A #8 or #10 stonefly nymph is a good choice early in the day, and once the switch is made to fishing the riffles, dry flies like Royal Wulffs or Adams are productive.

If spinning tackle is preferred, tiny in-line spinners are good. Most anglers prefer dark colors. Live bait angling can be the most productive way to prospect unknown water. Worms and crickets are both good baits.

GA~G grid: 14, B-1

General information: The Jacks River is designated as seasonal trout water. The stream is open to fishing during trout season only; when trout season is closed no fishing is allowed on the stream. All anglers must meet Georgia licensing requirements and possess a valid Georgia trout stamp. Fishing is allowed 30 minutes before sunrise to 30 minutes after sunset; night-fishing is prohibited. Any type of bait, natural or artificial, may be used. Trout may be harvested following standard Georgia creel limits. Consult the *Georgia Sport Fishing Regulations* pamphlet for more information on the Jacks River and trout fishing rules and regulations.

Some trailheads and recreation areas in the Chattahoochee National Forest charge a daily use fee. Be sure to check information boards for rules and regulations on arrival.

Food, lodging, and supplies are 17 miles away in Blue Ridge.

Nearest camping: Primitive camping is allowed throughout the Cohutta Wilderness Area. The nearest developed camping is on the western boundary of the wilderness area at the USDA Forest Service's Lake Conasauga Campground.

Directions: Travel north from Blue Ridge on Georgia Highway 5 for 3.5 miles. Turn left onto Old Highway 2. Continue on this road after it turns to gravel. At the intersection between Old Highway 2, FR 64, and FR 22, turn left onto FR 64 to reach the Jacks River headwaters or turn right onto FR 22 to reach the wilderness area trailheads.

For more information: Contact the Wildlife Resources Division Fisheries Section Office in Calhoun. For information about the Lake Conasauga Campground and Cohutta Wilderness Area rules and regulations, contact the USDA Forest Service Cohutta Ranger District.

15 Lower Toccoa River—Blue Ridge Dam to State Line

Key species: rainbow trout, brown trout, smallmouth bass.

Overview: The Toccoa River below Blue Ridge Dam is arguably the best tailwater trout fishery in Georgia. Plenty of feisty fish and little fishing pressure make the Toccoa a good choice for big-water trout fishing.

Best way to fish: wading, float tube, canoe.

Best time to fish: April through October.

Description: From Blue Ridge Dam to where it crosses into Tennessee (and takes on the name "Ocoee River"), the Toccoa River offers about 15 miles of good fishing for trout and perhaps even a few smallmouth bass. Compared to most Georgia trout streams, the Toccoa is big water. Long, deep pools separated by rocky shoals make the river perfect for floating using a tube or canoe. At high water, wading can be a problem. At low water, expect to do some dragging if you are in a canoe. Low water conditions are best fished by floating in a canoe and then getting in the water to fish.

Because this section of the Toccoa River flows through private lands, access is limited. However, several public parks and road crossings provide angler access to the river and make floating from one point to another an option. Since the operation of Blue Ridge Dam significantly affects the water level, safety should always be foremost. The onset of generation, unannounced and sometimes unscheduled, brings sudden and dramatic changes in the river. When wading, always keep a close eye on a benchmark rock, fallen tree, or other objects in the river. At the first hint that the water is rising, immediately head for higher ground. Wearing a personal flotation device (PFD) when wading makes good sense anywhere on the river, especially during cold weather, and the Tennessee Valley Authority (TVA) requires it for anglers entering the river at the dam access point.

Since natural reproduction in the tailwater is negligible, most of the trout caught will be stockers around 9 inches. However, some holdover does occur and larger fish are a possibility. The tributaries to the river do produce some stream spawned fish and these occasionally make their way down into the river. In the fall and winter months, big brown trout will migrate out of the tributaries and into the main river to take advantage of a more abundant food supply. When river temperatures begin to rise in early summer, the fish will migrate back into the tributaries in search of cooler water.

Although predominantly a trout fishery, the lower Toccoa River offers opportunities to catch warm-water species including black bass and sunfish. As

Lower Toccoa River—Blue Ridge Dam to State Line

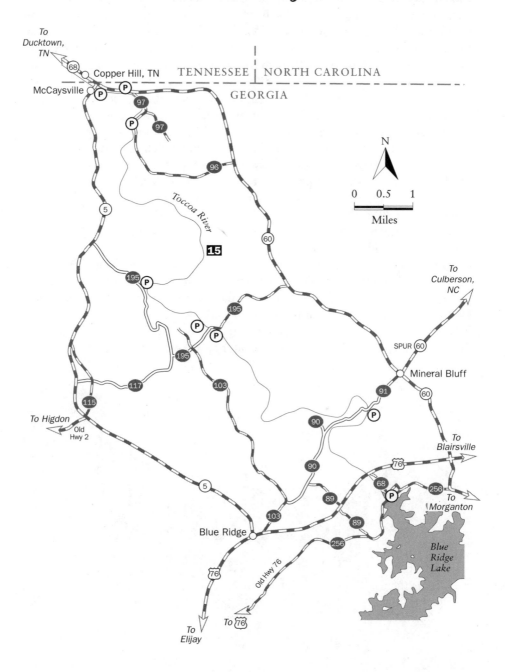

with trout fishing, floating will be the most effective way to find and catch fish.
The fishing: Successful fishing on the lower Toccoa is directly tied to what is occurring at Blue Ridge Dam. The best fishing occurs during the falling water that comes when generation ceases. Make the most of these favorable conditions by either hopscotching access points down the river to keep pace with falling water, or timing your float to follow the falling water. When the water is at its lowest point, fishing is usually slow.

When conditions are right and fish are actively feeding, nearly any trout-sized bait, spinner, plug, or fly will draw strikes. One factor to keep in mind during lure selection is bigger water requires a bigger bait if for no other reason than to maintain contact. Tiny spinners that work well in mountain brooks will be difficult to fish in the deeper, swifter water of the river. An eighth-ounce spinner is a good starting point, although conditions may allow you to go lighter or may require an even heavier bait. Flycasters may want to consider stonefly nymphs early in the year and then switch to dry flies later in the season. Good choices would include a #16 or #18 caddis or mayfly, especially early in the morning or near sunset.

Although not the best season for numbers of fish, winter offers some interesting possibilities. Holdovers from the summer stockings and fish that have migrated out of the tributaries provide an opportunity for the biggest fish of the year. The key to catching fish is to make a presentation on or near the bottom. Weighted nymphs in stonefly patterns, Gold-Ribbed Hare's Ears, and Pheasant Tails are good choices. For spinning afficionados, a small plug that

The lower Toccoa River is some of the best big-water trout fishing in Georgia.

imitates a minnow or crayfish, favorite foods of big wintertime brown trout, may produce a fish to remember.

GA~G grid: 14, B-3

General information: The Toccoa River downstream of Blue Ridge Dam is designated as year-round trout water. However, all tributaries to the river, unless specifically listed as year-round, are seasonal trout water. All anglers fishing the Toccoa River must meet Georgia licensing requirements and possess a valid Georgia trout stamp. Night-fishing is allowed. Any type of bait, natural or artificial, may be used. Trout may be harvested following standard Georgia creel limits. Consult the *Georgia Sport Fishing Regulations* pamphlet for more information on the Toccoa River and trout fishing rules and regulations.

Food, lodging, and supplies are available in nearby Blue Ridge.

Nearest camping: From Blue Ridge Dam, the USDA Forest Service's Morganton Point Campground is only 3 miles away on the shores of Blue Ridge Lake. Tent and RV sites are available, although there are no hookups. Walk-in tent camping sites are also available. The campground has drinking water, hot showers, and flush toilets.

Directions: The lower Toccoa River is enclosed on the west by Georgia Highway 5 and on the east by GA 60. Several county roads intersecting these highways provide access to the river. Refer to the site map to reach the stretch of river you want to fish.

For more information: Contact the Wildlife Resources Division Fisheries Section Office in Calhoun. For Morganton Point Campground information, contact the USDA Forest Service Toccoa Ranger District. The generation schedule at Blue Ridge Dam is available from the TVA by phone or on the Internet.

16 Blue Ridge Lake

Key species: smallmouth bass, largemouth bass, walleye, white bass, bluegill.

Overview: Located close to the meeting place of the Georgia, Tennessee, and North Carolina borders, Blue Ridge Lake is one of north Georgia's mountain treasures and is arguably the best destination in the state for catching smallmouth bass.

Best way to fish: boat.

Best time to fish: October through May.

Description: With a normal pool elevation of 1,687 feet, Blue Ridge is the highest major reservoir in northwest Georgia. Impounded in 1930 by damming the Toccoa River, a tributary of the Tennessee River, the Tennessee Valley Authority (TVA) operates the reservoir for flood control and hydropower. Blue Ridge is also the oldest major reservoir in northwest Georgia.

Although Blue Ridge is a relatively small reservoir with 3,290 acres at full pool, it stretches over 12 miles and has about 100 miles of shoreline. With depths greater than 120 feet near the dam, Blue Ridge is also a deep lake. Blue Ridge has very little in the way of woody cover; instead the lake bottom is

Blue Ridge Lake

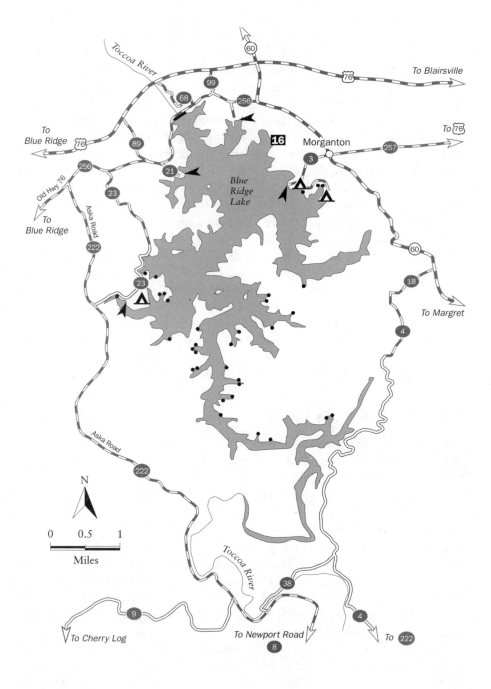

composed of rock, shale, and sand. For the uninitiated, the lack of cover can make Blue Ridge a difficult lake to fish.

Since one of the lake's primary purposes is to prevent flooding, the lake undergoes a significant drawdown every fall to provide storage for spring rains. Beginning as early as September, the lake level begins to drop. By the New Year, the lake may be as much as 50 feet below normal pool. With the warming rays of spring, however, come heavy rains and the lake is usually full again by the beginning of April. The fish seem to take the annual drawdowns in stride and simply move to deeper homes as the water begins to drop. At low water, only a few boat ramps are useable, all on the lower end of the lake. This is not too much of a burden, however, since Blue Ridge is a relatively small lake and fishing pressure is never all that heavy, especially in the dead of winter.

Since its clear, infertile waters are so attractive, Blue Ridge is a favorite with pleasure boaters in the summer. During this time, angling at night can provide welcome relief from the summer heat and constant boat traffic. Although there are some lakeside homes and cabins, the public lands of the Chattahoochee National Forest surround much of the lake.

The fishing: Georgia only has a handful of places to catch smallmouth bass, and Blue Ridge Lake is at the top of a short list. Around 25 percent of the black bass in Blue Ridge are smallmouth bass, with largemouths comprising most of the remainder.

With the lack of woody cover, structural features like points, drops, humps, and channels become very important to finding fish.

Although smallmouths are the main drawing card at Blue Ridge, the lake also offers good angling for walleye and white bass. At certain times of year, all three species will be using the same habitat and can all be caught in the same place with the same approach.

Favorite tactics for fishing Blue Ridge include soft plastics or jigs fished on bottom, vertically jigging spoons, and casting or trolling crankbaits. The depth at which to start your search varies by season. Perhaps because the water is so clear, night-fishing really shines on Blue Ridge. During the summer months, night-fishing is not only a way to catch more fish, but to have more fun doing it since there is less boat traffic with which to contend. Artificials are not the only game in town at Blue Ridge. Spring lizards (salamanders), crayfish, crickets, and minnows all are productive baits, and may produce the most action.

Other angling possibilities at Blue Ridge include bluegill, flathead catfish, and channel catfish. Bluegills run big at Blue Ridge, and what they lack in numbers they make up for in size. Fish deep with natural baits to catch hand-sized bream. Flathead and channel catfish are the most overlooked fishery on the lake. Fishing near channel ledges with live or cut bait on or near bottom can produce some surprisingly large fish.

GA~G grid: 14, C-4

General information: Blue Ridge is managed under standard statewide creel and length limits with one exception. Because the lake is infertile and fish growth is slow, there is no minimum length limit on any black bass species (smallmouth, largemouth, or spotted bass). Anglers must meet standard Georgia licensing requirements to fish the lake.

Food, lodging, and supplies are available about 3 miles away in the town of Blue Ridge.

Nearest camping: The USDA Forest Service operates two public campgrounds on the shores of the lake. Morganton Point Campground (44 sites, drinking water, hot showers, flush toilets) is on the east side of the lake and the Lake Blue Ridge Campground (58 sites, drinking water, cold showers, flush toilets) is on the west side. Each site at both campgrounds is equipped with a tent pad, fire ring/grill, picnic table, and lantern post. Walk-in tent camping sites are available at Morganton Point.

Since Chattahoochee National Forest lands surround much of the lake, primitive boat-in camping is also a possibility. Finding flat ground may be difficult though, and since private land is interspersed with public land along the shores of the lake; take care to avoid trespassing.

Directions: Blue Ridge Lake is just south of the intersection U.S. Highway 76 and Georgia Highway 60 in Fannin County 3 miles east of the town of Blue Ridge.

For more information: Contact the Wildlife Resources Division Fisheries Section Office in Calhoun. For information about the Morganton Point and Lake Blue Ridge Campgrounds, contact the USDA Forest Service Toccoa Ranger District. The lake level and generation schedule at Blue Ridge Dam is available from the TVA by phone or on the Internet.

17 Upper Toccoa River

Key species: rainbow trout, brown trout, smallmouth bass.

Overview: From its headwaters in Union County, the upper stretch of the Toccoa River flows nearly 30 miles through a patchwork of public and private land before it reaches Blue Ridge Lake. The river's moderate rapids and lack of development make it a great choice for a float-fishing trip for trout or smallmouth bass.

Best way to fish: canoe.

Best time to fish: April through October.

Description: Although its extreme headwaters are in the Chattahoochee National Forest, the first 10 miles or so of the Toccoa River's journey to the Tennessee River is through private lands. From the USDA Forest Service's Deep Hole Recreation Area near the village of Margret downstream to Blue Ridge Lake, however, the river flows in and out of a patchwork of national forest lands. Since even this early on its journey the Toccoa is big water by trout stream standards, floating is the best way to fish the river; the river's size makes bank fishing ineffective, and wading can be difficult in places. Using public lands as starting and stopping points for a float avoids the problem of privately

Upper Toccoa River

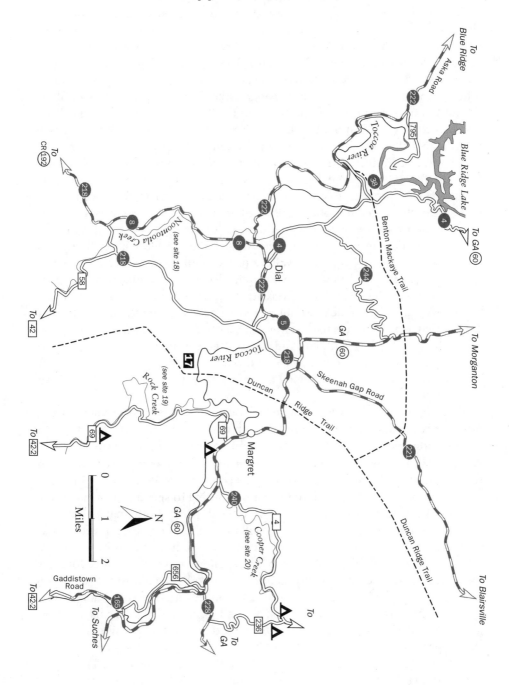

held bank access. Since the upper Toccoa River is not easily fished by bank or wading, it receives less pressure than other nearby trout streams.

The Toccoa River is a great class I/II paddle with a couple of borderline class III rapids thrown in, although both can be easily portaged. The developed canoe access at the Deep Hole Recreation Area is a favorite starting point, and the float from Deep Hole to Blue Ridge Lake is an excellent overnight trip. Otherwise, there are two good day trips; one from Deep Hole to Dial, and the other from Dial to just above Blue Ridge Lake. The last good take-out above the lake is at a rapid known as Noontootla Boil. This is where Aska Road parallels the river for about a half-mile. You can choose to finish your trip by running this class II+ rapid or you can take out above it.

Natural reproduction in the river is limited, so most of the trout caught from the Toccoa will be stocked rainbows, and a few of its tributaries are some of the heaviest stocked trout streams in Georgia. Trout in the Toccoa make good use of the abundant food supply, and quality fish are present. Some native browns and rainbows that have migrated out of the tributary streams are also possibilities. The closer you are to Blue Ridge Lake, the more likely that small-mouth bass and perhaps even a walleye or two will show up in the creel.

Although developed facilities on the upper Toccoa are limited, what is present is high quality. The Deep Hole Recreation Area not only has a paved canoe launch, but also a wooden fishing pier designed to provide physically challenged anglers with access to the river. Especially during the summer, the upper Toccoa is popular with paddlers and tubers. Recreational use of the river is not so heavy it takes away from the fishing though. Another interesting sight near Deep Hole is the 260-foot swinging bridge that carries the Duncan Ridge Trail over the river.

Except during high water, the upper Toccoa is well-suited to the novice or intermediate paddler. Keep in mind though that should misfortune befall you, help is a long way away. Plan carefully and be prepared for emergencies.

The fishing: Even with a canoe, time constraints will likely prevent you from thoroughly fishing every good-looking piece of water. One thing to keep in mind is whoever is in the back of the canoe is going to spend just as much time steering the canoe as they are fishing. In the still pools, both anglers will have a chance to fish. In the faster water, it will take at least one person's full attention to keep the canoe upright and headed in the right direction.

Since the river alternates between wide, shallow, and swift sections followed by deep, still pools, carry two ultralight spinning rods. Rig one rod for a shallow presentation and one for a deeper presentation. A one-sixteenth ounce in-line spinner (green is a local favorite) or a small gold or silver Rapala are both good lures. A sinking Rapala would be a good choice for reaching down into the deeper holes.

Flycasters will find the upper Toccoa well-suited to their art. The deeper slow-moving pools beg for the presentation of a dry fly when the mist is just beginning to burn off the water. Since major hatches are rare, an attractor pattern will serve you well. Nymphs can be used to comb the deeper water for bigger fish.

For flat out producing fish, nothing beats natural bait. Salmon eggs, corn, worms, or crickets bumped slowly along the bottom of pools is very effective.

On the lower sections of the river, if smallmouth bass are your game, a small floating or diving plug or a lead-head jig tipped with a plastic grub is hard to beat. Small topwater plugs are also good and can draw explosive strikes. Be sure to bring your polarized sunglasses. Good sunglasses will not only help you spot fish and good lies, but also submerged rocks that want to capsize your canoe.

GA~G grid: 14, D-4

General information: The upper Toccoa River is designated as year-round trout water. Fishing is allowed throughout the year, but all anglers must meet Georgia licensing requirements and possess a valid Georgia trout stamp. Night-fishing is allowed. All tributaries to the river are designated as seasonal trout waters unless *Georgia Sport Fishing Regulations* pamphlet specifically lists them as open to fishing year-round.

Some recreation areas on the Chattahoochee National Forest require a daily use fee. Be sure to check area rules and regulations upon arrival.

A good selection of food, lodging, and supplies are available about 21 miles away in Blue Ridge.

Nearest camping: The nearest developed camping is the USDA Forest Service's Deep Hole Campground. The campground is open seasonally and has eight sites equipped with a tent pad, picnic table, and grill. Restrooms and drinking water are available.

Primitive camping is allowed throughout the Chattahoochee National Forest unless specifically posted as closed to camping.

The privately-owned Toccoa Valley Campground is downstream of Dial and is also a good secure take-out point for a float. The campground even offers shuttle service up to the Deep Hole put-in.

Directions: To reach the Deep Hole Recreation Area, from Morganton drive 14.6 miles south on Georgia Highway 60 to the entrance road on the right. Other access points can be reached via county roads off GA 60 or from Blue Ridge by traveling south on Aska Road (CR 222).

For more information: Contact the Wildlife Resources Division Fisheries Section Office in Calhoun. For information about the Deep Hole Recreation Area, contact the USDA Forest Service Toccoa Ranger District. Contact the owners of the Toccoa Valley Campground for an explanation of services offered.

18 Noontootla Creek

Key species: rainbow trout, brown trout.

Overview: Managed under a set of special regulations that restrict anglers to artificial lures only and prohibits harvest of all but trophy fish, Noontootla Creek is the premiere stream of the Blue Ridge Wildlife Management Area in Fannin County. Access to the creek is excellent, with almost the entire watershed on public land.

Best way to fish: wading.

Best time to fish: year-round.

Description: From its headwaters near Winding Stair Gap, Noontootla Creek flows northward through the lands of the Chattahoochee National Forest and Blue Ridge Wildlife Management Area. Although the stream's lower half is mostly on private land, the upper half and its tributaries offer plenty of public owned opportunities for trophy trout fishing. Since no stockings have taken place since the mid-1960s, all the fish caught will be stream-bred brown and rainbow trout. Native brook trout may be possible in the extreme headwaters of small tributaries, but the browns and rainbows are what draw anglers to the stream.

Although access to Noontootla Creek is easy since a national forest road parallels the stream's course, angling pressure is surprisingly light. The special regulations in effect on Noontootla Creek make it virtually a catch-and-release stream only, and undoubtedly have something to do with the lack of pressure.

Another interesting thing about Noontootla Creek is many anglers prefer to approach the stream with a fly rod versus ultralight spinning gear. Except the small tributaries and the extreme headwaters of the creek upstream of the Appalachian Trail crossing, the main stem of the creek is open enough for fly fishing, although it is not an easy go.

Noontootla Creek is not for everyone but it is perfect for some, especially fly anglers seeking an interesting challenge with a reward of small-stream, big trout.

The fishing: Most of the keeper-size fish caught from Noontootla Creek will be brown trout. However, harvesting fish is not what draws anglers to the stream. The drawing card is catching 10- to 14-inch wild rainbows and browns with the very real chance of going head-to-head with something larger in the tight confines of the creek.

Fly fishers should choose a general "buggy-looking" pattern instead of trying to exactly match a hatch that is probably close to nonexistent. The trout in Noontootla are wary, and are much more likely to be put off by a clumsy approach and cast than a perfect presentation of an insect they are not used to seeing. Adams and caddis patterns are good choices, and an Irresistible is easy for both the fish and the angler to track and keep in sight. If nymphs are the choice of the day, try a Hare's Ear, Prince, or Pheasant Tail. If fly fishing is not your forte, or you plan to fish the tight headwaters or tributaries, go with an

116

Noontootla Creek • Rock Creek (Fannin County)

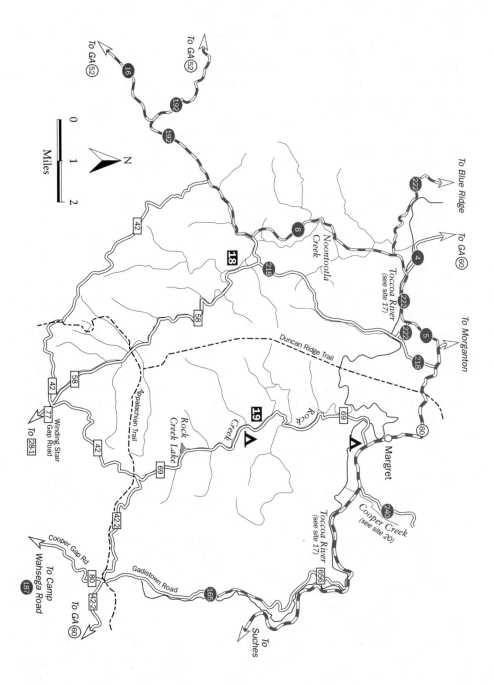

ultralight spinning outfit and the smallest spinner you can get away with. Casts are not going to be long, and in fact will probably be short underhand flips, so extra weight is not needed for casting distance.

GA~G grid: 14, E-5

General information: Noontootla Creek is designated as year-round trout water; however, several special regulations are in effect for the portion of the stream and its tributaries that are within the Blue Ridge Wildlife Management Area. One restriction is only artificial lures may be used; see the *Georgia Sport Fishing Regulations* pamphlet for the definition of an artificial lure. In addition, only fish more than 16 inches in length may be harvested. Keep in mind it is illegal to possess a trout less than 16 inches while fishing Noontootla Creek, no matter where you harvested it.

All anglers must meet Georgia licensing requirements and possess a valid Georgia trout stamp.

Food, lodging, and supplies are available in either Ellijay or Blue Ridge, both about 20 miles away.

Nearest camping: The USDA Forest Service's Deep Hole and Frank Gross Campgrounds are both within 10 miles. The sites at both campgrounds are equipped with a tent pad, grill, and lantern post. Primitive camping is allowed throughout the Chattahoochee National Forest unless otherwise posted. Some areas around the creek are posted closed to camping, so pay close attention to the signs before setting up camp.

Directions: Depending upon which direction you are coming from, there are several ways to access Noontootla Creek. Be aware that the southern and eastern approaches through Winding Stair Gap can be rough travel and the roads may be closed due to bad weather. Refer to the site map to plan your route.

For more information: Contact the Wildlife Resources Division Fisheries Section Office in Calhoun. For information about the Deep Hole and Frank Gross Campgrounds or Chattahoochee National Forest rules and regulations, contact the USDA Forest Service Toccoa Ranger District.

19 Rock Creek (Fannin County)

See map on page 117

Key species: rainbow trout, brown trout.

Overview: With the Chattahoochee National Fish Hatchery just a short drive down the road, it is no wonder Rock Creek is one of the most heavily stocked trout streams in Georgia. The creek's tame nature together with the heavy stocking combine to make Rock Creek very popular with families and those after an easy trout supper.

Best way to fish: bank, wading.

Best time to fish: April through September.

Description: A tributary to the Toccoa River, Rock Creek is a small- to medium-sized stream that sees a lot of use. The entire stream flows through lands of the Chattahoochee National Forest and Blue Ridge Wildlife Management Area.

The Chattahoochee National Fish Hatchery is located on one of the tributaries to the creek. The easy access, heavy stocking, and a streamside campground make Rock Creek very popular with trout fishing families and anglers interested in catching trout without having to go to the trouble of reaching more remote waters.

Although wild trout may be possible in the upper reaches of the stream and its tributaries, it is the 9-inch stocked trout that bring people to Rock Creek. Most of the fish caught will be rainbows. With the heavy use it receives, angling at Rock Creek is a community affair. There are plenty of fish for everyone though, and success rates are high. Rock Creek is an excellent place to introduce youngsters to the sport of trout fishing. The fish are plentiful, can be caught with a variety of techniques, and reaching and fishing the stream is easy.

Besides the stream itself, 13-acre Rock Creek Lake also offers trout fishing.

The fishing: Just about any method should work on Rock Creek. Fish fresh out of the hatchery are suckers for anything resembling the food pellets that have been the standard fare for all their lives. Kernel corn, salmon eggs, commercially produced trout candy, worms, and crickets fished on a light spinning or spin-casting outfit will all catch fish. Present the bait on or near the bottom in the pools.

If you prefer artificials, small spinners would be the top choice. A small Rapala or other minnow imitator can also be good. Present these lures at the base of plunge pools and riffles. In deeper pools, let the lure sink before beginning an erratic retrieve.

Fly fishing is not that common here, but the number of targets present does make the stream a good choice for the budding flycaster. Any fly pattern stands a good chance. Although not commonly found in tackle shops, a fly that resembles a food pellet would work especially well. Something dark brown and the shape and size of a pencil eraser will suffice. Even the novice fly tier can produce a reasonable facsimile with materials found around the house.

If escaping the crowds is your goal, fish the extreme headwaters of the creek or its tributaries. Native trout are possible in these tiny rivulets, and some brook trout might even be available. The fishing in these tiny waters will be much more challenging than the main creek, and the fish much smaller.

GA~G grid: 14, E-5

General information: Rock Creek and Rock Creek Lake are both designated as year-round trout water. Rock Creek is open to night fishing, however, night-fishing is prohibited on Rock Creek Lake. Private boats are allowed on Rock Creek Lake, but are limited to electric motors only. All anglers fishing Rock Creek or the lake must meet Georgia licensing requirements and possess a valid Georgia trout stamp. Standard statewide creel and length limits are in effect on Rock Creek and Rock Creek Lake; see the *Georgia Sport Fishing Regulations* pamphlet for more information.

Food, lodging, and supplies are available 25 miles away in Blue Ridge.

Nearest camping: The USDA Forest Service's Frank Gross Campground is on the banks of Rock Creek. All nine sites have a tent pad, fire ring, and lantern pole. Toilets and drinking water are available. The campground is open seasonally. In addition, there are many primitive campsites up and down the stream.

Directions: From Morganton, travel 14.4 miles south on Georgia Highway 60 to Forest Road 69 on the right. A short distance after crossing the Toccoa River on FR 69, Rock Creek will appear on the right side of the road.

For more information: Contact the Wildlife Resources Division Fisheries Section Office in Calhoun. For camping information, contact the USDA Forest Service Toccoa Ranger District.

Northeast Georgia

Northeast Georgia is the center of Georgia trout fishing. Most of Georgia's best trout streams are found in this mountainous portion of the Peach State. The region offers more than just trout fishing though, there are several sprawling impoundments nationally known for excellent spotted and largemouth bass fishing.

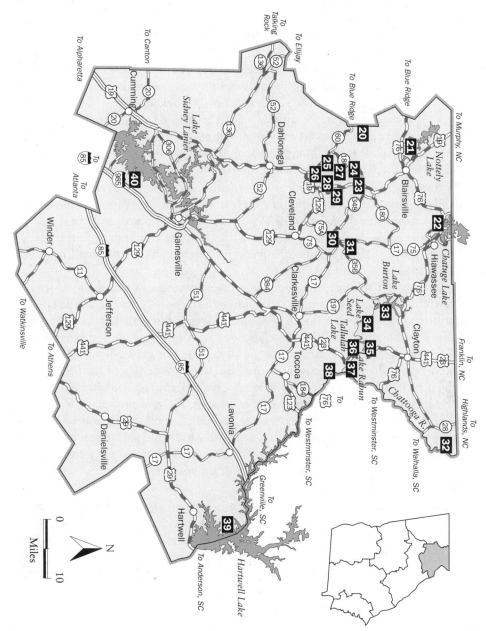

20 Cooper Creek

Key species: rainbow trout, brown trout.

Overview: Cooper Creek runs though public land for most of its length and offers a good mix of both the easy and difficult brands of Georgia trout fishing.

Best way to fish: wading.

Best time to fish: April through October.

Description: Cooper (often called Coopers) Creek is a tributary to the Toccoa River. Except the lowermost segment and one other small area, the creek flows over lands of the Chattahoochee National Forest. Cooper Creek provides something for everyone, no matter what style of trout fishing you prefer. The lower reaches of the stream around the two USDA Forest Service campgrounds can be very crowded angling, especially right after opening day and on summer weekends. This portion of the stream is heavily stocked. Farther up the creek, access becomes much more difficult and the crowds drop off dramatically. Both stocked and native trout are possible here. The small tributaries to Cooper Creek also provide trout fishing opportunities. These waters are small though, and fishing them can be hard work.

The fishing: The lower section of the stream near the campgrounds is perfect for sharing the camaraderie of other anglers while pursuing a limit of fat stocker trout. Access is much easier here, heavy stocking takes place, and the stream is tame with some deep holes. Wading is the best way to approach the creek. Canned corn, worms, commercially prepared trout bait, and small spinners are all good bets to try.

If you prefer solitude, the middle to upper portions of Cooper Creek are for you. Access to these portions is more limited. The middle section of the stream that flows through the Cooper Creek Scenic Area is the most remote. The creek is more rough-and-tumble in these sections with faster water and overgrown, steep banks. Since these portions of the stream are not as heavily stocked, your quarry is more likely to be a stream-bred fish that is not going to fall for the first thing that plunks down on top of its head. Try small spinners on ultralight tackle or fly fishing here. Keep in mind that at its best, Georgia mountain-stream fly fishing means little room for casting. If your skills with the fly rod are not so great, it is probably a better idea to stick with ultralight spinning tackle. If you go with fly fishing gear, do not get too hung up on fly selection. Any pattern that presents a buggy look has a good chance of drawing strikes.

GA~G grid: 15, D-6

General information: Cooper Creek is seasonal trout water and is only open to fishing during the trout season. All anglers must meet Georgia licensing requirements and must have a valid Georgia trout stamp. Consult the *Georgia Sport Fishing Regulations* pamphlet for more information on trout fishing rules and regulations. Several short hiking trails start near the Cooper Creek Scenic Area parking area. All of the trails are moderate to difficult and none run directly alongside Cooper Creek itself, although a few tributaries are crossed.

Cooper Creek • Lake Trahlyta • Lake Winfield Scott

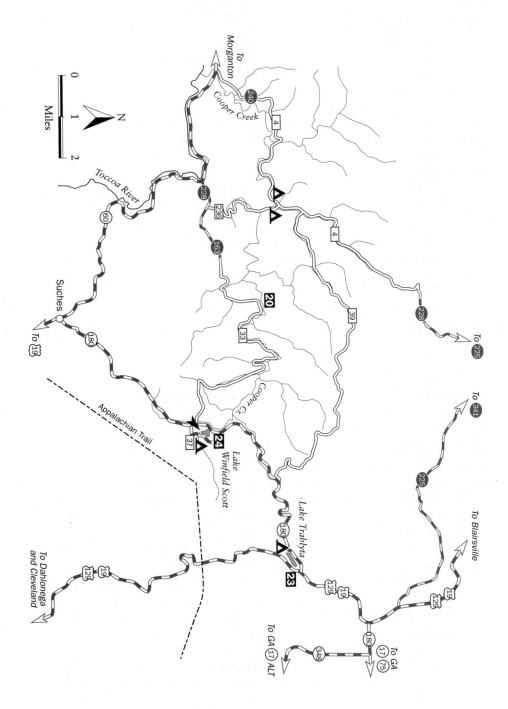

Day-use areas contain no facilities other than parking and information boards. A daily or annual parking fee is required.

Food, supplies, and lodging are available about 15 miles (via secondary roads) away in Blairsville. Other options are Blue Ridge and Dahlonega, both within 30 miles via primary roads.

Nearest camping: Both very near the creek, the USDA Forest Service's Cooper Creek and Mulky Campgrounds offer 17 and 11 campsites respectively. Each site consists of a tent pad, picnic table, and grill. Drinking water and toilets are available at both campgrounds. A fee is charged for camping. The campgrounds are open seasonally from late March through the end of October. Some parts of the Cooper Creek Recreation Area and all of the Cooper Creek Scenic Area are closed to primitive camping. Primitive camping is allowed anywhere on the Chattahoochee National Forest unless otherwise posted.

Directions: From Morganton, head south 14.6 miles on Georgia Highway 60 to Cooper Creek Road (CR 240) on the left. CR 240 turns into Forest Road 4. Drive 5 miles to Mulky Campground. Continue 1 mile past Mulky Campground to Cooper Creek Campground at FR 246. To reach the parking area for the Cooper Creek Scenic Area, turn left off FR 4 onto FR 236 and travel 0.5 mile to the entrance on the left.

For more information: Contact the Wildlife Resources Division Fisheries Section Office in Gainesville. For information about the Cooper Creek and Mulky Campgrounds or Chattahoochee National Forest rules and regulations, contact the USDA Forest Service Toccoa Ranger District.

21 Lake Nottely

Key species: largemouth bass, spotted bass, crappie, striped bass.

Overview: Fertile waters and low fishing pressure combine to make Nottely one of the best bass fishing lakes in north Georgia.

Best way to fish: boat.

Best time to fish: March through October.

Description: Lake Nottely is a 4,180-acre TVA reservoir on the Nottely River constructed for power generation, navigation, and flood control. Lake Nottely is one of the few places in Georgia where bass anglers have a realistic chance of catching three black bass species from the same lake. Largemouth bass make up about 70 percent of the bass population in Nottely and support most of the fishery. Spotted bass are a distant second at 25 percent, and smallmouth bass pick up the remaining 5 percent. Nottely is one of only three major reservoirs in Georgia to have bronzebacks (Blue Ridge and Chatuge are the others), but their numbers in Nottely have fallen to the point that they are not really a player anymore. If your goal is to catch a Nottely smallmouth, stay downlake near the dam.

For bass fishing, Lake Nottely is known more for size than numbers. Traditionally, the average largemouth bass caught will weigh more than 2

Lake Nottely

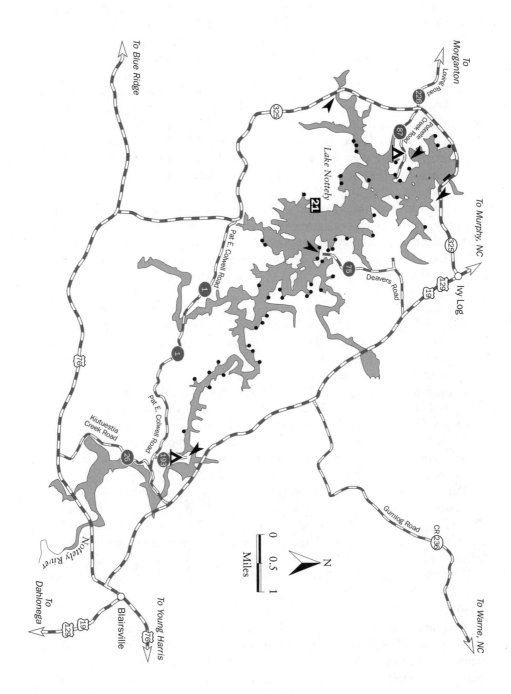

pounds, with spots lagging behind at about a pound each. Any largemouth even approaching the 10-pound range is going to be a fish of a lifetime, but there are good numbers of 2- to 4-pound fish and some more than 5 pounds.

Like most mountain lakes, Nottely lacks the type of cover preferred by largemouths; wherever you can find it, you need to fish it thoroughly. In an attempt to improve the lunar-surface nature of Nottely's bottom, government agencies and local anglers have worked to place and maintain cove fish attractors around the lake.

Since Lake Nottely is far removed from major population centers, the fishing pressure is not that heavy. The lake has several boat ramps, but access can be a problem during much of the year. Beginning in late summer, the lake is gradually drawn down 30 to 40 feet and is not usually back to full pool until mid-spring. At the height of the drawdown, finding a usable boat ramp may be a problem.

The fishing: At Nottely, cover is the key, especially for largemouths. Specific places to try are Ivy Log and Young Cane Creeks and the Canal Lake area. Don't overlook the small pockets on the main channel where debris collects and provides cover where there would otherwise be none. Flipping a jig into the tangled mess can result in some good bites. On the lower lake, try the back end of Conley Creek. Jigs or medium-diving crankbaits are good lure choices. If the water is dingy, use a lure with brown, chartreuse, and orange. In clearer water, shad patterns work well.

For spotted and smallmouth bass, concentrate on the lower lake's rocky points and deep banks. Marked points 2 and 3 have traditionally produced. A plastic grub threaded on a light jighead and worked along the bottom is a good technique any time of year.

Early in the spring, look for stripers making their way up the river on a false spawning run. The rest of the year, search for stripers around deep points in the main lake. A large surface lure can draw explosive strikes early and late in the day. Shad and small bream are two favorite live baits when fish are deep.

March and April are the best time to catch hefty Nottely crappie. Present a jig or small minnow in and around the marked fish attractors or any other woody cover you can find.

Other species available on Nottely include walleye, white bass, bluegill, and catfish. The best bluegill and catfish angling is on the upper end of the lake. Bluegill concentrate around shallow cover. Catfish will be found on feeding flats beside the channel. Nightcrawlers and shiners are favorite live baits for walleye. For white bass, fish upriver in March and April as the fish make their upstream spawning run. Later in the year, search for them in the more open waters of the lower lake.

GA~G grid: 15, B-6

General information: Lake Nottely is managed under standard Georgia state-wide creel and length limits. All anglers must meet Georgia licensing requirements. Food, lodging, and supplies are about 10 miles away in Blairsville.

Nearest camping: Camping is allowed seasonally at the TVA's Poteete Creek Recreation Area.

A striped bass is about to be gaffed and brought aboard before being released.

Directions: Lake Nottely can be reached via secondary roads off U.S. Highways 19/129 and 76 or Georgia Highway 325, near Blairsville.

For more information: Contact the Wildlife Resources Division Fisheries Section Office in Gainesville or the TVA.

22 Lake Chatuge

Key species: spotted bass, hybrid striped bass, largemouth bass, white bass.

Overview: Despite being an infertile mountain reservoir, Lake Chatuge has produced several state record fish, including the hybrid striped bass and smallmouth bass.

Best way to fish: boat.

Best time to fish: March through November.

Description: Lake Chatuge is a 7,050-acre TVA reservoir constructed on the Hiwassee River for hydropower and flood control. Impounded in 1942, Chatuge is an old lake and has always been popular with vacationers. Cabins and houses line much of the shoreline, and summertime traffic on the lake and the surrounding roads is heavy. The lake sprawls across the Georgia–North Carolina border with both states having an almost equal-sized portion.

Nestled in the Blue Ridge Mountains, Lake Chatuge is breathtaking. Since the lake is infertile, its waters are usually clear and add to the attractiveness of the surroundings. Chatuge has a fair amount of stumps, logs, and brush in places, but is not rife with cover. The water is deep, and fishing depths of 25 feet or more is common on Chatuge. The lake undergoes a winter drawdown every year, but plenty of water is still available for you to fish.

Lake Chatuge has undergone some dramatic changes in its life. For much of its history, Lake Chatuge was the best place in Georgia to catch smallmouth bass. The long-standing state record smallmouth of 7 pounds, 2 ounces, came from Chatuge. In the mid-1980s, spotted bass were introduced into the lake by unknown means, and the smallmouth began a precipitous decline. To add insult to injury, blueback herring were introduced into the lake in 1990s, again an unauthorized stocking, and the jury is still out on what the effects may be.

The ever increasing problem of species introductions has decimated what once was a unique and productive fishery on Lake Chatuge. Bronzebacks are still available, but make up only a slight fraction of the total black bass population; spotted bass have replaced them. Largemouths have always been present in Chatuge and some manage to grow to astonishing sizes. As unlikely as it may seem, one of Georgia's top-10 largemouth bass is a documented 16 pounds, 11 ounces, mossyback caught from Chatuge in 1976.

While the lake does not produce a trophy bass on every cast, Chatuge is nonetheless a good fishery. Spotted bass weighing 0.5 to 2 pounds are abundant and make up the bulk of the black bass catch. Largemouths are fewer, but are often quality fish of 2 to 3 pounds. Smallmouth bass are now so uncommon that catching one is a notable event; if you do manage to catch one, it is likely to be a solid fish of 1 to 4 pounds.

Lake Chatuge

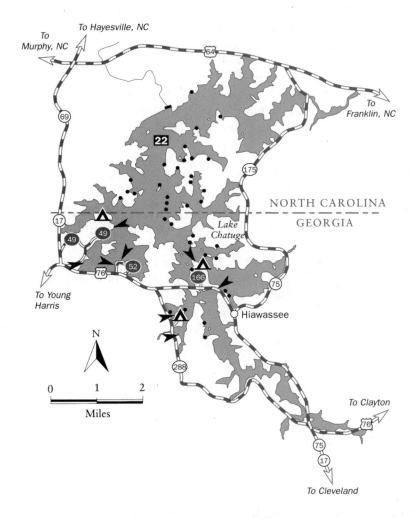

These same waters once held the world record for hybrid striped bass and still hold the Georgia record at 25.5 pounds. Since hybrids are sterile and do not reproduce, their numbers are totally dependent on stocking. If forage is becoming too abundant, then stocking numbers go up; if forage declines to a level barely sufficient to support the existing fishery, then the stocking numbers go down or stocking is halted. The use of hybrid stocking as a dynamic management tool benefits all species, but does result in some up and down hybrid fishing. Other species popular with anglers on Lake Chatuge are white bass, walleye, channel catfish, and sunfish.

Food, lodging, and supplies are available in the town of Hiawassee right on the lake. Interestingly, the town's name is spelled differently than the name of the river feeding the lake.

The fishing: To catch Chatuge spotted bass, target main-river shorelines and points in 15 to 25 feet of water. A rocky bank is best, and if stumps or brush are present, all the better. From the U.S. Highway 76 bridge north to the dam and the Bell Creek arm midway up on the east side of the lake are good places to find spotted bass. Fish these areas with small topwater plugs or shallow-diving crankbaits early in the day and then switch over to a deeper presentation once the sun is on the water.

For bronzebacks, fishing the same areas one would for spotted bass may result in the occasional fish, but the junction of the Bell Creek and Hiwassee River channels is proven for smallmouth. Here the depth abruptly drops off from 25 feet to 80 feet. Fish a jigging spoon along the walls.

If largemouth bass are your quarry, cover is the key. Topwater baits are good early in the morning. Later in the day, fish a purple or black plastic worm in depths of 10 to 25 feet. Shad and shiners are favorite live baits, as are commercially grown rainbow trout, locally available. The best time for trophy hybrids is at night during the full moon in April and May, when they move onto points and bars. A live bait or a diving plug at night gets trophy results.

Other good bets on Chatuge include white bass and walleye. Early in the spring, look for white bass upriver as the fish make their spawning run. For walleye, cast or troll crankbaits along rocky shorelines and points. Nighttime is the best fishing. Nightcrawlers and shiners fished on the bottom are also good choices.

The best crappie fishing on Chatuge will be around the cove fish attractors and other woody cover in the early spring. Minnows and small jigs are favorite baits. Bluegill and other sunfish can be caught throughout the summer from shallow spawning areas and around shoreline cover. Crickets, red wigglers, small spinners, or popping bugs are all good choices. Channel catfish are abundant in the lake and can be caught nearly anywhere on chicken liver, worms, or other smelly bait fished on the bottom.

Plan to fish at night or very early in the morning during the summer to avoid heavy boat traffic.

GA~G grid: 15, A-9

General information: Georgia and North Carolina have a reciprocal agreement allowing license holders from either state to fish by boat the waters of the lake and all tributaries reachable by boat from the main body of the lake without having to purchase the other state's license. However, if you are on the shoreline or your boat is anchored to the shore or a pier or dock connected to the shore, you must have appropriate license for the state you are in.

Standard Georgia creel and length limits apply to the Georgia portion of Chatuge. Be aware that North Carolina creel and length limits differ from Georgia's, and anglers must follow the regulations of whatever state they are in no matter where the fish were caught.

Nearest camping: Several county and USDA Forest Service campgrounds are found on the lake's shores besides private marinas and fish camps. The USDA Forest Service's Lake Chatuge Campground has 30 campsites with tent pads,

Fly fishing is a great way to fish for a variety of species including bass, bream, and trout.

grills, and picnic tables. Some sites can accommodate trailers. Restrooms, drinking water, and cold showers are available. The campground is open from late April to late October. The Towns County Park and Georgia Mountain Fair has 189 sites with utilities and is open year-round. Camping is also available at the Chatuge Woods County Park.

Directions: The Georgia portion of Lake Chatuge is reachable from U.S. Highway 76 and Georgia Highways 17, 75, and 288, near Hiawassee.

For more information: Contact the Wildlife Resources Division Fisheries Section Office in Gainesville. For lake levels and generation schedules, contact the TVA. For information on county parks and other Towns County opportunities, contact the Towns County Chamber of Commerce. USDA Forest Service campground information is available from the Brasstown Ranger District Office.

23 Lake Trahlyta (Vogel State Park)

See map on page 123

Key species: rainbow trout, largemouth bass, bluegill.

Overview: Named for a Cherokee maiden buried nearby, Lake Trahlyta is a 22-acre lake in Vogel State Park, one of Georgia's oldest and most popular parks. The popularity of the park and the lake means that fishing is a community affair shared with swimmers and paddleboaters.

Best way to fish: bank.

Best time to fish: April through October.

Description: Established in the 1930s and within the Chattahoochee National Forest, Vogel State Park is one of the most popular parks in Georgia. The beautiful mountain scenery and cool climate make Vogel State Park a favorite summer getaway for Georgia families.

Although the park is small at 280 acres, it has plenty of attractions. Anglers will be most interested in Lake Trahlyta and its feeder stream, Wolf Creek. Both bodies of water receive periodic stockings of rainbow trout. Warm-water species including largemouth bass and sunfish are also abundant in Lake Trahlyta.

Along with fishing, Vogel State Park offers activities for the whole family. Camping, hiking, swimming, picnicking, miniature golf, and paddleboats are all available. Appropriately, since Civilian Conservation Corps (CCC) workers built the lake and the original cabins during the Great Depression, the park also contains a small museum chronicling the history and accomplishments of the CCC in the area. Every autumn thousands of Georgians make their annual pilgrimage to the north Georgia mountains to see a natural palette of countless shades of yellow, orange, and red as the leaves begin to turn.

The fishing: Since Lake Trahlyta is only 22 acres, it is easily covered in a day. The best fishing is on the south end of the lake where Wolf Creek enters. For trout, an ultralight spinning outfit with small spinners or small minnow-imitators like Rapalas and Rebels is a good way to go. Fly anglers can also draw strikes casting any variety of streamers, nymphs, or dry flies. For the bait angler, the usual trout fare of whole kernel corn, worms, or crickets can be productive.

Warm-water species are also available in Lake Trahlyta. Any standard bass lure fished around structure should draw strikes. If you are after the biggest bass in the lake, go with a large lure that closely imitates a rainbow trout. Worms and crickets, besides being good trout baits, will also attract strikes from sunfish. Fish these live baits around shallow cover for the best results.

For anglers who prefer to stream fish, there is about a mile of fishable moving water in the park in Wolf Creek and its tributaries. These streams are small and overgrown, making casting awkward. In the summer, the water level in these small streams can get extremely low, making angling difficult. Tiny spinners are the most effective lures for these small waters.

Since Vogel State Park receives such heavy use, you may want to consider a trip early or late in the year. Although fishing is a secondary diversion for many park visitors, the lake is small and the fish become educated very quickly.

GA~G grid: 15, D-7

General information: The regulations governing Lake Trahlyta and Wolf Creek are somewhat different. Anglers fishing the lake for trout or other species must meet Georgia licensing requirements, but are not required to possess a trout stamp since the lake is within a state park. Fishing is open year-round on Lake Trahlyta.

Wolf Creek is seasonal trout water and all anglers must meet Georgia licensing requirements and possess a valid Georgia trout stamp. The stream is closed to all fishing when trout season is closed.

Private boats are not allowed on Lake Trahlyta, and fishing boats are not available for rent. However, a trail and perimeter roads give anglers easy access to the whole lake. Most of the shoreline is cleared or only lightly forested, so a boat is not really necessary. All vehicles parked in the area must have a daily or annual Georgia Parks Pass.

Beyond what is available in the park itself, food, lodging, and supplies are about 10 miles away in Blairsville.

Nearest camping: A variety of camping opportunities are available at Vogel State Park. There are tent/RV sites with electricity and water, walk-in tent sites, primitive group camping, and cottages. More than 100 campsites are available, but on busy weekends the campground will be full, so you may want to consider calling ahead for reservations.

Directions: The entrance to Vogel State Park (Lake Trahlyta) is south of Blairsville, on U.S. Highway 19/129, 0.3 mile south of that highway's intersection with Georgia Highway 180.

For more information: Contact the Wildlife Resources Division Fisheries Section Office in Gainesville. For information on facilities and park rules and regulations, contact the Park Superintendent's Office.

24 Lake Winfield Scott

See map on page 123

Key species: rainbow trout, largemouth bass, bluegill.

Overview: The USDA Forest Service's Lake Winfield Scott is an 18-acre lake at the headwaters of Cooper Creek. Periodically stocked with trout, and surrounded by beautiful scenery, the small lake is popular with anglers, picnickers, and campers.

Best way to fish: shore, boat.

Best time to fish: April through October.

Description: Lake Winfield Scott is completely surrounded by the Chattahoochee National Forest. Since it is situated high in an undeveloped watershed, the waters in Lake Winfield Scott are usually ultraclear. The sometimes steep shoreline is forested, but there are plenty of openings to fish from, making a boat more of a luxury than a necessity.

The Civilian Conservation Corps built the lake in the 1930s and it has been popular ever since. The scenery is outstanding and the lake offers good fishing for both stocked rainbow trout and warm-water species including largemouth bass and sunfish.

The Appalachian Trail runs nearby, and two approach trails start at the lake and eventually join the main trail. In addition, a trail circles the lake giving anglers an easy walk from one spot to another.

The fishing: Lake Winfield Scott offers a good mix of angling. Fishing with worms or crickets is just as likely to produce a sunfish as it is a trout. Small spinners are also a good choice to catch nearly anything that swims in the lake. Largemouth bass are found in the lake and can be caught using standard bass fishing tactics. A technique for catching the biggest bass in the lake would be to use a lure that closely resembles a rainbow trout, a favorite food of bass wherever the two species coexist. This technique is not going to produce many strikes, but when you get one, it likely will be big enough to justify the wait.

Some more popular spots to fish are from the fishing pier and the area near the dam. Most trout caught will be around 9 inches, but bigger holdover fish are not out of the question. Fly fishing from a canoe would be a good choice, but most anglers opt for spinning gear.

GA~G grid: 15, E-7

General information: As a trout stream impoundment, the trout fishing regulations on Lake Winfield Scott are different than those of streams. The lake is open to fishing year-round and night-fishing is allowed. Anglers can fish for species other than trout without having a Georgia trout stamp; however, any trout caught must be immediately released if you do not have a stamp. To fish for or possess trout, you must have a valid trout stamp. All other Georgia licensing requirements apply.

Some areas of the Chattahoochee National Forest charge a daily use fee. Be sure to check area rules and regulations upon arrival. The lake has a boat ramp, but all boats are limited to electric motors only.

Food, lodging, and supplies are available within 20 miles in either Blairsville or Dahlonega.

Nearest camping: Camping is allowed at Lake Winfield Scott. The campground is open from May through October. Two camping loops offer 36 sites on a first-come, first-served basis. Each campsite is equipped with a tent pad, grill, lantern post, and picnic table. Drinking water, hot showers, and flush toilets are available during the open season. A group camping area is also available. During the closed season 16 campsites are available, but there is no drinking water and the restroom is a privy.

Directions: From the intersection of U.S. Highway 19/129 and Georgia Highway 180, drive 6.1 miles west on GA 180 to the day-use entrance on the left. For the campground and the boat ramp, continue another 0.7 mile to the second entrance.

For more information: Contact the Wildlife Resources Division Fisheries Section Office in Gainesville or the USDA Forest Service Brasstown Ranger District Office.

25 Dockery Lake

Key species: rainbow trout.

Overview: Situated high on a small tributary to Waters Creek, Dockery Lake is a 3-acre pond that offers good fishing for rainbow trout. The lake, campground, and other facilities are popular with people searching for a peaceful and relaxing place.

Best way to fish: shore, float tube.

Best time to fish: April through October.

Description: In the shadow of the Appalachian Trail within the bounds of the Chattahoochee National Forest and Chestatee Wildlife Management Area,

Dockery Lake • Waters Creek • Dicks Creek
Frogtown Creek • Boggs Creek

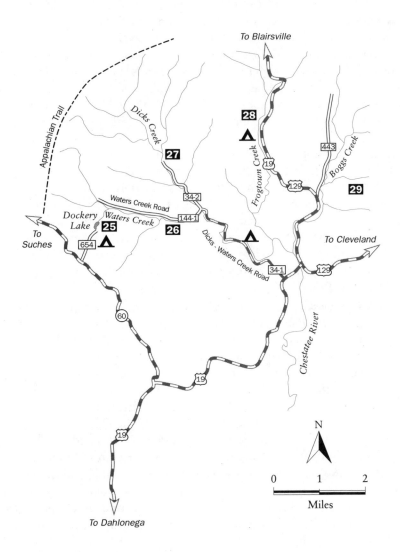

Dockery Lake is a peaceful oasis. Dockery Lake is noted for its attractive shore-line campground offering above-average privacy and spacious sites.

The lake receives periodic stockings of catchable-sized rainbow trout throughout the trout season. Warm-water species including bass and bream are also found in the lake, but trout are the favorite with anglers. Several small piers have been constructed to help give anglers unrestricted access to the lake.

In addition, an angler's trail completely circles the lake never straying more than a few feet from the water's edge.

Bear, deer, and wild turkeys can all be seen on the area at times. In fact, visitors should take extra precautions with their food and supplies to discourage any marauding by bruins with a hungry stomach.

The fishing: Dockery Lake is strictly a put-and-take trout fishery. Most of the fish caught will measure around 9 inches. However, since some winter hold-over is possible, larger fish are not out of the question. The best trout fishing will be midseason. Although the trout season runs through October, the year's stocking has been wrapped up well before then, and by autumn, trout will be scarce. Other warm-water species are available though, so one should not rule out Dockery Lake for a relaxing day of fishing simply because it is late in the season.

Most anglers approach Dockery Lake with light spinning gear and natural or artificial baits. Corn, worms, and crickets are all good selections for natural bait. Those who prefer to fling artificials will find small spinners and tiny minnow-imitating plugs to be effective. Fly fishing is also a possibility at Dockery Lake. Even an angler confined to the shoreline should find plenty of places with room to cast. Although shoreline access is good, the ideal way to approach fly fishing the small lake would be with a float tube. Flycasters should have luck with any variety of dry flies, small streamers, or nymphs.

GA~G grid: 15, E-7

General information: Unlike most trout stream impoundments, Dockery Lake is designated as seasonal trout water and is only open to fishing during trout season. When trout season is out, no fishing is allowed on the lake. No night-fishing is allowed. All anglers must meet Georgia licensing requirements and possess a valid Georgia trout stamp. Standard statewide creel and length limits are in effect on the lake.

Private boats are allowed on the lake, but only electric motors may be used. There is a carry-down boat access. Some areas of the Chattahoochee National Forest require a daily use fee. Be sure to check area rules and regulations upon arrival. Food, lodging, and supplies are 13 miles away in Dahlonega.

Nearest camping: Camping is allowed at Dockery Lake, and along with the fishing, is a main attraction in the area. The campground consists of 11 very nice sites each with a tent pad, picnic table, fire ring, and lantern post. Drinking water and flush toilets are available. The campground is open seasonally from mid-April through the end of October.

Directions: From Dahlonega, travel north on U.S Highway 19/Georgia Highway 60 until GA 60 splits off to the left. Bear left onto GA 60 and travel 3.6 miles to Forest Road 654 on the right. Follow this gravel road for 0.9 mile to the entrance of the area.

For more information: Contact the Wildlife Resources Division Fisheries Section Office in Gainesville or the USDA Forest Service Brasstown Ranger District Office.

26 Waters Creek

See map on page 135

Key species: rainbow trout, brown trout, brook trout.

Overview: Waters Creek is one of Georgia's special-regulation trout streams. Although the fishing in Waters Creek has fallen off from its heyday in the 1980s, the creek still offers the potential for trophy trout.

Best way to fish: wade, bank.

Best time to fish: April through October.

Description: Waters Creek is in the Chestatee Wildlife Management Area and is jointly managed as a trophy trout stream by the Georgia Wildlife Resources Division and USDA Forest Service with the Georgia Council of Trout Unlimited cooperating. The creek is small but has produced trophy trout, including a state record brook trout. Special regulations strictly curtail harvest of fish from the stream. Also, a supplemental feeding program is used to help the fish grow to trophy class in these infertile waters.

Waters Creek anglers have a shot at all three Georgia trout species. Rainbow trout successfully reproduce in Waters Creek, but maintaining a fishable population of brookies and brown trout requires periodic stocking.

Waters Creek was treasured by Georgia trout anglers following a decade of stellar trophy trout fishing, but in recent years the stream has been rocked by a series of blows to its special fishing. The first blow was a well-publicized poaching incident that took place while the caretaker was out sick. A band of poachers either netted or gigged nearly all the trophy trout from the stream. Trout Unlimited and the state offered a substantial reward, but no one was ever charged with the crime. A few years later, while the fish population was being rebuilt, a tornado struck the area and downed many trees into the lower section of the stream, making already challenging fishing conditions almost impossible. Then, the blizzard of the century in 1993 virtually filled the stream with fallen trees. The next few years brought significant flood events and Hurricane Opal.

Waters Creek never returned to its former glory. Some blame continued poaching or the natural expansion of river otters into the stream for the continued lack of monster trout. Studies on how trout fit into river otters' diet were inconclusive, with only trout less than 6 inches showing up in roughly 50 percent of scat samples. For those inclined to blame the otters, it is also speculated that perhaps the otters are eating up the crayfish and other forage once available to large trout.

Whatever the reason, the fishery in Waters Creek has changed. It is still a good place to catch larger than average fish, and definitely is less crowded with anglers than it once was, but trout meeting the stream's minimum length limits are rare.

The fishing: If catching 12-inch native rainbow trout will satisfy your urges, carefully fish good holding areas with a tiny spinner or attractor pattern fly. Waters Creek is an artificials-only stream so natural bait is not an option. Wade carefully and keep a low profile to prevent spooking the fish. Fish each pool thoroughly then move to the next one.

If your game entails a serious attempt at catching one of the trophy fish in Waters Creek, then a different strategy is called for. These fish are extremely wary. Full camouflage attire in a woodland green pattern is a necessity. Anglers after trophy trout prefer not to be in the stream while working a big trout. The best strategy is to conceal yourself alongside the stream well before daylight and quietly wait for legal fishing hours to arrive. Once the time to fish is at hand, you should make very careful intermittent presentations of a spinner or fly. Try not to show the fish the same thing too often. Preferred spinners are those that imitate small minnows. A favorite fly is one that resembles a food pellet. A floating fly that looks like a food pellet is a killer on trout accustomed to getting their meals in a neat, compact package.

One other thing to keep in mind about fishing Waters Creek is stream manners. The nature of the fishing does not lend itself to standing elbow-to-elbow with other anglers or sloshing your way upstream while hailing everybody you see to inquire if the fish are biting. Give other anglers a wide berth as they go about their intent pursuit of big trout and they will show you the same courtesy.

GA~G grid: 15, E-7

General information: Waters Creek is designated as seasonal trout water and several special regulations are in effect. The creek is open to fishing from 6:30 A.M. to 6:30 P.M. on Wednesdays, Saturdays, and Sundays during the trout season. Only artificial lures with a single barbless hook no larger than No. 6 may be used. Only one lure can be used at a time. Landing nets cannot exceed 2 feet in length. No illegal bait, lure, landing net, or other gear can be possessed on the stream. No night-fishing is allowed.

All anglers fishing the creek must meet Georgia licensing requirements, possess a valid Georgia trout stamp, and have a Georgia Wildlife Management Area stamp unless they hold a Senior Lifetime or Honorary fishing license. The minimum size limits for the stream are 22 inches for rainbow and brown trout, and 18 inches for brook trout. All trout caught not meeting these limits must be immediately released. Anglers may possess one keeper trout daily but no person can take more than three keeper trout per season.

Some areas in the Chattahoochee National Forest require a daily use fee. Be sure to check area rules and regulations upon arrival.

Food, lodging, and supplies are within 17 miles in Dahlonega or Cleveland.

Nearest camping: Despite its name, the USDA Forest Service's Waters Creek Campground is right on the banks of nearby Dicks Creek. The campground has eight sites consisting of a tent pad, picnic table, fire ring, grill, and lantern post. Chemical flush toilets are available. Drinking water is provided. The campground is open seasonally from April through October.

Primitive camping is allowed in the Chattahoochee National Forest unless posted otherwise.

Directions: From the intersection of U.S. Highway 19 and US 129 northwest of Cleveland, go 0.5 mile west on US 19 to Dicks-Waters Creek Road (Forest Road 34-1) on the right. Follow this road for 2.8 miles and then bear left to reach the check station at Waters Creek.

For more information: Contact the Wildlife Resources Division Fisheries Section Office in Gainesville. For information on Waters Creek Campground or Chattahoochee National Forest rules and regulations, contact the USDA Forest Service Brasstown Ranger District Office.

27 Dicks Creek

See map on page 135

Key species: rainbow trout, brown trout.

Overview: With both stocked and wild rainbow and brown trout, Dicks Creek offers the opportunity to catch a quick limit of stockers or a wild trophy trout. The creek produces some surprisingly large trout every year and is a favorite with Georgia trout anglers.

Best way to fish: wading.

Best time to fish: April through October.

Description: Dicks Creek is one of Georgia's more popular trout streams. The headwaters are small overgrown brooks that eventually join together to form a large and open creek at lower elevations. The creek joins with several others to form the Chestatee River.

Most of the Dicks Creek watershed is on public land. There are some private holdings both upstream and downstream of the USDA Forest Service campground on the lower portion of the creek. Most of the private land along the creek is well posted as such, but be sure not to trespass.

Dicks Creek receives heavy stockings of catchable-sized trout throughout the season. The creek is also home to native trout, mostly in the higher elevations. Dicks Creek is known for the inordinate number of trophy fish it produces each season although no special regulations are in effect. Some of these large fish may be coming from Waters Creek (see Site 26), a tributary to Dicks Creek managed as a trophy stream. However, trout exceeding 20 inches have been caught well upstream of where Waters Creek enters the stream, and above several waterfalls that virtually eliminate Waters Creek as the source of these trophy fish. No matter where they are coming from, trophy trout are available in Dicks Creek, and every season brings reports of some monster fish.

Like many Georgia trout streams, the fishing spot you pick on Dicks Creek has a direct relationship to what sort of trout fishing you can expect. Where access is easy, both for the angler and the stocking truck, most of the available fish will be stocker trout. Where access is difficult, the probability of encountering wild trout increases considerably. On Dicks Creek, this means the lower reaches of the creek near the road will see the most anglers and stocked fish, and the remote headwaters get very little fishing pressure and have wild trout.

Dicks Creek is not only a favorite with anglers. Some pools on the lower section, especially near the falls, are popular swimming holes. During hot summer weekends, your energy is best focused farther upstream.

The fishing: Nearly any standard trout fishing technique should work in Dicks Creek. The stream's middle to lower reaches are open enough for fly fishing, but the fly fisher is the exception in this area. Most anglers after stocked trout

Dicks Creek in the Chestatee Wildlife Management Area is known for producing a few trophy trout every year.

prefer spinning gear and either small in-line spinners or natural bait. Good choices for natural bait include whole-kernel corn, worms, crickets, and commercially prepared trout bait. When casting spinners, use the lightest one that you can cast that will run at the desired depth.

If fly fishing gear is the route you choose on the lower section, nearly any fly, nymph, or small streamer stands a chance of catching fish. Trout that have spent their lives in a hatchery have not learned to be picky eaters and will strike at anything resembling food, whether or not it "matches the hatch."

Farther upstream, where native trout are the target, a little more cunning is needed. Small spinners on ultralight gear are still a good choice, and worms or crickets are good natural baits. Flycasting in these smaller waters can be difficult, but if you decide to give it a go, try a generic attractor pattern. These tiny-water trout are very skittish and a heavy footfall will send them scurrying. Try to make your approach as quiet as possible, keep sudden movements to a minimum, and wear clothes that will blend into the surroundings.

GA~G grid: 15, E-8

General information: Dicks Creek is within the Chestatee River watershed upstream from Tate's Bridge, and therefore is designated as seasonal trout water. Fishing of any type is allowed only during the designated trout season. All anglers fishing the creek, whatever species they are after, must meet Georgia licensing requirements and possess a valid Georgia trout stamp. No special regulations are in effect on Dicks Creek; standard trout fishing creel limits apply. As noted above, most of the watershed is on public land. There are some private streamside holdings though, and trespassing is definitely frowned upon. Be sure you stay on public lands as you work your way up or down the creek.

Some areas in the Chattahoochee National Forest require a daily use fee. Be sure to check area rules and regulations upon arrival.

Food, lodging, and supplies are within 15 miles in Dahlonega or Cleveland.

Nearest camping: Despite its name, the USDA Forest Service's Waters Creek Campground is right on the banks of Dicks Creek. The campground has eight sites consisting of a tent pad, picnic table, fire ring, grill, and lantern post. Drinking water and chemical flush toilets are available. The campground is open seasonally from April through October.

Primitive camping is allowed in the Chattahoochee National Forest unless posted otherwise. There are several established primitive campsites along Dicks Creek that receive heavy use.

Directions: From the intersection of U.S. Highway 19 and US 129 northwest of Cleveland, go 0.5 mile west on US 19 to Dicks-Waters Creek Road (Forest Road 34-1) on the right. Follow this paved road and the creek will soon appear on the right. After 1 mile, the campground will appear on the right.

For more information: Contact the Wildlife Resources Division Fisheries Section Office in Gainesville. For Waters Creek Campground information or Chattahoochee National Forest rules and regulations, contact the USDA Forest Service Brasstown Ranger District Office.

28 Frogtown Creek

See map on page 135

Key species: rainbow trout.

Overview: A small stream that supports both stocked and native trout, Frogtown Creek runs through the USDA Forest Service's DeSoto Falls Campground and Recreation Area.

Best way to fish: wading.

Best time to fish: April through October.

Description: Frogtown Creek is a small stream mentioned here more for its location than any other reason. From a purely fishing standpoint, the creek is overshadowed by its more popular neighbors to the east and west. However, the stream runs through the DeSoto Falls Campground.

Although the creek runs right through a popular campground, fishing pressure is surprisingly light once you have taken a few steps away from the obvious access points. The stream is small, but tiny overlooked waters can sometimes hold big fish that live out their lives unmolested by anglers.

Except for the lowermost portion of the stream, Frogtown Creek is within the boundaries of the Chattahoochee National Forest and Chestatee Wildlife Management Area. Some stocking takes place, and the fish caught will be a mix of wild and hatchery-raised rainbow trout. The farther you stray from the road access points, the greater percentage of wild trout in the creel.

The fishing: Since Frogtown Creek is small water, ultralight spinning gear is the way to go. There are no special bait restrictions; both natural bait and artificials are good choices.

If you decide to go with artificials, small in-line spinners are best. Many anglers prefer a dark pattern with a gold blade. Tiny plugs that closely mimic a grasshopper or other insect can also be cast with ultralight gear and should prove appealing.

On the natural side of things, whole-kernel corn, worms, and crickets are favorite baits. Natural bait cannot be beat for producing numbers of fish and is a good choice when prospecting unfamiliar water.

Since Frogtown Creek is small, be sure to keep the tackle as light as possible. Heavy tackle will deaden the action of the little lures that can be so effective in these small waters.

GA~G grid: 15, E-8

General information: Since it is within the Chestatee River watershed upstream from Tate's Bridge, Frogtown Creek is designated as seasonal trout water. Angling is only allowed during the trout season. All anglers must meet Georgia licensing requirements and possess a valid Georgia trout stamp. There are no special regulations on Frogtown Creek; standard trout fishing creel limits apply. See the *Georgia Sport Fishing Regulations* pamphlet for more information on trout fishing rules and regulations.

Some areas in the Chattahoochee National Forest require a daily use fee. Be sure to check area rules and regulations upon arrival.

Food, lodging, and supplies are about 15 miles away in Cleveland.

Nearest camping: Frogtown Creek runs through the USDA Forest Service's DeSoto Falls Campground. The campground offers 24 sites equipped with tent pads, picnic tables, and grills. Hot showers, flush toilets, and drinking water are available.

Primitive camping is allowed throughout the Chattahoochee National Forest unless otherwise posted.

Directions: From the intersection of U.S. Highway 19 and US 129 northwest of Cleveland, go 4.1 miles north on US 19/129 to the DeSoto Falls Campground and Recreation Area on the left.

For more information: Contact the Wildlife Resources Division Fisheries Section Office in Gainesville. For information on the DeSoto Falls Campground or Chattahoochee National Forest rules and regulations, contact the USDA Forest Service Brasstown Ranger District Office.

29 Boggs Creek

See map on page 135

Key species: rainbow trout, brown trout.

Overview: A small creek overshadowed by its more popular neighbors to the west, Boggs Creek offers good fishing for both stocked and native trout.

Best way to fish: wading.

Best time to fish: April through October.

Description: Boggs Creek is part of the upper Chestatee River watershed. Most of the creek is within the Chattahoochee National Forest and Chestatee Wildlife Management Area, but the stream's lower portion flows through private lands.

Both stocked and native trout can be caught from Boggs Creek. Stocking primarily occurs on the accessible portions of the creek near the road, and the more remote areas depend on Mother Nature to produce enough fish to maintain a limited but viable fishery. Boggs Creek receives fairly heavy fishing pressure, especially after the periodic stockings as anglers flock to the stream in search of uneducated trout.

Although both brown trout and rainbows are found in the stream, rainbows will make up most of the catch. The stream is rumored to contain some monster brown trout that have grown fat by competing with the angler for a supper of stocker-sized rainbows. Rumors and fish tales aside, most fish caught from the stream will be less than 10 inches.

The fishing: On the stocked portion of the stream, natural bait is the favorite. The usual assortment of corn, worms, and crickets will do the trick. For artificials, a small in-line spinner like a Rooster Tail or Panther Martin is a good choice. For monster browns, a floater-diver plug that mimics a small rainbow trout would be a good choice. The strikes may be few, but they should be ones to remember.

The farther you fish upstream, the smaller the stream gets. These narrow waters are no place for fly fishing gear, and are best suited to a short ultralight spinning outfit. Small spinners and natural baits are the best choices for numbers of fish, but big brown trout can inhabit unbelievably small waters, so do not eliminate the diving plugs from your wading box if you are in search of a trophy.

Since access is so easy on most of the stream, just a little bit of effort to get away from the crowds can pay tremendous rewards. Often, a 100-yard walk away from the road will put you in virtually untapped water, though the rest of the stream may be heavily fished.

GA~G grid: 15, E-8

General information: Boggs Creek is within the Chestatee River watershed upstream from Tate's Bridge, and therefore is designated as seasonal trout water. Fishing is allowed only during the trout season. All anglers must meet Georgia licensing requirements and possess a valid Georgia trout stamp. There are no special regulations on Boggs Creek; standard trout fishing creel limits apply. See the *Georgia Sport Fishing Regulations* pamphlet for more information on trout fishing rules and regulations.

Some areas in the Chattahoochee National Forest require a daily use fee. Be sure to check area rules and regulations upon arrival.

Food, lodging, and supplies are about 12 miles away in Cleveland.

Nearest camping: The nearest developed camping is about 3 miles north on U.S. Highway 19/129 at the USDA Forest Service's DeSoto Falls Campground. The campground offers 24 sites equipped with tent pads, picnic tables, and grills. Hot showers, flush toilets, and drinking water are available.

Primitive camping is allowed throughout the Chattahoochee National Forest unless otherwise posted. There are several established primitive campsites along Boggs Creek.

Directions: From the intersection of U.S. Highway 19 and US 129 northwest of Cleveland, go 1.4 miles north on US 19/129 to Forest Road 443 on the right. Turn on this gravel road and the creek will soon appear on the right.

For more information: Contact the Wildlife Resources Division Fisheries Section Office in Gainesville. For information on the DeSoto Falls Campground or Chattahoochee National Forest rules and regulations, contact the USDA Forest Service Brasstown Ranger District Office.

30 Dukes Creek (Smithgall Woods–Dukes Creek Conservation Area)

Key species: rainbow trout, brown trout.

Overview: Arguably Georgia's premiere public-water destination for trophy trout, Dukes Creek is managed under special regulations to maintain and protect the excellent fishing the area offers.

Best way to fish: wading.

Best time to fish: year-round.

Description: More than 7 miles of Dukes Creek and its tributaries flow through the 5,562-acre Smithgall Woods–Dukes Creek Conservation Area.

Although some stocking has taken place over the years, the current management scheme is dependent upon natural reproduction to replenish the population. Since the portion of Dukes Creek contained within the area is catch-and-release only, overharvest is not a threat. Both rainbow and brown trout are found in the stream, and supplemental feeding is used to maintain high numbers of large fish. On the very first day the creek was open to public fishing, most anglers caught at least one trout measuring more than 20 inches! As one might expect, the glory days of everybody catching huge trout were short-lived, but fish of that size are still a fairly regular occurrence and the stream has given up specimens of more than 26 inches. Even if the lunkers have gotten harder to catch, plenty of 12- to 18-inch fish are available to keep you busy while waiting for the fish of a lifetime.

Since Dukes Creek flows gently through a level valley, wading the creek is easy. The creek is large and open enough to allow careful flycasting.

The fishing: Trout are abundant throughout Dukes Creek. The upper portions of the creek are likely to contain more rainbows, with brown trout preferring the deeper pools of the lower end. Because of special restrictions in place, natural bait is not an option on Dukes Creek. Anglers are restricted to artificial lures only, and all hooks must be barbless.

Anglers preferring spinning gear will find small in-line spinners to be an effective choice. Especially if the target is a large brown trout, a small Rapala or other minnow-imitator would also be a good bet.

Standards with flycasters include Wooly Buggers, caddis nymphs, and attractor pattern dry flies. The stream's gentle nature makes it easy wading and fishing, and means that extra stealth is required in the calm waters of the stream.

Fish are distributed throughout the creek, but the feeding stations attract the greatest concentrations of fish. Where the fish are obvious though, you can expect the anglers to be close behind, and the fish that lounge around the feeding stations receive the most pressure. With more than 7 miles of fishable water and only a few anglers allowed on the stream at any one time, there is plenty of room to spread out and be off to yourself. Of course this means no one may be around to witness your triumphs, but they will not be around to witness your blunders either.

Since these waters are catch-and-release only, bring your camera.

GA~G grid: 15, E-9

General information: A host of special regulations are in place to make Dukes Creek the unique fishery it is. All trout caught from Dukes Creek and its tributaries in the Conservation Area must immediately be released. Only artificial lures with barbless hooks may be used. Possession of any trout or illegal bait, lure, or gear is prohibited in the Conservation Area.

A permit system is in place to limit the number of anglers on the stream at any given time. Fishing is only allowed on Wednesdays, Saturdays, and Sundays. Reservations may be made in advance and are strongly recommended. During most months of the year, there are two half-day shifts of anglers; a morning session and an afternoon session. In the shorter days of winter, there is only

Dukes Creek • Unicoi Lake • Smith Creek
(Unicoi State Park)

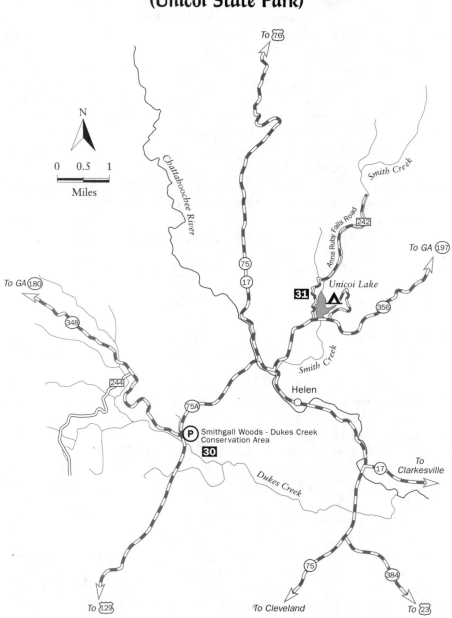

one day-long shift. All anglers are required to meet Georgia licensing requirements and possess a valid Georgia trout stamp.

Since the area is operated by the State Parks and Historic Sites Division, a daily or annual Georgia Parks Pass is required to park in the area. Private vehicles are prohibited from using area roads. A shuttle is operated from the visitor center to drop off and pick up anglers. All visitors must sign in at the visitor center.

Nearest camping: The only camping in the area is a group camp consisting of 10 tent pads, a fire ring, and pit toilets. Primitive camping is allowed throughout the Chattahoochee National Forest unless specifically posted. Unicoi State Park, 5 miles northeast of Dukes Creek, offers a variety of tent, RV, and cottage camping.

Directions: From the intersection of Georgia Highway 75 and GA 75 Alternate north of Helen, travel southeast on GA 75A for 2.5 miles to the Conservation Area entrance on the left.

For more information: For information about the area, rules and regulations, or to make reservations contact the Smithgall Woods–Dukes Creek Conservation Area Office. For information on nearby camping opportunities, contact the USDA Forest Service Chattooga Ranger District Office or the Unicoi State Park Superintendent's Office.

31 Unicoi Lake / Smith Creek (Unicoi State Park)

See map on page 146

Key species: rainbow trout, largemouth bass, bluegill, channel catfish.

Overview: The waters of Unicoi State Park offer a variety of fishing opportunities both for warm-and cold-water species.

Best way to fish: wading, bank, boat.

Best time to fish: year-round.

Description: Though not quite in the Blue Ridge Mountains, 1,081-acre Unicoi State Park has a definite mountain feel, with surrounding ridges, tumbling waterfalls, and the nearby alpine village of Helen. There are angling opportunities on both the 44-acre Unicoi Lake and roughly 2 miles of Smith Creek, a designated trout stream.

Unicoi State Park is one of the most popular parks in Georgia. A variety of recreational opportunities for the whole family are available either in the park or only a short distance away. Unicoi sees heavy use for most of the year, but during the brief days of the fall leaf season, thousands of people flock to Helen and the surrounding area to see the fantastic fall colors.

The fishing: A lazy day spent along the shores of Unicoi Lake with worms or crickets will produce some sort of action whether it is from stocked rainbow trout, bluegill, or channel catfish. If you favor fooling fish with artificial baits, and trout and sunfish are your primary quarries, then small spinners would be a good choice.

The largemouth in Unicoi Lake are susceptible to any of the usual bass-fishing lures, but the biggest bass have learned trout are a quick and tasty treat.

Both boat and shoreline fishing are popular on Unicoi Lake. Several shoreline fishing platforms give the nonboating angler good access to the lake. Although private boats are not allowed, johnboats and canoes are available for rent.

The other option for fishing Unicoi State Park is Smith Creek. About 1 mile of the creek is in the state park upstream of Unicoi Lake, and another mile is available downstream of the lake. Most trout caught from Smith Creek are stockers, but a few wild trout are possible, especially upstream of the lake. Fly fishing is possible on Smith Creek, although casting may be tight in places. Presentation is more important than fly selection. Smith Creek upstream of the lake offers the opportunity of a trophy trout.

If you prefer casting gear, spinners and natural baits are good choices on Smith Creek upstream of the lake. Especially on the portion of the stream just upstream from the lake, where stocked trout are common, whole-kernel corn is one of the best natural baits around.

The stretch of Smith Creek downstream of Unicoi Lake Dam to the state park boundary is under special seasonal delayed-harvest regulations. During the nonrestricted season, any type of gear can be used on the stream. Flies, spinners, tiny plugs, or natural baits are all good choices.

GA~G grid: 15, E-9

General information: Anglers fishing Unicoi State Park lake can fish for and possess trout without a Georgia trout stamp. All anglers must, however, meet standard Georgia fishing license requirements.

Smith Creek above Unicoi Lake is seasonal trout water. The creek is only open to fishing during the designated trout season. Part of the stream immediately downstream of Anna Ruby Falls is permanently closed to angling. Smith Creek downstream of Unicoi Lake Dam to the park boundary is open to fishing year-round. From November 1 to May 14, anglers must immediately release any trout caught. Also during this time, anglers cannot possess or use anything other than artificial lures with a single hook. From May 15 through October 31, the creek is open to fishing following standard Georgia trout fishing regulations. During this time fishing is allowed with artificial or natural bait, and anglers may harvest trout within the standard creel limit. All anglers fishing Smith Creek must meet Georgia licensing requirements and have a valid Georgia trout stamp.

A daily or annual Georgia Parks Pass is required for all vehicles parked in Unicoi State Park. A parking permit is also required at Anna Ruby Falls; however, this permit is different from the Georgia Parks Pass.

Food, lodging, and supplies are 3 miles away in Helen. In addition, a 100-room lodge and 30 cottages are available at Unicoi State Park.

Nearest camping: Unicoi State Park has 84 tent, trailer, and RV sites. The campground is equipped with all the amenities including restrooms, running water, and utilities.

Directions: From the intersection of Georgia Highway 75 and GA 75 Alternate north of Helen, travel southeast on GA 75 for 0.4 mile and turn left GA 356. Follow this road 2.4 miles to the park.

For more information: For information about Unicoi State Park, contact the Park Superintendent's Office. For fisheries information, contact the Wildlife Resources Division Fisheries Section Office in Gainesville. For information on Anna Ruby Falls, contact the USDA Forest Service Chattooga Ranger District Office.

32 Chattooga River

Key species: brown trout, rainbow trout, redeye bass.

Overview: Designated by Congress as a Wild and Scenic River, the Chattooga River is known for its whitewater paddling, trout fishing, and primitive setting.

Best way to fish: wading.

Best time to fish: year-round.

Description: From its headwaters in the North Carolina Appalachians, the Chattooga River travels a rugged 50-mile journey before ending in the still waters of Lake Tugalo. For much of its path, the Chattooga forms the state line between South Carolina and Georgia.

On May 10, 1974, Congress designated the Chattooga as a National Wild and Scenic River because of its outstanding scenery and recreational, wildlife, geologic, and cultural values. With this designation came the protection of a river corridor a quarter-mile wide on each side of the river. No motorized equipment is allowed within the corridor. Developed facilities are minimal, consisting mostly of hiking trails.

The river is split into several management sections, with the upper section from Ellicott Rock to Georgia Highway 28 being of most interest to anglers. Ellicott Rock, the boulder that marks the point where Georgia, North Carolina, and South Carolina all meet, is named for Andrew Ellicott, an early eighteenth-century surveyor commissioned with the daunting task of surveying this rugged parcel of Southern Appalachia. This section is the best trout water on the whole Chattooga. Downstream of GA 28, the river becomes marginal trout water and redeye bass are more common. No boating is allowed on this section, so it escapes the heavy activity of canoes, whitewater rafts, and kayaks of the lower sections.

The lower section of the Chattooga River is a favorite with whitewater thrill seekers. There are some very dangerous class V rapids that should only be attempted by those completely confident in their ability to handle what the wild river throws at them. Many lives have been lost on the Chattooga River, not just by boaters, but also by hikers and others walking and playing in and around the river. Some stretches of the river below GA 28 are relatively tame and good for the novice or intermediate paddler.

Anglers wading the upper section should have no problem if they use common sense and stay out of places where they have no business being. The stretch upstream of Burrells Ford is still big water by Georgia trout fishing standards, 50 to 60 feet wide in most places, and is predominantly a wild brown trout fishery. This is probably one of the best places in Georgia to catch a double-digit stream-reared brown trout. Downstream of Burrells Ford, the river widens to almost 100 feet, and rainbows become much more common. Stocked fish are also plentiful downstream of Burrells Ford, where natural reproduction is limited. To augment the population, subadult trout are stocked by helicopter and quickly learn the wary ways of wild fish.

The Chattooga's reputation as a whitewater river is based on the lower sections; anglers should have no problem fishing the upper reach of the river characterized by big deep pools separated by shallow shoals. Some areas too rough or deep to wade may be encountered, but a short hike around should put you back into wadeable water. One area to take special care with is known as "Rock Gorge" and is a short distance upstream of where the Bartram Trail intersects the Chattooga Foothills Trail. Although the gorge's deep pools hold some of the biggest brown trout in the river, anglers need to use extreme caution here. Violent rapids, undercut rocks, drop-offs, and wading paths that dead-end into deep water or cliff walls are common in the gorge. Never go into this area alone. Having a partner is really a good idea for fishing any of the Chattooga; not only may you save each other's life, but you will have someone with whom to share the river's majestic wildness.

The film *Deliverance* was filmed on the lower Chattooga River, and the

The Chattooga River is not only a favorite with anglers, it is also a favorite destination for whitewater paddlers.

Chattooga River

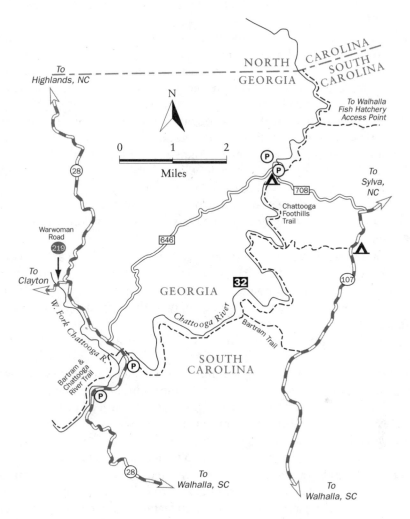

river today remains as rough as it was in the early 1970s when film crews were forced to use rafts to get them and their gear on location.

The Chattooga is one of Georgia's wildest rivers and should be on the list of any angler who wants to see what Appalachian highland trout fishing is all about. Both the river and the brown trout are big and brawny, and fishing the river is an experience that will stay with you for some time.

The fishing: The Chattooga is year-round trout water. Keep in mind though the weak winter sunshine is not going to warm up the mostly shaded gorges of the Chattooga. The weather can feel pleasant in Atlanta but bone-chilling in the north Georgia mountains. Anglers willing to brave the cold should find at least a few trout. In the winter, slowly fish weighted nymphs along the bottoms of deep pools. A #8 or #10 gold and black stonefly nymph is a good choice. If the fish want something a little smaller, drop down to a #12 or #14 beadhead Gold-Ribbed Hare's Ear.

Later in the year and throughout the warmer months, the Gold-Ribbed Hare's Ear nymph is still a good choice for catching fish. For dry flies, try a Light Cahill or Parachute Adams. For casting gear, try small spinners like a white Rooster Tail or Panther Martin. Small plugs that imitate a minnow or crayfish are also a good choice.

The best time to fish for the Chattooga's big browns during any season is first and last light. Overcast days are also good.

The easiest fishing in the summer is right around Burrells Ford, but it also will be the most crowded. A short walk will usually outdistance most anglers though, and you should have the river to yourself.

Fall fishing can be the best of both worlds. The weather is crisp, the foliage brilliant, and spring and summer anglers have moved on to other pursuits.

GA~G grid: 16, B-5

General information: The Chattooga River upstream of the mouth of Warwoman Creek (between GA 28 and U.S. Highway 76) is designated as year-round trout water. Downstream of this point, the river is seasonal trout water. Standard trout fishing regulations and creel limits apply to the Chattooga River; see the *Georgia Sport Fishing Regulations* pamphlet for more information.

Georgia and South Carolina have a reciprocal agreement worked out regarding license requirements for the Chattooga River. All anglers fishing the main river who meet the licensing requirements of either state are in compliance with the law. This agreement only applies to the main river channel; tributaries are not covered. Upstream of Ellicott Rock, you are in North Carolina and must meet that state's licensing requirements; this section of the river is not shared water so no reciprocal agreement is in effect.

Food, lodging, and supplies are available 21 miles away in Clayton.

Nearest camping: Primitive camping is permitted anywhere in the Chattooga River corridor not otherwise posted as closed to camping. Campsites must be at least 0.25 mile from a road and at least 50 feet from any trail, stream, or the river. A semi-developed campground is available at Burrells Ford on the South Carolina side. The campground is a 350-yard walk from the parking area and offers several good flat places to pitch a tent. Some campsites have lantern posts and picnic tables. A hand pump for water and pit toilets are available. The campground is open year-round.

Another option is the USDA Forest Service's Cherry Hill Campground off South Carolina Highway 107. Following the trail 2.8 miles from the trailhead near the campground will put you on the river.

Directions: To reach Burrells Ford, from U.S. Highway 441 in Clayton take Warwoman Road (County Road 219) 14 miles to GA 28. Turn right and drive 1.8 miles to the gravel Forest Road 646 on the left. Follow FR 646 to the parking area on the right just before the bridge. To get to the campground parking, cross the bridge into South Carolina and the parking area will be on the right.

For more information: Contact the Wildlife Resources Division Fisheries Section Office in Gainesville. Information on recreation in the Chattooga National Wild and Scenic River corridor is available from the USDA Forest Service Tallulah Ranger District Office.

33 Lake Burton

Key species: spotted bass, largemouth bass, crappie, bluegill, yellow perch.

Overview: A Georgia Power hydropower reservoir, Lake Burton is a deep, infertile impoundment on the Tallulah River in northeast Georgia. Although the lake supports a variety of sport fish, steep shorelines with little underwater cover make Lake Burton challenging angling.

Best way to fish: boat, shore.

Best time to fish: April through October.

Description: Created in 1919 with the construction of 128-foot high Burton Dam, which spans 1,100 feet across the Tallulah River, Lake Burton's purpose was to meet Georgia's growing demand for electricity. Burton Dam and its sister dams on the Tallulah River were considered engineering marvels of the time, and are still impressive today.

Burton has 2,775 surface acres and 62 miles of shoreline. Like many older reservoirs opened to shoreline development, Lake Burton is almost completely surrounded by lakeshore homes and summer cabins. The beauty of the lake and its deep, clear water makes it a favorite with pleasure boaters. The lake gets very crowded during the summer months, making night-fishing an option that should be strongly considered.

The fishing: Although Lake Burton supports a diverse fishery of many species, the lack of bottom cover makes finding and catching fish difficult. Both spotted bass and largemouth bass are present, with spots making up most of the creel. The average spotted bass will measure around 12 inches. Largemouths, although fewer, run larger. The average largemouth caught from Lake Burton will be in the 15-inch range and weigh upwards of 2 pounds. Spotted bass can be caught from offshore structure like points and humps throughout the year. Anglers targeting largemouths should concentrate their efforts around the limited shallow cover in spring and fall and fish deeper during the summer and winter months. A topwater bait that mimics a small yellow perch is a good choice to catch these actively feeding fish. Whenever bass are concentrated over deep structure in summer and winter, vertically jigging spoons is a productive technique.

Spotted bass exceeding 5 pounds and largemouths well into the double-digits have been caught from the lake.

Crappie are often overlooked by Burton anglers intent on other species, but Lake Burton is a good choice for catching some real slabs. Fish in the 10- to 12-inch range are abundant and easily caught by concentrating on cover,

Lake Burton

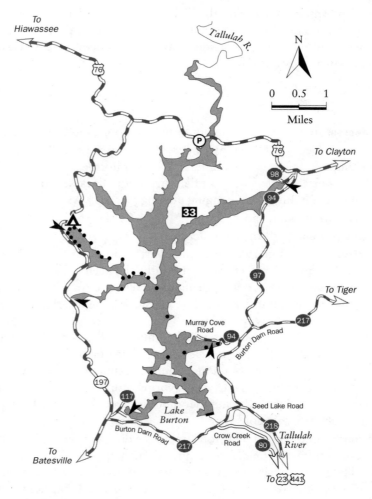

especially downed trees, in the 5- to 15-foot depth range. Medium-sized shiners are the best bait.

Other good choices at Lake Burton are bluegill and yellow perch. These species are easily caught using worms or crickets around any shallow cover such as fallen trees and docks.

GA~G grid: 16, C-1

General information: Anglers fishing Lake Burton must meet all Georgia licensing requirements. Creel and length limits follow standard statewide regulations with one exception; since growth is so slow there is no minimum length limit on black bass harvested from Lake Burton. Several Georgia Power, state, and private access points are available. Anglers using Moccasin Creek State Park as an access point must possess a valid daily or annual Georgia

LaPrade's Marina on Lake Burton has been in continuous operation since the 1920s.

Parks Pass to park a vehicle in the area. Some Georgia Power parks, access points, and camping areas charge a small reservation or parking fee. Be sure to check area rules and regulations upon arrival.

Although the nearest town of any size is about 15 miles away from most of the lake, lodging and supplies are available at several private marinas. Of particular note is LaPrade's, on the west side of the lake off Georgia Highway 197. Originally built as a camp for dam construction workers in the 1910s, LaPrade's has been in continuous operation as a fish camp since the 1920s. The camp offers meals, lodging, and marina service.

Nearest camping: Moccasin Creek State Park is on the shores of Lake Burton. The 32-acre park contains 54 tent, trailer, and RV sites with restrooms, water, and utilities present. A boat ramp is also available in the park.

Directions: Lake Burton is 10 miles west of Clayton off U.S. Highway 76.

For more information: Contact the Wildlife Resources Division Fisheries Section Office at Lake Burton Hatchery. Lake information is available from the Georgia Power North Georgia Land Management Office. For information about camping at Moccasin Creek State Park, contact the Park Superintendent's Office.

34 Lake Seed

Key species: spotted bass, largemouth bass, walleye, yellow perch.

Overview: A narrow Tallulah River impoundment of 240 acres with 13 miles of shoreline, Lake Seed is one of Georgia Power's chain of north Georgia hydroelectric lakes.

Best way to fish: boat.

Best time to fish: April through October.

Description: The Nacoochee Hydroelectric Plant is on the Tallulah River downstream of Burton Dam. The name "Nacoochee" comes from the Cherokee language and means "evening star." The plant's dam impounds the waters of Lake Seed. The Nacoochee Plant was completed in 1926, and was the last in a chain of Tallulah River developments built by the Georgia Railway and Power Company.

Lake Seed is probably the most overlooked link in the Tallulah River chain of lakes, except for tiny, undeveloped Tallulah Lake. However, Lake Seed receives a fair amount of use in the summer, when boat traffic from visiting pleasure boaters, anglers, and those fortunate enough to live on the lake can make the narrow lake appear very busy.

Both spotted bass and largemouth bass are present, with spots making up most of the fish caught. Spotted bass in the 2- to 4-pound range are common, with even larger fish a possibility. Other species popular with anglers are yellow perch and walleye. Rounding out the list of target species are various species of panfish including sunfish and crappie.

Access to Lake Seed is limited to one boat ramp on the upper north side of the lake. The small size of the lake makes it a short boat ride to anywhere you want to fish.

The fishing: Lake Seed fishes more like a river than a reservoir. When current is running, expect the fish on the downstream side of points and in any cover to ambush prey swept past.

Good lures are small soft-plastics retrieved slowly along bottom and diving plugs in chartreuse patterns. Although the lake is usually clear, yellow or chartreuse are good color choices since they imitate a small yellow perch, a favorite prey item of largemouth and spotted bass.

Walleye will also relate to points and can be caught using the same general approach used for Lake Seed bass. Crankbaits, plastic grubs, or spoons are good lure choices; nightcrawlers and medium-sized minnows are best on the natural side of things.

Panfish in Lake Seed are easily caught around shallow cover. Since the lake has no real coves, anglers should concentrate their efforts around dock pilings and fallen trees. A worm, cricket, or small minnow fished a few feet deep around shallow cover will draw strikes. Small spinners, either safety-pin or in-line, are also good choices.

Especially during the busy summer months, anglers may want to consider night-fishing to avoid the heavy boat traffic. Summer fish are more active during the hours of darkness. Nighttime is always a good choice when fishing for the highly nocturnal walleye.

GA~G grid: 16, D-2

General information: Lake Seed is open to fishing year-round and all hours of the day. The lake is not hard to reach, but the paved road leading to the ramp is narrow and extremely winding as it follows the shorelines of Lake Seed and its downstream neighbor, Lake Rabun.

Lake Seed • Lake Rabun • Tallulah Lake
Lake Tugalo • Lake Yonah

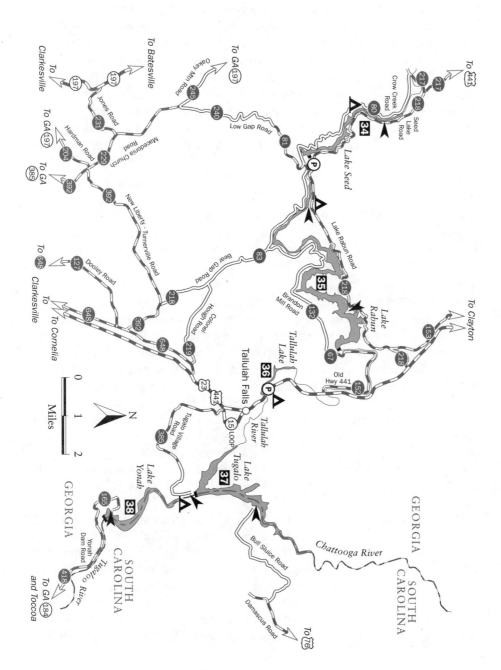

Standard Georgia creel and length limits are in effect on Lake Seed. All anglers must meet Georgia licensing requirements. Some Georgia Power parks, access points, and camping areas charge a small reservation or parking fee. Be sure to check area rules and regulations upon arrival.

Food, lodging, and supplies are 15 miles away in Clayton.

Nearest camping: Georgia Power operates Lake Seed Campground on the western shore of the lake. The campground includes a white sand beach, primitive campsites, a picnic area, and latrines. No running water is available.

Directions: From Tallulah Falls, drive north 1.7 miles on U.S. Highway 23/441 to Old Highway 411 on the left. A brown Rabun Beach sign marks this road. Turn left and drive 2.6 miles to Lake Rabun Road (CR 218). Turn left and follow this narrow and winding shoreline road along Lake Rabun to Lake Seed.

For more information: Contact the Wildlife Resources Division Fisheries Section Office at Lake Burton Hatchery. For information about the lake or its facilities, contact the Georgia Power North Georgia Land Management Office.

35 Lake Rabun

See map on page 157

Key species: largemouth bass, spotted bass, crappie, bluegill, redear sunfish, walleye, yellow perch.

Overview: Ten miles long, 834 acres, and 25 miles of shoreline, Georgia Power's Lake Rabun is a tremendously diverse fishery.

Best way to fish: boat.

Best time to fish: April through October.

Description: Lake Rabun was created in 1915 by the completion of 108-foot high Mathis Dam and is the third largest of the Tallulah River chain. Boaters and anglers both enjoy the clear, deep waters of the lake but the boating traffic on the lake can make midday summer angling a nerve-racking proposition. Most anglers prefer to ply the lake's waters by night in the summer season. The lake's shorelines are heavily developed with homes and cabins.

Although both largemouth and spotted bass are found in the lake, unlike in the two lakes immediately upstream, Burton and Seed, largemouth bass dominate in Lake Rabun. Like most mountain lakes, Rabun's bass population is low compared to more fertile waters. However, Lake Rabun is known for the quality fish it produces. Largemouths weighing more than 12 pounds have been caught from the lake.

Big bass are not the only trophy fish in Rabun. Bluegill and redear sunfish weighing up to 1 pound are common, and walleye in the 10-pound class are occasionally caught. Walleye were introduced into the lake in 1994 and 1995 when high waters washed them down from upstream reservoirs. They have successfully reproduced in the lake but receive very little fishing pressure and are a virtually untapped resource.

Blueback herring also were introduced into the lake in the mid-1990s through unknown means, and the population has expanded. The predatory fish in Rabun have developed a taste for bluebacks though, and so far their numbers have not risen to a level that negatively affects the native sport fish species.

The fishing: Anglers after largemouths should focus their effort on the lake's upper half, while spotted bass are more common in the deeper waters of the lower end. This lake is especially known for exciting topwater fishing in May and June. During the summer night-fishing period, topwater plugs, dark spinnerbaits, large plastic worms, or a jig-and-pig worked around shallow cover or the base of points can be very productive, especially for big fish.

The most consistent places to find Rabun bass are small pockets where tiny feeder streams enter the lake. These pockets are shallower than the main lake and usually hold baitfish. Use lures that imitate small sunfish or yellow perch in the spring and summer. In cooler weather, go with something that imitates a crayfish, shad, or blueback herring.

Lake Rabun walleye fishing is still in its infancy since the species is a relative newcomer to the lake. Walleye are highly nocturnal, and the best fishing will be from dusk to dawn.

Panfish such as bluegill, redear sunfish, yellow perch, and crappie are all present in Lake Rabun, and the average size is as good as or better than any other lake in the area. Spring and fall crappie fishing is especially good in the shallower upper half of the reservoir. The best fishing for sunfish is in the summer when the fish congregate around boat docks in search of cover, food, and shade. Bluegill will readily strike a cricket fished under a float around the docks, while redear sunfish prefer a worm fished on the bottom in slightly deeper water. Weedlines along the uplake river channel are prime for yellow perch. Nacoochee Park is also a great place for catching a mess of panfish from the shore. Live bait or small spinners are the local favorites.

GA~G grid: 16, D-2

General information: Lake Rabun is open to fishing year-round. All anglers must meet Georgia licensing requirements. The shoreline is covered with private homes, and public access is fair. Although not surrounded by the Chattahoochee National Forest, one small area of the forest does join the shoreline. Several boat ramps owned and operated by private individuals or public agencies are available. Nonboating anglers will find the best access at Georgia Power's Nacoochee Park or the USDA Forest Service's Rabun Beach Campground and Recreation Area.

Some USDA Forest Service and Georgia Power parks, access points, and camping areas charge a small reservation or parking fee. Be sure to check area rules and regulations upon arrival.

Food, lodging, and supplies are 10 miles away in Clayton.

Nearest camping: The USDA Forest Service's Rabun Beach Campground, found on the north side of the upper end of the lake, has 80 campsites, some with electricity. Drinking water, hot showers, and flush toilets are available.

Directions: From Tallulah Falls, drive north 1.7 miles on U.S. Highway 23/441 to Old Highway 411 on the left. A brown Rabun Beach sign marks this road. Turn left and drive 2.6 miles to Lake Rabun Road (County Road 218). Turn left and follow this narrow and winding shoreline road along Lake Rabun. The entrance to the Rabun Beach Campground is 4.6 miles on the right.

For more information: Contact the Wildlife Resources Division Fisheries Section Office at Lake Burton Hatchery. For information about the lake or Georgia Power facilities, contact the Georgia Power North Georgia Land Management Office. Chattahoochee National Forest recreation information is available from the USDA Forest Service Tallulah Ranger District Office.

36 Tallulah Lake

See map on page 157

Key species: largemouth bass, spotted bass, sunfish.

Overview: The smallest of the Tallulah River lakes at only 63 acres, Georgia Power's Tallulah Lake is an old lake with little angling history. For many years, a complete lack of improved access allowed little Tallulah Lake to stay in the shadow of its larger companions.

Best way to fish: canoe, shore.

Best time to fish: April through October.

Description: Impounded by a 126-foot high dam just upstream of Tallulah Falls across what is basically the extreme upper end of Tallulah Gorge, a chasm 2 miles long and nearly 1,000 feet deep, Tallulah Lake is the oldest of Georgia Power's chain of north Georgia hydropower developments.

Until the recent development of Tallulah Gorge State Park, which was created through a partnership between the state of Georgia and Georgia Power Company, the tiny lake had no improved public access. The opening of the park has improved bank access on the upstream side of the dam, but there is no improved boating access. Anglers should have no problem sliding in a canoe, though, and the ambiance of the little lake somehow best lends itself to this sort of fishing.

Since the little lake does not have a long history of development and easy access, it has seen very little fishing pressure throughout its life. With no access and virtually no use by anglers, the lake has not been the subject of extensive studies by biologists either.

The fishing: Since Tallulah Lake is a basically a flooded gorge, the banks drop off very quickly into deep water. Anglers should focus their efforts on the narrow shelf of shallow water next to the shoreline. Any fallen trees or patches of weeds are prime targets for both bass and sunfish.

Both shoreline and boat anglers will find the best access from Tallulah Gorge State Park. A fishing pier and easy shoreline access make this area the best for trying your luck from shore or slipping in a canoe to explore the whole lake.

Because fishing pressure on the lake has always been nonexistent to light, no special techniques or favorite areas are well known. The best approach for fishing the lake is to make your best guess. Small lures and light line, always a good choice in deep and clear lakes, should produce the most strikes.

GA~G grid: 16, D-3

160

General information: Visitors to Tallulah Gorge State Park are required to have a valid daily or annual Parks Pass to park a vehicle in the area. For safety and to protect fragile ecosystems, a permit is required to hike down into the gorge or pursue other activities like rock climbing. All anglers must meet Georgia licensing requirements and standard creel and length limits apply.

Food, lodging, and supplies are 11 miles away in Clayton.

Nearest camping: Tallulah Gorge State Park has 50 tent, trailer, and RV sites. The site also has hiking trails, a swimming beach, overlooks, and a visitor center with cultural, historical, and natural resource exhibits, and an award-winning film about Tallulah Gorge.

Directions: Tallulah Lake and Tallulah Gorge State Park are on U.S. Highway 23/441. Drive south from Clayton for about 11 miles until you see the sign marking the entrance to the area.

For more information: Contact the Wildlife Resources Division Fisheries Section Office at Lake Burton Hatchery. For information about the lake or Georgia Power facilities, contact the Georgia Power North Georgia Land Management Office. Tallulah Gorge State Park information is available from the Park Superintendent's Office.

37 Lake Tugalo

See map on page 157

Key species: largemouth bass, bluegill, redear sunfish, crappie.

Overview: Arguably the most scenic lake in Georgia, 597-acre Lake Tugaloo is also one of the most remote. The incredible beauty of 1,000-foot walls rising straight up from the water's edge and the possibility of truly trophy-sized largemouth bass make Lake Tugalo an interesting trip indeed.

Best way to fish: boat.

Best time to fish: April through October.

Description: Georgia Power's 155-foot high Tugalo Dam forms Lake Tugalo on the Tugaloo River. Oddly, the spelling of the river differs from the spelling of the lake and dam. In the Cherokee language "Tugalo" means "fork of a stream." The dam is just downstream of where the Tallulah and Chattooga rivers join to form the Tugaloo River.

Since it is so remote and nearly inaccessible, Tugalo does not receive heavy fishing pressure. What access points there are require a steep and winding drive on unpaved roads. Kayakers and whitewater rafters use the access point on the South Carolina side as a take-out after braving the class V rapids of the Chattooga River upstream of the lake.

The fishing: Of all the lakes in the Tallulah River system, Tugalo offers the best chance for catching a truly trophy-sized bass. Large plastic worms and jig-and-pig combinations are good choices for catching big bass. Topwater baits are also good choices from spring to early summer.

Bluegill, shellcracker, and redbreast sunfish also offer good possibilities. During the summer, fishing worms or crickets around shoreline cover can result in a good mess of fish. If artificials are preferred, chartreuse Beetle Spins worked on light spinning tackle, or popping bugs or weighted nymphs on a fly outfit are local favorites. With all the shoreline cover, finding the fish can sometimes be a problem. Make presentations to different parts of the blowdowns until you find the most productive pattern. Some days the fish will be holding near the shore, other days they may be in deep water at the very end of the tree, or anywhere between. Half-pounders are common, and even larger fish are possible.

The best crappie fishing is in the spring and fall near woody structure in 5 to 15 feet of water. White bass are also present in the lake, and are easily caught during their spring upstream migration to the headwaters. A white jig or a jig-and-minnow combination are good bets for catching these feisty members of the temperate bass family.

Several catfish species are found in Lake Tugalo, with white catfish making up most of the creel. The area around the boat ramp on the South Carolina side of the lake is the most productive.

GA~G grid: 16, E-3

General information: Part of Tugalo Lake forms the Georgia–South Carolina border. The two states have a reciprocal agreement that allows anglers holding either a Georgia or South Carolina fishing license to fish the waters of the lake. Standard Georgia creel and length limits apply in the Georgia portion of the lake. Of special note, South Carolina does not have a minimum length limit on largemouth bass harvested from the lake, but the Georgia largemouth length limit is 12 inches. Anglers should keep this difference in mind if they have harvested any short bass and enter Georgia waters. Consult the *Georgia Sport Fishing Regulations* pamphlet for more information about the reciprocal agreements between states regarding angling.

Some Georgia Power parks and overnight camping facilities charge a small reservation or camping fee. Be sure to check area rules and regulations upon arrival.

Food, lodging, and supplies are available 15 miles away in Clayton.

Nearest camping: Tallulah Gorge State Park has 50 tent, trailer, and RV sites. The site also has hiking trails, a swimming beach, overlooks, and a visitor center with cultural, historical, and natural resource exhibits, and an award-winning film about Tallulah Gorge.

Directions: To reach the Chattooga River arm access point in South Carolina, from the U.S. Highway 76 Chattooga River bridge southeast of Clayton, travel 4.5 miles to paved Damascus Road on the right. Stay on the paved road for 4.8 miles to gravel Bull Sluice Road (Tugalo Lake Road) on the right just past Damascus Church. Take Bull Sluice Road 3.8 miles to the lake.

For more information: Contact the Wildlife Resources Division Fisheries Section Office at Lake Burton Hatchery. For information about the lake or Georgia Power facilities, contact the Georgia Power North Georgia Land Management Office. Tallulah Gorge State Park information is available from the Park Superintendent's Office.

Key species: largemouth bass, bluegill, redear sunfish, crappie.

Overview: Lake Yonah is the final link in the chain of small hydropower developments in north Georgia. Like its five sister lakes upstream, Lake Yonah offers good fishing for a variety of species and receives relatively little fishing pressure.

Best way to fish: boat.

Best time to fish: April through October.

Description: The Yonah Hydroelectric Plant was completed and placed in operation in 1925. A Tugaloo River impoundment, 325-acre Lake Yonah is the downstream terminus in Georgia Power's string of north Georgia hydropower lakes. Like most Georgia Power hydro projects in northeast Georgia, the name of the lake comes from Native American language. "Yonah" is a Cherokee word meaning "big black bear." Below Yonah Dam is the beginning of Lake Hartwell, a sprawling USACE hydropower reservoir.

The fishery in Yonah is similar to the lakes above it. The total standing crop of fish in the lake is low compared to the more fertile waters of the Piedmont and Coastal Plain, but there are still plenty of fish to interest the angler, some trophy-sized. The lake gets little fishing pressure, and is a good destination if you want to get off the beaten path but not go to much trouble doing it.

The fishing: The operation of Yonah and Tugalo Dams plays a large part in what the fish in the lake will be doing. An increase in current stimulates feeding

The author displays a chunky largemouth bass.

behavior and pulls the fish away from cover. When there is good current in the lake, for bass try a crankbait or spinnerbait around fallen trees, especially the outer edges. Do not overlook the very top of the tree that is out over deeper water. Fish will hold loosely around deeper cover waiting for the current to wash prey over their heads. During slack-water times, fish will still be using the trees but will be buried deep in the twisted branches. This is a good time to carefully cast or flip a Texas-rigged plastic worm or a jig-and-pig. Fish each spot thoroughly, and pitch into the tightest cover you can find.

Spring and early summer can be the best topwater fishing of the year. Try chuggers and minnow-imitators around submerged cover. A soft-plastic weightless "trick worm" is also very productive this time of year when twitched slowly through little cuts and pockets.

Anglers will find summer the best time to target bluegill and redear sunfish. Worms or crickets fished near shallow cover are effective, and casting small spinners or fly fishing with popping bugs are good choices for fooling aggressive sunfish.

Crappie are easiest caught during the early spring spawn when they move into shallow woody cover to spawn. A small minnow or light jig fished around shallow brush during this time is almost guaranteed to draw strikes. Summer crappie fishing can be difficult since the fish suspend over deep water, but autumn sees a return of the fish to woody cover as they feed heavily in preparation for the coming winter.

Access to Lake Yonah is fair with a public boat ramp at both the extreme upper and lower ends of the lake on the Georgia side.

GA~G grid: 16, E-3

General information: Yonah Lake forms part of the Georgia–South Carolina border. The two states have a reciprocal agreement that allows anglers holding either a Georgia or South Carolina fishing license to fish the waters of the lake. Standard Georgia creel and length limits apply in the Georgia portion of the lake, including a 12-inch minimum length limit on largemouth bass. South Carolina does not have a minimum length limit on largemouth bass harvested from the lake. Anglers should keep this difference in mind if they have harvested any short bass and cross into Georgia waters. Consult the *Georgia Sport Fishing Regulations* pamphlet for more information about the reciprocal agreements between states regarding angling.

Some Georgia Power parks and overnight camping facilities charge a small reservation or camping fee. Be sure to check area rules and regulations upon arrival.

Food, lodging, and supplies are about 18 miles away in Clayton or Toccoa.

Nearest camping: Primitive camping is available at Georgia Power's Tugalo Park on the very upper end of Lake Yonah immediately below Tugalo Dam. Tallulah Gorge State Park is also nearby.

Directions: To reach the Lake Yonah ramp at Tugalo Park, from the Georgia Highway 15 Loop in Tallulah Falls take Tugalo Village Road (CR 385) until it ends at the lake. To reach the ramp on the lower end of the lake, travel north from Toccoa on Georgia Highway 184. Bear left onto the last road (Yonah

Dam Road (CR 418)) in Georgia before crossing the Tugaloo River bridge into South Carolina. Follow this road to the boat ramp.

For more information: Contact the Wildlife Resources Division Fisheries Section Office at Lake Burton Hatchery. For information about the lake or Georgia Power facilities, contact the Georgia Power North Georgia Land Management Office. Tallulah Gorge State Park information is available from the Park Superintendent's Office.

39 Lake Hartwell

Key species: largemouth bass, hybrid striped bass, striped bass, crappie, channel catfish.

Overview: Lake Hartwell is a 55,950-acre USACE reservoir on the Savannah River in northeast Georgia. The lake receives moderate fishing pressure and is good angling for largemouth bass, crappie, and other species.

Best way to fish: boat.

Best time to fish: year-round.

Description: Situated 7 miles below the point where the Tugaloo and Seneca rivers come together to form the Savannah River, Hartwell Dam impounds 55,950 acres of water for power generation, flood control, and recreation. The lake stretches 49 miles up the Tugaloo River valley and extends 45 miles up the Seneca River valley into South Carolina. Hartwell Dam is an amazing 3 miles long, with the concrete portion measuring 1,900 feet and rising 204 feet above the riverbed. The entire project encompasses 76,450 acres of land and water.

The topography around Lake Hartwell transitions from Piedmont-type terrain on its lower end to rugged foothill country on the upper end. The lake's shoreline has some development, but most of the backdrop is forested hillsides. If you could look below the lake's surface, you would see essentially the same thing. During construction, the trees near the shoreline were cleared in the Tugaloo and Seneca arms of lake; in the main body of the reservoir the trees were simply flooded. The result is an expansive forest of trees hidden below the surface anywhere from 10 to 100 feet down.

Like most reservoirs constructed with flood control in mind, Lake Hartwell undergoes a winter drawdown every year. The lake is usually down 10 to 12 feet by mid-December and reaches full pool again in March.

Lake Hartwell is one of the most visited USACE lakes in the United States, but fishing pressure is surprisingly light despite the good access and excellent angling. Largemouth bass are one of the most popular species in the lake, but there is also decent fishing for redeye bass, which is unusual since redeye are a stream species and typically do not do well in reservoirs. Lake Hartwell is known for numbers of bass instead of size. The lake has produced largemouth bass weighing in the double digits, but they are very rare; anything more than 4 pounds is a good catch.

Crappie and hybrid striped bass are the other two major game species in Lake Hartwell. Some striped bass are present and provide a trophy fishery that

Lake Hartwell

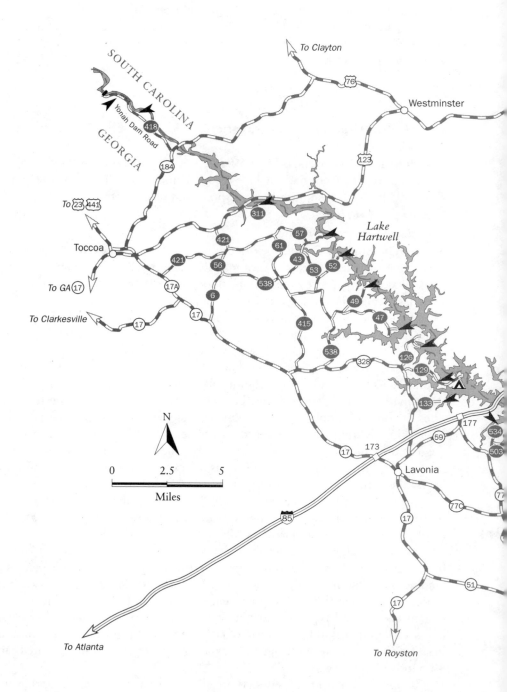

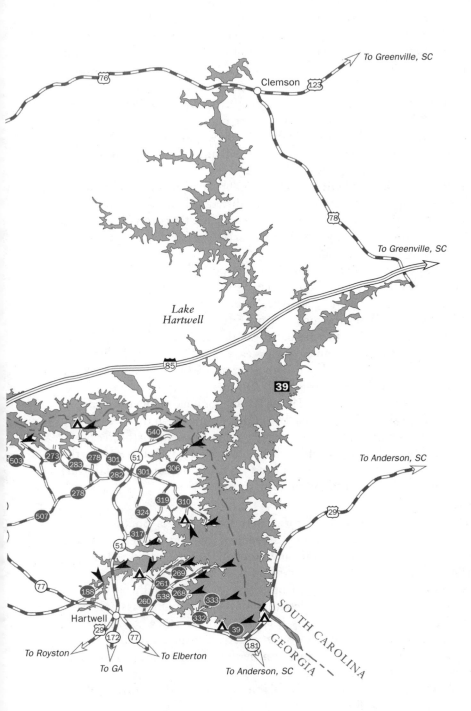

To Greenville, SC

Clemson

To Greenville, SC

To Anderson, SC

Lake Hartwell

To Royston

To GA

To Elberton

To Anderson, SC

Hartwell

SOUTH CAROLINA

GEORGIA

complements the fine hybrid striped bass angling in the lake. Hartwell has some huge stripers and hybrids. Striped bass weighing more than 50 pounds have been caught from the lake as have monster hybrids in the 20-pound class. Lake Hartwell is a diverse fishery, and offers a variety of other species overlooked by anglers intent on the glamour species. Bluegill, redear sunfish, channel catfish, flathead catfish, walleye, yellow perch, white bass, and others are all possible.

The fishing: Spring fishing on Hartwell can be great. As the spawn approaches, look for bass in the pockets. Twitching a weightless plastic worm just below the surface will draw vicious strikes. Topwater plugging can be excellent for much of the year, especially early and late in the day. Look for long, flat points or humps with nearby deep water where bass will ambush schools of baitfish.

Summertime bass anglers catch fish by jigging a spoon in the deep timber or concentrating on fishing lighted docks at night. Focus your effort on small isolated patches of trees or anything that is different from the surrounding area. When fishing docks at night, concentrate on those that drop off into deep water. A soft-plastic jerk bait twitched on top or a Texas-rigged worm crawled along bottom are both good choices.

Redeye bass are most abundant in the lower portions of the lake. A small crankbait or topwater lure is a good choice.

Striped bass and their hatchery-spawned hybrid are extremely popular with Lake Hartwell anglers. When the surface temperature creeps above 50 degrees F, live bait fishing picks up. The fish are usually at depths of 20 feet or less during this time, and getting a bait down to them is easy. The first step to finding fish is to look for long points and other offshore structure. Once found, check the area for baitfish. If there is no bait, go find another point.

A relatively infertile lake, Hartwell is not known for huge numbers of crappie, but rather for large sizes. The best places to find crappie are in the creek arms.

Lake Hartwell is home to huge channel catfish and has some flathead catfish. For fiddler-sized channel catfish, fish chicken livers or nightcrawlers on the bottom near creek channels. Bigger fish can be taken on cut bait. Flatheads prefer live bait and are often found in deeper water.

GA~G grid: 16, 17, 23

General information: Lake Hartwell forms part of the Georgia–South Carolina border. The two states have a reciprocal agreement that allows anglers holding either a Georgia or South Carolina fishing license to fish the waters of the lake. Standard Georgia creel and length limits apply in the Georgia portion of the lake, including a 12-inch minimum length limit on largemouth bass. South Carolina does not have a minimum length limit on largemouth bass harvested from the lake. Anglers should keep this difference in mind if they have harvested any short bass and cross over into Georgia waters. Consult the *Georgia Sport Fishing Regulations* pamphlet for more information about the reciprocal agreements between states regarding angling.

Food, lodging, and supplies are available on the Georgia portion of the lake in Toccoa or Hartwell.

Nearest camping: There are five USACE campgrounds and two state parks on the Georgia side of the lake.

Directions: Lake Hartwell, outside of the city of Hartwell, is crossed by U.S. Highways 123 and 29 and Interstate 85. Reach the lake off these and other connecting highways.

For more information: Contact the Wildlife Resources Division Fisheries Section Office at Lake Burton Hatchery. For information about USACE facilities on the lake, including campgrounds, contact the Hartwell Project Office. For information about camping opportunities at Hart or Tugaloo State Parks, contact the Park Superintendent's Office.

40 Lake Sidney Lanier

Key species: spotted bass, largemouth bass, striped bass, crappie, white bass, channel catfish.

Overview: Lake Lanier is one of the most heavily used USACE lakes in the country. The lake offers great fishing for a variety of species, and its proximity to metro Atlanta makes it a popular destination with both anglers and pleasure boaters.

Best way to fish: boat.

Best time to fish: year-round.

Description: Lake Sidney Lanier is named for the nineteenth-century Georgia poet, Sidney Clopton Lanier. The poet's love of the area inspired him to write his famous "Song of the Chattahoochee." Lake Lanier's Buford Dam was completed in 1956 as part of a comprehensive development plan for the Chattahoochee River. The lake's purposes are flood control, hydropower, navigation, recreation, and fish and wildlife management. It is the largest lake found entirely within Georgia's borders.

Lake Lanier is not the place for solitude and undisturbed vistas. There are an estimated 7,500 boat docks on the lake's 38,000 acres, and homes occupy much of the shoreline. As Atlanta has spread north, much of Lake Lanier has become part of suburbia. Recreational use of the lake is extremely heavy on summer weekends, and the lake traffic begins to resemble the notorious traffic jams on Atlanta's freeways. Even during the week, boating traffic is heavy. Besides the thousands of personal watercraft buzzing around, there are plenty of inland yachts that throw quite a wake.

Despite all the use, the lake consistently produces good fishing and is nationally known. Lake Lanier is a frequent stop on national bass tournament trails. Although summertime angling basically becomes a nighttime proposition because of the heavy use, in the cooler months anglers have the lake to themselves.

Though a variety of species are found in the deep, clear waters, Lake Lanier is best known for spotted bass and striper fishing. The lake has produced state record spotted bass weighing more than 8 pounds. The biggest largemouth to come from the lake weighed more than 17 pounds, and was caught in 1965.

Lake Sidney Lanier

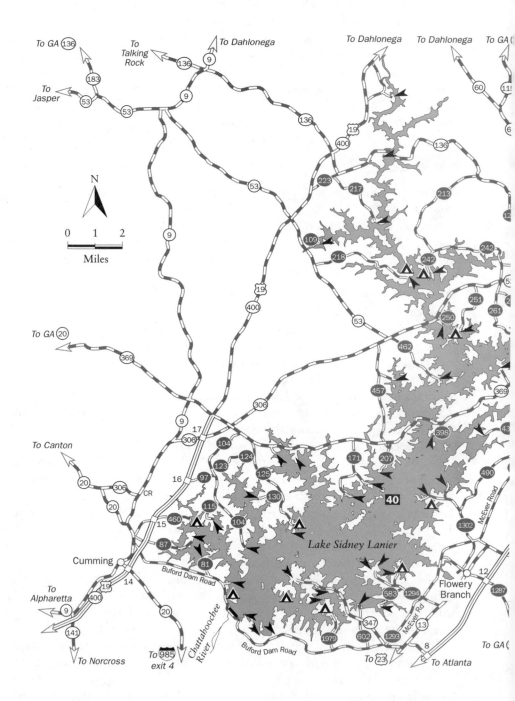

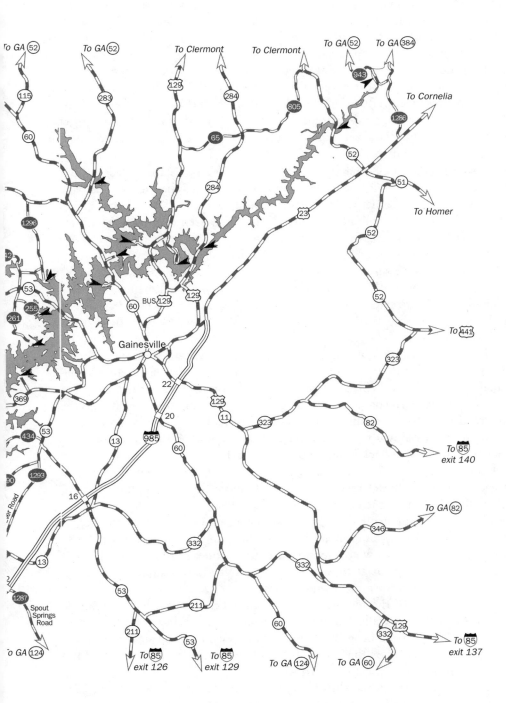

To GA 52
To GA 52
To Clermont
To Clermont
To GA 52
To GA 384

115
283
129
284
943
60
805
To Cornelia
65
1286
284
52
1296
23
51
To Homer
52
53
255
60 BUS 129
129
261
52
Gainesville
369
22
323
434 53
129
To 441
1293
20
11
985
323
82
13
60
To 85
exit 140
16
To GA 82
1287
332
346
Spout
Springs
Road
13
332
211
53
To GA 124
211
53
60
129
To 85
To 85
To 85
exit 126
exit 129
To GA 124
To GA 60
exit 137

Spotted bass dominate the Lake Lanier black bass fishery. About 90 percent of the bass caught will be spots, with the remainder largemouths and perhaps a few shoal bass far up the rivers. Most spots will weigh 1 to 2 pounds, but good numbers of 3- and 4-pound fish are available. Even with all the fishing pressure, Lake Lanier has a lot of fish.

Striped bass fingerlings are stocked into Lake Lanier as a forage management tool and to support a very popular fishery. Striper fishing techniques have probably been refined on Lake Lanier more so than any other Georgia reservoir where these hard-fighting game fish are found. As one might expect on such a heavily used reservoir, access is excellent with many marinas, boat ramps, and shoreline parks.

The fishing: A couple of general rules apply to Lanier bass fishing. Uplake (above Georgia Highway 369) is best for largemouths; downlake is best for spotted bass.

Bass fishing on Lanier really starts to heat up in April. The fish will spawn toward the end of the month, and are shallow in search of nesting locations. Prespawn fish are aggressive, and this is one of the few times of the year you can expect to find spotted bass in less than 5 feet of water.

In the heat of the summer, night-fishing is the way to go. Start your trip in the evening just before dusk as boat traffic dies down. Cast a buzzbait across long, deepwater points to catch schooling fish. Once the sun goes down, switch over to a Texas-rigged plastic worm or a spinnerbait and fish deep, rocky points in 18 to 25 feet of water.

Lake Lanier is arguably the best striper lake in Georgia. Nothing in freshwater pulls harder than a striped bass, but finding and catching them is sometimes difficult. From February until May, look for stripers in the creeks and upriver. The urge to spawn drives them upstream during this period, and the key to finding fish is finding bait. Expect the shad to be holding anywhere from the surface down to 25 feet. Start your search at the creek mouths and then work your way back in until you find bait. Free-line a live shad or bream behind the boat and use the trolling motor to move very slowly through the area. If the depth finder reveals the baitfish and stripers are holding deeper, down-line the bait to the desired depth using a heavy egg sinker.

Lanier is an underrated crappie lake. From mid-February to the beginning of May, look for crappie in the upper lake and tributary creeks. These areas have more shallow cover, and during this time, shallow cover is what crappie are looking for as they prepare to spawn. Cast a small jig or fish a minnow and bobber around woody cover.

Lanier is one of the few lakes in Georgia where anglers have a realistic chance of catching a walleye. Both the Chattahoochee and Chestatee arms are good, but the Chattahoochee probably holds a few more fish since it is larger. A nightcrawler fished on the bottom is a good natural bait, and crankbaits and jigs are tops in the artificials department.

Lake Lanier has a good white bass population. The best time to catch them is in March and April when they migrate up the rivers on their spawning run. Cast a jig around shoals and eddies. Later in the year, look for schools of fish in the main lake following the baitfish. Catching them feeding on top early or late in the day is the best way to fill the livewell in a hurry.

GA~G grid: 21

General information: All anglers fishing Lake Lanier must meet Georgia licensing requirements. Standard Georgia fishing regulations are in effect with one exception; all black bass harvested from the lake must be a minimum of 14 inches. This regulation applies to largemouth bass, spotted bass, and shoal bass.

Boat traffic on the lake is extremely heavy in the summer. All boaters should make sure they know the boating rules of the road and follow them. Navigation hazards are well marked, and should cause no problem to the angler if a little common sense is exercised. Some USACE facilities charge a daily use fee; be sure to check area rules and regulations upon arrival.

Food, lodging, and supplies are available around the lake and along the Georgia Highway 400 and Interstate 985 corridors.

Nearest camping: Camping is available at nine USACE campgrounds found around the lake. County- and state-owned campgrounds are also available.

Directions: Northeast of Atlanta, GA 400 and I-985 (U.S. Highway 23) roughly parallel the lake on the west and east. Refer to the site map to reach the area you want to fish.

For more information: Contact the Wildlife Resources Division Fisheries Section Office in Gainesville. For lake and USACE facility information, contact the Resource Manager's Office.

Lake Sidney Lanier is one of the best spotted bass and striped bass fisheries in Georgia.

East Central Georgia

East Central Georgia has some of state's most popular large reservoirs and several smaller waters that are excellent angling. The region also contains the state's southernmost trout water, the Chattahoochee River, which is just north of Atlanta and is a popular trout anglers' destination.

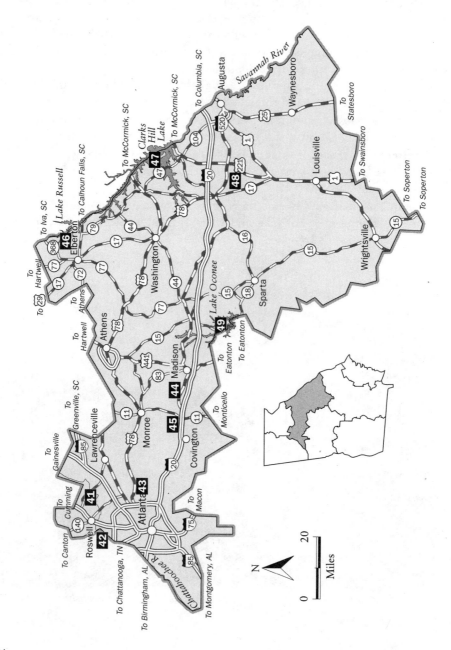

41 Chattahoochee River National Recreation Area

See maps on pages 177-179

Key species: rainbow trout, brown trout.

Overview: Managed by the National Park Service, the Chattahoochee River National Recreation Area consists of 16 land units along a 48-mile stretch of the Chattahoochee River north of Atlanta. Releases from Lake Sidney Lanier's Buford Dam keep the river cold, allowing it to sustain trout even in the heat of the summer.

Best way to fish: float tube, wading, canoe.

Best time to fish: good year-round, but April through July is prime.

Description: The lands of the Chattahoochee River National Recreation Area (CRNRA) are managed as nine park units. The units are scattered along the river from Buford Dam downstream to Interstate 75 and make up most of the public lands along the river.

The CRNRA receives about 3.5 million visitors annually. The river and its banks are a popular place to hike, picnic, float tube, and sightsee. Although fishing pressure on the river is heavy, so is the stocking. Some evidence suggests trout reproduction occurs in the river, but it is limited. The fishery is almost entirely supported by stocked rainbow and brown trout. Unlike many stocked Georgia trout streams, winter holdover of 9- to 12-inch stocked fish is common. The Chattahoochee River is one of the premiere destinations in Georgia for trophy trout, especially big browns. Huge rainbows and browns weighing in the double-digits have been taken from the river.

The Chattahoochee River below Lake Lanier is usually cold, clear, and slow-moving, but it can also be a muddy torrent. Besides the effects of Mother Nature, the operation of Buford Dam dictates the character of the river. When the turbines come on, the river can jump up several feet in a matter of minutes, making the danger of being swept away or swamped very real. The wading angler should never be far from a quick and easy escape route to higher ground. Although the water release schedule is available by telephone, and sirens on the river announce impending water releases, all anglers should keep track of the water level by noting a benchmark rock or stick. If the water starts to creep up on the benchmark, be prepared for much higher and faster water coming in just a matter of minutes. The river is full of slippery rocks, and wading conditions can be treacherous. Because it comes from deep below the surface of Lake Lanier, the Chattahoochee's water is extremely cold and hypothermia is a threat. Anglers should always keep safety in mind on the Chattahoochee. The closer to the dam you are, the more dangerous the river.

Besides preserving the natural aspects of the river corridor, the CRNRA has preserved history as well. Rock shelters used by nomadic Native American families and hunting parties are found on several units. The Chattahoochee was once a dividing line between the Cherokee and Creek Indian Nations, and after the Native American inhabitants of the area were forced west, settlers established several mills and ferries along the river.

Many road names and place names are taken from these early developments along the river's course.

The fishing: The best way to fish the Chattahoochee is to float and fish whatever looks good, then stop and wade the best shoals. The shoals and rocky areas make a canoe or float tube the best choice of craft. Wading up the middle and casting toward the trough of deeper water along the bank is a good approach. Use caution and be prepared to retreat if the water begins to rise. The best fishing is when the turbines are silent and the water is low and clear.

One section of the stream is restricted to artificial lures only, but other than that, anything from corn to crickets and worms to the tiniest dry fly stands a chance of catching fish.

The river immediately below Buford Dam is good for numbers, but trophies are rare. Insects are scarce, and regulars swear by a gold, eighth-ounce Little Cleo spoon.

Around the Jones Bridge weeds and insects increase, and so do trophy trout. The Little Cleo is still good, but in-line spinners and small minnow-imitators are most commonly used. Fly fishers should try midges and caddis, but presentation is more important than pattern.

From Jones Bridge to Bull Sluice Lake is probably the stretch for trophy trout. Fish plugs that imitate a small fish or crayfish, or a nightcrawler bumped along the bottom.

Downstream of Bull Sluice Lake and Morgan Falls Dam is arguably the best fly fishing in Georgia. Good wadeable water and abundant hatches provide exciting fishing. Stocked fingerlings grow quickly.

An angler tries his luck on the Chattahoochee River below Lake Sidney Lanier.

Chattahoochee River National Recreation Area

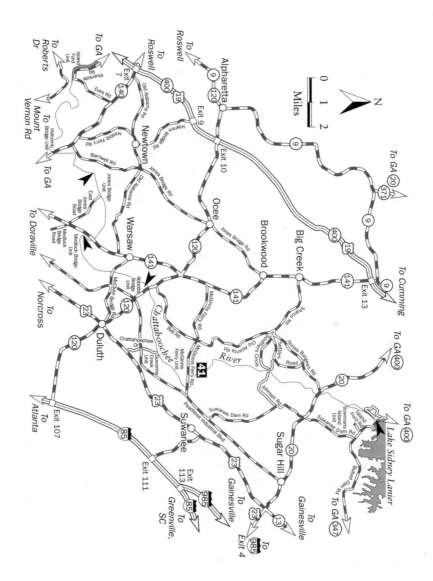

Chattahoochee River National Recreation Area • Bull Sluice Lake

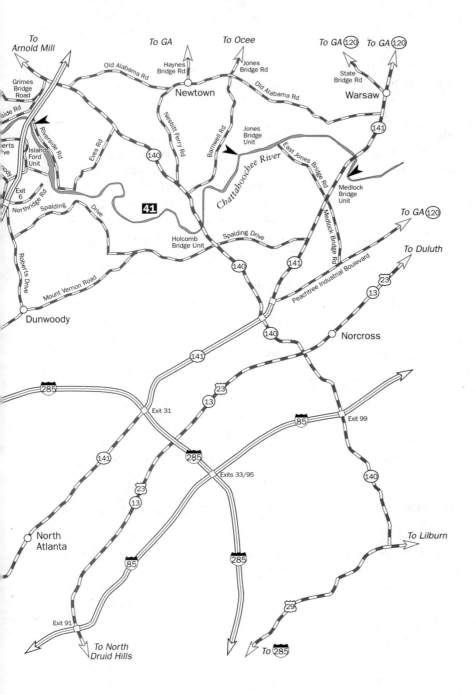

To Arnold Mill

To GA

To Ocee

To GA 120   To GA 120

Old Alabama Rd

Haynes Bridge Rd

Jones Bridge Rd

Old Alabama Rd

State Bridge Rd

Grimes Bridge Road

Newtown

Warsaw

...side Rd

Riverside Rd

141

Island Ford Unit

...erts ...ve

...ody

Eves Rd

Nesbitt Ferry Rd

140

Barnwell Rd

Jones Bridge Unit

East Jones Bridge Rd

Chattahoochee River

Medlock Bridge Unit

Exit 6

Northridge Rd

Spalding

Drive

41

Holcomb Bridge Unit

Spalding Drive

141

Medlock Bridge Rd

To GA 120

Roberts Drive

Mount Vernon Road

140

141

Peachtree Industrial Boulevard

To Duluth

23

13

Dunwoody

140

Norcross

141

285

Exit 31

23

13

85

Exit 99

141

285

Exits 33/95

140

23

13

North Atlanta

85

285

To Lilburn

29

Exit 91

To North Druid Hills

To 285

Trout in the Chattahoochee are usually not picky, but they can be hard to find. Once fish are found, a good presentation will draw strikes. For most of the year, the shoals are the best places to fish. One exception would be the dog days of summer when flycasters should bump nymphs along the bottom, and spinning anglers should fish lures deep.

The banks of the river are full of fallen trees which trout use for resting and feeding. Pulling fish out of the limbs can be difficult, but the trees are consistent producers.

GA~G grid: 20, 21

General information: This section of the Chattahoochee River is designated as year-round trout water; however, some special regulations are in effect. Anglers fishing the river from Georgia Highway 20 to the boat ramp at the CRNRA Medlock Bridge unit are restricted to artificial lures only; natural baits cannot be used or possessed in this stretch. The Chattahoochee River within the CRNRA is closed to any use at night. Anyone in or on the river between Buford Dam and the GA 20 bridge must wear a personal flotation device at all times. Live fish may be used as bait downstream of GA 9 (Roswell Road). All anglers must meet Georgia licensing requirements. A trout stamp is required to fish designated trout water, regardless of the species being pursued.

A daily parking fee is charged on the CRNRA. Contact the CRNRA Office for more information on other rules and regulations, and to obtain an excellent map of the river corridor. A variety of food, lodging, and supplies are available in the Greater Atlanta Metropolitan Area.

Nearest camping: Camping is not allowed on the CRNRA. The nearest public campgrounds are at Lakes Allatoona and Lanier.

Directions: Refer to the site map for roads leading to the stretch you are interested in.

For more information: Contact the CRNRA Superintendent's Office. For fisheries information, contact the Wildlife Resources Division Fisheries Section Office in Social Circle.

CHATTAHOOCHEE RIVER NATIONAL RECREATION AREA AT A GLANCE

Bowman's Island Unit — The northernmost unit of the CRNRA extends downstream for about 2 miles from Buford Dam. The bottom is heavily scoured and the rugged banks are thickly wooded. The mouth of Haw Creek on the north side of the river near the dam is popular with bank anglers. There is a lot of wadeable water in this section, and the shoals around Bowman's Island are very productive. This unit has some developed facilities including restrooms and a paved launching ramp.

McGinnis Ferry Unit — A small, undeveloped unit, its 161 acres stretch along 2 miles along the river about 9 river miles south of Buford Dam. There is no parking lot and access to the river is along undeveloped pathways. This unit is within the artificials-only portion of the river.

Suwanee Creek Unit — Another small, undeveloped unit about 10 miles below the dam. There is no parking or facilities, and access to the river is along undeveloped trails. This unit is within the artificials-only portion of the river.

Abbotts Bridge Unit — About 12 river miles downstream of the dam, this unit has developed facilities including restrooms and a launch ramp and is within the artificials-only portion of the river.

Medlock Bridge Unit — This unit is only about 43 acres, but has improved facilities including a launching ramp. The ramp is the downstream cut-off point for the artificials-only stretch of the river. This unit is about 17 river miles below Buford Dam. It's a good tube trip from here to Jones Bridge Unit.

Jones Bridge Unit — About 20 river miles below the dam, this is a popular unit with developed facilities including a paved launching ramp, restrooms, and hiking trails. The shoals in this area offer good fishing. Jones Bridge Park, part of the Gwinnett County Park System, is directly across the river. It's a good tube trip from here to Holcomb Bridge Unit.

Holcomb Bridge Unit — This is a small unit with no developed facilities located about 23 miles downstream of Buford Dam.

Island Ford Unit — The CRNRA headquarters is on this unit. The island and surrounding shoals offer great fishing. Facilities include a carry-down launch ramp, restrooms, hiking trail, parking, and observation deck. Native Americans once used the huge rock outcroppings found on this unit for shelter while on hunting trips.

Vickery Creek Unit — This 254-acre unit has some developed facilities including parking and hiking trails. The unit is about 30 river miles downstream of Buford Dam. Ruins of mills built in the mid-1800s are found on the unit, including the Roswell Cotton Mills. At 254 acres, this is a fairly large unit but much of it is along the banks of the creek, with little river frontage.

Chattahoochee River Park — Managed by Fulton County Parks and Recreation and not part of the CRNRA, this 770-acre park's facilities are extremely popular with visitors. The launch ramp here is the last take-out above Bull Sluice Lake and Morgan Falls Dam.

Gold Branch Unit — This unit is along the shores of Bull Sluice Lake. Facilities include hiking trails and parking. No boat ramp is present.

Morgan Falls Park — Though not part of the CRNRA, this public park offers a boat ramp and parking right below Morgan Falls Dam. Most of the facilities are directed toward athletics and playing fields.

Johnson Ferry Unit — This is a large unit divided into North and South sections by Johnson Ferry Road; this area is great fishing. Canoe launching is easy here, and the unit is a popular starting point with people rafting or tubing down the river. Facilities include restrooms, hiking trails, raft rentals and shuttles, and a concession stand with food and drinks. This unit roughly covers the first 2 river miles downstream of Morgan Falls Dam. Wading opportunities are limited; it's best approached by tube or canoe.

Sope Creek Unit — This unit connects with the Cochran Shoals Unit and does not directly border the river. However, it has a very interesting history. Sope Creek is reportedly named for a full-blooded Cherokee Indian who somehow managed to avoid being forcibly moved west in 1838. Legend has it that area youngsters would sneak from their homes to go visit the kindly man who told them stories and taught them Cherokee words. Also along the creek are the ruins of the paper mill that produced much of the South's paper from 1855 to 1902. Union troops razed and burned the mill in 1864. It was rebuilt, however, and the ruins of the second incarnation of the mill are still visible today.

Cochran Shoals Unit — This is a large unit that is popular with hikers, trail bikers, and walkers. The shoals here offer good fishing and can easily be waded at low water. Restrooms are available.

Powers Island Unit — This unit lies across the river from Cochran Shoals and is a popular put-in point for kayakers, canoeists, and floaters. Raft rentals, shuttles, and concessions are available. This area of the river is heavily used during the summer, especially on the weekends.

Palisades Unit — This is a large unit that spans the river with good wading and good shoals. Float-tubing from here down to Paces Mill is a good, short trip of a couple miles. When tubing traffic is heavy, this section of the river can be a never-ending parade of one group of fun-seekers after another.

Paces Mill — Downstream end of CRNRA and take-out point for tubers and rafters. Restrooms are present. Shuttle service available. A lot of good wading available to the angler.

42 Bull Sluice Lake

See maps on pages 177-179

Key species: bluegill, redear sunfish, largemouth bass.
Overview: On the north side of metropolitan Atlanta and in the middle of the prime trout fishing water of the Chattahoochee River, Bull Sluice Lake is a series of shallow sloughs that offer good fishing for bream and other warm-water species.
Best way to fish: boat.
Best time to fish: April through October.
Description: Bull Sluice Lake (also known as Morgan Falls Lake or Lake Roswell) is a 500-acre lake upstream of Georgia Power's small hydroelectric dam on the Chattahoochee River. The dam goes by the name Morgan Falls,

hence the confusion about the name of the lake. The lake is generally recognized to be the stretch of the Chattahoochee River from Georgia Highway 9 (Roswell Road) downstream to Morgan Falls Dam.

Although the lake is just a stretch of the Chattahoochee River and a collection of several shallow sloughs, the fishing here is very different from the rest of the Chattahoochee around Atlanta. The current in the lake can be very strong, depending on what is taking place at Buford and Morgan Falls Dams.

Anglers should use extreme caution navigating the lake. Much of it is extremely shallow and sandbars and shoals lie hidden just below the surface. In most places, the main channel will have 4 to 8 feet of water, but once you get out of the channel, watch out. Use your trolling motor to navigate your way up the narrow side channels leading into the sloughs. Lest you throw caution to the wind and operate your boat in a manner resulting in an unplanned swim, another factor to keep in mind is that even in the summer months, this water is cold. Releases from Buford Dam usually keep the temperature around 60 degrees F in the main channel, with the sloughs slightly warmer.

Although Bull Sluice Lake has some of Georgia's most popular trout water both upstream and downstream of it, most of the fishing in the lake is for warm-water species. Bream are probably the best choice, but largemouths better than 8 pounds have also been caught.

The fishing: Fishing for bream near shallow beds in the spring is the fastest fishing of the year. Spawning sunfish are aggressive and readily take live bait or small artificials. A red wiggler or cricket fished under a small bobber is a good choice, as is a Beetle Spin bumped along the bottom. When fish are off the beds, look for them to concentrate around shallow cover.

Largemouth bass are also available in Bull Sluice. The shallow sloughs are prime in the spring, but later in the year the mouths of the sloughs and feeder creeks are the best places to try. Any standard bass fishing technique stands a good chance of garnering strikes. Topwaters, shallow-diving plugs, and soft plastics fished on the bottom and around cover should produce.

Although not technically within Bull Sluice Lake, the tailwaters below Morgan Falls Dam offer good fishing for a variety of species. Trout, warm-water species, and maybe even a few striped bass are possible.

GA~G grid: 20, G-3

General information: Although Bull Sluice Lake is on the portion of the Chattahoochee River designated as trout water, no trout stamp is needed to fish the lake (defined as GA 9 [Roswell Road] downstream to Morgan Falls Dam). Anglers fishing the Morgan Falls tailwater are required to possess a trout stamp since they are not within the defined boundaries of Bull Sluice Lake. However, anglers fishing the lake must meet all other Georgia licensing requirements and a trout stamp is required to harvest trout. If you do not possess the trout stamp, any trout caught must be immediately released. Standard Georgia creel and length limits apply on the lake.

Access on the lake is limited to one public boat ramp on the upper end of the lake at Chattahoochee River Park. Although larger boats can be used, the lake lends itself to a small aluminum johnboat. Water release schedules are available by phone, see the Appendix for more information. Food, lodging, and supplies are just a few miles away in Roswell.

Georgia Power has a public access park at Morgan Falls Dam on the east side of the river. A boat ramp is present at the park and is downstream of the dam. There is no portage around Morgan Falls Dam.

Nearest camping: There are several public campgrounds operated by the USACE within 25 miles at Lakes Allatoona and Lanier.

Directions: From Atlanta, travel north on GA 9 (Roswell Road). Immediately after crossing the Chattahoochee River, turn left onto Azalea Drive. Fulton County's Chattahoochee River Park borders the lakeshore along Azalea Drive. To reach the Georgia Power public use area at Morgan Falls Dam, after crossing the Chattahoochee River traveling southbound on GA 9 (Roswell Road), continue 3 miles to Morgan Falls Road on the left. Follow this road to the park.

For more information: Contact the Wildlife Resources Division Fisheries Section Office in Social Circle.

43 Stone Mountain Park Lakes

Key species: largemouth bass, bluegill, redear sunfish, crappie, catfish.

Overview: Home to the largest exposed piece of granite in the world, with the Dixie equivalent of Mount Rushmore carved into it, Stone Mountain Park is one of Georgia's most popular destinations, hosting more than 4 million visitors annually. The park is 3,200 acres and includes two lakes open to public fishing.

Best way to fish: boat, shore.

Best time to fish: March through October.

Description: Although not a state park per se, Stone Mountain Park is near and dear to Georgians' hearts and is a popular family destination. The park's nightly laser show is a spectacle all should see. Besides fishing, plenty of other activities are available. Every member of the family should find something they enjoy doing.

The Confederate Memorial Carving on Stone Mountain is the largest relief sculpture in the world. Conceived in 1912, the project took nearly 60 years to complete. The figures of Confederate President Jefferson Davis, General Robert E. Lee, and General "Stonewall" Jackson, all mounted on horseback, cover nearly 3 acres of the mountain's north face.

Surprisingly, for being in the middle of one of the busiest recreation facilities in metro Atlanta, the lakes at Stone Mountain do not receive that much dedicated fishing pressure. With all the other things to do on the park, angling is simply an afterthought for most visitors. Overlooking the lakes' angling potential is a mistake since both have produced largemouth bass in the 10-pound range. In addition, bream and other panfish are abundant and easily caught.

Stone Mountain Park Lakes

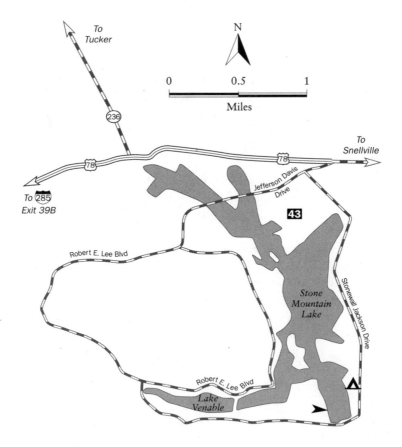

The fishing: Bass anglers who like fishing the shoreline find Stone Mountain the place to be. Shoreline blowdowns and overhanging brush consistently produce. Skipping a plastic worm up under the brush and working it back slowly is a favorite tactic. Buzzbaits, spinnerbaits, and other shallow-water favorites are also good on the Stone Mountain lakes.

If things are not happening in the shallows, try a crankbait or Carolina-rigged soft plastic in deeper water. If a depth finder is not available, study the lay of the land to make an educated guess about what is beneath the surface. Both the crankbait and Carolina rig are good at quickly covering deeper water, which is important when searching for a needle in the haystack. If you luck upon some offshore structure though, you may find that it is stacked full of fish.

For bream and other panfish, try fishing crickets or worms around shoreline cover. If you prefer artificials, cast small spinners or flycast a popping bug. The blowdowns are good for crappie in the early spring when the spawn pulls them shallow. The rest of the year, crappie can be difficult since they suspend in deeper water. Small minnows and jigs are good crappie baits.

Catfish are best caught on chicken livers or worms fished on the bottom near deeper water. Commercial catfish baits are also productive.

GA~G grid: 26, A-5

General information: Stone Mountain Park is open daily from 6 A.M. until midnight. Fishing at Stone Mountain Park is free but a fee is charged to bring a vehicle into the park. Private boats are allowed on Stone Mountain Lake, which is open year-round. Outboard motors less than 10 horsepower can be used, and larger boats are allowed on the lake but must use electric motors only. During peak-season weekends, private boats must be off the lake by 11 A.M. A boat ramp is available. Smaller Lake Venable is open seasonally and only rental boats may be used.

Nearest camping: The campground at Stone Mountain has 441 wooded campsites. There are 191 sites with full hookups, 197 with water and electricity, and 53 primitive tent sites. Comfort stations and a trading post with groceries and supplies are also available.

Directions: In Atlanta, take Interstate 285 North to exit 39B, the Stone Mountain Freeway/Highway 78 East. Travel 7.7 miles and exit at the Stone Mountain Park East Gate Entrance. Follow this exit around a long curve to the East Gate entrance of Stone Mountain Park.

For more information: Contact the Stone Mountain Park Office.

Two anglers try their luck on one of the lakes at Stone Mountain Park.

44 Lakes Rutledge and Brantley (Hard Labor Creek State Park)

Key species: largemouth bass, bluegill, redear sunfish, channel catfish.

Overview: This state park contains two impoundments on Hard Labor Creek; 275-acre Lake Rutledge and 40-acre Lake Brantley. Both lakes offer good fishing from the shore or a small boat. Many other outdoor recreation opportunities are available on-site, making the park a great choice for a family trip.

Best way to fish: boat, shore.

Best time to fish: March through October.

Description: Hard Labor Creek State Park is one of the largest parks in Georgia. The park came into being during the Great Depression when the National Park Service acquired 44 parcels of land that formed the Hard Labor Creek Recreation Demonstration Area.

With its proximity to Atlanta and the variety of activities available, the state park receives heavy use. However, most fishing pressure on the lakes is from the shoreline around the picnic areas and campgrounds. Anglers who are willing to hike or who use a small boat should find uncrowded conditions. Especially on Lake Brantley, which has no boat ramp, sliding in a canoe or small johnboat will give you the best access to the lake.

Since the lakes are old, they are heavily silted. Any offshore depth breaks or channels have long since been buried under a load of silt. The lake basins were completely cleared during construction, so most woody cover is near the shoreline where wind, bank erosion, and time have done their share to add some fallen trees to the lake. Lake Rutledge has a couple of marked fish attractors. Both lakes are shallow; you will find depths to 10 feet in Lake Rutledge, but most of the lake is much shallower.

Largemouths are the only black bass species found in the lakes. Lake Rutledge was traditionally known for producing many bass in excess of 8 pounds, but by the mid-1990s rough fish had nearly taken over the lake and it was drained and restocked. Since the fish population has been restored to balance, the lake should again produce good fishing with the opportunity for a trophy fish.

The fishing: Since the lakes are shallow, with little structure, fishing the shoreline is the best approach on Lakes Rutledge and Brantley. Fallen trees are good targets for a plastic worm, spinnerbait, or topwater plug. The most obvious trees are the heaviest fished. A sharp eye and a little deduction might lead you to some cover that gets less pressure. Look for stumps on the shore that might suggest a fallen tree in deeper water. Often this will be a fruitless search, but when structure is found, it pays tremendous dividends. The shoreline around the islands in Lake Rutledge is also a good place to try your luck.

Shallow lakes like Rutledge and Brantley warm quickly and produce when larger, deeper lakes are still locked in the winter doldrums. Try shallow areas on the north side of the lakes to find the warmest water and the most active fish in early spring. Large lures like a jig-and-pig are good choices for tempting a trophy during this prespawn period.

Lakes Rutledge and Brantley
(Hard Labor Creek State Park)

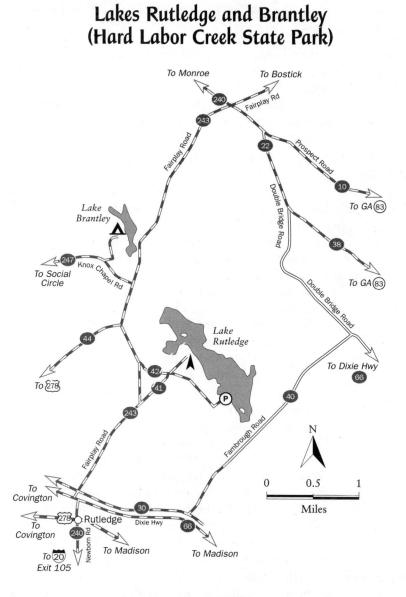

Bluegill and redear sunfish are easily caught from shoreline cover. Bluegill will be shallow right in the cover, while shellcrackers prefer slightly deeper water. Crickets and worms, small spinners and popping bugs can be very effective. The best bream fishing will be when the fish are on the bed. Search the back of shallow coves for saucer-shaped spawning beds.

Channel catfish can be caught anywhere on the lakes, with the deeper water near the dam being a prime location. Nightcrawlers and chicken livers fished on the bottom are local favorites.

GA~G grid: 28, C-1

General information: A daily or annual Georgia Parks Pass is required for all vehicles parked on the area. All anglers must meet Georgia licensing requirements. Private boats are allowed on the lakes, and Lake Rutledge has a boat ramp. Lake Brantley does not have a boat ramp, but anglers should have no trouble sliding in a canoe or small johnboat. Only electric motors may be used on Lake Brantley; gasoline motors 10 horsepower or less are allowed on Lake Rutledge. Johnboats and canoes are available for rent. Bank fishing is allowed from 7 A.M. to 10 P.M. and boat fishing hours are from 7 A.M. until sunset.

Other recreation opportunities include camping, picnicking, hiking, horseback riding (riders must provide their own mount), swimming, and golf. Hard Labor Creek State Park is open year-round.

Food, lodging, and supplies are available in the park or 3 miles away in Rutledge.

Nearest camping: Hard Labor Creek State Park offers 51 combination tent and trailer sites with water and electric hookups, picnic tables, and grills. Comfort stations provide hot showers and flush toilets. Both developed and primitive group camps are available for use by organized groups. The park has 20 cottages for rent each equipped with a stove, refrigerator, air conditioning, fireplace, kitchen supplies, linens, and towels.

Directions: From Atlanta, go east on Interstate 20 and take exit 105 (Newborn Road (CR 240)). Drive north 2.4 miles to Rutledge. In Rutledge follow the signs through several quick turns and continue north on Fairplay Road (CR 243) to the park entrance.

For more information: Contact the Wildlife Resources Division Fisheries Section Office in Social Circle or the Hard Labor Creek Park Superintendent's Office.

45 Lake Varner

Key species: largemouth bass, bluegill, redear sunfish, crappie.

Overview: An 850-acre drinking water reservoir owned by Newton County, Lake Varner opened to the public in 1992 and has produced excellent fishing ever since.

Best way to fish: boat, shore.

Best time to fish: March through October.

Description: First known as "Cornish Creek Reservoir," this 850-acre impoundment was built in 1991 to provide an additional source of water for county residents. The lake opened to public fishing in 1992 and although some unique regulations are in place, anglers continue to flock to the lake to get in on the hot action.

Much of Lake Varner remains virtually uncharted water. Since all boats are limited to electric motors only, the upper ends of the lake distant from the single access point get very little fishing pressure. Also, prospecting for offshore structure is a time-consuming task without a gasoline motor.

Lake Varner is not an extremely deep lake. In the main creek channels, the water is close to 20 feet deep. The deepest point on the lake is near the dam and has 38 feet of water. Lake Varner's waters are usually clear, and aquatic vegetation is abundant.

The lake has one public access point on the east side near the dam. The access point has a paved boat ramp, parking, fishing pier, and shoreline fishing area.

The lake offers good fishing for several panfish species, and specimens up to 10 inches are common. Anglers targeting bluegill, redear sunfish, and crappie should have no problem finding the main ingredient needed for a fish fry.

The bass fishing in Lake Varner has been excellent from the start. Several ponds were flooded when the lake was built and trophy fish were possible from opening day. In the years since the lake opened, fish populations have expanded to fill the lake, and since growth is good, even more trophies are available. Several bass weighing more than 13 pounds have been caught, and many of the bass weigh 2 pounds or more.

The fishing: Some of the best fishing holes are within sight of the boat ramp. The old pond dams flooded at impoundment offer very good fishing. Both dams are in about 8 feet of water and provide bass the type of structure they love. One dam is in the boat ramp cove just east of the ramp, while the other is across the lake to the right of the long point with a gazebo. Both locations can be fished in a variety of ways. A jig-and-pig, Texas-rigged plastic worm, or crankbait are all good choices.

The coves on either side of the gazebo point offer good bream fishing. Starting in May, keep a close eye out for beds. Redear sunfish spawn as early

A view of Lake Varner from near the dam.

Lake Varner

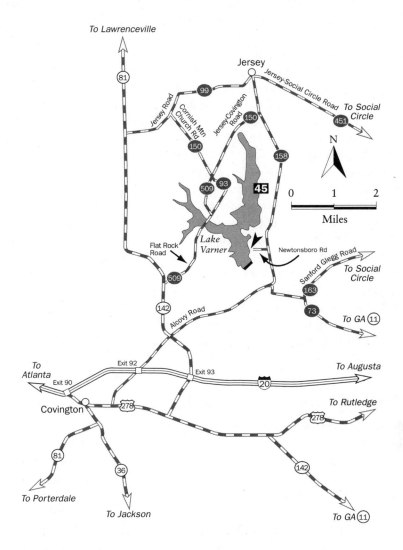

as April and only spawn once, but bluegill spawn repeatedly throughout the summer. Whether you are lucky enough to catch redear sunfish on the beds or have to settle for bluegill, expect some fast fishing for hand-sized bream. Red wigglers or crickets are the best for live bait, and casting spinners or a popping bug can produce a good stringer of fish.

Crappie begin to move shallow in March and the spawning peak usually comes sometime in early April. Spawning crappie are drawn to wood like a magnet, and when they are shallow, any piece of cover is likely to produce. Small minnows or jigs are standard baits with crappie anglers.

GA~G grid: 27, C-9

General information: The most important thing to realize when planning a trip to Lake Varner is the lake is limited to electric motors only. Gasoline motors or gas tanks are not allowed on the lake, even if they are not used. Anglers living outside Newton and Walton Counties must pay a $5 daily parking fee and a separate $5 boat launch fee; local residents are exempt from the fees. Lake hours vary seasonally and are posted along with other rules and regulations. All anglers fishing the lake must meet standard Georgia licensing requirements.

Nearest camping: The nearest camping is about 15 miles away at Hard Labor Creek State Park. The park has 51 sites with water and electric hookups, picnic tables, and grills. Comfort stations have hot showers and flush toilets. In addition, the park has 20 cottages for rent each equipped with a stove, refrigerator, air conditioning, fireplace, kitchen supplies, linens, and towels.

Directions: From Interstate 20, near Covington, take exit 92 (Alcovy Road). Travel northeast 3.3 miles to the entrance road on the left just after crossing the bridge over Cornish Creek.

For more information: Contact the Newton County Parks and Recreation Department or the Wildlife Resources Division Fisheries Section Office in Social Circle. For camping information, contact the Hard Labor Creek State Park Superintendent's Office.

46 Lake Richard B. Russell

Key species: largemouth bass, spotted bass, crappie.

Overview: Georgia's newest large reservoir, Lake Richard B. Russell reached its full pool of 26,650 acres in December 1994. The reservoir is an USACE multipurpose project on the Savannah River in Georgia's Piedmont region.

Best way to fish: boat, shore.

Best time to fish: year-round.

Description: Because Lake Russell is managed for fish and wildlife and is undeveloped, it escapes much of the boat traffic that Georgia anglers are so familiar with on other reservoirs.

Lake Russell impounds the Savannah River and the Rocky River. About 25 miles of the lake's Savannah River arm is part of the Georgia–South Carolina border. The Rocky River flows into Lake Russell from Lake Secession in South Carolina.

The needs of fish and anglers were kept in mind during the construction of the lake. Some forested areas were left standing, and thousands of acres of trees were topped at 12 to 35 feet below normal pool level. The cutting pattern

Lake Richard B. Russell

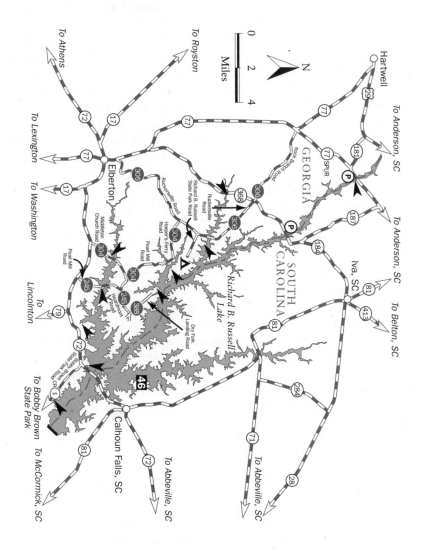

left a ring around the lake from the shoreline out to about the 30-foot depth that is mostly free of trees, but anglers have rectified this situation by placing brush piles in this generally narrow band of water. In addition, both Georgia and South Carolina fisheries agencies have placed fish attractors around the lake. Russell is a deep lake and its waters stay relatively clear year-round. Most of the fishing takes place offshore in the flooded timber.

The placement of numbered marker poles has made navigation on Lake Russell easy and safe. Marker poles, which are also lighted at night, reveal how the channels run and where the ledges are. For most of the year, a first-time angler would do well just casting to the poles. Since they are found on the breaks and are cover themselves, a few fish should always be available.

Lake Russell has been a bass lake from the start. Most of the fish caught in the lake will be largemouth bass, but spotted bass are starting to come on strong. Just after impoundment, redeye bass were plentiful but have since declined, probably because they are primarily a stream fish and usually do not do well in reservoirs. Although Lake Russell has produced largemouth bass weighing more than 13 pounds, the lake is known mostly for producing high numbers of quality-sized fish up to 5 pounds. Crappie are another popular species in Lake Russell, with many fish measuring more than 10 inches. Bream and catfish are also present, as are a few striped bass and hybrid striped bass that make their way into the lake from upstream reservoirs.

The fishing pressure is light for a lake of this size and quality. To get to Russell, you have to drive by other fine lakes, which could explain the uncrowded angling on Lake Russell. Access is good with many public access points on both the Georgia and South Carolina sides of the lake.

The fishing: From late-October through March, the simple jigging spoon will outproduce nearly any other lure. Look for the bass between 20 and 55 feet deep on the flats next to the main channels. The presence of baitfish is key for this pattern to work. A Carolina-rigged soft plastic can also be effective. Cast the lure shallow and work it back down the drops.

Another good tactic for cool-water bass is to work the submerged trees with a deep-diving crankbait or heavy spinnerbait. This pattern works best when water temperatures are in the mid-50s or warmer. Secondary points are good for prespawn bass. Look for these points in the tributary arms. As the lake warms and the spawn gets closer, go to the backs of tributary creeks and cast a spinnerbait to visible cover.

May is topwater time. Fish riprap banks, hard clay bottoms, or the pockets for best action. A good offshore topwater bite usually occurs early in the morning, but then the bass suspend in the submerged forests. When not actively feeding, a school of fish may be holding 20 feet down in the trees over 50 feet of water. When they decide it is time to eat, the fish will slide up onto the nearest hump or point to fill their bellies before sliding back to their deepwater forest haunts.

Winter crappie anglers would do well to concentrate on deep brush piles and tributary channels by trolling a spread of tiny jigs. When the crappie get ready to spawn in the spring, look for blowdowns and other shallow, woody cover. Cast a jig or fish a minnow under a bobber for best results. Summer and fall crappie fishing is best at night under bridges. Using floating lights or lanterns, anglers draw in baitfish and crappie. The best bridges cross the tributaries instead of the main channel. The best place to put the lights is right next to pilings. Fish a minnow straight down and set rods at different depths to find the fish.

Catfish are overlooked on Lake Russell. Channel cats dominate, but bullheads, white catfish, and a few flatheads are possible. The best place to look for big channel cats is the upper end of the lake and the tributaries. Expect big catfish to hold on the ends of points and near channel edges during the day, and then venture into shallow water to feed at night. If just catching a mess of fish is your goal, you can fish nightcrawlers, chicken liver, or commercially prepared catfish bait nearly anywhere on the lake and expect to get a few bites.

Panfish like bluegill, redear sunfish, and yellow perch are all common in Lake Russell but receive almost no fishing pressure. A few walleye are available, but most catches come accidentally for anglers casting a crankbait or jigging a spoon for bass.

GA~G grid: 23

General information: Lake Russell forms part of the Georgia–South Carolina border. The two states have a reciprocal agreement that allows anglers holding either a Georgia or South Carolina fishing license to fish the waters of the lake. Standard Georgia creel and length limits apply in the Georgia portion of the lake, including a 12-inch minimum length limit on largemouth bass. South Carolina does not have a minimum length limit on largemouth bass harvested from the lake. Anglers should keep this difference in mind if they have harvested any short bass and cross over into Georgia waters. Consult the *Georgia Sport Fishing Regulations* pamphlet for more information about the reciprocal agreements between states regarding angling.

Food, lodging, and supplies are within 15 miles in Elberton.

Nearest camping: Richard B. Russell State Park has 28 campsites and 10 cottages for rent.

Directions: From Elberton, Lake Richard B. Russell can be reached from Georgia Highways 72 and 368.

For more information: Contact the Wildlife Resources Division Fisheries Section Office in Thomson. For camping information, contact the Park Superintendent's Office at Richard B. Russell State Park. For information about the lake and USACE facilities, contact the Richard B. Russell Project Office.

47 Clarks Hill Lake

Key species: largemouth bass, crappie, redear sunfish, striped bass, hybrid striped bass, channel catfish, flathead catfish.

Overview: Clarks Hill Lake is one of the largest inland bodies of water in the South. With 71,535 acres of water, the lake offers almost unlimited angling opportunities for a variety of species.

Best way to fish: boat, shore.

Best time to fish: year-round.

Description: Clarks Hill Lake officially known as the J. Strom Thurmond Project, stretches 40 miles up the Savannah River valley and 26 miles up the Little River valley.

The 1,200-mile shoreline is covered with mixed pine and hardwood and more than 100 islands dot the lake's surface. Clarks Hill sees heavy use but its size allows plenty of room to spread out and find your own honey hole. Access

Clarks Hill Lake

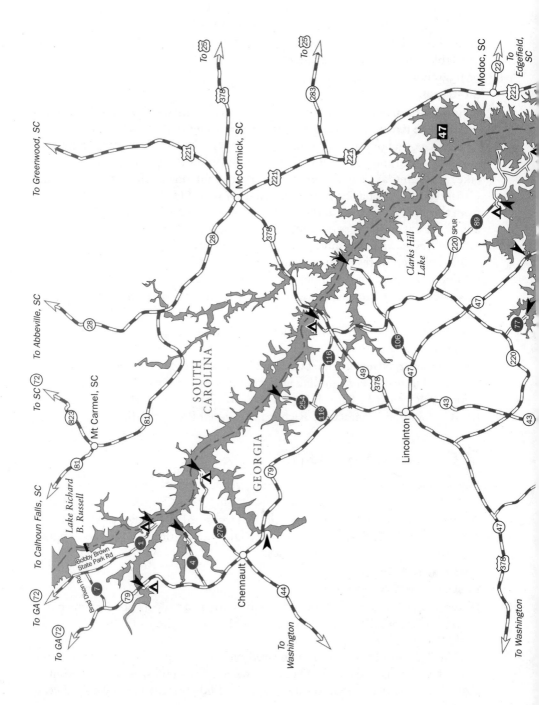

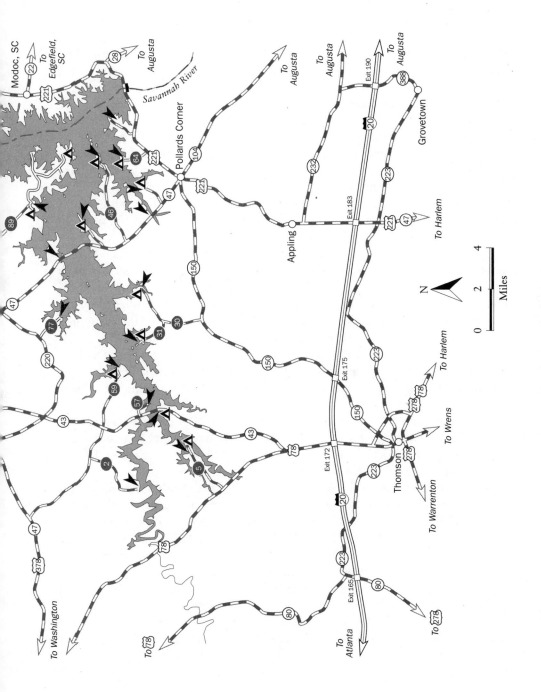

197

to the lake is excellent, with more than 30 access points on the Georgia side. The lake is well marked for navigation.

Clarks Hill anglers reportedly invented "Carolina-rigging" a soft-plastic bait. Since it is steadily retrieved right along the bottom, a Carolina rig covers a lot of water, and is a great way to fish expansive points and flats, of which Clarks Hill has plenty.

Like most older lakes, the basin was almost completely cleared of trees and stumps before impoundment. The lake has many submerged building foundations though, including what once was the town of Petersburg at the confluence of the Savannah and Broad rivers. To help anglers find fish, the agencies responsible for managing the lake maintain about 30 marked fish attractors on the lake; in addition, anglers have placed hundreds of unmarked brush piles. Also, hundreds of shoreline trees have been felled into the lake. One other form of cover is hydrilla. This exotic aquatic plant first appeared here in the 1990s. Although popular with anglers, hydrilla is a hardy plant that quickly spreads, and can require thousands of dollars and hours of effort to keep it under control and to prevent heavy weed growth from choking off access. The spread of non-native plants and fish species is a growing problem that concerns lake managers everywhere.

Clarks Hill is a fertile lake and is known as some of the best bass fishing in Georgia. The lake record specimens for a variety of species bears out the lake's ability to produce big fish: largemouth bass, 14 pounds, 14 ounces; striped bass, 55 pounds, 12 ounces; black crappie, 4 pounds, 8 ounces; flathead catfish, 63 pounds.

The fishing: Springtime is the right time for big bass on Clarks Hill. Beginning in March, cast a spinnerbait around wood on secondary points in the creeks. Digging a crankbait along the bottom on points is also productive. The bass hold on these points before moving onto the spawning grounds. The best points are those with plenty of cover and deep water nearby. A Carolina-rigged soft plastic is also a good choice.

When the fish move in to spawn, fish around the button bushes in the backs of coves. Just about any lure stands a chance of catching fish during this time, but soft-plastic jerk baits and spinnerbaits are both good choices. Do not overlook topwater plugs for some exciting fishing.

The summer months will find bass on deep structure. Anglers can catch a few fish shallow early and late in the day, but the best tactic is to target deeper water with deep-diving crankbaits or a soft-plastic bait worked along the bottom.

October to December can be some of the best bass fishing of the year. The narrow cuts and steep banks in the lake's Little River arm are productive in the fall. This arm is full of bends, and the deeper water on the outside bends is prime. Start early in the day with a buzzbait worked around shallow cover and then switch to a jig-and-pig combo or medium-diving crankbait later in the day. Since the bass are feeding heavily on shad this time of year, choose a color that closely matches the forage. Although the shorelines in this area quickly drop to 15 to 25 feet, depths in the 7- to 10-foot range are the best places to find feeding fish.

During the winter, look for schools of bass in deep water. Humps and channel ledges that top out 20 to 40 feet below the surface are good places to try. Use a depth finder to survey potential areas for baitfish, and once you find the right combination of structure and bait, lower down a jigging spoon. Start off vertically jigging the spoon just above the bait, and if that does not produce, then drop the spoon down another foot or so. Once you figure out the right depth, you can pretty much count on it holding up for the rest of the day.

Clarks Hill is an excellent choice for crappie anglers. Late March and April are the best times for crappie fishing, especially in the creek arms. When the water hits 55 degrees F, expect the crappie to be shallow in preparation for the spawn. Search depths 5 feet or less around woody cover. Cast a jig-and-grub combo to shoreline cover. Or, a live minnow fished under a bobber is always hard to beat for crappie. If a cold front moves fish out of the shallows, troll small jigs in about 10 feet of water near good spawning shorelines.

When they are shallow to spawn, or during the hottest part of summer and the coldest days of winter, look for crappie around brush piles in 12 to 14 feet of water. When it is extremely hot or cold, the fish will move deeper and will be hard to catch, but fortunately these times are few. Cast to the brush piles with a small jig or fish a live minnow straight down into the brush. Bridge pilings are also good places to find fish.

Fishing for hybrids and striped bass on Clarks Hill is excellent. Both shad and blueback herring are present in the lake, and if you are not fishing where the bait is, you are not going to catch fish. Very early in spring, look for stripers and hybrids on shallow main-lake points. The best points are rocky and slowly gain depth as they taper toward the channel and deeper water. Trolling live bait, either free-line or under a float, is productive. Once the water warms to the low-60s, start to search the flats for bait. Clarks Hill is loaded with expansive flats in the 5- to 12-foot range that gradually slope toward the channel. Good flats are those close to a main channel and with some secondary structure or cover like ledges or rock piles. When bait shows up on the flats, the stripers and hybrids will not be far behind. Some anglers like to move along the flat with their trolling motor and cast artificials. Probably the most productive technique is to fish live or cut bait. A live shad or blueback herring fished on the bottom will catch fish when they are feeding on the flats. For anglers wanting to catch a big striper on flycasting gear, this is the time to do it. The fish are shallow and ready to eat. Try a large streamer fished in the mid-depths over good flats and points. Shallow fish are a double-edged sword. The shallow water makes both presentation and spooking fish easier. Hybrids and stripers are skittish and will quickly depart an area if you make your presence known.

In the summer and early fall, look for surface feeding activity early and late in the day. This type of fishing is very exciting but usually short-lived. Plugs are the best way to go when the fish are tearing up bait on the surface. If the fish are not on top, try a live shad or blueback herring down deep. Use a depth finder to find the combination of deep structure and baitfish. Humps and deep channel ledges are good places to look; then simply lower the bait down to the depth the baitfish are holding and let the wind or trolling motor slowly move you around the structure. Expect to fish from 25 to 50 feet deep in the summer. The hotter it gets, the deeper you need to go. Fishing at night is usually best. Many anglers mount powerful lights on their boats that shine down into the water to attract baitfish and hopefully stripers and hybrids.

As the water cools in early winter, expect the stripers to begin moving up the tributary rivers and large creeks. The Little River arm is a favorite with anglers. Search deep holes for schools of bait and stripers and hybrids. Downlining live bait is still a good technique, and trolling large plugs is also effective. The winter months are when the shoreline angler has a legitimate chance of catching a big striper. Fish far up lake right below Richard B. Russell Dam. This tailwater is a consistent producer of fish and is very popular with anglers, so expect some company. Fish live bait or cast a large plug or bucktail jig into the eddies below the dam.

Redear sunfish are the best choice for bream fishing at Clarks Hill. Shellcrackers will bite year-round, but the best time to catch them is when they are spawning from mid-April to May. Like all game fish, the key to finding shellcracker is finding the bait. The good thing about shellcracker fishing, though, is once you have found the bait, you do not have to worry about finding it again the next day, next month, or even next year. As their name suggests, shellcrackers feed on snails and small freshwater mussels, which are not known for their mobility, so when you find them, they are going to be there for a while. Search along the shores of islands and cove pockets for shells washed up on the shoreline by wave and wind action. When you find a shoreline littered with broken and bleached shells, you can bet a good shell bed is just offshore. Fish a red wiggler worm on the bottom. Worms will catch shellcrackers better than any other bait, and fishing is simply a matter of casting out a few baits, tightening up the line, and waiting for a pickup. Shellcracker get big on Clarks Hill and are strong fighters. They also are excellent eating.

Clarks Hill also has a good catfish population. Channel catfish make up the bulk of the creel, and are most popular with anglers, but big flatheads are also available. The lake has produced state record flatheads. Along with channels and flatheads, anglers can expect to catch white catfish and several bullhead species. The best catfishing is up the tributary arms, with Little River being a favorite. Fish a smelly bait on the bottom for fiddler-sized channel cats, white catfish, and bullheads. For big flatheads and channel cats, target deeper channels with a live shad or small bream. Catfishing is usually best at night.

GA~G grid: 30, 31

General information: Clarks Hill Lake forms part of the Georgia–South Carolina border. The two states have a reciprocal agreement that allows anglers holding either a Georgia or South Carolina fishing license to fish the waters of the lake. Standard Georgia creel and length limits apply in the Georgia portion of the lake, including a 12-inch minimum length limit on largemouth bass. South Carolina does not have a minimum length limit on largemouth bass harvested from the lake. Anglers should keep this difference in mind if they have harvested any short bass and cross over into Georgia waters. Consult the *Georgia Sport Fishing Regulations* pamphlet for more information about the reciprocal agreements between states regarding angling.

Some USACE facilities charge a daily use fee; be sure to check area rules and regulations on arrival.

Food, lodging, and supplies are found around the lake and within 20 miles in Augusta, Thomson, and Lincolnton.

Nearest camping: Camping is available on the Georgia side at Bobby Brown, Elijah Clark, and Mistletoe State Parks and 9 USACE campgrounds.

Directions: Clarks Hill Lake is about 20 miles north of Augusta. Refer to the site map to find the best route to the part of the lake you wish to fish.

For more information: Contact the Wildlife Resources Division Fisheries Section Office in Thomson. For lake and USACE facility information, contact the Project Manager's Office.

48 McDuffie Public Fishing Area

Key species: largemouth bass, bluegill, redear sunfish, channel catfish.

Overview: This state-owned facility is important to anglers in two ways: The tract includes not only McDuffie Public Fishing Area, but also one of the State of Georgia's warm-water fish hatcheries.

Best way to fish: shore, boat.

Best time to fish: February through October.

Description: McDuffie Public Fishing Area contains more than 10 fishing ponds. The ponds range in size from 1 to 30 acres and offer good angling for several different species. The 700-acre area not only contains one of Georgia's best public fishing areas, it is also home to McDuffie Hatchery, an important source of warm-water fish for the stocking of waters throughout the state. The topography is typical of the upper coastal plain with longleaf pines and sandy soil. Lilypads and other aquatic vegetation are common in the lakes.

The fishing: No matter how you like to fish, or for what species, McDuffie Public Fishing Area has a lake for you. Several lakes are managed intensively for channel catfish. Chicken livers, commercial stink bait, or the tried and true nightcrawler are all good bets. Since the catfish ponds are heavily stocked, one spot is likely to be as good as another. Pick a spot and try it for 30 minutes, and if things do not go in your favor, pack up and try another one. Catfish usually let you know in short order whether they are in the vicinity and in the mood to bite.

For bluegill and redear sunfish, it is unlikely you can make a bad choice on what pond to fish or how to catch them. All of the ponds are intensively managed and provide good fishing. Fishing worms or crickets below a small bobber near any shoreline cover will produce fish. For a little more sport, consider a fly rod. Especially in the evening when hatches are occurring, a dry fly, popping bug, or sponge spider will draw surface strikes and provide lots of fun.

McDuffie Public Fishing Area

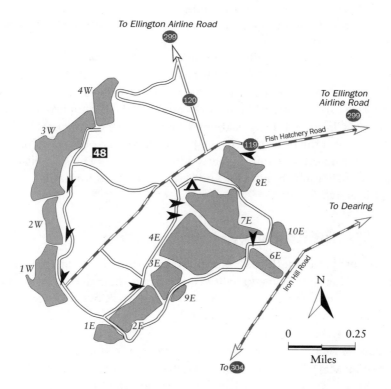

During times when the fish seem a little reluctant to come to the top, try a wet fly around woody cover or weedlines.

McDuffie Public Fishing Area produces big largemouth bass every year. Again, all of the ponds offer a shot at a trophy bass. February and March probably are the best times to catch a real wallhanger, but fishing is good throughout the year. For the most success, concentrate your efforts on one pond and really try to learn it. Anglers who bounce from pond to pond hitting only the obvious targets will not do as well as those who invest the time to find more subtle fish-holding areas.

Any bass lure may work at a given time of year; a plastic worm is hard to beat, though. Rigged weedless, the worm can be worked through thick cover or weeds, shallow or deep. Topwaters, crankbaits, and spinnerbaits are also good choices. Topwater baits may draw fewer strikes, but the excitement factor of seeing a big fish smash a plug on top is worth the cost to many anglers.

GA~G grid: 30, G-2 (not shown in GA~G)

General information: McDuffie Public Fishing Area offers a variety of well-maintained facilities for the angler and outdoor enthusiast. Many larger ponds have concrete boat ramps. Shoreline access is good on the ponds, especially those with fishing piers. Restrooms and picnic tables are available, as are camping facilities. Other facilities include a nature trail and archery range.

McDuffie Public Fishing Area is open from sunrise to sunset every day. During the fall and winter months, anglers wanting to camp should call ahead to check on the status of the seasonally open campground.

Standard Georgia Public Fishing Area regulations are in effect. A Wildlife Management Area stamp is required to fish the area. Refer to the *Georgia Sport Fishing Regulations* pamphlet for more information on rules, regulations, and license requirements.

Food, lodging, and supplies are available 10 miles away in Thomson.

Nearest camping: Camping is allowed at McDuffie Public Fishing Area in designated areas. Campsites range from primitive to RV.

Directions: From Thomson, go south on Georgia Highway 17 to U.S. Highway 278; turn left (east) onto US 278 and travel 5.6 miles to Ellington Airline Road on the right. Travel 2.8 miles on Ellington Airline Road to Fish Hatchery Road on the right. Continue 0.8 mile on Fish Hatchery Road to the entrance of the area.

For more information: Contact the McDuffie Public Fishing Area Office.

49 Lake Oconee

Key species: largemouth bass, crappie, hybrid striped bass, white bass.

Overview: Georgia Power's Lake Oconee is the second-largest lake found entirely within Georgia and is very popular with anglers and boaters alike. Impounded in 1979, Oconee is also one of the youngest reservoirs in the state.

Best way to fish: boat, shoreline.

Best time to fish: year-round.

Description: Lake Oconee sprawls across 18,791 acres with 374 miles of shoreline and impounds the Oconee River. "Oconee" is a Creek Indian word meaning "great waters."

Since it is one of the most popular lakes in Georgia, development is heavy on some parts of the lake. In contrast though, a good portion of the lake lies within the bounds of the Oconee National Forest, and is virtually undeveloped. When the lake basin was cleared, construction crews removed most of the timber. Some large stands escaped the saw, and others were topped out 10 feet below full pool. The lake bottom is mostly clay with plenty of rocky outcroppings. Very little aquatic vegetation grows in Oconee.

Oconee is a consistent year-round producer. Although the lake has produced largemouth bass weighing more than 12 pounds, Oconee is not famous for the numbers of trophy fish it produces. Like its sister lake to the south, Lake Sinclair, Oconee is a frequent stop on the Georgia bass tournament trail. Though the lake is popular with weekend tournament anglers, the best fishing is through the work week. Most generation and pumpback occurs Monday

Lake Oconee

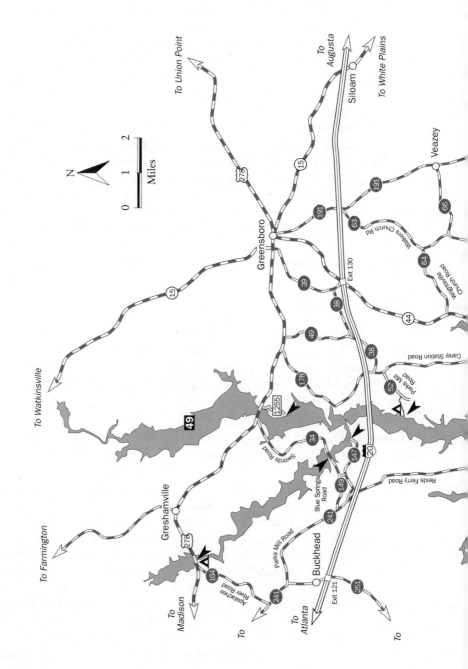

through Friday, and when the dam is silent on the weekends, there is no current and the bass become lethargic and finicky.

Oconee is the only large reservoir in Georgia where largemouth bass are managed under a slot limit. Largemouth bass must measure less than 11 inches or more than 14 inches to be legally harvested from the lake. The popularity of catch-and-release angling, while a boon to bass populations in other lakes, is not the best philosophy on Oconee. Largemouth bass grow slowly in Oconee, so the slot limit is in place to encourage selective harvest, or thinning, of the bass population so the remaining fish will have less competition for food and exhibit faster growth. Anglers can sometimes play a large and beneficial role in the management of a lake simply by harvesting some fish.

Oconee is a fine crappie lake with good numbers of fish 10 inches or better. White bass and hybrid striped bass are also good bets on Oconee, especially in the early spring. Both species are great fighters and are easily caught at certain times of the year.

Public access is good on Lake Oconee with several Georgia Power and USDA Forest Service access points available. The lake also has some private marinas. Because of its popularity and lakeshore development, avoid Lake Oconee in the summer if your goal is solitude and peace and quiet. The boat ramps and the lake are crowded on summer weekends, making fishing early in the morning or at night a good decision.

The fishing: Oconee is one of the best summer bass lakes in Georgia for two reasons: current and structure. Keeping cool in Georgia takes a lot of electricity, and when it is hot, you can bet the dams are generating. Since Oconee is a pump-back operation, not only is there current on hot afternoons and evenings, current flows the other direction during the night and early morning as the lake is filled back up. Bass feed best when the current is running, and it runs more at Oconee than nearly any other lake in the state. Fishing deep structure is a must if you want to consistently catch summer and winter reservoir bass.

Using a good map and a depth finder, look for offshore structure in the 15- to 18-foot range and fish the upstream side first to find the most aggressive fish. Deep-diving crankbaits, a jigging spoon, or a Carolina-rigged soft plastic are all good lures. Bridge crossings that constrict the lake are always good places to fish.

In fall and winter, look for deep structure and fish a jigging spoon. A backup pattern is to fish deep docks with a jig-and-pig or spinnerbait worked very slowly and thoroughly around the dock. Docks that end in 12 feet or more of water are best. Riprap bridges are always good, especially in the afternoon on sunny days when the rocks warm up and attract baitfish.

Crappie run a close second to largemouth bass in popularity at Lake Oconee; the best fishing is in the winter and early spring. When the water starts to warm in late February, try shooting docks. Use a slingshot cast to shoot a small jig up under docks and slowly work it back to the boat. In March and early April, the crappie are shallow spawning and the fishing is easy. Fish a jig or a minnow under a bobber around blowdowns and other shallow woody cover. A sandy bottom with plenty of woody cover is a good place to find crappie this time of year.

Anglers after white bass and hybrid striped bass should start in March, when fish begin to migrate up the river to spawn. White bass are usually ahead of the hybrids and can be caught on jigs and a curly-tail plastic grub. Look for hybrids in deep holes or bends. Bridge crossings are also good since the fish have to pass through the area to get upstream. Fish a live shad on the bottom or cast a bucktail jig.

Other species available in Lake Oconee are bream and catfish. Fish worms, crickets, or small spinners around shallow cover for bluegill and redear sunfish. Several species of catfish are found throughout the lake including bullheads and channel cats. Blue catfish can be taken from deep channels and holes and will hit live shad or cut bait.

GA~G grid: 28, F-4

General information: Lake Oconee is managed under standard Georgia creel and length limits with one exception. Largemouth bass harvested from the lake must measure less than 11 inches or greater than 14 inches. Anglers are encouraged to harvest fish less than 11 inches to thin the bass population to allow better growth of the remaining fish. All anglers fishing Lake Oconee must meet Georgia licensing requirements.

Food, lodging, and supplies are found around the lake in Greensboro, Madison, or Eatonton.

Nearest camping: Georgia Power's Lawrence Shoals, Old Salem, and Parks Ferry Recreation Areas all have campsites with utilities and also primitive camping.

Directions: West of Greensboro, Lake Oconee can be reached from Georgia Highways 16, 44, and 15 and U.S. Highways 129/441 and 278.

For more information: Contact the Wildlife Resources Division Fisheries Section Office in Social Circle. For information on the lake or Georgia Power recreation areas, contact the Lake Oconee/Sinclair Land Management Office. Contact the USDA Forest Service Oconee Ranger District for information on recreation opportunities in the Oconee National Forest.

West Central Georgia

Reservoir anglers have a lot to choose from in west central Georgia. The region contains several large reservoirs sprawling across many miles, and many medium-sized lakes just right for finding an out of the way place to spend a relaxing day fishing for bass, crappie, bream, and other species. West central Georgia also contains the upper reaches of the Flint River, which is the best place in the state to spend a hot summer day wading shoals in search of the hard-fighting shoal bass, also known as "Flint River smallmouth."

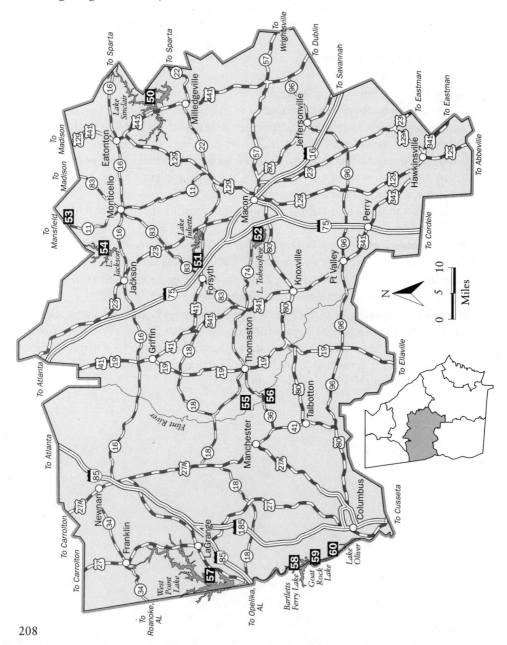

50 Lake Sinclair

Key species: largemouth bass, crappie.

Overview: With 15,330 acres of water and excellent access, Georgia Power's Lake Sinclair is a favorite with Georgia anglers.

Best way to fish: boat, shore.

Best time to fish: year-round.

Description: Lake Sinclair is a 15,330-acre hydropower impoundment at Furman Shoals on the Oconee River. The Georgia Power Company began building Sinclair Dam in 1929, but construction was suspended in 1930 as the Great Depression took hold. Work on the plant resumed in 1949, and the plant was placed into operation in 1953. Lake Sinclair is named for B.W. Sinclair, Georgia Power's superintendent of power plant construction and operations during the completion of the project.

Several factors make Lake Sinclair a somewhat unusual lake. The first is that Lake Oconee is just upstream of Lake Sinclair. Oconee's Wallace Dam separates the two lakes. Wallace Dam is operated as a pump-back operation, meaning that at times of peak electrical demand water is released through the dam into Lake Sinclair. At times of low demand, the Wallace Dam turbines are reversed and pump water from Lake Sinclair back up into Lake Oconee. The result is that the current can flow either way in Sinclair depending on the operation of Wallace Dam. The other factor is that Lake Sinclair serves double duty for Georgia Power. Not only does the water running through Sinclair Dam generate power, but the waters of the lake are used in the cooling towers of Plant Harlee Branch, a coal-fired generation plant in the Beaverdam Creek area of Lake Sinclair. The water returning to the lake from the plant is 5 to 10 degrees warmer than the lake itself, making the area around the hotwater discharge a great place for wintertime angling.

Lake Sinclair is known for consistency and numbers rather then huge fish. Although the lake record largemouth bass weighed more than 13 pounds, trophies are rare on Sinclair. You can expect lots of action from 1- to 2-pound bass. Crappie are also popular with Sinclair anglers, and provide better than average fishing with lots of harvestable-size fish available.

Lake Sinclair's shoreline is heavily developed with private homes, especially on the lower portions of the lake. Public access is excellent, however, with many public boat ramps and private marinas.

The fishing: The lake is a frequent stop on the Georgia tournament trails. Bass anglers have found Sinclair to be a good place for limits of keeper-sized fish with a few trophies thrown in. April is prime. Look for small pockets with plenty of grass, boat docks, and other cover. This combination draws shad in the spring, and the bass move right along with them. A chartreuse spinnerbait or Texas-rigged soft plastic is a good choice for fishing this shallow cover.

Autumn may be the best time to load up on numbers of bass. When the water starts to cool, expect the fish to move into the backs of creeks to feed on shad. A buzzbait followed by a spinnerbait or big plastic worm is a good combination. Early in the day, start in the backs of creeks and then work your way out toward

Lake Sinclair

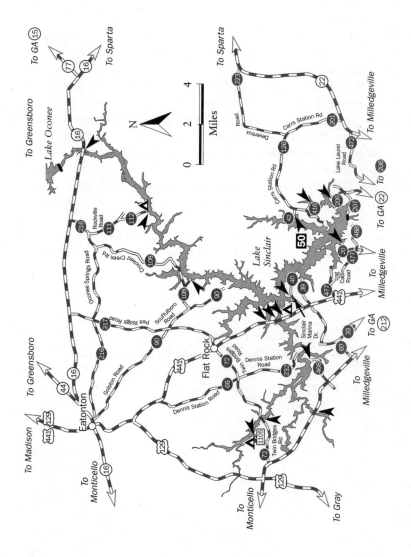

the main body of the lake as the day progresses hitting boat docks and brush.

An effective method for catching Sinclair crappie is shooting docks. Sling-shot a jig under the dock and let it sink, paying close attention for a strike on the fall. If nothing happens, slowly retrieve the jig back along the bottom with short twitches of the rod. A medium-heavy rod and light spinning reel works best for this technique.

Once spring arrives, crappie move shallow to spawn around wood, docks, brush piles, and blowdowns. If most of the fish you are catching are small males, the big females are probably still holding deep. Back off the shoreline and fish deeper for the bigger fish.

The Georgia DNR maintains several marked fish attractors on Lake Sinclair. These brush piles are marked by a white buoy and will hold at least some crappie and bass year-round. Since they are so easy to find, the attractors are heavily fished but seem to keep on producing despite the pressure.

GA~G grid: 35, B-9

General information: All anglers fishing Lake Sinclair must meet Georgia licensing requirements. The lake is managed under standard Georgia creel and length limits. Boaters upstream of Georgia Highway 16 are required to wear a life jacket at all times.

Some recreation areas on Lake Sinclair charge a daily use fee, be sure to check area rules and regulations upon arrival.

Food, lodging, and supplies are found on the north and south side of the lake in Eatonton and Milledgeville.

Nearest camping: The USDA Forest Service's Lake Sinclair campground is on the west side of the lake just off GA 212. The campground is open seasonally from mid-April to mid-December. There are 44 campsites with picnic tables and grills; sites do not have utilities. The area has drinking water and showers. An RV dump station is also available.

Several private-owned marinas on Lake Sinclair also offer camping opportunities.

Directions: Southeast of Eatonton, Lake Sinclair can be reached from U.S. Highways 129 and 441 and GA 16 and 22.

For more information: Contact the Wildlife Resources Division Fisheries Section Office in Fort Valley. Information about the lake and Georgia Power facilities is available from the Lake Oconee/Sinclair Land Management Office. Contact the USDA Forest Service Oconee Ranger District for information on Lake Sinclair Campground and other recreation opportunities in the Oconee National Forest.

51 Lake Juliette

Key species: largemouth bass, striped bass, redear sunfish.

Overview: Lake Juliette is a 3,600-acre Georgia Power Company reservoir that provides cooling water for Plant Scherer, a coal-fired power plant. The Georgia Wildlife Resources Division manages the lands around Lake Juliette as the Rum

Creek Wildlife Management Area. A development-free shoreline and use restrictions favoring the angler make Lake Juliette a favorite in central Georgia.

Best way to fish: boat.

Best time to fish: year-round.

Description: Lake Juliette was impounded in 1980 by damming Rum Creek. Since Rum Creek is a small stream, water must be pumped from the nearby Ocmulgee River to keep the lake full. With a small watershed and limited natural inflow of water, Lake Juliette is an infertile lake by central Georgia standards. The water is usually very clear and while the lake is known for producing some huge stripers and largemouth bass, the fish population is low compared to other nearby lakes.

Aquatic weeds thrive in Juliette and often can be found growing as deep as 30 feet. Plenty of timber was left in Lake Juliette at impoundment. On the lake's lower half, the timber was topped off 35 feet below full pool leaving a submerged forest with open water above it. However, the timber in the upper lake was not topped and careful navigation is required if you venture out of the channels. A 25 horsepower motor restriction eliminates all of the summertime pleasure boat traffic that can be annoying on other lakes. There is absolutely no shoreline development other than the power plant.

Although the clear waters make angling a challenge most of the time, Lake Juliette is a good choice early in the year when other lakes are muddied by heavy spring rains. Juliette's water rarely can be called anything worse than slightly stained.

A still, summer morning on Georgia Power's Lake Juliette.

Lake Juliette

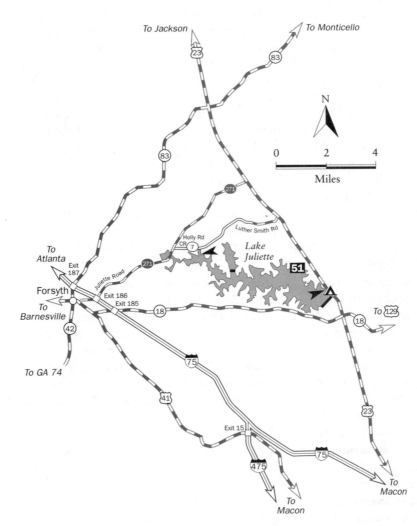

Although the lake is infertile, it does produce some trophy fish. The lake has a proven ability to produce largemouth bass weighing more than 15 pounds and striped bass to 37 pounds. Lake Juliette is not a numbers lake, but what it lacks in numbers it makes up for in size and quality of the experience.

The fishing: Lake Juliette's clear waters make it excellent topwater fishing for largemouth bass but the action is usually limited to the early morning, before the sun really begins to beam down on the clear waters of the lake. Once the sun is up, switch to deep-diving crankbaits and Carolina-rigged soft plastics. Even with the clear water, chartreuse is a favorite crankbait color. Good plastic worm colors are pumpkinseed and June bug. By summer, the weedbeds will be thriving and have distinct edges. Weedline irregularities, points, and humps are all good places to fish.

Winter fishing on Juliette can be good for monster bass. Strikes are not going to come quickly this time of year, but when they do come they are likely to be good ones. Troll a deep-diving crankbait or fish a live shad deep just over the top of the timber for both largemouth and stripers.

Striper fishing on Lake Juliette is very popular. Even in the heat of the summer, live shad fished 20 to 40 feet deep over points and humps will catch these hard-fighting fish. Winter is a good time for stripers too. Stripers can come up anytime on Juliette, so no matter what you're fishing for, it pays to have a heavy outfit rigged with a bucktail jig or large surface plug standing by to take advantage of unexpected opportunities.

Juliette's bluegill tend to run small. However, Lake Juliette is excellent fishing for redear sunfish which can provide nonstop action, although most will be average-sized fish around 6 inches. In the springtime, search shallow weedy coves for collections of spawning beds. Worms and small spinners are good choices for bait. Almost every cast will bring a strike once fish are found.

GA~G grid: 34, D-4

General information: The use of outboard motors greater than 25 horsepower is prohibited on Lake Juliette. Boats with larger motors are allowed on the lake, but are restricted to operating electric motors only. Boating access is limited to two Georgia Power launching facilities. Both facilities offer paved launch ramps, picnic tables, and latrines. Night-fishing is allowed.

The lake is managed under standard Georgia creel and length limits with the exception that there is no minimum length limit on largemouth bass harvested from the lake. All anglers must meet Georgia licensing requirements to fish the lake.

Food, lodging, and supplies are 10 miles away in Forsyth.

Nearest camping: Georgia Power's Dames Ferry Park on Lake Juliette offers full-service campsites with water, electricity, picnic tables, and grills. A comfort station with showers is available.

Directions: Lake Juliette can be reached off U.S. Highway 23 north of Macon or by taking Juliette Road (County Road 271) northeast from Forsyth.

For more information: Contact the Wildlife Resources Division Fisheries Section Office at the Charlie Elliott Wildlife Center or Georgia Power's Land Management Office at Lake Jackson.

52 Lake Tobesofkee

Key species: hybrid striped bass, largemouth bass, crappie, channel catfish.

Overview: Lake Tobesofkee, a 1,750-acre lake near Macon owned and operated by Bibb County, is the perfect place to take the whole family. With fishing, swimming, picnicking, boating, camping, and even a water park, everyone can find something they like to do.

Best way to fish: boat, shore.

Best time to fish: October through April.

Description: Lake Tobesofkee is a watershed impoundment on Tobesofkee Creek. The lake was a joint project between the Bibb County Commission and the U.S. Soil Conservation Service. Construction began in 1963, the dam was completed in 1967, and the lake and its facilities opened to the public in 1969. Since its inception, Lake Tobesofkee Recreation Area has been extremely popular with visitors. Creel surveys have shown that on a per-acre basis, Tobesofkee is one of the hardest-fished lakes in Georgia.

The lake is becoming heavily developed, especially on the lower end, and boat traffic is heavy during the summer months. The heavy pleasure-boat traffic makes Tobesofkee a better fall and winter lake for the angler. Fish can be caught year-round, but most anglers prefer to seek out less-crowded waters during the spring and summer months. During this time, limit your fishing to very early or late in the day, or better yet, at night.

Tobesofkee is not just for the boating angler. The lake has plenty of access for shoreline anglers, and when looked at on a per-acre basis, Tobesofkee may be one of the best big lakes in the state for shore anglers. The area on the upper end of the lake known as the "the fingers" or "the duck pond" is a series of canals left over from the lake's construction. This area is maintained for shore fishing and can be some of the best fishing on the lake.

Tobesofkee has the reputation of being a hard lake to fish. One reason is the heavy boat traffic. Another reason may be that consistent success on Lake Tobesofkee requires structure fishing. Not all anglers are comfortable with using contour maps and a depth finder to find and fish a small area well offshore; their confidence and comfort factor is much better when casting to visible shallow stumps and other shoreline cover, although it may not be nearly as productive.

A good way to break into offshore fishing on Tobesofkee is to fish the marked fish attractors. There are eight state-maintained fish attractors that consist of suspended Christmas and cedar trees. The attractors, marked by white buoys with orange markings, give the novice structure angler easy to find deep-water targets.

Tobesofkee is not known for the trophies it produces, but the fish are not small either. Hybrid striped bass will average 12 to 16 inches, with plenty of fish up to 20 inches available. Even larger hybrids are not out of the question. For hybrid striped bass fishing, Tobesofkee is arguably one of the best destinations in middle Georgia.

Largemouth bass of 1 to 2 pounds will make up most of the bass angler's creel, but fish weighing up to 4 pounds are common. Every year a few lucky anglers manage to catch Tobesofkee bass approaching the 8- to 10-pound range. Bass weighing more than 12 pounds have been caught from the lake, but it is an exceptionally rare event.

Crappie and catfish are also popular with lake regulars. Most channel catfish will weigh less than 2 pounds, with decent numbers of 5- to 10-pound fish available. Although not the best lake for big crappie, Tobesofkee has many harvestable-sized fish measuring 8 inches or better.

The fishing: Fish in Tobesofkee have seen it all, probably more than once. Find hidden offshore structure; fish finesse baits and concentrate hard on detecting strikes others miss; and fish all night when most anglers are home in bed. These are all strategies that require time and dedication, but will increase your fishing success on Tobesofkee.

Tobesofkee bass fishing kicks off in late February. With the coming of spring, the topwater bite arrives and anglers will experience the best shallow-water fishing of the year. Check out shallow points, boat docks, and any other shallow-to medium-depth cover or structure.

Fishing at night is productive, and some of the best places are the easiest to find. Find a creek channel, bend areas are especially good, and slowly drag a plastic worm or jig-and-pig along the bottom. Making a vertical presentation with a jigging spoon can also be productive.

As in most lakes, crappie are a three-season proposition. Slowly trolling a spread of light jigs over channel ledges and other deep structure is good in the fall and winter. In the early spring, the crappie are spawning and the fishing is easy. Cast a light jig or bobber-and-minnow setup around shallow woody cover and docks. Summer crappie are hard to catch since they usually are suspended in open water. Although heavily fished, the fish attractors are always good for a few strikes.

Catfish are a staple of shoreline anglers and can be caught nearly anywhere in the lake. Fish nightcrawlers, chicken livers, or commercially prepared stink bait on bottom. The best areas are those with nearby deep water. Catfish are highly nocturnal and anglers may want to consider waiting for sunset before venturing out, especially in the summer.

GA~G grid: 34, G-4

General information: The Bibb County Recreation Department charges an admission fee and boat launch fee. Be sure to check area rules and regulations upon arrival. All anglers must meet Georgia licensing requirements to fish the lake. The Lake Tobesofkee fishery is managed under standard Georgia statewide creel and length limits.

Food, lodging, and supplies are available within 3 miles along the Interstate 475 corridor.

Nearest camping: Public camping is available in the Lake Tobesofkee Recreation Area at both Arrowhead and Claystone Parks. Both campgrounds are open year-round, have a full-time staff, and offer sites with water and electricity, grills, and picnic tables. Sanitary dump stations, bath facilities, and coin-operated laundries are also available.

Directions: From I-475 in Macon, Lake Tobesofkee is easily reached by taking exits 3 or 5 to U.S. Highway 80 or Georgia Highway 74.

For more information: Contact the Tobesofkee Recreation Area or the Wildlife Resources Division Fisheries Section Office in Fort Valley.

Lake Tobesofkee

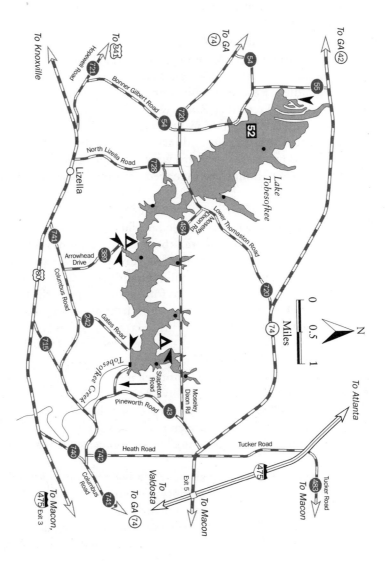

53 Marben Public Fishing Area

Key species: largemouth bass, bluegill, redear sunfish, channel catfish.

Overview: Marben Public Fishing Area is part of the Georgia Wildlife Resources Division's Charlie Elliott Wildlife Center. Visitors to the center can enjoy a variety of outdoor recreation and education opportunities.

Best way to fish: boat, shore.

Best time to fish: March through November.

Description: The Charlie Elliott Wildlife Center, named for the noted outdoor writer and former director of the Georgia Game and Fish Commission (now known as the Wildlife Resources Division), includes the Clybel Wildlife Management Area, the Preaching Rock Wildlife Education Center, and the Marben Public Fishing Area. The Center contains 6,400 acres of rolling Piedmont hills. There are 22 ponds and lakes totaling about 300 acres. Some lakes have developed facilities, some are walk-in, some are for group fishing by reservation, and some ponds are managed to provide the best fishing for certain species.

The fishing: The fishing at Charlie Elliott varies with each lake. Refer to the sidebar to get an idea of which may be the best lake for you.

Spinnerbaits, plastic worms, and crankbaits are all good bass lures. Lipless rattling crankbaits like a Rat-L-Trap are local favorites because they can be retrieved at a variety of depths from burning the surface to slowly bumping the bottom. Spring and fall are the best months for bass fishing. For the best chance at a trophy bass, anglers should concentrate on fishing the smaller ponds on sunny days in late winter or very early spring. Marben bass have filled as many as two of the top five slots in Georgia's all-time bass records. One fish exceeded 17 pounds and the other weighed an incredible 18 pounds plus.

For bluegill and other sunfish, the summer months are most productive. May through September, anglers fishing live bait like worms or crickets (live fish are not allowed as bait) around shallow cover should have no problem catching a mess of fish. Anglers who prefer artificials should find small spinners effective. Fly anglers should try a popping bug or sponge spider early or late in the day in the shallows.

Anglers can catch channel catfish nearly anywhere on anything. These opportunistic feeders will eat a variety of baits, both live and dead. Nightcrawlers and chicken livers are two favorites.

If possible, fish during the week. Weekends are the most crowded and fishing always seems better during the week on heavily fished waters. Also, take advantage of the walk-in ponds. For many anglers, if it takes more than a few steps to get to the water's edge, then they are not interested in fishing. Even on ponds with vehicle access, walk around to the side of the pond opposite of the parking area, and you may find the fish much more willing to strike.

Anglers should keep in mind not all lakes have the same species. Use the information provided here and on the information boards to find the best lake for you.

GA~G grid: 27, F-9

Marben Public Fishing Area

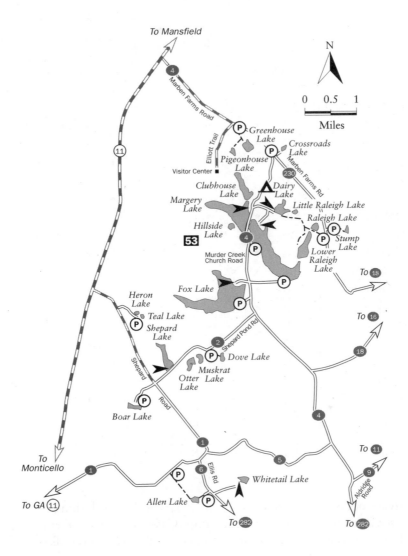

General information: Marben Public Fishing Area is open year-round from sunrise to sunset. Anglers 16 years of age and older must have a valid fishing license and Wildlife Management Area stamp. Senior Lifetime, Honorary, Sportsman's, and 1-Day license holders do not need the WMA stamp.

With some exceptions posted on-site, creel and length limits in the area follow Georgia Public Fishing Area regulations. Consult the *Georgia Sport Fishing Regulations* pamphlet for more information.

Marben Public Fishing Area at a Glance

	Size (acres)	Bass	Bream	Catfish	Crapple	Boat Ramp	Restrooms	Vehicle Access	Walk-in Only	Pier	Picnic Area	Group Fishing Only	Universally Accessible
Allen	5.0	•	•						•		•		
Bennett	69.0	•	•	•	•	•		•		•	•		
Boar	5.0	•	•	•			•	•			•	•	•
Clubhouse	8.3	•	•	•				•		•		•	•
Crossroads	2.0	•	•						•		•		
Dairy	7.2	•	•	•		•		•		•	•		
Dove	2.0			•					•		•	•	•
Fox	95.0	•	•			•	•	•		•	•		•
Greenhouse	5.8	•	•	•					•		•		
Heron	1.0		•					•				•	
Hillside	2.4	•	•	•					•		•		
Little Raleigh	2.0	•	•						•				
Lower Raleigh	15.0	•	•		•				•	•			
Margery	41.2	•	•	•		•	•	•		•	•		•
Muskrat	1.0		•						•			•	
Otter	3.0								•				
Pigeonhouse	1.0		•					•		•	•	•	
Shepherd	18.0	•	•	•		•	•	•		•	•		•
Stump	3.1	•	•						•				
Teal	1.0			•					•			•	
Upper Raleigh	3.8	•	•						•				
Whitetail	4.0	•	•			•		•		•	•		

Private boats are allowed on all the Marben Public Fishing Area lakes. However, not all lakes have a boat ramp. Gasoline motors operated at idle speed are allowed on lakes posted as open to such. Boats on all other lakes must use electric motors only.

Visitors are requested to sign in at the information boards at the start of each visit. While doing so, be sure to check the listing of open and closed ponds and any special regulations in effect. Some ponds are occasionally closed for improvements, and changing fish populations sometimes dictate a change in regulations.

Food, lodging, and supplies are available 15 miles away in Covington and along the Interstate 20 corridor.

Nearest camping: Primitive camping is allowed in the area. The nearest public developed campground is Hard Labor Creek State Park (see Site 44) about 20 miles north of the area. Hard Labor Creek State Park offers 51 combination tent and trailer sites with water and electric hookups, picnic tables, and grills. Comfort stations provide hot showers and flush toilets. The park has 20 cottages for rent.

Directions: From I-20, east of Covington, take exit 98 and travel south 9.4 miles on Georgia Highway 11 to Marben Farm Road on the left. Follow this road into the area.

For more information: Contact the Charlie Elliott Wildlife Center.

54 Lake Jackson

Key species: largemouth bass, redear sunfish, crappie, channel catfish, hybrid striped bass.

Overview: Created in 1911 with the closing of Lloyd Shoals Dam on the Ocmulgee River, 4,750-acre Lake Jackson is the oldest major reservoir in Georgia. The lake is very fertile, and up through the 1970s, Lake Jackson was one of the hardest-fished reservoirs in Georgia.

Best way to fish: boat.

Best time to fish: year-round.

Description: Lake Jackson was constructed by the Central Georgia Power Company. After a 1928 consolidation of power companies, the lake came under the auspices of today's Georgia Power Company. The lake is operated as a hydropower reservoir and is part of Georgia Power's Central Georgia Hydro Group.

The waters of the Yellow, Alcovy, and South rivers join in the lake. Below Lake Jackson's Lloyd Shoals Dam, the waters leaving the lake become the Ocmulgee River. Since flood control is not one of Lake Jackson's primary duties, the lake's water level usually varies only 3 to 4 feet throughout the year. The lowest water is from December to March.

Since Jackson is an old reservoir, the bottom is heavily silted and little of the original cover remains. Anglers and shoreline residents have rectified this situation by placing numerous brush piles in the lake. In addition, the Georgia Wildlife Resources Division maintains 15 fish attractors. The attractors are marked by a white buoy and are easy to find.

Summertime boat traffic on Jackson is heavy. Access to the lake is good with several public boat ramps. During more extreme drawdowns approaching 8 feet, only a few ramps remain useable.

Lake Jackson is known for producing big bass. Largemouth bass exceeding 14 pounds have come from the lake, and Jackson is famous for the number of bass weighing more than 5 pounds it gives up every year. Jackson is one of the better bream lakes in central Georgia and specimens that weigh 1 pound or more are not uncommon. Other popular species are catfish, crappie, and hybrid striped bass.

The fishing: The best bass fishing on Jackson is from October through February. The sun is the key factor because although the water may be cold, sunny conditions will pull baitfish onto the shallow points and the bass will follow.

Lake Jackson

A medium-diving crankbait cast to the shore and slowly worked back to the boat will draw strikes. If the water is clear, go with a natural or chrome pattern. In dirty water, try something with a lot of chartreuse and brown or black for contrast. Depths of 8 feet or less are the best place to find shallow wintertime bass.

During springtime, look for bass to be spawning shallow or near deeper staging areas. Any lure is likely to work during this time if it is fished in the right place. Docks and shallow brush are two good areas to try, along with shallow flats and pockets.

Once warm weather sets in for good, switch over to night-fishing to avoid the boat traffic. For Lake Jackson's big bream, the best fishing is from April through June when the heaviest spawning occurs. Shellcrackers prefer a worm to a cricket, and are suckers for a small Beetle Spin bounced along the bottom.

Catfish are popular with Jackson anglers and several different species of these whiskered fish are available. Several bullhead species, white catfish, and channel catfish will all show up in the creel. A juicy nightcrawler is a hard bait for catfish to resist.

Crappie anglers should have no problem catching a mess of slabs to take home for the skillet. Winter is the best time to fish and trolling a spread of light jigs is the way to go.

Hybrid striped bass are stocked in Lake Jackson and have a dedicated following of anglers. Although Jackson is not known for producing big hybrids, the fish are abundant and provide exciting fishing.

GA~G grid: 27, G-8

General information: Lake Jackson is managed under standard Georgia creel and length limits. All anglers fishing the lake must meet Georgia licensing requirements.

Food, lodging, and supplies are found around the lake in Jackson, Monticello, or Covington.

Nearest camping: Camping is available at several private marinas on Lake Jackson. The nearest public campground is Indian Springs State Park, about 12 miles from the lake. The 538-acre park has eight campsites with utilities and ten cottages for rent.

Directions: South of Covington, Lake Jackson can be reached from Georgia Highways 36, 212, or 16.

For more information: Contact the Wildlife Resources Division Fisheries Section Office at the Charlie Elliott Wildlife Center or the Georgia Power's Lake Jackson Land Management Office. For camping information, contact the Park Superintendent's Office at Indian Springs State Park.

55 Upper Flint River

Key species: shoal bass, redbreast sunfish, flathead catfish, channel catfish.

Overview: This section of Flint River contains some of the best shoals the river has to offer. Shoal bass and redbreast sunfish are abundant: floating and wading the river for them is a great way to spend a hot summer day.

Best way to fish: canoe, wade.

Best time to fish: May through October.

Description: The Flint River arises on the grounds of Atlanta's Hartsfield International Airport and flows south through western Georgia and Lakes Blackshear and Chehaw before joining with the Chattahoochee River to form the Apalachicola River below Lake Seminole. Shoal bass, sometimes known as "Flint River smallmouths," are found throughout the river. Although the Flint is not the only river in Georgia where shoalies are found, it is certainly the most fabled flow they inhabit.

The northern half of the river is rife with shallow rocky shoals ideal for the wading angler. Once it flows over the Fall Line near U.S. Highway 80, the river's character changes. The current slows, the river channel deepens, and the shoals end. Below the Fall Line, shoal bass are still present in good numbers but begin to more equally share the river with largemouth bass.

With a few notable exceptions, the banks of the Flint are privately owned. Anglers are restricted to accessing the river at a few public boat ramps, road crossings, Sprewell Bluff State Park, and Big Lazer Creek Wildlife Management Area. Fortunately, the Sprewell Bluff and Big Lazer Creek stretches both have some good shoals, and offer the best combination of easy access and good fishing. Since it is easily reached, the Sprewell Bluff stretch is the most heavily used by anglers, paddlers, and swimmers.

Floating, wading, or a combination of both is the best way to approach fishing the Flint. Some stretches can be fished from a canoe, but other shoals will require beaching the canoe and wading. See the sidebar for information on what to expect when floating each section of the river.

Shoal bass and redbreast sunfish are the most popular species on this stretch of the Flint River. Channel and flathead catfish are also popular, and largemouth bass and other sunfish species will show up in the creel.

The Georgia record shoal bass weighing 8 pounds, 3 ounces, came from the Flint River at Big Lazer Creek. This fish also held the world record until a fish from Florida's Apalachicola River bested it.

The fishing: As their name suggests, shoal bass love current. The best fishing is in areas where the water is fast and tumbles over drops and boulders. Early and late in the day, a topwater bait like a Rapala is hard to beat. Especially at low flows, once the sun is on the water, the fish will snuggle down into the shelter of the rocks and must be coaxed out. Small crayfish-imitating crankbaits and Texas-rigged soft plastics worked on bottom are excellent choices. Spinnerbaits are also a good all-around choice. Usually, the bigger the bait, the fewer the strikes, but the better the fish. Small shoalies are abundant in the river, and sometimes it seems like the big fish never have a chance to strike because the little ones get there first.

If wading with a fly rod is your passion, you've found the right place. A #4 or #6 white popper is a good choice, especially at low light levels. Later in the day, a big nymph or streamer will also draw strikes from shoal bass. If you do not mind catching redbreast sunfish along with your shoal bass, try a #12 or

225

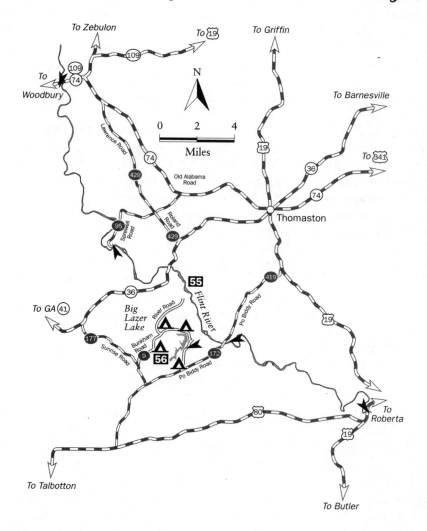

#14 dry fly (any visible pattern) with a #8 or #10 black Wooly Worm on a 24-inch dropper. Hooking up a double with this rig is a distinct possibility.

For redbreast sunfish, fish the side-current areas near cover and the shoals. Redbreasts will readily strike artificials. A small spinner or popping bug is a good choice. For natural bait, go with a cricket or worm fished under a small float.

GA~G grid: 33

General information: With the few exceptions mentioned above, the banks of the Flint River are privately owned. If you are out of the river channel, you are on private land and must have permission to be there to avoid trespassing. All anglers fishing the Flint River must meet Georgia licensing requirements. The Flint River conforms to standard Georgia creel and length limits with one

An angler admires a small blue catfish.

Section	Length of Float	Notes
GA 18 to Sprewell Bluff State Park	14 miles	Long for a day trip. Heavily fished. Best shoal near end of trip about 3 miles upstream of Sprewell Bluff.
Sprewell Bluff State Park to GA 36	5.5 miles	Heaviest-used section of Flint River. Some good shoals and small islands.
GA 36 to Po Biddy Road	6 miles	Full of shoals. At high flows, even experienced paddlers should be careful. Excellent fishing. Early take-out possible at Big Lazer Creek Wildlife Management Area.
Po Biddy Road to US 80	14 miles	Long stretch. Numerous shoals downstream of Po Biddy Bridge. Least-fished section; best chance for a trophy shoal bass. Last half of trip slow-moving water without any shoals. A motorized boat can be used with care to reach the shoals by motoring upstream from US 80.

exception. All shoal bass taken from the Flint River and its tributaries must be a minimum of 12 inches in length.

Food, lodging, and supplies can be found in Thomaston, Manchester, or Talbotton.

Nearest camping: Because it's a new park, at the time of this writing camping is not available at Sprewell Bluff State Park. Primitive camping is available at Big Lazer Creek Public Fishing Area. The nearest public developed campground is about 25 miles away at F. D. Roosevelt State Park. This 10,000-acre park has 140 campsites and 21 cottages for rent.

Directions: To reach Sprewell Bluff State Park, from the intersection of Georgia Highway 74 and U.S. Highway 19 in Thomaston, travel west 5.7 miles on GA 74 to Old Alabama Road on the left. Follow this paved road 5.3 miles to the park entrance. Refer to the map for other access points.

For more information: Contact the Wildlife Resources Division Fisheries Section Office in Manchester. For other information, contact the Park Superintendent's Office at F. D. Roosevelt or Sprewell Bluff State Parks. For river information and services offered, contact the Flint River Outdoor Center.

56 Big Lazer Creek Public Fishing Area

See map on page 226

Key species: bluegill, redear sunfish, largemouth bass, channel catfish.

Overview: This 195-acre public fishing lake is on Big Lazer Creek Wildlife Management Area near the Flint River in Talbot County.

Best way to fish: shore, boat.

Best time to fish: March through October.

Description: Big Lazer Creek Public Fishing Area is on a 5,984-acre state Wildlife Management Area of the same name. The lake is 195 acres and was first opened to fishing in 1989. The lake is intensively managed to provide good fishing for bream, largemouth bass, and channel catfish.

Anglers will find plenty of structure in the lake. About 15 acres of timber were left during construction. You'll find the timber around the old creek channel and a small island. In addition, the lake is full of submerged cover. Fish attractors have been constructed and placed near the fishing pier. The upper end of the lake is shallow, averaging around 5 feet in depth. Near the dam, depths are more than 30 feet.

The fishing: Big Lazer Creek is perhaps best known for its bream fishing. Good bets for bream are near any woody structure or weeds. Crickets and worms fished below a float on ultralight tackle are good choices. If artificials are preferred, small plastic grubs and spinners can also be good. When the bream are concentrated in spawning colonies, flycasting a small popping bug over the spawning beds is very productive and great fun.

Channel catfish are popular with anglers at Big Lazer Creek Public Fishing Area. They can be caught from nearly anywhere in the lake, but flats adjacent to the old creek channel should top the list of places to try. Chicken livers, nightcrawlers, and "stink bait" fished on bottom are all good choices.

Largemouth bass are plentiful in the lake. Although a few trophies are caught every year, Big Lazer Creek is not known for producing truly huge bass. Good areas to try for bass are along the edge of the standing timber around the island and the edges of the creek channel. A 6-inch plastic worm fished on the bottom around submerged cover is hard to beat for drawing strikes.

GA~G grid: 33, H-7 (not shown in GA~G)

General information: Facilities at Big Lazer Creek Public Fishing Area include a paved double-lane launching ramp with plenty of parking, picnic tables, universally accessible restrooms, and a universally accessible fishing pier. The area is open year-round from sunrise to sunset. Standard Georgia Public Fishing Area regulations apply. A Wildlife Management Area stamp is required to fish on the area. See the *Georgia Sport Fishing Regulations* pamphlet for more information. The lake has no outboard motor horsepower restriction, but motors more than 10 horsepower must be operated at idle speed only. To prevent the introduction of unwanted species, anglers are restricted from using live fish as bait in the lake.

Big Lazer Creek Public Fishing Area is on the same tract of land that provides some of the best public access to the Flint River (Site 55). A trip to this area will provide options for both still-water and river fishing.

Food, lodging, and supplies are about 12 miles away in Talbotton.

Nearest camping: Primitive camping is allowed in designated areas at Big Lazer Creek Public Fishing Area. The nearest developed campsites are at F. D. Roosevelt State Park, about 35 miles west of the area.

Directions: From Talbotton travel east on U.S. Highway 80 for 4 miles to Po

Biddy Road (County Road 172). Turn left and travel 6.3 miles on Po Biddy Road to Bunkham Road (CR 8) on the left. Turn left onto Bunkham Road, go 1.5 miles and then turn left into the area at the sign.

For more information: Contact the Wildlife Resources Division Fisheries Section Office in Manchester. For information on camping at F. D. Roosevelt State Park, contact the Park Superintendent's Office.

57 West Point Lake

Key species: largemouth bass, spotted bass, hybrid striped bass, crappie, channel catfish.

Overview: West Point Lake is a 25,900-acre USACE reservoir that extends 35 miles along the Chattahoochee River southwest of Atlanta. The lake spans the Georgia-Alabama border, and is a popular destination with anglers of both states.

Best way to fish: boat, shore.

Best time to fish: year-round.

Description: Impounded in 1974, West Point Lake is one of the few Georgia reservoirs managed under a special regulation for largemouth bass. The minimum length limit is 16 inches. Although many think the limit is in place to produce a trophy bass fishery, the main reason for its implementation was to maintain a higher predator population of sufficient size to keep the gizzard shad population in check.

There are numerous launch sites and shoreline fishing areas on West Point Lake. About 25 percent of the lakeshore is open to development, but the remainder is in mixed pine and hardwood forest. The lake also provides flood control and hydropower. During the critical flood season of December through April, the lake is drawn down about 10 feet to provide storage for the heavy winter and spring rains. Hydropower plays a role in the fishing at West Point. When water is released through the dam during generation, it creates a current in the lake and the fish become more active. Plenty of fish can still be caught when the turbines are silent, but during generation is the best time to fish. Most generation takes place Monday through Friday when demand for electricity is high.

West Point Lake receives heavy fishing pressure because of its excellent reputation, good access, and proximity to metro Atlanta. Summertime boat traffic on the lake is high, but does not approach that of Lake Allatoona and Lake Lanier north of Atlanta. The lake is filled with cover and good structure including submerged ponds and roadbeds. The agencies responsible for managing the lake have taken steps to add even more cover by planting cypress, maiden cane, and banker's willow at several locations throughout the reservoir.

West Point produces above-average largemouth bass, and some real lunkers are possible. The lake regularly gives up 6- to 8-pound bass, and 10-pound largemouths are not uncommon. The lake record largemouth bass weighed more than 14 pounds. Spotted bass are found in the lake but comprise only about a fourth of the black bass population; largemouth bass make up the rest, although a few shoal bass are possible.

Access is excellent on West Point Lake. The USACE alone maintains almost 30 access points around the lake, not to mention state, county, and private facilities.

The fishing: Once winter begins to give way to spring, the best bass fishing is found up the creek arms. Buck brush fills the backs of many small coves on West Point. Fishing this cover with a buzzbait early in the day then switching to a Texas-rigged plastic lizard or a jig once the sun gets strong is a good technique during and after the spawn.

West Point is a great summer bass lake. The key is being able to find and fish offshore structure that drops from 10 feet down to 20 feet or more. Some anglers prefer to down-line live shad during this time.

Although daylight fishing is still good on West Point even in the summer, the usual night-fishing pattern of finding lighted boat docks to find the bass is effective for anglers wanting to avoid the heat and boat traffic of a Georgia summer afternoon.

In winter, look for bass on deep structure. Cold water concentrates the fish making them harder to find than in summer, but once you do find them, vertically jigging a spoon or slowly fishing a jig-and-pig combo can result in the best catches of the year.

White bass are abundant in West Point and their behavior pretty much mirrors that of hybrid striped bass, which are stocked heavily in this lake. Expect the fish to run up the tributaries in early spring to spawn, and spend the rest of the year in the open water of the main lake. White bass do not grow as large as hybrids, so downsize your baits to target this species. When they are on their spawning run up the river, white bass are suckers for a plastic shad body threaded on a small lead-head jig. Cast this rig to sandy banks and bars, and you are almost guaranteed to catch fish.

West Point is an excellent crappie lake, and they can be caught year-round just about any way you want to do it.

Although overlooked by most anglers, West Point is probably one of the best channel catfish lakes in Georgia. To catch really big fish, use live shad or cut bait fished on the bottom in deep channels.

GA~G grid: 24, 32

General information: West Point Lake spans the Georgia-Alabama border. The two states have worked out a reciprocal agreement allowing an angler holding a valid fishing license from either state to fish the waters of the lake. The waters covered by this agreement do not include other streams or tributaries which flow into the Chattahoochee River or its impoundments. The portion of the lake upstream of the Georgia Highway 109 bridge on the Chattahoochee River arm is not included in the reciprocal agreement; all anglers fishing this part of the lake must possess a Georgia license. Georgia creel and possession

West Point Lake

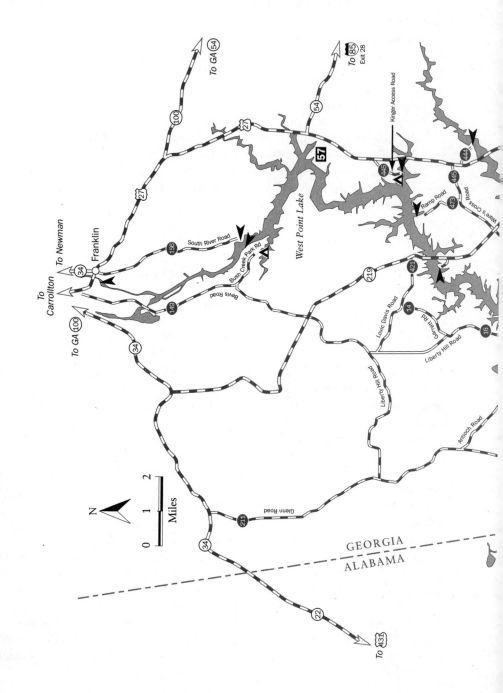

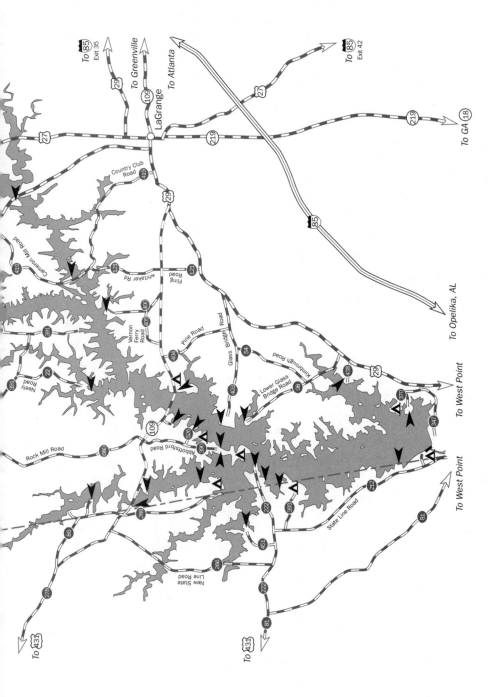

limits apply to the waters covered by the agreement. Largemouth bass must be a minimum of 16 inches to harvest from any part of the lake. All other Georgia fishing laws and regulations apply to Georgia waters.

Nearest camping: Camping opportunities are good at West Point Lake with a selection of private and public campgrounds found around the lake.

Directions: North of West Point, West Point Lake can be reached from U.S. Highways 27 and 29 and GA 109 and GA 219.

For more information: Contact the Wildlife Resources Division Fisheries Section Office in Fort Valley. Information about the lake and USACE facilities is available from the West Point Project Management Office.

58 Bartletts Ferry Lake (Lake Harding)

Key species: largemouth bass, spotted bass, white bass, striped bass, crappie, channel catfish.

Overview: A 5,850-acre hydropower reservoir on the Chattahoochee River owned and operated by Georgia Power Company, Bartletts Ferry offers good angling for a several different species. The lake is especially known for good night-fishing for bass in the summer.

Best way to fish: boat, shore.

Best time to fish: year-round.

Description: Originally constructed by the Columbus Electric and Power Company, the generating plant at Bartletts Ferry began producing electricity in 1926. Georgia Power acquired the lake and generating plant in 1930 and has operated it ever since. Bartletts Ferry is also known as Lake Harding, named for an executive who worked for the original owners of the lake. Most Georgians call the lake Bartletts Ferry, a mispronunciation of a man named Bartley who once ran a ferry across the Chattahoochee in the area where the lake now stands.

Bartletts Ferry is a relatively deep and rocky lake and basically follows the path of the river channel. Houses line the lakeshore and docks and piers provide plenty of cover. Any cover left at impoundment has long since rotted away, making the docks and other shoreline cover the best thing going for both the fish and the angler.

Bartletts Ferry is known more for the good average size of its bass than for the chances of catching a real lunker. Both largemouth and spotted bass are found in the reservoir, with largemouth being the most abundant. Although good numbers of 3- to 5-pound largemouths are available, anything approaching 10 pounds is a real trophy. Catching a shoal bass far up the lake's tributaries is possible, but shoalies are not a significant part of the fishery.

Being a relatively small lake with a power-generating dam on either end, the water level in Bartletts Ferry can fluctuate up or down as much as 3 feet in short order. When upstream West Point Lake is releasing water but Bartletts Ferry is not, the lake comes up. Reverse the situation and exactly the opposite happens; the water goes down. When both dams are running, the water level will stay fairly constant but there will be a strong current. A change in the water level usually changes the fishing. What was a solid pattern will evaporate in minutes. Simply shifting a little bit deeper or shallower will usually put you right back on fish though.

Bartletts Ferry receives heavy fishing pressure due to the proximity of Columbus and Atlanta. However, the lake has always been a consistent producer. In the summer, boat traffic is extremely heavy, making night-fishing the best way to go.

Access to the lake is good with several paved boat ramps and recreation areas.

The fishing: Spotted bass provide nearly year-round action at Bartletts Ferry. During the winter, search for drop-offs and breaklines on main-lake or secondary points. Vertically jig a spoon over structure to catch fish. As the water begins to warm, the fish begin a slow migration to shallow water. As the spawn approaches, switch over to faster-moving baits like crankbaits and spinnerbaits and fish the coves.

Once the weather begins to cool and the boat traffic falls off, fishing secondary points with crankbaits and spinnerbaits is a good way to take advantage of bass feeding heavily before winter. Bass really key in on shad this time of year, and the crankbait is a good way to quickly cover ground looking for feeding fish.

Striped bass are doing well in Bartletts Ferry and are popular. The best way to hook up with a striper is to fish live shad near the dam in the winter or far upstream in the spring. Live shad and bucktail jigs are good choices. After the fish have returned to the main lake, use a depth finder to search points, channels, and humps for schools of shad with stripers hanging below them. Down-line a shad or fish a jigging spoon at the same depth the stripers are holding.

The best fishing for white bass is upriver in the early spring as the fish make their annual spawning migration. A jig with a curly-tail grub or shad body is a good lure. Later in the summer, look for white bass to be surfacing early and late in the day over open water. Fish the jumps with lures that can be cast a long distance to avoid approaching the school too closely.

Bartletts Ferry is a good crappie lake known for numbers of big fish. The best times to catch them are during the winter and spring. From February through April, the marked fish attractors are good places to try.

GA~G grid: 40, A-1

General information: Bartletts Ferry Lake forms part of the Georgia-Alabama border. The two states have worked out a reciprocal agreement allowing an angler holding a valid fishing license from either state to fish the waters of the lake. The waters covered by this agreement do not include other streams or tributaries which flow into the Chattahoochee River or its impoundments. Standard Georgia statewide creel and possession limits apply to the waters covered by the agreement. Largemouth bass possessed in Georgia waters must be 12 inches no matter where they were caught, and all other Georgia fishing laws and regulations apply to Georgia waters.

Bartletts Ferry Lake (Lake Harding)
Goat Rock Lake • Lake Oliver

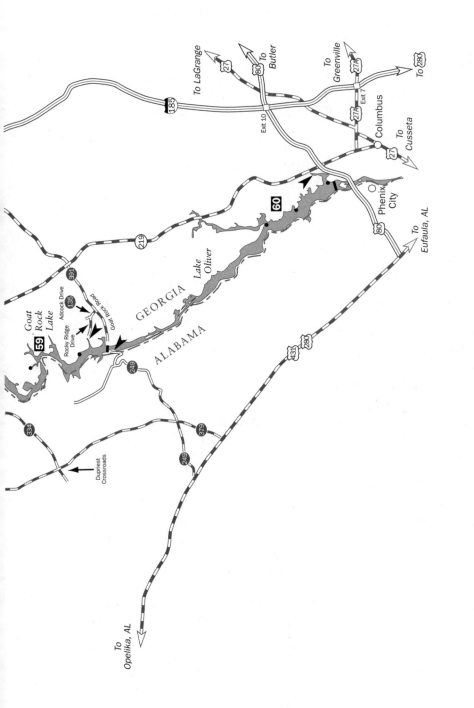

Boaters should have no problem navigating the lake other than far upriver where shoals and sandbars are common. Some Georgia Power Recreation Areas charge a daily parking fee. Be sure to check area rules and regulations upon arrival.

Food, lodging, and supplies are available 20 miles away in Columbus.

Nearest camping: Georgia Power's Blanton Creek Park is on the east side of Bartletts Ferry Lake. The campground includes full-service sites with water and electricity, picnic tables, and grills. Comfort stations with hot showers and flush toilets are also available. Campsite reservations must be made at least 10 days in advance and require a two-night stay. The campground is open seasonally from the first Friday in April through Labor Day.

Directions: Northwest of Columbus, Bartletts Ferry access points can be reached off Georgia Highway 103 and Lee County (Alabama) Road 379.

For more information: Contact the Wildlife Resources Division Fisheries Section Office in Manchester. Contact Georgia Power for information on Blanton Creek Park and generation schedules.

59 Goat Rock Lake

See map on page 236

Key species: largemouth bass, redear sunfish, bluegill, hybrid striped bass, channel catfish.

Overview: With only 940 acres, Goat Rock Lake is one of the smallest lakes on the Chattahoochee River and is virtually unknown to all but local anglers.

Best way to fish: boat.

Best time to fish: March through November.

Description: Situated between Lakes Bartletts Ferry and Oliver, Goat Rock Lake is very riverine in nature. The lake is basically the Chattahoochee River channel with a few flooded backwaters. Goat Rock is one of the oldest hydropower lakes in Georgia. The lake and powerhouse were constructed in 1912 by the Columbus Electric and Power Company and acquired by Georgia Power in 1930. The story behind the lake's unique name is that a local family once saw a group of goats jumping onto a rock in the river.

Unlike its upstream and downstream neighbors, Goat Rock sees little public use. Access on the lake is very limited, and that together with its small size, out-of-the-way location and mostly undeveloped shoreline, make the lake a peaceful summer retreat for anglers. On the Georgia side, access is limited to the privately owned Goat Rock Marina on the lower end of the lake. On the Alabama side, there is a public ramp at Georgia Power's Sandy Point Recreation Area on the upper end of the lake just downstream of Bartletts Ferry Dam.

The activity of Bartletts Ferry Dam on the upper end of the lake significantly affects the water level in the lake. Water level fluctuations of 3 to 4 feet are common. Due to the releases from Bartletts Ferry Dam, and the narrow nature of the lake that does not allow for much warming, springtime water temperatures in Goat Rock will often lag a few weeks behind other nearby waters. Since the lake is so old, very little cover remains on the bottom. Blowdowns along the banks are the most common woody cover. To help anglers find fish, the Georgia Wildlife Resources Division maintains several fish attractors, which are marked with white buoys.

Although not really known as a trophy lake, Goat Rock offers good angling for quality-sized fish in an uncrowded setting. The lack of fishing and boating pressure gives the fish more time to grow before being caught and also results in less wary fish. Largemouth bass weighing more than 14 pounds have been caught from the lake and hybrid striped bass weighing more than 20 pounds are known to swim in its waters.

If Goat Rock Lake is renowned for anything, it is bream and catfish angling. Goat Rock is arguably the best catfish reservoir in Georgia. Channel catfish up to 10 pounds are common, with the average fish weighing 2 to 3 pounds. White catfish are also common, and the average fish will weigh about a pound.

The fishing: Three species of black bass are found in Goat Rock Lake: largemouth, spotted, and shoal bass. The largemouths support most of the fishery, with spots coming in second. A few shoal bass are available below Bartletts Ferry Dam, or up Mulberry Creek, a major tributary about halfway up the lake on the Georgia side.

The best way to target largemouths is to fish shallow water in the spring. Spotted bass tend to hold a little deeper. A spinnerbait or jig-and-pig combo worked around shallow cover in the coves and pockets is a good choice early in the year.

From after the spawn until the dog days of summer, twitch Rapalas or small topwater chuggers around blowdown trees and other shallow cover. Do not overlook rocky points.

Once summer sets in, focus on deeper water for bass. Channel ledges are always good summer spots, especially if stumps or other cover are present. Deep-diving crankbaits or Carolina-rigged soft plastics cover a lot of water, and are good choices for fishing ledges. In autumn, search the creek arms and coves for bass feeding on shad. Spinnerbaits and crankbaits are good choices, with blue and chartreuse patterns the local favorites.

Hybrid striped bass and white bass fishing is best in early spring and throughout the summer. In early spring, concentrate on the headwaters of the lake just below Bartletts Ferry Dam. A lead-head jig with a soft-plastic curly-tail grub or shad body is the best all-around lure. Keep a sharp eye out for jumps of surfacing bait and hybrids, and make long casts into the frenzy with a heavy spoon or jig. Fishing a jump is usually short-lived, but it is fast while it lasts.

Catching Goat Rock's abundant catfish is simply a matter of soaking bait on the bottom until a fish decides to bite. The best places to try are transition areas from deep water to shallow flats. Especially at night, catfish will move up onto shallow flats to feed. Chicken livers, a gob of worms, or prepared catfish baits are all good choices.

General information: Goat Rock Lake forms part of the Georgia-Alabama border. The two states have worked out a reciprocal agreement allowing an angler holding a valid fishing license from either state to ply the waters of the lake. The waters covered by this agreement do not include other streams or tributaries which flow into the Chattahoochee River or its impoundments. Standard Georgia statewide creel and possession limits apply to the waters covered by the agreement. Largemouth bass possessed in Georgia waters must be 12 inches no matter where they were caught, and all other Georgia fishing laws and regulations apply to Georgia waters.

Care should be taken when navigating the lake. Shallow areas are not marked, and running up on a shoal or stump field is a sure way to turn a good fishing trip sour.

Some Georgia Power Recreation Areas charge a daily parking fee. Be sure to check area rules and regulations upon arrival.

A launch fee is charged at Goat Rock Marina. An information sign at the entrance to the marina lists area rules and regulations. The road to the marina is rough in places, but even a full-sized truck and trailer should have no problem reaching and using the boat ramp.

Food, lodging, and supplies are available 12 miles away in Columbus.

Nearest camping: The nearest public campground is about 15 miles away at Georgia Power's Blanton Creek Park on Bartletts Ferry Lake (Lake Harding). The campground includes full-service sites with water and electricity, picnic tables, and grills. Comfort stations with hot showers and flush toilets are also available. Campsite reservations must be made at least 10 days in advance and require a two-night stay. The campground is open seasonally from the first Friday in April through Labor Day.

Directions: To reach Goat Rock Marina, from the intersection of Georgia Highways 315 and 219 north of Columbus, take Goat Rock Road (County Road 391) west to the second road on the right, Adcock Drive (CR 135). Once on Adcock Drive, look for Rocky Ridge Road on the left and follow it to the marina.

To reach Georgia Power's Sandy Point Recreation Area, take U.S. Highway 280/341 northwest from Phenix City, Alabama, to Lee County (Alabama) Road 379 on the right. Follow this road about 5.4 miles to Dupriest Crossroads. Turn right onto Lee County (Alabama) Road 334 and travel about 3.6 miles to the gravel road on the right that leads to the boat ramp.

For more information: Contact the Wildlife Resources Division Fisheries Section Office in Manchester. Information on access and what is biting is available from Goat Rock Marina. Contact Georgia Power for information on Blanton Creek Park, Sandy Point Recreation Area, and generation schedules.

60 Lake Oliver

See map on page 236

Key species: largemouth bass, bluegill, redear sunfish, hybrid striped bass, white bass.

Overview: A 2,150-acre Georgia Power hydropower impoundment on the Chattahoochee River, Lake Oliver is one of the newest of Georgia Power's 19 hydroelectric generating plants.

Best way to fish: boat.

Best time to fish: October through April.

Description: Since its lower end is within the Columbus city limits, Lake Oliver receives heavy recreational boating use in the summer. The lake is long, narrow, and only 2,150 acres, so it cannot absorb much boat traffic without feeling crowded. Houses and cabins line the lake's shoreline, and nearly all of them have at least one boat tied up. Lake Oliver gets about as much summer boat traffic as it can stand. The arrival of cooler weather brings a respite from the boat traffic and Lake Oliver's main clientele becomes the angler.

Public access on Lake Oliver is only fair, but since the lake is so small, not many ramps are needed. At the lower end of the lake on the Georgia side is the Columbus City Marina with paved boat launching facilities. Georgia Power's Goat Rock Recreation Area is on the upper end of the lake just below Goat Rock Dam on the Alabama side. This ramp is narrow and gravel-surfaced.

Lake Oliver is best known for its bream fishing with plenty of fish in the 6- to 8-inch range, and some much larger. Both largemouth and spotted bass are found in the lake, but largemouths support the bulk of the fishery. A lucky angler will occasionally catch a largemouth bass in the 10-pound range, but most fish will average less than 2 pounds. The average spotted bass will measure around 12 inches and weigh less than a pound.

Hybrid striped bass and white bass populations are good. The average hybrid weighs 2 to 3 pounds and whites weighing more than a pound are not uncommon. Crappie are also available. Most crappie will weigh about half a pound, but larger fish are common.

The fishing: Lake Oliver has plenty of cover and structure. Rocky points are good before and after the spawn. When they pull off the beds, bass often go no farther than the first major depth break, which in many cases is going to be a rocky point. Docks line the shoreline, and fishing them with a Texas-rigged plastic worm is a good late-spring tactic. If you find any brush piles around the dock, fish them thoroughly. The combination of dock pilings, shade, and brush is a bass magnet.

Current plays a role in fishing Lake Oliver. Note the generation schedule, and if Goat Rock Dam is generating, head uplake to take advantage of the feeding binge caused by the sudden increase in current. Rocks are good places to fish when the current is moving, and a diving plug that just barely reaches to the rocks will produce fish. The downstream side of the small island below Goat Rock Dam is a good place to try when the dam is generating.

Below the dam is also a good spot for hybrid striped bass and white bass, especially in the early spring as the urge to spawn pulls the fish upstream. Since Goat Rock Dam marks the upper end of the road for Lake Oliver fish, just below the dam often holds a concentration of fish like nowhere else on the lake. Minnows are good bait, but a lead-head jig and plastic shad body is even better.

Bluegill and redear sunfish are the bread-and-butter fish for most Lake Oliver anglers; the lake produces a bunch of bream, many larger than what you typically find in reservoirs. Worms are the best bait, with crickets a close second. Worms known as Louisiana pinks are favorites with anglers. From late spring through summer, search the backs of small coves and sloughs for bream beds. If the fish are not on the beds, expand your search to shoreline cover like boat docks and blowdowns. Shellcrackers are usually found a little deeper than bluegill and prefer a juicy worm over anything else. If you prefer to do your bream fishing with artificials, consider a small Beetle Spin bumped along the bottom with an ultralight spinning outfit.

GA~G grid: 40, C-1

General information: Since Lake Oliver forms part of the Georgia-Alabama border, the two states have worked out a reciprocal agreement allowing an angler holding a valid fishing license from either state to fish the waters of the lake. The waters covered by this agreement do not include other streams or tributaries which flow into the Chattahoochee River or its impoundments. Standard Georgia statewide creel and possession limits apply to the waters covered by the agreement. Largemouth bass possessed in Georgia waters must be 12 inches no matter where they were caught, and all other Georgia fishing laws and regulations apply to Georgia waters.

Some Georgia Power Recreation Areas charge a daily parking fee. Be sure to check area rules and regulations upon arrival. Food, lodging, and supplies are all available in Columbus.

Nearest camping: The nearest public campground is about 25 miles away at Georgia Power's Blanton Creek Park on Bartletts Ferry Lake (Lake Harding). The campground includes full-service sites with water and electricity, picnic tables, and grills. Comfort stations with hot showers and flush toilets are also available. Campsite reservations must be made at least 10 days in advance and require a two-night stay. The campground is open seasonally from the first Friday in April through Labor Day.

Directions: To reach the City Marina, take the Georgia Highway 219 exit off U.S. Highway 80 on the north side of Columbus. After exiting, go north on GA 219. The entrance road to the marina is on the west side of GA 219 just north of the US 80 overpass.

To reach the Goat Rock Recreation Area, take US 280/341 northwest from Phenix City, Alabama, to Lee County (Alabama) Road 379 on the right. Once on this road, take the first paved road on the right, Lee County (Alabama) Road 249. Stay on this road after it turns to gravel until reaching the entrance road for the Goat Rock Recreation Area on the right.

At Lake Oliver, both boat and shorebound anglers will find access at the city docks near the U.S. Highway 80 bypass in Columbus.

For more information: Contact the Wildlife Resources Division Fisheries Section Office in Manchester. Information on access and what is biting is available from the Columbus City Marina. Contact Georgia Power for information on Blanton Creek Park, Goat Rock Recreation Area, and generation schedules.

Southwest Georgia

This is a land of huge reservoirs and big largemouth bass. Trying your luck for black bass on nationally renowned big reservoirs like Seminole and Walter F. George is a popular pastime in southwest Georgia. Anglers who like fishing smaller, more secluded waters should try fishing some of the rivers in this part of the state. The Ochlockonee River is the best place in Georgia to catch a Suwannee bass, a diminutive member of the black bass family whose range is very limited.

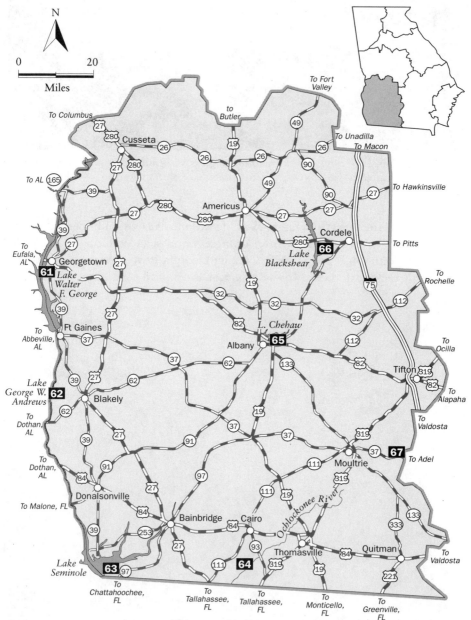

61 Lake Walter F. George

Key species: largemouth bass, crappie, hybrid striped bass.

Overview: A 45,180-acre USACE reservoir on the Chattahoochee River, Lake Walter F. George, also known as Lake Eufaula, is a nationally known destination for anglers in search of largemouth bass.

Best way to fish: boat, shore.

Best time to fish: year-round.

Description: Lake Walter F. George, named in honor of a Georgia Senator from the post–World War II era, is better known among anglers as Lake Eufaula. The name Lake Eufaula comes from a town of the same name on the Alabama side of the lake. Lake George was impounded in 1963 for the purposes of navigation and hydropower. The USACE maintains a channel 100 feet wide by 9 feet deep through the lake for barge traffic. The lake is long and narrow and follows the old Chattahoochee River channel. Lake George stretches across 85 miles from the dam to the headwaters, with the upstream half very riverine in nature, and forms part of the Georgia-Alabama border.

Because of its clay bottom and fertile watershed, heavy rains can quickly muddy the lake's water. When the lake basin was cleared, all the trees within 20 feet of the shoreline were removed, and the remainder topped off 10 feet below full pool level. Shoreline cover on the lake is sparse. Agencies responsible for the management of the lake have taken several steps to improve this situation though. More than 20 fish attractors are maintained around the lake, and some shallow water areas have received plantings of cypress trees.

Like many Georgia reservoirs, Lake George undergoes a winter drawdown, usually about 5 feet. Especially when the lake is down, boaters unfamiliar with the lake should stay in the marked channels. Even well offshore, Lake George's bottom can get shallow in a hurry and is full of stumps.

Bass fishing on the old lake has been an up and down proposition over the years. Overharvest, out-of-control gizzard shad populations, and disease outbreaks have hurt the largemouth bass population. In an attempt to address the first two problems, the lake is managed under a 16-inch minimum length limit on largemouth bass. By raising the minimum length limit, more and bigger fish are kept in the lake to prey on the larger-sized gizzard shad. Without adequate predation, the shad would overpopulate, and the population would be made up solely of large adults with almost no production of the fingerling shad that are such good forage for smaller bass and crappie.

Although shoal bass, spotted bass, and largemouth bass are all present in the lake, largemouths make up the vast majority of the catch. In its glory days, the lake was known for pumping out incredible numbers of 5- and 6-pound fish, with plenty of larger ones available. On the high end of the trophy scale, the lake has produced several fish weighing more than 14 pounds. Although the current fishery is a far cry from the heady early days, Lake George is still a productive fishery and the potential for a lunker is still there.

Lake Walter F. George

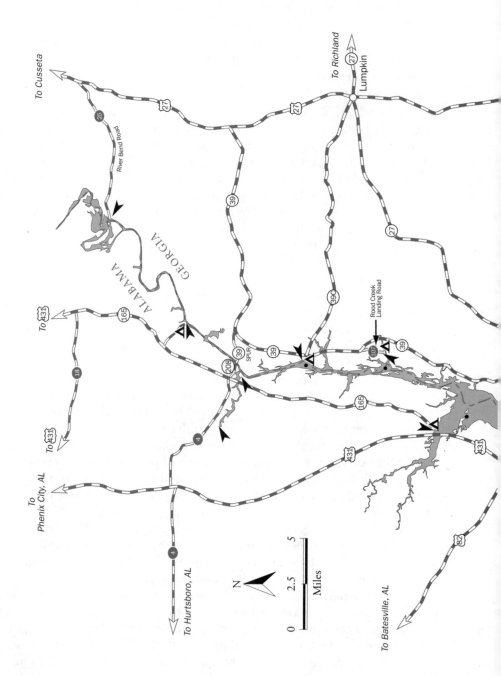

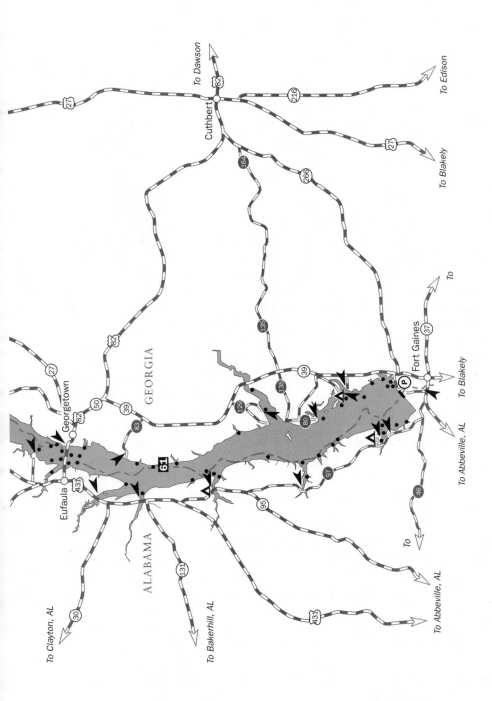

The fishing: The favored largemouth spawning places on Lake George are grassy, sandy-bottomed areas in the backs of small coves and pockets. Between the spawn and the onset of really hot weather, the topwater fishing can be good around shallow weedbeds and other cover, especially early in the morning.

In summer, concentrate on the ledges, either the main river channel or the countless ditches and creeks along the main channel. Drag a Carolina-rigged worm along the bottom or fish a deep-diving crankbait.

Crappie fishing at Lake George really begins to pick up in early February. A couple of warm days in a row will turn on the fish. As usual, the ledges are the place to be. When crappie are spawning, they are easily caught on small jigs or minnows fished around shallow cover. Night-fishing with lanterns under the bridges is the best approach to catching summer crappie.

For hybrid striped bass, follow the usual springtime strategy of intercepting them at shoals and deep holes in the headwaters as they make a false spawning run up the lake. Live shad or a bucktail jig is a good choice for bait. For the rest of the year, expect the fish to be in the main lake following the shad around. Early and late in the day, you may find some fish feeding on top, but most of the time they will be on deep channel ledges and points.

Catfish are virtually overlooked on Lake George. The fish will bite year-round, but summer is probably the best fishing. Bluegill and redear sunfish are abundant at Lake George but generally run small. Try live bait around shallow cover during the summer months.

GA~G grid: 48

General information: Since Lake Walter F. George forms part of the Georgia-Alabama border, the two states have worked out a reciprocal agreement allowing an angler holding a valid fishing license from either state to fish the waters of the lake. The waters covered by this agreement do not include other streams or tributaries which flow into the Chattahoochee River or its impoundments. Standard Georgia statewide creel and possession limits apply to the waters covered by the agreement with the exception of an increased minimum length limit on largemouth bass. All other Georgia fishing laws and regulations apply to Georgia waters.

Food, lodging, and supplies are available around the lake in Fort Gaines and Georgetown, Georgia, and Eufaula, Alabama.

Nearest camping: The USACE maintains seven campgrounds around the lake. In addition, there are two state parks on the Georgia side of the lake, Florence Marina State Park at the north end of the lake, and George T. Bagby State Park on the southern end. Both parks offers a variety of camping and lodging options.

Directions: From Georgetown, access points on the lake can be reached from U.S. Highways 431 and 82, and Georgia Highway 39. From Eufala, Alabama, access points can be reached from Alabama Highway 95.

For more information: Contact the Wildlife Resources Division Fisheries Section Office in Albany. For information on USACE facilities, contact the Resource Site Office. Information on Florence Marina and George T. Bagby State Parks is available from the Park Superintendent's Office.

62 Lake George W. Andrews

Key species: largemouth bass, bluegill, channel catfish, blue catfish.

Overview: Lake George W. Andrews is a 29-mile long stretch of the Chattahoochee River sandwiched between Lake Walter F. George to the north and Lake Seminole to the south.

Best way to fish: boat.

Best time to fish: February through November.

Description: Lake Andrews, known as Columbia Lake on the Alabama side of the river, is probably Georgia's least-known major reservoir. The Mobile District of the USACE operates this Chattahoochee River impoundment, named after an Alabama Congressman who played a prominent role in getting the lake constructed.

Although fishing pressure is light, the lake is known to pleasure boaters and water-skiers and its narrow nature can lead to crowded conditions on summer weekends. Fishing early or late in the day will avoid much of the pleasure-boating traffic. The shoreline is largely undeveloped, and access points, while sufficient, are limited. Andrews is very riverine in nature, to the point it should hardly be called a lake. The lake has no significant area of open water and at least some current is always flowing, so anglers should plan to approach the fishing as they would in any other large river. Usually, more current is present during the week because of more barge traffic.

Among those familiar with the lake, Andrews is known more for the size of the fish it produces than pure numbers. Largemouth bass in the 6- to 8-pound range are common, and trophies weighing more than 10 pounds are occasionally caught. The light fishing pressure and abundant forage base of threadfin and gizzard shad allow for the growth of the large fish. Largemouth bass make up a great majority of the black bass population. A few spotted bass and shoal bass are likely present, since they are found in the drainage, but neither makes a significant contribution to the angler's creel.

During the summer, when fishing on other Georgia lakes is slow, Lake Andrew keeps on producing. Fishing moving water is always a good strategy in the dog days of summer, and Lake Andrews in no exception. A likely explanation of why Andrews is such a good summer lake is that the lake's inflow comes from the Walter F. George Dam, so the water coming in is cooler than normal. Also, since Andrews is narrow and does not have extensive shallow flats, the sun does not get the opportunity to heat the water to the usual summertime boil. Finally, the undeveloped shoreline is forested with plenty of shade. These factors combine to keep the water a few degrees cooler than one would expect, and the fish stay more active during the summer.

Although not technically part of Lake Andrews, the tailwaters below the dam offer good fishing too. A fishing pier and boat ramp are available. Anglers should be aware that sudden water level fluctuations of 8 feet are possible and take due precautions.

The fishing: Current is key to catching fish on Lake Andrews. During high flows, most species will take up feeding stations like the outer branches of

Lake George W. Andrews

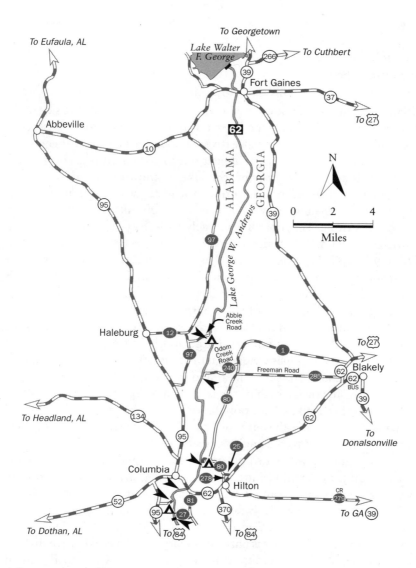

fallen trees, sand bars, and creek mouths. Most of the fishing on Lake Andrews takes place along the shoreline. Cover in the lake is limited, and ideal feeding stations are scarce, so when one is found, fish it thoroughly.

When the current falls off, slack water brings some new options. Blowdowns on steep banks are a favorite target, and plastic worms or a topwater bait worked through and around the tree should produce.

Striped bass, white bass, and their hatchery-spawned hybrid are all present in good numbers. Reserve the smallest lures for white bass and the larger for hybrids and stripers. Live or cut shad is by far the best choice for natural bait.

The best crappie fishing takes place in early spring. Small minnows or jigs fished around woody cover in the main river or the flooded creeks are a sure thing. The best time for sunfish is summer. Live bait fished under a float around shallow cover is the best approach. A variety of catfish are found in the lake, but the favorite with most anglers is the channel catfish which is abundant, grows big, fights hard, and tastes great. Concentrate around creek mouths, deep holes, and below the dam. Catfish usually will let you know pretty quickly whether or not they are willing to bite; fish a good hole for 30 minutes and if you do not get any action, pull up the anchor and go try another spot.

One final note—anglers on Lake Andrews prefer heavier tackle than the norm. Big fish and strong current are no place for finesse gear.

GA~G grid: 56, B-1

General information: Since Lake George W. Andrews forms part of the Georgia-Alabama border, the two states have worked out a reciprocal agreement allowing an angler holding a valid fishing license from either state to fish the waters of the lake. The waters covered by this agreement do not include other streams or tributaries that flow into the Chattahoochee River or its impoundments. Standard Georgia statewide creel and possession limits apply to the waters covered by the agreement. Largemouth bass possessed in Georgia waters must be 12 inches no matter where they are caught, and all other Georgia fishing laws and regulations apply to Georgia waters. From Columbia Dam downstream, the striped bass season is closed from May 1 to October 31.

Since navigation is an authorized use of the lake, the USACE maintains a navigable channel of 100 feet by 9 feet, allowing commercial traffic as far north as Columbus, Georgia. Boaters should be extra cautious because of the commercial boat traffic using the waterway.

Food, lodging, and supplies are available within 15 miles in Blakely or Fort Gaines.

Nearest camping: Camping is allowed at the Coheelee Creek and Omussee Creek access points.

Directions: From Blakely, the lake's public access points can be reached from Georgia Highways 62 and 39 and Alabama Highways 95 and 10.

For more information: Contact the Wildlife Resources Division Fisheries Section Office in Albany. For lake and facility information, contact the Resource Site Office.

63 Lake Seminole

Key species: largemouth bass, hybrid striped bass, crappie, bluegill, redear sunfish.

Overview: A 37,500-acre USACE impoundment on the Chattahoochee and Flint rivers in the southwest corner of Georgia, Lake Seminole is nationally renowned for its angling, especially for largemouth bass.

Best way to fish: boat.

Best time to fish: year-round.

Lake Seminole

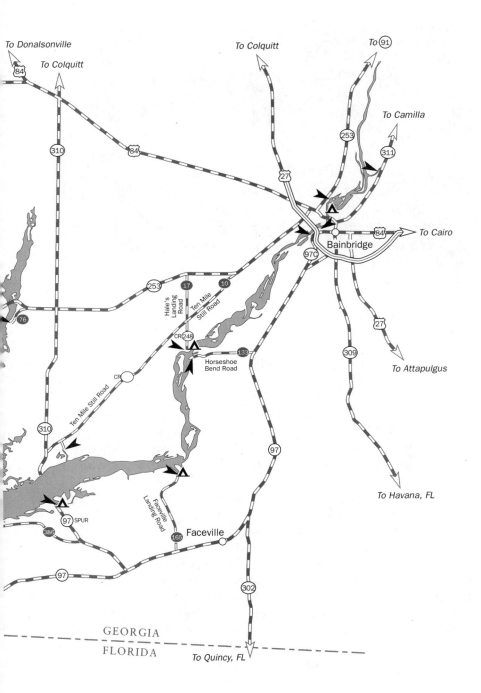

To Donalsonville

To Colquitt

To Colquitt

To 91

84

To Camilla

310

253

84

311

27

To Cairo

84

Bainbridge

97C

253

17

10

27

Hale's Landing Road

Ten Mile Still Road

309

To Attapulgus

CR 248

133

Horseshoe Bend Road

76

CR

Ten Mile Still Road

310

97

To Havana, FL

97 SPUR

Faceville Landing Road

386

97

165

Faceville

97

302

GEORGIA

FLORIDA

To Quincy, FL

The tally board at Jack Wingate's Lunker Lodge, a popular jumping-off point for bass tournaments on Lake Seminole.

Description: Lake Seminole was originally authorized as the Jim Woodruff Lock and Dam Project by the River and Harbor Act of 1946. The project took its name from a Columbus businessman and engineer who helped convince others of the need for the project. Seminole was the first of three projects authorized to improve navigation, provide hydropower, and add to the recreational opportunities in the Apalachicola, Chattahoochee, and Flint River basins. The lake sprawls across parts of Georgia and Florida, with the majority lying within the Peach State.

The introduction of non-native aquatic plants has significantly affected Lake Seminole over the years. Eurasian watermilfoil first made an appearance in the mid-1960s, with another exotic species, hydrilla, following a few years later and becoming even more of a problem. The effects of these weeds have been mixed. Although they are excellent cover for the fish, and fishing the weeds is a favorite strategy with anglers, at times thick weed growth has covered almost the entire lake, making navigation and angling difficult. Aggressive control of the weeds by a combination of chemical, biological, and mechanical methods has reduced coverage in recent years and opened up more of the lake. However, during the height of the growing season, weeds can cover nearly half the lake. Boaters visiting the lake are encouraged to clean off their boat and trailer before venturing to other waters to prevent the spread of these exotic nuisance plants.

Along with the weeds, Lake Seminole has plenty of stumps and sunken logs. Boaters unfamiliar with the lake need to take care when navigating its relatively shallow waters.

Although largemouth bass support most of the fishery, good numbers of shoal bass are available for anglers willing to run up the river and fish the rocky headwaters of the lake upstream of Bainbridge.

Seminole has produced some huge fish. The lake record largemouth bass weighed more than 16 pounds, and hybrid striped bass in the same range are possible. Seminole has given up striped bass nearing 40 pounds. Three-pound crappie and shellcrackers weighing more than a pound are common. Whatever species you choose to fish for, the chances of a trophy are very real. There are five marked fish refuges in Lake Seminole. Springs are found in these areas and coolwater-loving striped bass congregate around the springs in the summer. In an attempt to restore the population, Gulf Coast–strain striped bass are stocked into the lake. To prevent overfishing of this recovering stock, the spring refuges are closed to all fishing from May 1 to October 31.

The fishing: Anglers from all over the state make a pilgrimage to Seminole in January and February to get a dose of the cure for cabin fever. If the fish are not actively fanning beds yet, Carolina-rigging a soft-plastic worm or lizard around submerged timber and ledges can be productive, as can fishing a small crankbait over submerged weed beds. During the spawn, fish a Texas-rigged lizard in the bedding areas for a chance at a real lunker.

Summertime bass angling on Seminole basically means fishing the deep weed edges with a plastic worm or crankbait. Autumn finds the bass feeding over the weedbeds. Once cold weather arrives, expect fish to be deep in the timber or on the channel ledges.

Hybrid striped bass are an overlooked fishery on Lake Seminole. In the spring, fish below the dams on the extreme upper end of the lake in the Chattahoochee and Flint River arms below Lake Andrews and Lake Chehaw.

Crappie fishing on Lake Seminole is a little bit different than most Georgia lakes. Not only do the fish spawn earlier in the year, but they tend to relate to grass more than wood. Seminole crappie like to feed on grass shrimp, and casting a small jig that imitates this forage will catch shallow, spawning fish. After the spawn, the fish come out the same way they went in and spend the rest of the year in the deep water around the channels.

Although a variety of catfish species are found in the lake, channel catfish are a favorite with anglers. Technically, the Flint and Chattahoochee rivers below the dams on the upper end of Seminole are part of the lake. However, the habitat is riverine and the catfish love the moving water.

Although bream are overshadowed on Lake Seminole by other more popular species, some big ones are available, and they are easy to catch during a few prime times. Redear sunfish begin to bed in early April. The second good time for Seminole bream is whenever the mayflies are hatching. Starting sometime in May, every few weeks will bring a new hatch of the short-lived mayfly.

GA~G grid: 64

General information: Georgia and Florida have worked out a reciprocal agreement regarding the fishing regulations on Lake Seminole. Refer to the *Georgia Sport Fishing Regulations* pamphlet for more information.

Five marked fish refuges are closed to all fishing from May 1 to October 31. The striped bass season in the Flint River from the U.S. Highway 84 bridge upstream to the dam at Albany, the Chattahoochee River from Georgia Highway 91 upstream to Columbia Dam, and Spring Creek upstream of GA 253 is closed from May 1 to October 31. All tributaries to these waters are also included in this regulation.

The minimum length limit for all shoal bass caught from the Flint River and its tributaries is 12 inches. Other than the special regulations mentioned, Lake Seminole conforms to standard Georgia fishing regulations.

Food, lodging, and supplies are available at private establishments around the lake or in Bainbridge, Georgia, and Chattahoochee, Florida.

Nearest camping: The USACE maintains 5 campgrounds around the lake. The Georgia Department of Natural Resources' Seminole State Park is found on the shores of the lake. Camping is also available at some private marinas and county recreation areas.

Directions: Lake Seminole is southwest of Bainbridge and can be accessed from GA 97 and GA 253.

For more information: Contact the Wildlife Resources Division Fisheries Section Office in Albany. For information on the lake and USACE facilities, contact the Resource Management Office. Information on Seminole State Park is available from the Park Superintendent's Office.

64 Ochlockonee River—U.S. Highway 84 to State Line

Key species: Suwannee bass, largemouth bass, redbreast sunfish, channel catfish.
Overview: Although it's a small river, it's the best place in Georgia to catch a Suwannee bass.
Best way to fish: small boat or canoe.
Best time to fish: May through November.
Description: The Ochlockonee would go virtually unnoticed with Georgia anglers if Suwannee bass did not swim in its waters. Besides their native Suwannee River drainage in extreme southeastern Georgia, the Ochlockonee River is the only other place where Suwannee bass are relatively common. In fact, just based on ease of access and numbers of fish available, the Ochlockonee is arguably the best place in Georgia to go catch this rare little member of the black bass family.

Although Suwannee bass are the most notable residents of the river, large-mouth bass outnumber them. Distinguishing between the two is easy since the Suwannee's jaw does not extend behind the eye as does a largemouth's, and Suwannees often are bluish on the lower rear half of the body.

This far south in Georgia, the fishing is good year-round. However, ideal river fishing conditions call for clear water and medium flows. During the winter and early spring frequent heavy rains muddy the river and bring it up.

Ochlockonee River—U.S. Highway 84 to State Line

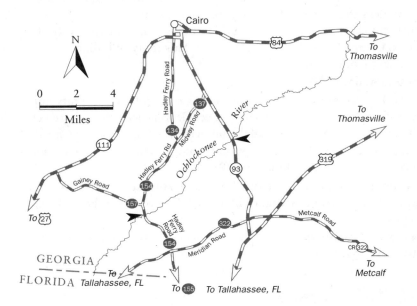

The Ochlockonee is a medium-sized river at best, and the fish are sized accordingly. Most largemouth caught will average well below 3 pounds, although fish twice as big are possible. Suwannee bass will average 12 inches or less and weigh somewhere close to a pound. The Georgia record Suwannee bass, at 3 pounds, 9 ounces, caught in 1984, came from the Ochlockonee though, and at one time was recognized as the undisputed world-record Suwannee bass.

The best fishing and virtually the only improved access will be found in the section of the river downstream of U.S. Highway 84. This stretch of the river has two public boat ramps. The river is filled with stumps and blowdowns, so expect to do some bushwacking, especially if the river is low.

The fishing: Anglers can target Suwannee bass by ignoring the usual blowdowns and other bank cover favored by largemouths and concentrating on midchannel areas. Suwannee bass prefer to hold in the current along rocky areas and under overhanging willow trees. Small crankbaits or topwater lures are local favorites for catching both species. Bass-sized in-line spinners like the venerable Snagless Sally should also work, although the simple baits of that period have fallen into disfavor and been forgotten by today's high-tech bass angler. Interestingly, Suwannee bass are not reported to be fond of plastic worms.

If the bass will not cooperate, anglers may want to focus their attention on bream. Redbreast sunfish, bluegill, and a variety of other sunfish species are generally always willing to hit a well-placed spinner, popping bug, cricket, or worm. Live bait works the best in the spring, with artificials taking the lead in the summer months. Bream can save the day on a float trip when the bass will not cooperate and there is still a long way to go to the take-out point.

Anglers after catfish should try fishing their favorite catfish bait on bottom. The best fishing is after the spring rains are over and the river is back within its banks. Channel catfish, white catfish, and a variety of bullhead species can all be caught from the Ochlockonee.

GA~G grid: 65, C-10

General information: Georgia statewide creel and length limits apply on the Ochlockonee River. All anglers must meet Georgia licensing requirements. Food, lodging, and supplies are available in nearby Thomasville or Cairo.

Nearest camping: The nearest public campground is at Lake Seminole, about 40 miles west of the Ochlockonee River.

Directions: From Cairo, the two boat ramps on the lower Ochlockonee River can be reached from Georgia Highway 93 and Hadley Ferry Road (County Road 154).

For more information: Contact the Wildlife Resources Division Fisheries Section Office in Albany.

65 Lake Chehaw (Lake Worth)

Key species: hybrid striped bass, largemouth bass, channel catfish, flathead catfish.

Overview: Lake Chehaw is a 1,400-acre Georgia Power hydropower development on the Flint River.

Best way to fish: boat, shore.

Best time to fish: year-round.

Description: Impounded in 1919 by damming the Flint River, Lake Chehaw went by the name of Lake Worth for many years. A good portion of the lake lies within the City of Albany, so as one might expect, houses line the shoreline and summer boat traffic is heavy. A very riverine-type impoundment, Lake Chehaw stretches out about 10 miles east to west and is a shallow lake full of islands and sloughs. To provide flood storage, the lake is drawn down almost 10 feet every winter in preparation of spring rains. Access can be difficult during these times, but the fishing is usually good since the low water concentrates the fish.

Although historically known as an average fishing lake at best, the flood of 1994 and subsequent drawdowns for dam repair turned an aged, tired reservoir into a nearly new one.

Besides the Flint River, Kinchafoonee and Muckalee Creeks on the west side of the lake are the two other major tributaries. The area of the lake where these two creeks come together is known as "Muckafoonee" and traditionally has produced the biggest bass.

Lake Chehaw (Lake Worth)

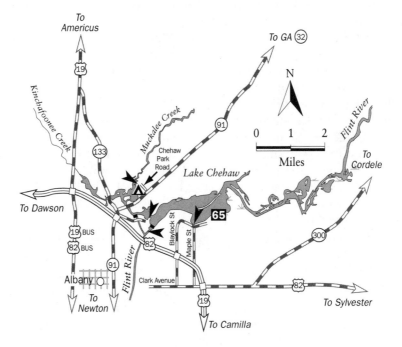

Surprisingly, given the lake's urban location, fishing pressure is moderate. Part of the reason is that little Lake Chehaw is up against some tough competition from its more famous neighbors like Lakes Walter F. George, Seminole, and Blackshear. In addition, the heavy boat traffic can make summer angling a rock-and-rolling proposition, and access during the winter drawdown can be difficult. Despite these hurdles, anglers manage to find some good, although not fantastic, fishing, especially for largemouth bass and hybrid striped bass.

Although not technically in Lake Chehaw, the tailwater below the dam is known for big striped bass and flathead catfish. Flatheads weighing in the double-digits are common, and stripers in the 20-pound range also show up in the spring as they make a spawning run up from Lake Seminole. See the general information section for special regulations on striped bass fishing in the Flint River.

The fishing: Bass love docks and piers, and Lake Chehaw has plenty. A good bet would be to start in the spring with topwater plugs or a Texas-rigged worm fished from 1 to 5 feet deep. As summer arrives, if you can tolerate the boat traffic, fish the main-channel stumpfields and ledges with crankbaits. Autumn is spinnerbait time, with chartreuse and white being two local favorites. In the winter, a Carolina-rigged soft plastic is a good choice.

Hybrid striped bass are stocked into Lake Chehaw and are a popular fishery. Most hybrid fishing is done in the summer and is simply a waiting game. Early and late in the day, schooling hybrids will jump to the surface to feed on shad.

Casting a topwater plug, spoon, or bucktail jig into the fray will result in some fast action. One spot that is consistently good for schooling action is a shallow flat at the mouth of Muckalee Creek. This flat is by far the best one on the lake and sees consistent schooling action all summer long.

Lake Chehaw has both channel cats and flatheads. For flatheads, concentrate on fishing a live shad or bream along channel drop-offs; channel catfish like dead bait. Nightcrawlers and chicken livers fished on the bottom near channels is a productive technique.

Bluegill, redear sunfish, and crappie do not grow that large in Chehaw. All three species are easily caught during their spawning season—early spring for crappie, spring and summer for bream. Minnows, worms, and crickets are good natural baits, and small spinners get the nod in the artificial department.

When fishing the tailwater, shad and shiners are good live baits for both flathead catfish and striped bass. Besides live bait, a bucktail jig is always hard for a striped bass to resist. Fish the eddies in the fast water for the best results.

GA~G grid: 49, H-10 and 50, H-1

General information: Anglers on Lake Chehaw must meet standard Georgia licensing requirements. Several special regulations are in effect for Lake Chehaw as part of the Flint River drainage. The season for striped bass fishing from the Georgia Power Company dams at Albany downstream to U.S. Highway 84 is closed from May 1 to October 31. In addition, the minimum length limit for all shoal bass caught from the Flint River and its tributaries is 12 inches. Other than these two special regulations, Lake Chehaw and its tailwater conform to standard Georgia fishing regulations regarding seasons and creel and length limits.

Part of Lake Chehaw falls within the Albany city limits and there are many nearby choices for food, lodging, and supplies.

Nearest camping: Camping is available at Chehaw Park, a privately run recreation facility on the west side of the lake. RV and tent camping are available. The campground has utilities and comfort stations.

Directions: All the Lake Chehaw access points are a short distance off the US 82 Bypass, northeast of Albany.

For more information: Contact the Wildlife Resources Division Fisheries Section Office in Albany, Georgia Power, or Chehaw Park.

66 Lake Blackshear

Key species: largemouth bass, crappie, bluegill, redear sunfish, channel catfish.

Overview: Spreading over 8,515 acres, this Flint River impoundment is owned and operated by the Crisp County Power Commission. In the summer of 1994, floodwaters breached its dam. Once repairs were made though, the fishing quickly rebounded and Blackshear is a favorite destination with anglers in southwest Georgia.

Best way to fish: boat, shore.

Lake Blackshear

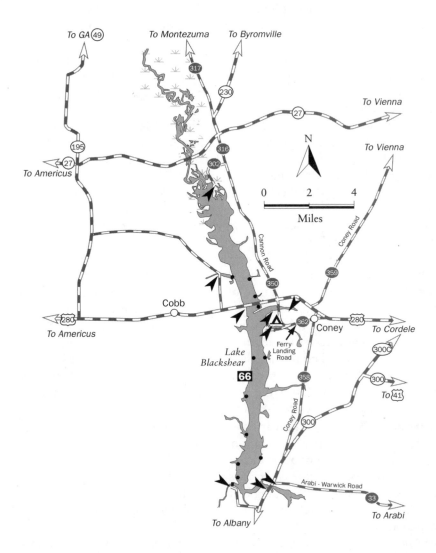

Best time to fish: year-round.

Description: Lake Blackshear was constructed by the Crisp County Power Commission in 1930 using private funding. The lake is named after General David Blackshear, a Revolutionary War–era soldier who blazed a trail through this part of Georgia when it was still the young nation's western frontier. Blackshear is a riverine lake, less than a mile in width, and stretches across more than 15 miles of the Flint River valley. When the lake was constructed, no timber was removed from the basin. While this was great for the fish, it made navigation difficult, sometimes with deadly results. In 1973 the lake was drawn down and the timber removed from the area downstream of the Georgia Highway 280 bridge. Upstream of the bridge, the timber was left untouched except for clearing a well-marked navigation channel. The results of these efforts were beneficial to both anglers and pleasure boaters. During the summer, the lake below the bridge is the usual three-ring circus of personal watercraft and pleasure boats, but upstream of the bridge anglers can find plenty of uncrowded water to fish. About a third of Blackshear's shoreline is taken up by houses, cabins, and other developments, while the rest remains mostly agricultural or undeveloped. There are about 1,200 docks on the lake, so for the dock-fishing specialist, Blackshear is the place to be.

The most significant event in Lake Blackshear's life undoubtedly was the flood of 1994. When the floodwaters receded, 80 percent of Lake Blackshear was high and dry. For more than a year, Lake Blackshear was 14 feet below full pool while the dam was repaired and rebuilt. The flood seemed to do the old lake good though. Many feel that the fishing has improved since the lake was refilled.

Blackshear is a unique lake. Not only is it a large reservoir owned by a county commission and the only major reservoir in Georgia ever to have its dam breached, but the lake also has three large springs set aside part of the year for fish refuges. In an attempt to restore them to their native range, Lake Blackshear receives annual stockings of Gulf Coast-strain striped bass. The springs are summertime refuges for these coolwater-loving fish. The area around each spring is closed to all fishing from May 1 to October 31.

Lake Blackshear receives moderate fishing pressure, and the lake is just as popular with bream and crappie anglers as it is with largemouth bass anglers. Never known as a trophy bass lake, Blackshear is nevertheless a fertile lake and produces lots of fish. Bass in the 7- to 9-pound range are common, and the lake has proven it can produce fish in the low double-digits.

The fishing: The key to Blackshear bass is cypress trees. Since Blackshear is a shallow lake, it warms up fast and fishing a topwater bait early in the morning next to a cypress tree is a popular tactic. Later in the day, the bass will retreat to the extensive root system that encircles the tree. A Texas-rigged plastic worm is the best way to penetrate the tangle of roots. If the cypress trees do not pan out, try fishing some of Blackshear's hundreds of boat docks with a spinnerbait or the plastic worm.

Blackshear is an excellent crappie lake and has a dedicated following of anglers. From late fall through early spring, trolling a spread of small jigs will usually fill the livewell with a limit of these tasty panfish. Yellow, white, or a combination of the two are good colors to try.

Fishing for hybrid striped bass on Lake Blackshear is good from early June well into the fall. Most of the activity takes place early and late in the day when the hybrids go on jumps and feed on the surface. Look for surface feeding activity on main lake points, humps, and channels.

Unlike most large reservoirs, Lake Blackshear is good fishing for bluegill and redear sunfish. The best time to catch fish is during the spawn. Bedding activity may start as early as April, but usually May and June are peak times.

Look for collections of spawning beds in shallow water or under docks and cypress trees. When fish are not spawning, they will still be around cover, but the bigger fish will likely be a little bit deeper. Good baits are worms, crickets, or a Beetle Spin. Do not overlook a fly rod and popping bug as a great way to enjoy these scrappy little fighters.

GA~G grid: 50, C-2

General information: Lake Blackshear is managed under general statewide regulations with a couple of exceptions. All largemouth bass harvested from the lake must be at least 14 inches, and all shoal bass harvested must be at least 12 inches. As mentioned above, several spring areas in Blackshear are set aside as coolwater fish refuges for much of the year. No fishing is allowed in these areas from May 1 through October 31. All anglers fishing Blackshear must meet Georgia licensing requirements.

Nearest camping: The nearest camping is at Georgia Veterans Memorial State Park midway up the lake's eastern shoreline. The 1,308-acre park has 77 campsites with utilities, primitive camping, and 10 cottages for rent. The park is open year-round.

Directions: Lake Blackshear is just west of Cordele off Interstate 75. Access to the lake is off U.S. Highway 280 and Georgia Highways 300 and 27.

For more information: Contact the Wildlife Resources Division Fisheries Section Office in Albany. For Georgia Veterans Memorial State Park information, contact the Park Superintendent's Office.

67 Reed Bingham State Park

Key species: largemouth bass, bluegill, redear sunfish.

Overview: Reed Bingham State Park surrounds a 375-acre lake that has become a major boating and waterskiing attraction in south Georgia. The lake is also popular with anglers and its waters are full of largemouth bass and sunfish.

Best way to fish: boat, shore.

Best time to fish: year-round.

Description: Reed Bingham State Park, named for a local activist who played a significant role in getting the park built, covers 1,620 acres on the coastal plain in south-central Georgia. Central to the park is a 375-acre impoundment of the Little River. The lake is very popular with pleasure boaters and water-skiers, but most of the activity takes place on the more open lower lake, leaving the lake's shallow upper end for anglers. Besides the lake itself, 3 miles of the Little River upstream of the lake are in the park and open to public fishing.

Nature lovers will enjoy visiting the Coastal Plains Nature Trail. The trail leads visitors through a cypress swamp, pitcher plant bog, sandhill area, and other unique habitats typical of south Georgia. Alligators and other wildlife are abundant.

The fishing: Largemouth bass, redear sunfish, and bluegill are the most popular species with anglers. The whole lake is good fishing, but the area around the

Reed Bingham State Park

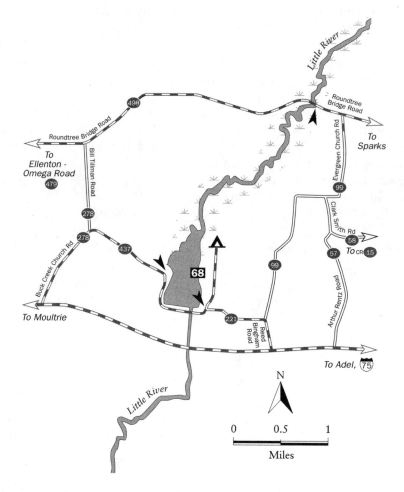

small islands on the west side of the lake is a favorite. Anglers will find plenty of aquatic vegetation to fish; floating frogs, weedless spoons, spinnerbaits, and Texas-rigged plastic worms are all good bass lures. Spinnerbaits are always a good choice for fishing moving waters, and should work well when fishing upriver. The venerable Snagless Sally is an often overlooked bait that can be a killer in small rivers.

Bream anglers will find the lake especially productive. Fishing worms or crickets around shallow vegetation and structure is sure to produce some fish. For even more fun, try a small popping bug on a lightweight flycasting outfit. During the spring and summer, be on the lookout for bream beds. When the spawn concentrates the fish together during spawning, they are very aggressive and easily caught. The spillway area just below the dam is especially good in the spring when a good flow of water is coming over the dam. This small area produces a lot of fish for shoreline anglers.

Other species popular with anglers are crappie and catfish. A small marabou jig cast around shallow cover in the early spring is a tried and true crappie technique. Catfish are usually found on the bottom near deeper water, and a gob of worms, chicken liver, or other strongly scented bait will attract fish.

GA~G grid: 59, E-6

General information: Access is excellent at Reed Bingham State Park. Several paved boat ramps, including one upstream on the river, are available. There are also fishing piers on the lake to give shoreline anglers easy access to good angling. The park is open to fishing year-round from 7 A.M. to 10 P.M. daily. All boats must be off the water by sunset. All anglers must meet Georgia licensing requirements, and a daily or annual Georgia Parks Pass is required to park a vehicle on the area.

Food, lodging, and supplies are 7 miles away in Adel.

Nearest camping: Reed Bingham State Park has 46 campsites. Utilities and comfort stations are available.

Directions: From Interstate 75 exit 39 in Adel, travel west on Georgia Highway 37 for 6.4 miles to County Road 221 on the left. Follow this paved road to the park.

For more information: For fisheries information, contact the Wildlife Resources Division Fisheries Section Office in Albany. For information on Reed Bingham State Park, contact the Park Superintendent's Office.

Southeast Georgia

Southeast Georgia does not have a single major reservoir, which to the uninformed might suggest fishing opportunities are limited in this area of the coastal plain. However, the long-standing world record largemouth bass was caught from an oxbow lake in southeast Georgia, and attempting to surpass this record is probably the most vigorously pursued task in the sport of fishing.

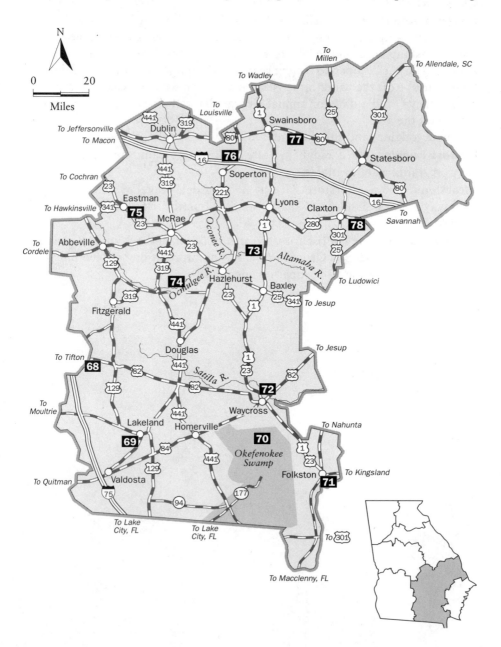

Many have tried, but none have been up to the task. Besides bass fishing, the rivers offer good opportunities for monster catfish, slab crappie, and many other species.

Still-water anglers will find many small lakes and ponds to choose from, and the Okefenokee Swamp, although not renowned for its angling, is still worth a try if for no other reason than to experience its unique collection of habitats.

68 Paradise Public Fishing Area

Key species: largemouth bass, bluegill, redear sunfish, channel catfish, crappie.

Overview: With 75 lakes encompassing 525 acres of water, Paradise Public Fishing Area is truly an angler's paradise.

Best way to fish: shore, boat.

Best time to fish: year-round.

Description: Owned and operated by the Georgia Wildlife Resources Division, Paradise Public Fishing Area contains enough ponds to keep an avid angler busy for weeks. Originally constructed in the 1940s and operated as a private pay-fishing site, the area was known as "Patrick's Fishing Paradise" and billed itself as "the home of the next world record bass." The area's heyday as a pay-fishing site peaked in the early 1970s and maintaining the large area became a burden on the owners. The state of Georgia purchased the area in 1989.

With so many lakes and ponds on more than 1,000 acres of land, Paradise Public Fishing Area offers many angling opportunities. Some lakes are managed for big bass, some for just catfish, some for good all-around fishing, and a few ponds are reserved for use by children and other special groups. Some lakes are periodically closed for maintenance, restocking, or simply to give the fish a rest from all the activity. Call ahead or check the information board at the entrance to find out what lakes are open and if any special regulations are in effect.

Anglers have caught some huge bass over the years at Paradise Public Fishing Area and it is arguably the best public trophy bass water in the state of Georgia. Fish weighing more than 10 pounds are not unusual, and 7- to 8-pounders are common.

Bluegill, redear sunfish, channel catfish, and crappie are also available here in good numbers and good size.

The fishing: To decide which pond to fish, talk to area staff. They can tell you which ponds are open, what fish live in them, and the best way to catch them. Traditionally, the larger lakes like Patrick, Bobbin, and Paradise have been the best bass fishing. Your best chance for a trophy bass is in late winter and early spring when the water starts to warm. Fat sow bass begin spawning, and on warm days they will be in the shallows looking for both prey and potential spawning areas. Slowly working a jig-and-pig along bottom around cover is a tried-and-true technique.

When fish are shallow, cast buzzbaits, spinnerbaits, or topwater plugs. Deeper summer and winter bass call for Texas-rigged soft plastics and

Paradise Public Fishing Area

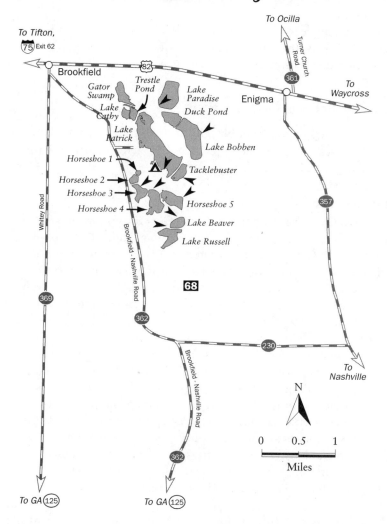

crankbaits. Another local favorite for shallow bass is a large plastic worm fished with little or no weight. Twitching the lure gives it a natural swimming action bass find hard to resist.

Bluegill and redear sunfish provide the most consistent fishing in the area. Most of the ponds and lakes have bream that are almost always willing to bite a cricket or worm. Small spinners like Beetle Spins and Rooster Tails are also productive and sometimes outfish natural bait. For loads of fun, unlimber a lightweight fly rod and present a popping bug on the surface in the evening.

Catfish will fall prey to anything stinky; try chicken livers, worms, or store-bought catfish baits. Fish the bait on the bottom and keep a tight line to detect nibbling strikes.

Crappie are only found in a few of the Paradise lakes. However, some of the Paradise lakes managed intensively for largemouth bass produce the added benefit of good crappie fishing. With high numbers of largemouth bass to prey on small crappie and control their numbers, there is less competition for food and crappie grow to keeper sizes. Minnows are not allowed as bait in any of the lakes on Paradise Public Fishing Area. Therefore, a small crappie jig is the best option. From February to April fish a jig around shallow woody cover to take advantage of the spawn. Later in the year, crappie are much more difficult to find and catch. Begin your search in open water around deep cover or channels.

GA~G grid: 59, B-8

General information: Paradise Public Fishing Area is open year-round from sunrise to sunset. Private boats are allowed and the larger lakes are equipped with paved boat ramps. Some lakes are limited to electric motors only; on waters posted as open to gasoline engines, all boats must be operated at idle speed. Anglers 16 years of age and older must have a valid fishing license and Wildlife Management Area stamp. Senior Lifetime, Honorary, Sportsman's, and 1-Day license holders do not need the WMA stamp. See the information board at the entrance to the area for more information on what lakes are open, any special regulations in effect, and general area rules and regulations.

Food, lodging, and supplies are available 10 miles away in Tifton.

Nearest camping: Primitive camping is allowed in designated areas at Paradise Public Fishing Area.

Directions: In Brookfield, turn south onto Whitley Road (County Road 369) and travel 0.1 mile to Brookfield-Nashville Road (CR 362) on the left. Follow this road 1.4 miles to the entrance on the left.

For more information: Contact the Paradise Public Fishing Area Office.

69 Banks Lake National Wildlife Refuge

Key species: largemouth bass, bluegill, redear sunfish.

Overview: Fantastic fishing for big bass and bream, Banks Lake is a natural "Carolina Bay" of ancient origin.

Best way to fish: boat.

Best time to fish: year-round.

Description: Banks Lake National Wildlife Refuge is part of a much larger blackwater system. The refuge contains many different habitats including 1,500 acres of marsh, 1,549 acres of cypress swamp, and 1,000 acres of open water. Small stands of upland pine and hardwood forest are scattered throughout. Cypress trees and stumps fill the lake. Weedbeds of coontail, milfoil, spatterdock, and water lilies are everywhere.

Banks Lake National Wildlife Refuge

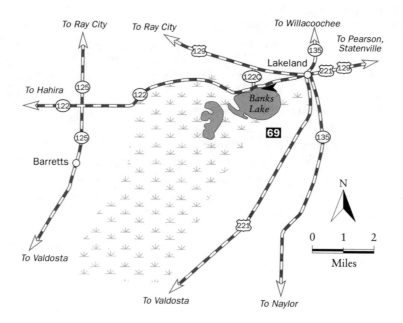

Banks Lake is a combination of the natural and the manmade. The natural part is the pocosin, or Carolina bay, a natural low-lying area that collects and holds rainwater. The manmade part is the earthen levee that was built in the 1840s.

Banks Lake averages around 5 feet deep, although a few holes go down to 15 feet. Banks Lake is less acidic than most blackwater systems, which allows largemouth bass and other sport fish to thrive in its waters. A fertile system with good water quality, plenty of forage, and a long growing-season make Banks Lake a great place to fish.

For the quality fishing it offers, Banks Lake is relatively unpressured water. Perhaps put off by its small size, many anglers overlook the lake as a prime destination for big bass and bream.

The fishing: No matter where you look on Banks Lake, you will see thousands of targets to cast to. Although every spot is not going to produce a lunker bass or trophy bream, Banks Lake is full of fish and one spot is just about as likely to produce as another.

For largemouth bass, the key is snagless lures. Plastic worms and lizards, spinnerbaits, and weedless spoons are all good choices. Topwater plugs are also good if cast accurately and retrieved with care. Diving plugs are not the best choice for Banks Lake. Unless you have a very deft touch with them, the multiple trebles on most diving plugs will result in more hangups than fish. Do not overlook live bait for trophy bass. Consider using large shiners under a float, especially in the winter and early spring.

During the summer months, nighttime topwater bassing can be tremendous but a test of nerves. Nothing gets the blood racing quite like an explosive topwater strike. Some special regulations apply to night-fishing at Banks Lake.

Whatever method you choose, stout tackle is required. You must immediately muscle fish out of the thick Banks Lake cover if you hope to land any.

Banks Lake is probably best known for its bream fishing. Spawning colonies of hundreds of chunky bluegills can be found all over the lake from spring through late summer. Standard live bait methods with worms or crickets will work. A popping bug on a fly rod or long, limber bream pole is an efficient way of fishing around the base of cypress trees where bream are bedding. The trick is to make the bug bounce off the tree and fall into the water only inches away from the trunk. The reward is often the loud "smack" of a bull bream taking the lure.

Other species you may run into are crappie, chain pickerel, gar, and bowfin. Plenty of alligators call Banks Lake home, and they are content to go about their business as you go about yours. Sometimes gators will strike at lures and, if hooked, pose an interesting dilemma: write off a favorite lure, or tangle with irate gator?

Fishing is good year-round, but the summer months are usually avoided because of heat, thick aquatic weeds, and biting insects. Most anglers prefer spring.

GA~G grid: 60, G-1

General information: The lake has one access point. Facilities include a paved boat launch, restrooms, universally accessible fishing pier, and a short walking trail. No entrance fee is charged. Camping is not allowed on the refuge. Swimming, wading, personal watercraft, and waterskiing are also prohibited, as are firearms, other weapons, and hunting.

No restriction is placed on the size of boats and motors used on the lake, but one look should convince the angler that Banks Lake is not the place to do speed trials. With all the shallow stumps and logs, slow speeds and common sense will serve you well and safely get you where you are going.

Night-fishing is allowed during certain months. Contact the Refuge Office for more information on night-fishing.

Along with fine fishing, Banks Lake National Wildlife Refuge offers good opportunities for viewing many bird species including red-tailed hawks, osprey, black and turkey vultures, American kestrel, barred owls, and wood ducks. During the winter, many wood storks use the area.

Food, lodging, and supplies are available 2 miles away in Lakeland. For greater selection or specialized services, Valdosta is about 20 miles away.

Nearest camping: No camping is allowed in the area, and no public campgrounds are found in the immediate vicinity. Several private campgrounds are available about 20 miles away in Valdosta.

This view of Banks Lake gives an idea of the vast expanses of flooded cypress available for anglers.

Directions: From Lakeland, travel about 1.3 miles west on Georgia Highway 122 to the access point on the left, just east of the intersection of GA 122 and GA 122 Connector.

For more information: Contact the Banks Lake National Wildlife Refuge Office in Folkston or Wildlife Resources Division Fisheries Section Office in Waycross.

70 Okefenokee Swamp

Key species: chain pickerel, bowfin, bream, largemouth bass.

Overview: The Okefenokee Swamp is 438,000 acres of peat bog in southeast Georgia. The Okefenokee is a unique and well-preserved ecosystem, and fishing is only one of the many rewarding experiences for visitors.

Best way to fish: canoe, johnboat.

Best time to fish: October through April.

Description: Established in 1936, the Okefenokee National Wildlife Refuge encompasses about 396,000 acres (650 square miles) of the Okefenokee Swamp. The swamp is roughly 38 miles long and 25 miles wide. Since 1974, much of the Okefenokee National Wildlife Refuge has been designated as a National Wilderness Area. The Okefenokee is estimated to be between 6,000 and 8,000 years old and lies in a saucer-shaped depression that was once part of the ocean floor. Elevations range from 103 to 128 feet above mean sea level. Drainage from the swamp flows into two rivers, the Suwannee and the Saint

Okefenokee Swamp

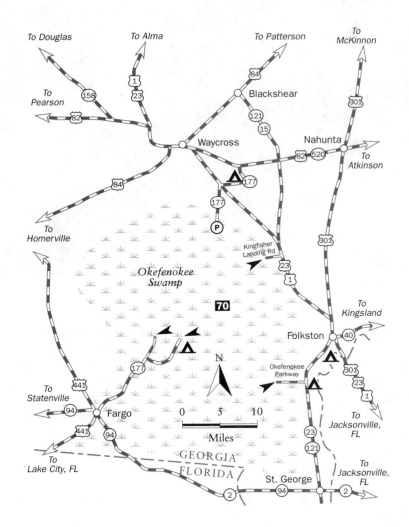

Marys. Native Americans inhabited the Okefenokee as early as 2500 B.C. and gave it its name, which means "land that trembles when you walk on it."

The swamp has many different habitat types including hummocks, prairies, marshes, and others. With such a variety of unique habitats, it is no wonder the area is home to so many different creatures. Visitors can look for at least 223 species of birds, 41 mammal species, 54 species of reptiles, and 60 species of amphibians.

The waters of the swamp are clear but stained the color of dark tea. Decaying vegetation produces tannins that give the water its distinctive color. Although the swamp looks like an angler's wildest dreams, fish populations

One of the most famous residents of the Okefenokee Swamp.

are actually quite modest. Tannic water is very acidic with a pH of about 3.7, well below the level preferred by most fish species. The swamp's waters are shallow, with depths more than 9 feet rare.

Although stories abound of huge bass pulled from the swamp's dark waters, the Okefenokee is a place that evokes legends, and most of the stories are just that, a legend. Documented catches of large bass are extremely rare. Chain pickerel and bowfin in the 10-pound range undoubtedly swim in the swamp, but most weigh much less.

The fishing: The swamp is full of rough fish like chain pickerel (jacks) and bowfin (mudfish). Both species are easy to find, strike viciously, fight strong, and have a mouth full of needle-like teeth. Fishing for jacks and mudfish is best done with standard bass tackle with one exception: a wire leader is a must.

For jacks, choose a large floating minnow lure or a large spinner briskly retrieved close to the surface around lilypads or other shallow cover. A spinner dressed with red, yellow, or white feathers is a local favorite. Jacks like flashy lures and seem to bite best on sunny days.

Mudfish are the biggest, meanest fish in the swamp. The state record mudfish was caught from the Okefenokee in 1976 and weighed 16 pounds. To target mudfish, retrieve large spinners close to bottom. Heavy-duty wire and hooks are required if you want to land a hard-fighting mudfish.

Bream and other sunfish can be caught using the usual techniques of worms, crickets, small spinners, or popping bugs. But, keep in mind that a jack or mudfish may take a liking to your bream offering and work a number on the lightweight bream tackle.

Largemouth bass are available in the swamp, although they are not nearly as abundant as jacks and mudfish. Use standard bass fishing techniques and be prepared for many more jack and mudfish strikes than bass strikes.

Although fish bite year-round, most anglers prefer early spring. Heat and insects can make a summer trip into the swamp an unpleasant experience.

GA~G grid: 61, 69

General information: All anglers fishing the Okefenokee Swamp must meet standard Georgia licensing requirements. Standard statewide creel and length limits apply. Private boats are allowed in the Okefenokee Swamp, but no motors more than 10 horsepower may be used. Some boat paths are restricted to nonmotorized boats only.

Access to the Okefenokee Swamp is limited to a few entrances. Stephen C. Foster State Park is the main entrance on the Okefenokee's west side. The park offers an interpretive center, a boat ramp, and boat rentals. Sill Landing near Stephen C. Foster State Park offers boat ramp facilities only. The north entrance of the swamp is the Okefenokee Swamp Park, a private not-for-profit attraction. This facility offers good wildlife viewing opportunities, boating tours of the swamp, and boardwalks. Okefenokee Swamp Park is excellent for those with limited time or who want a guided swamp experience. The park is not intended to be an access point for those wishing to explore and fish on their own. The east side of the swamp has a boat ramp at Kingfisher Landing. A boat ramp, boat rentals, visitor center, and other facilities are available at the Suwannee Canal Recreation Area, also on the east side of the swamp.

A daily use fee is charged. Be sure to check area rules and regulations upon arrival.

The Okefenokee is a special place, and human activities are closely managed to allow visitors to fully experience the wonders of the swamp without causing any damage to the fragile ecosystem. The Okefenokee National Wildlife Refuge publishes a wealth of information about the swamp and rules and regulations for its use.

Nearest camping: Primitive camping is allowed at designated campsites within the Okefenokee Swamp and is closely regulated. Reservations for overnight trips into the swamp are accepted and are absolutely necessary during the popular months.

Stephen C. Foster State Park on the west side of the swamp is the only public developed campground in the swamp. The state park has 66 tent, trailer, or RV sites with hookups, primitive camping, water, and comfort stations. Nine cabins are also available for rent.

Directions: From Fargo, access points to the Okefenokee Swamp can be reached from Georgia Highway 177; from Folkston, access points can be reached from GA 23 or U.S. Highway 1.

For more information: Contact the Okefenokee National Wildlife Refuge, Park Superintendent's Office at Stephen C. Foster State Park, or the Wildlife Resources Division Fisheries Section Office in Waycross.

71 Saint Marys River at Folkston

Key species: largemouth bass, redbreast sunfish, bluegill.

Overview: A blackwater river that drains part of the Okefenokee Swamp and serves as part of the Georgia-Florida border, the Saint Marys is one of Georgia's most beautiful coastal rivers.

Best way to fish: boat.

Best time to fish: year-round.

Description: The Saint Marys is a blackwater river. Very high dissolved organic carbon levels give the water its coffee-like appearance. The Saint Marys drainage is the smallest of Georgia's five coastal rivers. The river drains a part of the Okefenokee Swamp, and like the swamp, the water is acidic and fish populations are modest. However, this does not mean the Saint Marys is not a worthy destination. The river is unique, the scenery is outstanding, and while the Saint Marys is not known for the number of bass it gives up, it is known for larger-than-average fish. Besides bass, the river also contains large redbreast sunfish.

The Saint Marys is one of the few coastal plain rivers in southeast Georgia that have escaped colonization by non-native flathead catfish. Hopefully it will stay that way.

The Saint Marys is full of twists and turns. River bends and below sandbars are always good places to fish, and the Saint Marys has plenty of both. Where the river widens, patches of lilypads and other vegetation are common. Fishing is good at all but the highest river stages. Tidal influences in the river are strong. Even in the Traders Hill area, many miles away from the Atlantic and well upstream of the brackish water, when the tide comes in, the river current will go slack. Once the tide turns, the current picks back up.

The best fishing is from Folkston downstream. Access on the river is limited, but several ramps are found between Saint George and where the river turns brackish near the Interstate 95 crossing. Traders Hill Park is a good access point.

The fishing: The river supports good populations of largemouth bass, redbreast sunfish and bluegill. Although the best fishing, especially for bass, is from Traders Hill downstream, anglers should not totally shy away from the upper river near Saint George. The river is smaller here and makes a great canoe trip.

Anglers intent on catching largemouth bass should focus on casting spinnerbaits, plastic worms, or jigs around current breaks and heavy cover, both in the main river and the backwaters. Always retrieve your bait with the current to give it a lifelike appearance. Sharp casting is required to catch fish holding tight to a current break.

Redbreast sunfish grow big in the Saint Marys, with good numbers of fish exceeding 6 inches. You may not load the boat with fish, but the ones you catch are going to be larger than average. Worms and crickets fished under a float around heavy cover on the outside bends are productive. Casting small

Saint Marys River at Folkston

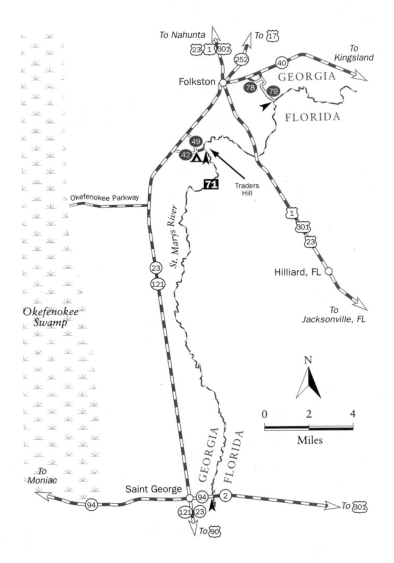

spinners and flycasting or dabbling a popping bug are also effective techniques.

Bluegill are more common in the backwaters than in the main river. Bluegill weighing 0.75 pound are common. Fish worms or crickets around shallow cover to catch these feisty panfish. Bluegill are great fun on a fly rod using a popping bug or sponge spider.

GA~G grid: 70

General information: Georgia and Florida have worked out a reciprocal agreement allowing anglers meeting the licensing requirements of either state to fish the waters and both banks of Saint Marys River; this agreement does not cover tributaries to the river. Regular Georgia creel and length limits apply on the waters covered by the reciprocal agreement.

Food, lodging, and supplies are available in Folkston about midway along the river's course.

Nearest camping: Owned and operated by Charlton County, the Traders Hill Park, Campground, and Recreation Area offers both primitive and developed camping. Restrooms are available.

Directions: The Saint Marys River can be reached from Georgia Highways 94, 23, and 40. To reach Traders Hill, from the intersection of U.S. Highway 301 and GA 23 in Folkston, travel south 2.9 miles on GA 23 to County Road 49 on the left. A sign for the area is at this intersection. Continue on this paved road after it runs into CR 42 until you reach the river.

For more information: Contact the Wildlife Resources Division Fisheries Section Office in Waycross. For information about facilities available at Traders Hill, contact the Folkston Chamber of Commerce.

72 Satilla River

Key species: redbreast sunfish, bluegill, largemouth bass, catfish.

Overview: Flowing 260 twisting and turning miles to the Atlantic Ocean, the Satilla is a blackwater river completely unimpeded by dams and is considered one of the most natural rivers in Georgia.

Best way to fish: boat.

Best time to fish: March through October.

Description: Although the Satilla is full of fish from start to finish, the section downstream of Waycross is the best for anglers. Upstream of Waycross navigation can be difficult at summer flows. Access on the river is good with many boat ramps scattered along its course. The first European to gaze upon the Satilla was the Spanish explorer DeSoto, but two French explorers, Admiral Gaspard Coligny and Jean Ribult, gave the river its name. The two named the river the Saint Ille, after a river in their homeland. "Saint Ille" was eventually bastardized into "Satilla."

The Satilla is known as a redbreast river. Redbreasts weighing more than a pound are possible. Bluegill are another popular target on the Satilla, and the average fish will measure 7 or 8 inches, with some larger fish possible. Although largemouth bass in the Satilla are overshadowed by the large and abundant sunfish, there are plenty of bass to make for a fun trip. Most fish will measure around 12 inches, with some larger specimens possible.

The fishing: The best redbreast fishing is from March to June. The fishing depends on the water level and most anglers believe the best time is when the river gauge at Waycross approaches 5 feet. The best section of the river for redbreast is from the U.S. Highway 301 crossing downstream to US 82. This stretch has everything redbreasts like: current, deep holes, and cover.

Satilla River

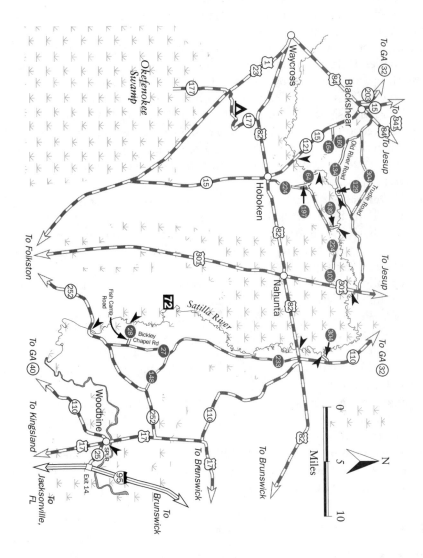

Downstream of this section is better bluegill fishing since the river has more wide, slow-moving sections and backwater sloughs. The same bait and lures will work for both redbreast sunfish and bluegill. Worms and crickets are the best natural baits, and small spinners and popping bugs the best artificials. What you are catching depends on where you are fishing; moving water around cover means redbreasts, slack-water cover means bluegills.

Largemouth bass can be caught throughout the Satilla, but the lower section, which has plenty of oxbows and backwater sloughs, is best. Floater/divers and spinnerbaits are good choices, as is a Texas-rigged plastic worm. Remember that largemouths do not like to fight the current and will always position themselves to take advantage of any current breaks.

The Satilla offers good fishing for channel catfish and a variety of bullhead species. Try worms, shrimp, or chicken livers on the bottom of deep holes.

Other species anglers may encounter are chain pickerel and several smaller sunfish species. Pickerel commonly strike bass lures, and the other sunfish species will result in a mixed creel by the end of a day of bream fishing.

Like most rivers, the fishing on the Satilla gets tough when the river is high. Not only are the fish hard to find, but if you venture into a flooded river swamp, you may have trouble finding the river again. Getting lost is extremely easy.

Although the best saltwater fishing in the Satilla is downstream of US 17, some tidal influences can be felt as far upstream as the Georgia Highway 252 crossing.

GA~G grid: 61, 62, 70

General information: The Satilla River is managed under standard Georgia creel and length limits with one exception regarding the harvest of striped bass, white bass, and hybrid striped bass; refer to the *Georgia Sport Fishing Regulations* pamphlet for more information. All anglers must meet Georgia licensing requirements.

Food, lodging, and supplies can be found at several locations along the river including Waycross and Woodbine.

The tide (Fernandina Beach Station) correction (Hr:Min) for the Burnt Fort area is Low +5:05, High +3:55.

Nearest camping: The nearest public campground is at Laura S. Walker State Park on GA 177 southeast of Waycross. The 626-acre park has 44 campsites with water and electricity.

Directions: From Nahunta, the Satilla River can be reached by secondary roads and state highways off US 82 and US 301; from Woodbine, the river can be reached from US 17.

For more information: Contact the Wildlife Resources Division Fisheries Section Office in Waycross. For camping information, contact the Park Superintendent's Office at Laura S. Walker State Park.

73 Upper Altamaha River

Key species: flathead catfish, largemouth bass, redbreast sunfish.

Overview: The upper Altamaha below the confluence of the Oconee and Ocmulgee rivers offers good fishing for a variety of species. You should have no problem finding a place to launch your boat in pursuit of monster flathead catfish or hefty largemouth bass.

Best way to fish: boat.

Best time to fish: year-round.

Description: Peaceful, full of fish, and laced with history, the Altamaha River is as close to perfection as one can get. The Altamaha is the largest river of the

Georgia coast, and one of few unimpounded rivers left in Georgia. With 137 miles of river downstream of where the Oconee and Ocmulgee meet, the Altamaha is the largest flow found entirely within the Peach State.

The Altamaha is a wide and meandering river. Bends and turns in the river channel are always the most productive areas to fish, and the Altamaha has plenty. That fact along with the fertile south Georgia soil may explain why the Altamaha is such a fine fishery.

Most of the land along the banks is undeveloped or used for agricultural purposes. Fishing pressure on the river is relatively light. Backwater lakes and sloughs can be just as good as or better than the river itself, depending on what species you are after and what the conditions are. Between the river itself and all the backwaters, there is a lot of water to explore.

Non-native flatheads were illegally introduced into the river sometime in the 1970s and have changed the fishing dramatically. The fishing for other species, notably redbreast sunfish, has suffered because of the flathead's predatory nature and booming numbers, but efforts to introduce anglers to flathead fishing have proved successful. Pulling huge flatheads from the Altamaha River's deep holes has become a favorite south Georgia pastime.

The fishing: The best time to fish is in late spring or early autumn when water levels are ideal and the heat and bugs tolerable. At high winter and springtime flows, the river becomes swollen with muddy water.

Although the best flathead fishing is found farther downstream, some of the biggest fish taken from the Altamaha have been caught from the upper section. Look for deep holes on the low end of sandbars, in the mouths of tributary creeks, and any outside bend. Lower a live bream or shiner on a heavy bottom-fishing rig into one of these holes and hold on. Heavy tackle is critical for subduing the Altamaha's big flatheads. Fish more than 60 pounds are a reality, and even larger fish have been boated using commercial fishing tactics.

Although flatheads are fast becoming the bread-and-butter fish of the Altamaha, largemouth bass are a close second. It was not too many miles away that the world-record bass was caught in 1932 from a slough on the Ocmulgee River. Truly trophy-sized fish are rare, but there are plenty of fish in the 5-pound range. The average bass will be 10 to 14 inches. What they lack in size they make up for in fight. A lifetime of struggling against the surprisingly strong current gives Altamaha bass impressive fighting abilities.

High water will push largemouths into the sloughs in the springtime. When water levels are normal, both the main river and the sloughs can be good. In the main river concentrate on eddies formed by blowdowns and sandbars. A spinnerbait is a good choice because it is virtually snag-free and covers a lot of water. Your casting needs to be right on the money. The lure should travel right alongside the cover just as if carried by the current. Another approach is to flip a jig-and-pig into the same areas. Flipping allows exact placement of the lure and a quiet entry.

The sloughs are also good during low water, but usually the fish will be closer rather than farther to the river. Just inside the mouth of the sloughs the

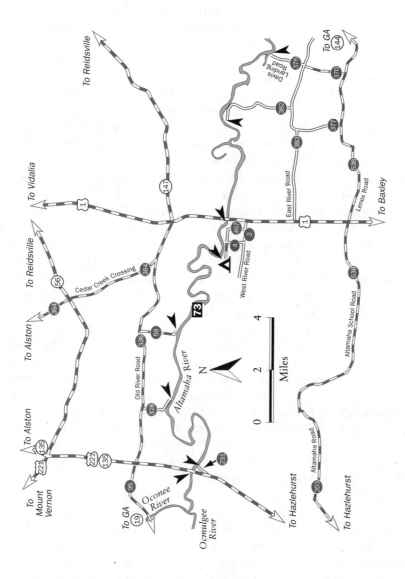

water quality is better, there is usually ample forage, and the fish are not continuously fighting the main-channel current. Spinnerbaits are still an excellent choice. A plastic worm or jig-and-pig bumped along bottom or through heavy cover is also productive, but will not cover nearly as much ground as a spinnerbait.

A creek mouth is always a good spot, and a band of incoming clear water will often hug the bank for a short distance before mixing with the dingier water of the main channel. Bass relate to this mud line just like they would any other cover. Try fishing these small pockets of clear water with a crankbait or spinnerbait. The fish will usually be positioned on the clear-water side of the transition.

Redbreast sunfish are seasonal favorites on the Altamaha. The best fishing is from April to June and is closely tied to water levels. If the water is high, fish for something else. Look for cover around the edges of deeper holes in the main river and use crickets or worms under a bobber in and around the cover. Small spinners, both in-line and safety-pin types, work well as do popping bugs. Light spinning tackle, a fly rod, or a long, limber bream pole will provide the most sport.

Other species anglers can expect to run into are channel catfish, bluegill, crappie, and redear sunfish.

The best fishing occurs when the U.S. Geological Survey gauge near Baxley reads 3.5 to 5.5 feet.

GA~G grid: 53, C-8

General information: The Altamaha River is managed under standard Georgia creel and length limits with one exception regarding the harvest of striped bass, white bass, and hybrid striped bass; refer to the *Georgia Sport Fishing Regulations* pamphlet for more information. All anglers must meet Georgia licensing requirements.

Food, lodging, and supplies are available within 20 miles in Hazlehurst or Baxley.

The Georgia Wildlife Resources Division publishes a *Guide to Fishing the Altamaha River*. The free guide includes a river map and has information on launch sites, camping, and fishing hints.

Nearest camping: Riverside camping is available at Deen's Campground. The nearest public campground is at Gordonia-Alatamaha State Park about 30 miles away. The park offers 26 sites for tents, trailers, and RVs; utilities and comfort stations are available.

Directions: This stretch of the Altamaha River is best reached from county roads off U.S. Highways 1 and 221 north of Hazlehurst and Baxley.

For more information: Contact the Wildlife Resources Division Fisheries Section Office in Waycross. For camping information, call the owner or Park Superintendent of the campgrounds listed.

74 Montgomery Lake (Lower Ocmulgee River)

Key species: largemouth bass, redbreast sunfish, bluegill, redear sunfish.

Overview: Not much more than a shallow, silted-in slough off the Ocmulgee River today, Montgomery Lake is hallowed ground. In 1932, these waters produced the world-record largemouth bass, and although many have tried, the record remains unbroken.

Best way to fish: boat.

Best time to fish: March through October.

Description: In all of freshwater fishing, no goal is pursued as vigorously as

Montgomery Lake (Lower Ocmulgee River)

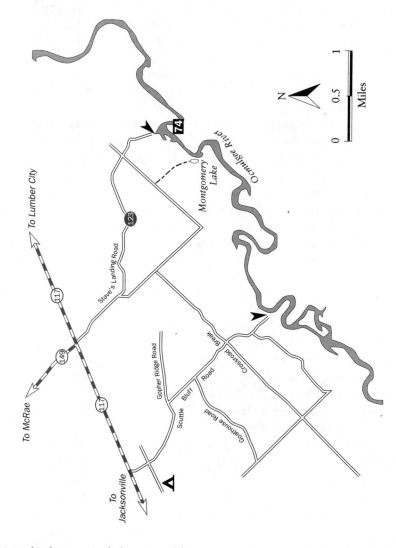

breaking the largemouth bass world-record weight of 22 pounds, 4 ounces. No one has been able to best the achievement of George W. Perry, a 19-year-old Georgia farm boy. On a June day in 1932, George Perry and his partner, Jack E. Page, fished from a 14-foot boat handmade from 75 cents worth of material. After a fruitless day of casting his one and only lure, a perch-pattern Creek Chub Wiggle-Fish, George Perry's fortunes changed. With a snap of the wrist he sent the Wiggle-Fish up next to a cypress log, and angling history was made. The monster fish weighed 22 pounds and 4 ounces, besting the previous world record by more than 2 pounds. The record bass was 32.5 inches long and 28.5 inches in girth.

The Ocmulgee River running high and muddy from spring rains.

Although it is estimated the next world-record bass will be worth a $1 million in endorsements to the lucky angler who catches it, fame and fortune was far from George Perry's mind on June 2, 1932. When Perry went to a country store in Helena to weigh his huge fish, someone mentioned that *Field and Stream* magazine was sponsoring a national fishing contest. The fish was weighed on certified scales and was the winning entry in the contest. For winning the contest George Perry received $75 worth of merchandise, including a new rod and reel. After the fish was weighed and measured, it was taken home, cleaned, and eaten by the Perry family. Although Montgomery Lake is in effect gone as a fishing hole, it is still there for the angler to see and envision a young Georgia farm boy standing the angling world on its ear.

Unless the river is extremely high, the best way to reach Montgomery Lake is on foot. The slough lies within the bounds of the Horse Creek Wildlife Management Area and is reachable by a short hike.

Montgomery Lake may be just a shadow of its former self, but many other sloughs and backwaters on the lower Ocmulgee River offer good fishing for bass and other species. Although the average bass will weigh only a couple of pounds, the Ocmulgee has proven that it can produce fish of tremendous size. Who knows, the tap-tap felt on the end of your line may signal the beginning of a new chapter in freshwater angling history.

The fishing: The best time to catch bass in the Ocmulgee River's backwater lakes is in April when the bass are spawning. Bass prefer to construct their nests in shallow, still water with a sandy bottom. When the water temperature stabilizes in the mid-60s, bass head to the backwaters to spawn, and the lakes provide the best fishing of the year. River level also plays a factor. If the river is too high, the backwaters flood and bass move into areas anglers cannot reach. When it is too low, the backwaters are almost dry and getting into them can be a problem. The ideal river stage for fishing the backwaters is between 3 and 8 feet on the U.S. Geological Survey gauge at Lumber City. A gauge reading between 4 and 6 feet indicates ideal conditions for spawning, assuming the temperature is right. Good lures are spinnerbaits, shallow-diving crankbaits, and floater/divers. The waters of the Ocmulgee are usually stained, especially in the spring, so a pattern that includes orange or chartreuse with plenty of contrast is a good choice.

Bluegill and redear sunfish are also common in the backwater lakes. Fish worms or crickets around shallow cover or spawning beds. Redbreast sunfish are more commonly caught in the moving waters of the main river channel. Outside bends and other deep holes that have woody cover are good places to try.

GA~G grid: 52, E-3

General information: The lower Ocmulgee River and its backwaters are managed under standard Georgia creel and length limits with a few exceptions. All largemouth bass harvested must be a minimum of 14 inches, and special regulations govern the harvest of striped bass, white bass, and hybrid striped bass; refer to the *Georgia Sport Fishing Regulations* pamphlet for more information. All anglers fishing the river must meet Georgia licensing requirements. Food, lodging, and supplies are 21 miles away in McRae.

Nearest camping: Camping is available in the Horse Creek Wildlife Management Area. The campsites are undeveloped, but the comfort station has running water, hot showers, and flush toilets.

Directions: From Lumber City, take Georgia Highway 117 west to its intersection with GA 149. Instead of turning right onto GA 149, turn left onto Stave's Landing Road (County Road 123). Follow this road to the river. To reach the Horse Creek Wildlife Management Area main entrance, follow the directions above except continue on GA 117 to the entrance on the left

For more information: Contact the Wildlife Resources Division Fisheries Section Office in Waycross.

75 Dodge County Public Fishing Area

Key species: largemouth bass, bluegill, redear sunfish, channel catfish.

Overview: Dodge County Public Fishing Area, operated by the Georgia Wildlife Resources Division, is on a 444-acre tract of gently rolling land nestled in Georgia's middle coastal plain. The centerpiece of the area is 104-acre Steve Bell Lake.

Best way to fish: shore, boat.

Best time to fish: year-round.

Description: Dodge County Public Fishing Area opened in 1992. The gently

Dodge County Public Fishing Area

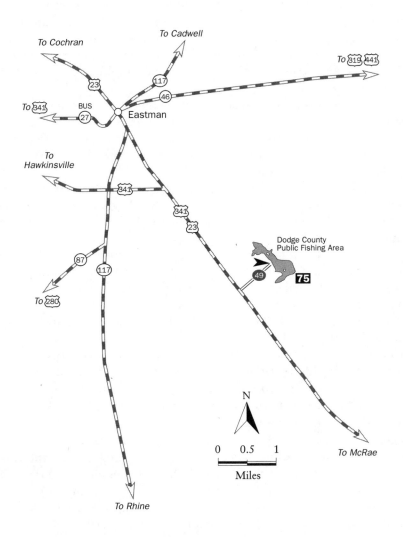

rolling tract of land contains a variety of habitats including mixed pine and hardwood stands, wiregrass/longleaf pine, planted pines, and hardwood bottoms. Steve Bell Lake has several coves and points, a small island, and some standing timber and submerged structure. The lake averages 10 feet deep, although depths of 28 feet are present at the dam. The area is intensively managed to produce quality angling for both boat and shore anglers.

Facilities for anglers include paved boat ramps, plenty of parking, restrooms, and a universally accessible fishing pier. Other facilities include picnic tables, an archery range, and a self-guided nature trail.

The fishing: Steve Bell Lake produces monster largemouth bass. Anglers have pulled several enormous mossybacks from the lake including one behemoth weighing more than 13 pounds. The best time for a truly huge bass is in very early spring. Prime areas include any shoreline structure on shallow banks, especially those found close to deeper water. The riprap dam can also be very productive, especially on sunny days. The warm sunshine on the rocks of the dam warms the water and bass will move in to bask and feed. A slow retrieve with a dark colored jig-and-pig combo or small crankbait can be very effective this time of year.

As spring turns into summer, the bass will move deeper in search of cooler water. Fishing the jig-and-pig or a Carolina-rigged soft plastic bait in deeper water should be productive. During autumn, bass again become active in shallow water where they feed heavily in preparation for winter. Spinnerbaits and small crankbaits are good bets during this fall feeding frenzy.

Bluegill and shellcracker are very popular here. The best action is when bream are spawning in April, May, and June. Find a colony of spawning sunfish by searching the upper end of the lake in 4 to 6 feet of water. Sometimes the spawning beds will be visible to the naked eye and appear as saucer-sized depressions that are lighter colored than the surrounding bottom. Sunfish weighing more than a pound are possible, but most are hand-sized. The favorite live baits are red wiggler worms and crickets. Good lures to try are small Beetle Spins in neon-yellow or yellow with black stripes.

Channel catfish are another sought-after species in the area. Almost any natural bait will work for channel catfish, but favorites are chicken livers, shrimp, or a gob of worms fished on bottom. Channel catfish rarely strike artificial baits. Although most catfish average around a pound, channel catfish up to 10 pounds are present. Good places to try for channel catfish are around the riprap dam and near the automatic fish feeders.

GA~G grid: 43, H-10 (not shown in GA~G)

General information: Dodge County Public Fishing Area is an excellent choice for a trip that includes the whole family. Any size boat and motor is allowed, but all boats are limited to idle speed. Anglers must meet Georgia licensing requirements and have a Wildlife Management Area stamp. Senior Lifetime, Honorary, Sportsman's, and 1-Day license holders do not need the WMA stamp. See the information board at the area for more information.

Food, lodging, and supplies are available 3 miles away in Eastman.

Nearest camping: Primitive camping is allowed in the area.

Directions: Dodge County Public Fishing Area is 3 miles southeast of Eastman on U.S. Highway 23/341. Look for the sign on the highway, and then turn left on Dodge Lake Road (County Road 49) and continue 0.6 mile to the area.

For more information: Contact the Dodge County Public Fishing Area Manager's Office.

76 Treutlen County Public Fishing Area

Key species: largemouth bass, bluegill, redear sunfish.

Overview: Operated by the Georgia Wildlife Resources Division, Treutlen County Public Fishing Area offers anglers a chance at a variety of fish species in a small lake setting.

Best way to fish: boat, shore.

Best time to fish: year-round.

Description: Commonly known as Sand Hill Lake among local residents, the Treutlen County Public Fishing Area offers anglers good fishing for a variety of species. Except for a small boat ramp, the lake is undeveloped and receives little fishing pressure. Most shoreline fishing is limited to a few easy access points, and anglers using a small boat or a canoe should have the lake virtually to themselves.

The 189-acre lake is shallow. Depths down to 9 feet are found in a few holes, for example around the old diving board. Shallow cover like stumps and lilypad fields are abundant. An old fence line runs through the middle of the lake and is one of the best places to find fish relating to deeper cover.

Although the lake gives up a few trophies, it is better known as a constant producer of fish. Most largemouth bass caught will be in the 1- to 3-pound range. The same holds true for the bream, crappie, and catfish in the lake; plenty of eating-size fish that are fun to catch, but trophies are rare.

The fishing: Anglers in search of the lake's largemouth bass should concentrate on woody cover and lilypads. A soft-plastic bait worked slowly along the bottom near any cover is sure to draw strikes. Fish the outside weedlines with a spinnerbait, plastic worm, or a Rat-L-Trap. When the weeds have topped out in the summer, slowly retrieving a floating frog over the matted vegetation can bring spectacular strikes. Be sure to hit any potholes or pockets in the weeds.

Bluegill, shellcracker, and other sunfish species including warmouth and flier are caught around shallow cover on worms and crickets. If fooling fish with artificials is your game, try casting a small Beetle Spin or fly fishing with a popping bug. During the spring and summer months, keep your eye peeled and your nose open in search of bream beds. The spawning beds are easily spotted in shallow water, and experienced bream anglers can even track them down by smell. When a bream bed is found, fast fishing is sure to follow.

Brown bullheads are common catches. A gob of worms or chicken liver fished on bottom should draw nibbling strikes from these bantam-sized members of the catfish family.

GA~G grid: 45, D-6

General information: Treutlen County Public Fishing Area is open year-round from sunrise to sunset. A paved boat ramp is available. All boats are limited to electric motors only. Anglers must meet Georgia licensing requirements and possess a Wildlife Management Area stamp. Senior Lifetime, Honorary, Sportsman's, and 1-Day license holders do not need the WMA stamp.

Treutlen County Public Fishing Area

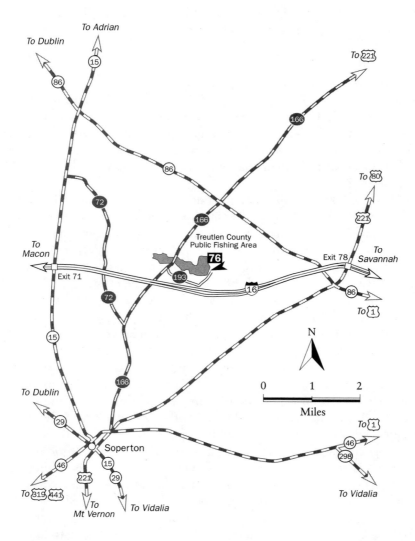

To Adrian

To Dublin

15

86

To 221

166

To 80

221

72

166

To
Macon

Treutlen County
Public Fishing Area

76

Exit 78

To
Savannah

Exit 71

193

16

86

72

To 1

N

15

0   1   2

Miles

To Dublin

166

To 1

29

46

Soperton

298

46

15

To Vidalia

221

29

To 819 441

To
Mt Vernon

To Vidalia

Creel and length limits for the area follow Georgia Public Fishing Area regulations. Consult the *Georgia Sport Fishing Regulations* pamphlet for more information.

Food, lodging, and supplies are 4 miles away in Soperton. More options are available in 22 miles away in Swainsboro.

Nearest camping: The nearest camping is 35 miles away at George L. Smith State Park (see Site 77). The park has 25 campsites with utilities and comfort stations available. Four equipped cottages are also available for rent.

Directions: From the intersection of U.S. Highway 221 and County Road 166 in Soperton, travel north 3.9 miles on CR 166 to the entrance sign on the right. Follow the dirt road to the boat ramp on the east side of the lake.

For more information: Contact the Wildlife Resources Division Fisheries Section Office in Metter. For camping information, contact the George L. Smith State Park Superintendent's Office.

77 Watson Mill Pond (George L. Smith State Park)

Key species: largemouth bass, bluegill, redear sunfish, crappie.

Overview: The 412-acre lake at George L. Smith State Park is actually a mill pond dating back to 1880. Much of the mill pond is studded with cypress trees, making the lake a haven for fish but a confusing maze for boaters.

Best way to fish: boat.

Best time to fish: year-round.

Description: One look at the lake in 1,638-acre George L. Smith State Park, named after one of Georgia's greatest legislators, and your mind will reel at the thought of all the fish that must live in the waters. The fishing is good, but it is not as easy as you might think. Simply navigating the lake can be difficult because of all the submerged stumps, and getting confused in the flooded cypress forest is very easy. To help with navigating the lake, more than 10 miles of boating trails are marked. Red signs show the main channel, and blue or yellow markings show the path of secondary channels and boat trails.

Unlike most cypress lakes, Watson Mill Pond is not a blackwater lake. These waters are much more fertile and sustain a high fish population. The mill pond is not deep; depths of 9 feet may be found in the channels, and there are a few holes that go to down nearly 20 feet. However, most of the lake averages less than 5 feet deep, with a very gradual slope away from the shore to deeper water.

Largemouth bass weighing more than 11 pounds have been documented, and local reports of fish weighing more than 15 pounds being pulled from the fertile waters are common. Most of the bass caught will weigh between 1 and 2 pounds. Since Watson Mill Pond is an extremely old lake and just a wide area on a natural stream, many different fish species live in the lake. Beyond key species listed above, anglers are likely to encounter crappie, a variety of smaller sunfish species, and bowfin.

The fishing: The problem with lakes like Watson Mill Pond is that everything looks so good, you do not know where to start. The best way to approach the lake is to pretend the thousands of cypress trees are not present. Close your eyes, picture the lake without the trees, and imagine where you would find bass that time of year. If the answer is in the channels, fish cypress trees on the channel edges. If the answer is on the shoreline, fish cypress trees near the shore.

Good places to try are the edges of the marked channels, especially where two channels come together, or in a channel bend. Lilypads are common and

Watson Mill Pond (George L. Smith State Park)

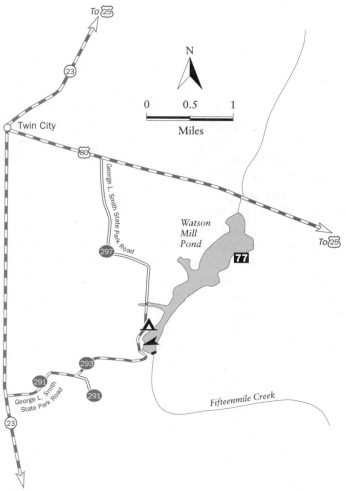

can produce heart-stopping action during the summer when a big bass blows through the overhead canopy of pads to smash a topwater bait.

Once you have decided where to fish, lure selection is the next hurdle. Whatever lure you choose must be able to come through heavy cover. Texas-rigged soft plastics, weedless spoons, and spinnerbaits are local favorites. Working the surface with topwaters or floater/divers is another way to avoid the submerged tangle of stumps and cypress knees, and can be very productive in spring and fall.

Catching bluegill and other sunfish is the same as bass fishing. Search for areas near a channel or where two types of cover come together. Live bait like

The old grist mill at George L. Smith State Park.

worms or crickets fished around cover is the most effective method for catching bream. Anglers may want to consider using a long bream pole to dabble live bait right in the cover with a vertical presentation. A good choice for artificials is a popping bug. Although most places have little room for traditional flycasting, use a popping bug and a fixed length of monofilament line slightly shorter than the rod to shoot the popping bug right to the target. Carefully hold the bug between your fingers, pull back to load up the rod, point the rod at the target, and let go. The energy stored in the bend of the rod will shoot the bug to its target without the need for casting. Bouncing the bug off the trunk of a tree so it falls naturally to the water can draw furious strikes from big bream.

GA~G grid: 46, B-1

General information: Private boats are allowed on Watson Mill Pond and a boat ramp is available. Rental fishing boats and canoes are also available. Gasoline motors are limited to 10 horsepower, and going slow is strongly recommended because of all the submerged cover. Although there is no restriction on the size of the boat, just the horsepower of the motor, the tight quarters of the flooded cypress forest lend themselves to a small, shallow-draft boat that can more easily negotiate the twists and turns needed to reach prime fishing areas.

Anglers on the lake must meet Georgia licensing requirements, and a valid daily or annual Georgia Parks Pass is required to park in the area. Standard Georgia creel and length limits apply. The lake is open year-round from sunrise to sunset.

Food, lodging, and supplies are available in the park or 4 miles away in Twin City.

Nearest camping: Camping is available in the park. The site has 25 campsites with utilities and comfort stations present. Four equipped cottages are also available for rent.

Directions: From Twin City, drive south 2.8 miles on Georgia Highway 23 to George L. Smith State Park Road on the left. Follow this paved road 1.6 miles to the park entrance.

For more information: Contact the Wildlife Resources Division Fisheries Section Office in Metter or the George L. Smith State Park Superintendent's Office.

78 Evans County Public Fishing Area

Key species: largemouth bass, bluegill, redear sunfish, channel catfish, crappie.

Overview: Operated by the Georgia Wildlife Resources Division, the Evans County Public Fishing Area offers good fishing for a variety of species. The site contains three small lakes open to public fishing.

Best way to fish: boat, shore.

Best time to fish: year-round.

Description: Evans County Public Fishing Area consists of three small lakes intensively managed for public fishing. The lakes are 8, 30, and 84 acres in size. All three lakes offer good fishing, but most anglers prefer to fish the largest lake. Although not a state-operated area from the beginning, the lakes have been under intensive management for many years. Weed control, facility maintenance and construction, and the placement of fish attractors make the area great fishing, especially for families. Besides fishing, families will find restrooms, picnic facilities, nature walks, and wildlife-viewing opportunities. Some facilities are accessible to those with disabilities.

On some days, especially during the week, yours may be the only boat on the water, and only a handful of anglers may be working the shoreline. On weekends, use is a little heavier, but there is still plenty of room for everybody.

The big lake offers a little bit of everything, including lilypads, cattail-lined shorelines, fallen and standing timber, flats, drop-offs, and channels. Although just a small boat is needed to fish the lake, a depth finder should be considered essential equipment to find offshore cover and structure.

Anglers have pulled largemouth bass weighing well into the double-digits from the Evans County Public Fishing Area lakes. Bluegill and shellcracker run big too, with half-pounders common. Channel catfish are popular with regulars in the area, and for good reason; monster cats weighing nearly 15 pounds have been caught from the lakes.

The fishing: Some of the biggest bass caught recently at the Evans County Public Fishing Area have come on topwater plugs. Late evening is a good time to toss topwaters around the willows and flats on the upper end of the lake. This far south, topwaters can be counted on almost year-round, but the spring

Evans County Public Fishing Area

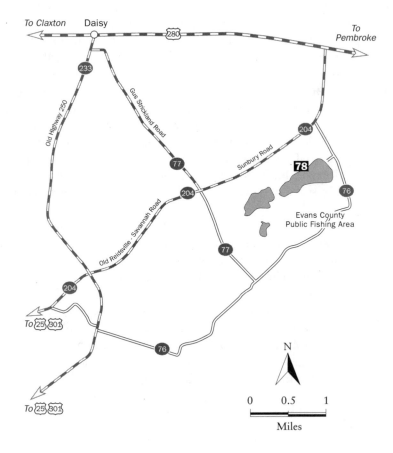

To Claxton   Daisy
To Pembroke
233
Gus Strickland Road
Old Highway 250
77
204
Sunbury Road
78
204
76
Evans County
Public Fishing Area
Old Reidsville - Savannah Road
77
204
To 25 301
76
To 25 301

N

0   0.5   1
Miles

and summer months, when the bream are spawning, are a prime time to find bass in the shallows chasing newly hatched sunfish. If you stand on the dam of the large lake and look down its length, the left side is shallow with depths around 6 feet. The right side of the lake has much deeper water with drops and channels down to 17 feet. Probe the deeper waters with jigs, soft plastics, and deep-diving crankbaits.

Bream fishing for bluegill and shellcracker is very popular at Evans County. Crickets and worms are favorite live baits, and a small spinner bumped briskly along the bottom is a good choice in the artificial department. Fly fishers will find a lightweight outfit paired with a small popping bug or sponge spider to be a productive combination. Since the bass at Evans County will not hesitate to take a lure off the top, a large popping bug or deer-hair bug can produce smashing strikes and a real battle on a fly rod. Bream can be found around any shallow cover. Potholes in stands of lilypads are a great place to find bream. During the spawn is the best fishing of the year since the fish are concentrated and very aggressive.

Many anglers in the area prefer catfish, and a favorite tactic is to fish smelly baits on the bottom. Chicken livers and shrimp are both popular. Soak the bait near channels or other areas with deep water nearby.

Some anglers like to chase crappie at Evans County. Small jigs trolled over the channel ledges or fished near shallow cover in early spring are productive.

GA~G grid: 46, H-4

General information: Evans County Public Fishing Area is open from sunrise to sunset, 365 days a year. Any size boat and motor is allowed, but all boats are limited to idle speed only. All anglers must meet Georgia licensing requirements and possess a Wildlife Management Area stamp. Senior, Lifetime, Honorary, Sportsman's, and 1-Day license holders do not need the WMA stamp.

Creel and length limits for the area follow Georgia Public Fishing Area regulations. Consult the Georgia Sport Fishing Regulations pamphlet for more information.

Food, lodging, and supplies are available 10 miles away in Claxton.

Nearest camping: Primitive camping is allowed in the area. The nearest developed campground is about 23 miles away at Gordonia-Alatamaha State Park near Reidsville. The park offers 26 campsites, and utilities and comfort stations are available.

Directions: From Claxton, go east on U.S. Highway 280 for 8.5 miles. Turn right onto Sunbury Road (County Road 204) and drive 1 mile. Turn left onto dirt Old Sunbury Road (CR 76) and drive 0.3 mile to the entrance on the right.

For more information: Contact the Evans County Public Fishing Area Manager's Office. For camping information, contact Gordonia-Alatamaha State Park.

Coastal Georgia

Coastal Georgia offers a good mix of both saltwater and freshwater angling opportunities. Georgia's saltwater fishing is underrated and often overlooked. Boating anglers will find good action near shore and offshore, and shorebound anglers should have no problem finding a pier or catwalk to take advantage of Georgia's coastal resources. The freshwater fishing in this part of the state takes place on beautiful coastal rivers and in small ponds and lakes that can grow some huge bass.

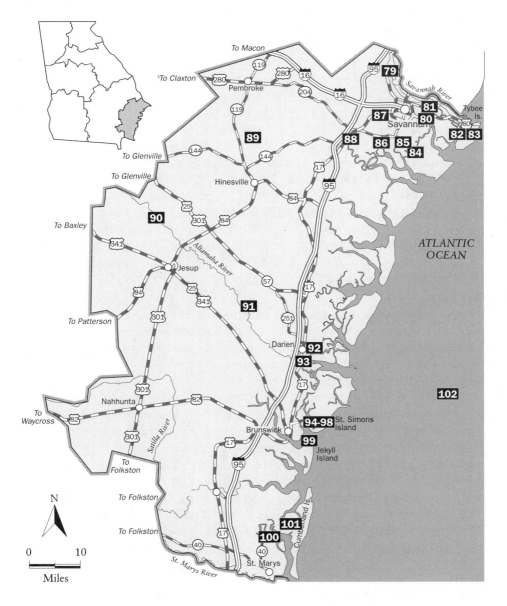

Key species: striped bass, white catfish, channel catfish.

Overview: This stretch of the Savannah River offers good year-round fishing for white and channel catfish and seasonal fishing for striped bass and other saltwater species.

Best way to fish: boat.

Best time to fish: October through May.

Description: The public boat ramp contains two double-lane ramps and a floating service dock. Easy access and the good fishing makes Houlihan Park a popular choice with anglers. Both freshwater and marine species are available depending on the tide.

The fishing: The Savannah River around Houlihan Park is predominantly a freshwater fishery, but when the tide brings the saltwater in, marine species that do not mind feeding in the transition zone will use the area. The most consistent angling at Houlihan Park is for white and channel catfish. Dead shrimp fished on bottom are a good choice for bait. Flounder fishing begins to pick up in September and the fish are available through fall. From November through January, occasional red drum and spotted seatrout are possible.

Mid-January to May is the best time for striped bass. One of the best places to fish is right around the Houlihan Bridge (Georgia Highway 25) itself. Large plugs or jigs retrieved at mid-depths should produce strikes when stripers are around. Special regulations govern the Savannah River striped bass fishery; be sure you know and understand the law before fishing. Largemouth bass are present in good numbers and can be caught when conditions are right.

Food, lodging, and supplies are available in Port Wentworth and along the Interstate 95 corridor.

GA~G grid: 47, H-10

General information: Manatees are sometimes in the area, so extra boating precautions are in order. Georgia and South Carolina have a reciprocal agreement allowing anglers meeting the freshwater license requirements of either state to fish on the banks and in the waters of all channels of the Savannah River from its mouth upstream. However, anglers fishing from a boat on the South Carolina side of the Savannah River downstream of where the CSX Railroad trestle crosses the Back River must have a South Carolina saltwater fishing license. No person may possess more fish in any state's water than the laws of that state allow no matter where the fish were caught. Some special regulations apply to the Savannah River. Be sure to see the *Georgia Sport Fishing Regulations* pamphlet for more information on the reciprocal agreement and both fresh and saltwater creel and length limits.

The tide (Savannah River Entrance) correction (Hr:Min) for the Port Wentworth area is Low +1:32, High +0:48, and Feet +0.2.

Nearest camping: The nearest public campground is at Skidaway Island State Park, about 22 miles away. The 533-acre barrier island park has 88 campsites,

Savannah River at Houlihan Park
Wilmington River at Thunderbolt Park
Wilmington River at F. W. Spencer Community Park
Lazaretto Creek
Tybee Island
Skidaway River Narrows
Moon River at Downing Piers
Little Ogeechee River at Bell's Landing
Salt Creek
Ogeechee River at Kings Ferry

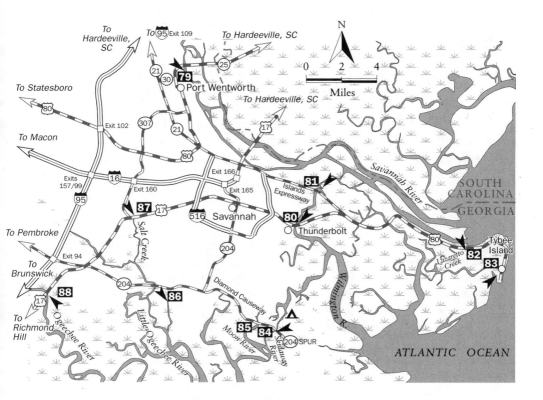

each with water, electricity, picnic table, and grill. The comfort stations have flush toilets and hot showers. Laundry facilities are available. The campground is open year-round.

Directions: From Interstate 95, north of Garden City, take exit 109 south on Georgia Highway 30 for 2.7 miles. Turn left and continue south on GA 30 for an additional 0.9 mile to GA 25. Turn left (north) for 0.8 mile. The park is on the right before crossing Houlihan Bridge (Savannah River).

For more information: Contact the Wildlife Resources Division Fisheries Section Office at Demeries Creek. For camping information, contact the Skidaway Island Park Superintendent's Office.

80 Wilmington River at Thunderbolt Park

See map on page 299

Key species: red drum, croaker, spot, sheepshead, spotted seatrout.

Overview: With both a boat ramp and fishing pier, the Wilmington River at Thunderbolt Park offers something for every inshore angler.

Best way to fish: boat, pier.

Best time to fish: year-round; species available are highly seasonal.

Description: Both boat and shore anglers will find good access at Thunderbolt Park. A single-lane paved launching ramp is on the east side of the river and across from it on the west side is a wheelchair-accessible fishing pier with handrails. Along with the fishing pier are restrooms, picnic tables, and a children's playground.

The fishing: The fishing for most species is highly seasonal. Check with local bait and tackle shops to find out what is biting at the time of your trip. A standard fish-finder rig baited with shrimp or a fiddler crab is a good all-around choice for catching many species found in the area.

GA~G grid: 39, B-8

General information: Anglers must meet all Georgia licensing requirements. Standard Georgia creel and length limits apply with the exception of special regulations governing the harvest of striped bass and hybrid striped bass; refer to the *Georgia Sport Fishing Regulations* pamphlet for more information.

The tide (Savannah River Entrance) correction (Hr:Min) for the Thunderbolt area is Low +0:12, High +0:32, and Feet +1.0.

Nearest camping: The nearest public campground is at Skidaway Island State Park about 12 miles away. The 533-acre barrier island park has 88 campsites, each with water, electricity, picnic table, and a grill. The comfort stations have flush toilets and hot showers. Laundry facilities are available. The campground is open year-round.

Directions: Thunderbolt Fishing Pier: from Interstate 95, west of Savannah, take exit 99 and travel east on I-16 for 7.8 miles to exit 165. Take the 37th Street Connector exit for 0.6 mile to 37th Street. Turn left on Georgia Highway 204 for 0.8 mile to Abercorn Street. Turn right and travel 0.3 mile to

U.S. Highway 80. Turn left on US 80 and travel 2.9 miles to Mechanics Avenue. Turn left on Mechanics Avenue for 0.3 mile to the pier.

Thunderbolt Boat Ramp: follow the directions above except continue 4 miles on US 80 to Macceo Drive on the left just past the Wilmington River bridge. Follow Macceo Drive 0.4 mile to the launch ramp.

For more information: Contact the Coastal Resources Division Office in Brunswick.

81 Wilmington River at F. W. Spencer Community Park

See map on page 299

Key species: red drum, croaker, spot, sheepshead, spotted seatrout.

Overview: A good access point on the Wilmington River not far from its confluence with the Savannah, F.W. Spencer Community Park has both a launching ramp and fishing pier.

Best way to fish: boat, pier.

Best time to fish: year-round; species available are highly seasonal.

Description: F.W. Spencer Community Park has everything you need for an inshore fishing trip. The fishing pier has handrails, and restrooms and picnic tables are available. The ramp is paved and has two lanes. Bait, fishing gear, food, and drinks are available on site.

The fishing: The old standby fish-finder rig and shrimp will serve you well on the pier at F.W. Spencer Community Park. What you can expect to catch depends on the season. Ask around in local bait shops or talk to other anglers on the pier to find out what is in and biting.

GA~G grid: 39, A-8

General information: Anglers must meet all Georgia licensing requirements. Standard Georgia creel and length limits apply except for special regulations governing the harvest of striped bass and hybrid striped bass; refer to the *Georgia Sport Fishing Regulations* pamphlet for more information.

The tide (Savannah River Entrance) correction (Hr:Min) for the Wilmington River–Thunderbolt area is Low +0:12, High +0:32, and Feet +1.0.

Nearest camping: The nearest public campground is at Skidaway Island State Park about 15 miles away. The park has 88 campsites with water, electricity, picnic tables, and grills; comfort stations have flush toilets and hot showers. Laundry facilities are available. The campground is open year-round.

Directions: From Interstate 95, west of Savannah, take exit 99 and travel east on I-16 for 7.8 miles to exit 165. Take the 37th Street Connector exit for 0.6 mile to 37th Street. Turn left on Georgia Highway 204 for 0.8 mile to Abercorn Street. Turn right and travel 0.3 mile to U.S. Highway 80. Turn left on US 80 and travel 6 miles to the Islands Expressway. Turn left on Islands Expressway and travel 1.5 miles to the park on the right.

For more information: Contact the Coastal Resources Division Office in Brunswick.

82 Lazaretto Creek

See map on page 299

Key species: whiting, sheepshead, spotted seatrout, red drum.

Overview: Lazaretto Creek is one of two creeks that make Tybee Island an island. With both a public fishing pier and a boat ramp, the Lazaretto Creek access point is a good choice for any type of angler.

Best way to fish: pier, boat.

Best time to fish: year-round; most species seasonal.

Description: The western end of Tybee Island once was a quarantine station for sick passengers coming in off ships. Unfortunate passengers thought to be carrying a communicable disease were quarantined for up to four months, and if they died, they were buried on the spot. "Lazaretto" is an Italian word for an institution or hospital for those with contagious diseases, and the name was applied to the creek that separated the quarantined Tybee Island from the mainland.

The Lazaretto Creek boat ramp is a good starting point if you intend to fish the Savannah River entrance or the open waters and tidal creeks around Tybee Island. Fishing from the pier provides a good view of the shrimp boats docked across the creek.

Food, lodging, and supplies are 2 miles away on Tybee Island.

The fishing: The fishing in Lazaretto Creek is seasonal. Fishing shrimp on the bottom is always a good bet for anything that is biting. For whiting, use small pieces no more than an inch long. For other species, larger bait can be used. Slowly working a jig along the bottom can also be effective.

For sheepshead around the pilings, use a small fiddler crab. Hook the crab by inserting the barb between the walking legs. Do not push the hook on through; leave the barb hidden inside the crab. Lower the bait to the bottom near pilings and other barnacle-encrusted structure, slowly raise and lower it, and if the slightest resistance or tug is felt, set the hook. Sheepshead are notorious bait thieves, and it takes almost a sixth sense to detect a strike.

Since the fishing for certain species is highly seasonal, check with local marinas and bait shops to see what is biting the best and plan your strategy accordingly.

GA~G grid: 39, B-10

General information: All anglers must meet Georgia licensing requirements. Standard Georgia saltwater creel and length limits apply except for special regulations governing the harvest of striped bass and hybrid striped bass; refer to the *Georgia Sport Fishing Regulations* pamphlet for more information.

The Lazaretto Creek Pier is equipped with handrails and the boat ramp has a floating courtesy dock. Restrooms are available.

The Savannah River Entrance tide chart will give you a good idea of tide height and when it will turn at Lazaretto Creek.

Nearest camping: The nearest public campground is at Skidaway Island State Park about 23 miles away. The park has 88 campsites with water, electricity, picnic tables, and grills; comfort stations have flush toilets and hot showers.

An excursion boat passes the shrimp boats moored in Lazaretto Creek.

Laundry facilities are available. The campground is open year-round.

A private campground is available on Tybee Island. The RV park has more than 150 sites with full utilities.

Directions: From Interstate 95, west of Savannah, take exit 99 and travel east on I-16 for 7.8 miles to exit 165. Take the 37th Street Connector exit for 0.6 mile to 37th Street. Turn left on Georgia Highway 204 for 0.8 mile to Abercorn Street. Turn right and travel 0.3 mile to U.S. Highway 80. Turn left on US 80 and travel 13.6 miles to Lazaretto Creek Boat Ramp located on the right. Follow the access road past the boat ramp for 0.4 mile to the pier.

For more information: Contact the Coastal Resources Division Office in Brunswick.

83 Tybee Island

See map on page 299

Key species: shark, whiting, sheepshead, flounder, Spanish mackerel, many others.

Overview: Jutting out into the Atlantic Ocean 18 miles east of Savannah, Tybee Island offers great saltwater fishing from a boat, pier, or in the surf.

Best way to fish: boat, pier, surf.

Best time to fish: year-round; species available are highly seasonal.

Description: Reputedly taking its name from a Native American word meaning "salt," Tybee Island's past is as colorful as its present. Known for its laid-back attitude and individuality, 2.5 miles long by 0.75 mile wide Tybee Island and its beaches are popular with tourists and day-trippers in the summer. The rest of the year, the island's 4,000 or so residents go about their business of enjoying their island community in their own unique way.

The first Europeans to lay claim to Tybee Island were the Spanish in the 1500s. They were followed 200 years later by General James Edward Oglethorpe, the founder of Georgia. Oglethorpe quickly realized the strategic importance of Tybee Island's location at the mouth of the Savannah and ordered that a lighthouse be built. Over the years, the lighthouse has been rebuilt several times due to wear from weather and wars. Although made obsolete with the coming of modern marine navigation electronics, the Tybee light still stands and is an interesting and historic focal point of the island. In the past, Tybee Island served as a quarantine station for sick passengers debarking off ships and as a duty station (Fort Screven) for then Lieutenant Colonel George C. Marshall, who later became a five-star general and served as Secretary of State, Secretary of Defense, and developed the Marshall Plan for rebuilding western Europe. The island is also known as a former hotbed of backroom gambling and illegal drinking, a summer home for Savannah residents, and a retreat for writers and artists.

Tybee Island has a lot to offer the angler. Several piers, public beaches, and marinas and boat launching facilities are all available to help the angler get to the fish. Food, lodging, and supplies are all available on the island.

The fishing: It is possible to find whiting, sharks, croaker, spot, black drum, flounder, spotted seatrout, red drum, and many other species in the waters around Tybee Island. The best thing to do is check with local bait and tackle shops for information on what may be biting and where. The good thing about fishing from a public pier is that you can see what is working for other anglers and adjust your technique accordingly.

A fish-finder or float rig baited with shrimp will catch many species found around Tybee Island. Other good baits are mud minnows, menhaden, and squid.

Tybee Island offers good shark fishing. Blacktips, sand sharks, and bonnetheads are all common. A good-sized chunk of cut bait should draw in a shark intent on an easy meal.

Whiting are a good fish for the whole family, and a summer fishing trip to a pier is a great way to try out saltwater fishing. A small piece of shrimp about an inch long fished on the bottom will draw strikes. Whiting do not get big, but they are abundant, easy to catch, and usually bite when nothing else will.

GA~G grid: 39, B-10

General information: All anglers fishing Tybee Island must meet Georgia licensing requirements. Standard Georgia saltwater creel and length limits apply except for special regulations governing the harvest of striped bass and hybrid striped bass; refer to the *Georgia Sport Fishing Regulations* pamphlet for more information.

The Tybee beaches are open to the public and fishing from the beach is allowed in most areas. Visitors to Tybee Island must pay to park in one of several public lots. Finding a space is usually no problem except on the busiest of summer weekends.

The Back River Pier has handrails, is wheelchair accessible, and has restrooms. The Tybee Island public boat ramp is recommended for small boats only. The Tybee Pier and Pavilion is a $2.5-million wooden pier, which was constructed in 1996 in almost the exact location of the Tybrisa, a historic Tybee Island pier and pavilion known for its Big Band concerts in days gone by. The original Tybrisa was destroyed by fire, but outdoor concerts still take place at the new pier and pavilion. Bait, tackle, food, and drinks are available on the pier.

The tide (Savannah River Entrance) correction (Hr:Min) for the Tybee Light area is Low -0:12, High -0:10, and Feet -0.1. The correction for Tybee Creek is Low +0:05, High -0:09, and Feet -0.1.

Nearest camping: The nearest public campground is at Skidaway Island State Park about 25 miles away. The park has 88 campsites with water, electricity, picnic tables, and grills. The comfort stations have flush toilets and hot showers. Laundry facilities are available. The campground is open year-round.

A private campground is available on Tybee Island. The RV park has more than 150 sites with full utilities and is within walking distance to good fishing.

Directions: From Interstate 95, west of Savannah, take exit 99 and travel east on I-16 for 7.8 miles to exit 165. Take the 37th Street Connector exit for 0.6 mile to 37th Street. Turn left on Georgia Highway 204 for 0.8 mile to Abercorn Street. Turn right and travel 0.3 mile to U.S. Highway 80. Turn left onto US 80 and travel 16.6 miles to Jones Avenue on Tybee Island. Turn right onto Jones Avenue and travel 1.6 miles to Chatham Avenue. Turn right onto Chatham Avenue and travel 0.1 mile to Alley Way Two. The pier is on the left at the end of the alley.

For the Tybee Island boat ramp, follow the directions above except continue on Chatham Avenue 0.2 mile to Alley Way Three. The boat ramp is at the end of the alley.

To reach the Tybee Pier and Pavilion, follow the directions above to reach Tybee Island. On the island, continue on US 80 (Butler Avenue) to 16th Street on the left. Follow 16th Street to the pier.

For more information: For information about Tybee Island, contact the visitor center or visit one of the web pages devoted to the island. For camping information, contact the Skidaway Island Park Superintendent's Office or the River's End Campground. For saltwater fishing information, contact the Coastal Resources Division Office in Brunswick.

Key species: spotted seatrout, red drum, striped bass, flounder, whiting.

Overview: Skidaway Narrows boat ramp is an excellent access point, and if you are camping, Skidaway Island State Park is just a few miles away.

Best way to fish: boat.

Best time to fish: highly seasonal depending on target species.

Description: With two triple-lane boat ramps, Skidaway Narrows boat ramp is a jumping-off point for anglers fishing the Skidaway, Little Ogeechee, and Vernon rivers and Green Island Sound. The Skidaway Narrows is part of the Intracoastal Waterway and offers good fishing for a variety of inshore species.

The fishing: Anglers starting their day at Skidaway Narrows are within reach of a variety of saltwater habitats and species. The species available are highly seasonal, so check with local bait shops on what is biting and where you should expect to find them. The best time to fish for trout and red drum up the rivers is in the fall and winter. A live shrimp or jig fished in deeper channels will produce when the water is cool. Look for sheepshead around the barnacle-encrusted pilings. Fiddler crabs are the best bait for these crafty bait thieves. Striped bass will use the area at times; fish live bait, a big diving plug, or a jig. Flounder, whiting, mullet, and a host of others are all available.

GA~G grid: 39, C-8

General information: All anglers must meet Georgia licensing requirements. Standard Georgia fishing regulations apply except for the striped bass and hybrid striped bass creel limit; see the *Georgia Sport Fishing Regulations* pamphlet for more information.

Bait, fishing gear, food and drinks, and ice are available. Restrooms and picnic tables are also present.

The tide (Savannah River Entrance) correction (Hr:Min) for the Vernon View area is Low +0:31, High +0:40, and Feet +0.7.

Nearest camping: The nearest public campground is at Skidaway Island State Park about 2 miles away. The park has 88 campsites with water, electricity, picnic tables, and grills; comfort stations have flush toilets and hot showers. Laundry facilities are available. The campground is open year-round.

Directions: From Interstate 95, west of Savannah, take exit 94 and travel 10.4 miles east on Georgia Highway 204 to Montgomery Crossroads. Turn right and travel 1.2 miles to Waters Avenue (Diamond Causeway). Turn right on Waters Avenue and travel 3.9 miles to the park on the right before crossing the drawbridge.

For more information: Contact the Coastal Resources Division Office in Brunswick or the Skidaway Island State Park Superintendent's Office.

85 Moon River at Downing Piers See map on page 299

Key species: spotted seatrout, red drum, croaker, spot.

Overview: With fishing piers situated on both sides of the river, the Downing Piers offer shoreline anglers a good chance at a variety of inshore fish.

Best way to fish: pier.

Best time to fish: most species seasonal.

Description: The Moon River joins with the Skidaway River before reaching the Little Ogeechee and Green Island Sound. There are fishing piers equipped with handrails on both sides of the river. No other facilities are present.

The fishing: Try fishing a shrimp on bottom with a fish-finder rig. The best fishing will be when the tide is running; dead low and dead high tides are not very productive. Although common species like croaker and spot will make up most of the catch, some spotted seatrout, juvenile red drum, and maybe even a striped bass are possible certain times of the year.

GA~G grid: 39, C-8

General information: All anglers must meet Georgia licensing requirements. Standard Georgia fishing regulations apply except for the striped bass and hybrid striped bass creel limit; see the *Georgia Sport Fishing Regulations* pamphlet for more information.

The tide (Savannah River Entrance) correction (Hr:Min) for the Vernon View area is Low +0:31, High +0:40, and Feet +0.7.

Nearest camping: The nearest public campground is at Skidaway Island State Park about 2 miles away. The park has 88 campsites with water, electricity, picnic tables, and grills; comfort stations have flush toilets and hot showers. Laundry facilities are available. The campground is open year-round.

Directions: From Interstate 95, west of Savannah, take exit 94 and travel east on Georgia Highway 204 for 10.4 miles. Turn right on Montgomery Crossroads and travel 1.2 miles to Waters Avenue (Diamond Avenue). Turn right on Waters Avenue and travel 3.3 miles to the Moon River Bridge.

For more information: Contact the Coastal Resources Division Office in Brunswick or the Skidaway Island State Park Superintendent's Office.

86 Little Ogeechee River at Bell's Landing See map on page 299

Key species: striped bass, spotted seatrout, red drum, flounder, catfish.

Overview: Deep in the marsh on the Little Ogeechee River, the facilities at Bell's Landing include a fishing pier and boat ramp.

Best way to fish: pier, boat.

Best time to fish: year-round; some species seasonal.

Description: Bell's Landing is a popular access point with anglers. The ramp's convenient location makes it a good choice for launching a boat and exploring the Little Ogeechee River marsh. A wheelchair accessible fishing pier with handrails is present for shoreline anglers. The double-lane launching ramp has a floating courtesy dock. Restrooms are present. Food, lodging, and supplies are all within a short distance along the Georgia Highway 204 corridor.

The fishing: To determine what is biting at Bell's Ferry pier, try fishing a dead shrimp on bottom with a fish-finder rig. Anglers lucky enough to own a boat can explore the vast expanses of fertile salt marsh that line the tidal creeks and rivers in the area. Look for oyster beds, points, and bars to catch spotted seatrout and young red drum. A live shrimp under a float rig is an effective way to fish the shallows for these species, although some anglers prefer to cast a plastic shrimp tail threaded on a lead-head jig.

GA~G grid: 55, B-10

General information: Anglers must meet all Georgia licensing requirements. Standard Georgia creel and length limits apply except for special regulations governing the harvest of striped bass and hybrid striped bass; refer to the *Georgia Sport Fishing Regulations* pamphlet for more information.

The tide (Savannah River Entrance) correction (Hr:Min) for the Coffee Bluff area downstream of Bell's Landing is Low +0:42, High +1:05, and Feet +0.7.

Nearest camping: The nearest public campground is at Skidaway Island State Park about 10 miles away. The park has 88 campsites with water, electricity, picnic tables, and grills. The comfort stations have flush toilets and hot showers. Laundry facilities are available. The campground is open year-round.

Directions: From Interstate 95, west of Savannah, take exit 94 and travel east on Georgia Highway 204 for 7.1 miles to Apache Avenue on the right. Travel 0.6 mile on Apache Avenue to the boat ramp and parking area on the left.

For more information: Contact the Coastal Region Fisheries Office. For more information on Skidaway Island State Park, contact the Park Superintendent's Office.

87 Salt Creek

See map on page 299

Key species: largemouth bass, red drum, striped bass, catfish.

Overview: The park at Salt Creek has both a fishing pier and a small launching ramp. The sheltered waters of Salt Creek are a good place to explore with a sea kayak.

Best way to fish: pier, small boat.

Best time to fish: most species seasonal.

Description: The Salt Creek access point is well inland. Both freshwater and saltwater species may be found in the area depending on the tide. With the child-friendly facilities, Salt Creek is a good place for a family outing.

The fishing: Anglers are liable to run into about anything at Salt Creek. Both freshwater and saltwater species that do not mind living in the transition zone will use the area. A shrimp fished on bottom with a fish-finder rig is a good way of prospecting to see what may be biting. Or, try rigging a shrimp or mud minnow on a float rig.

The winter months will be the best season for spotted seatrout and striped bass. The movements of these species are highly seasonal, and fall and winter are when they are most likely to use habitats like Salt Creek. Juvenile red drum are also a possibility. A lead-head jig is hard to beat as a consistent producer of strikes from nearly any fish that swims.

Catfish, either the freshwater or saltwater variety, should be the most consistent inhabitants of the area. Try a piece of shrimp fished on the bottom.

GA~G grid: 55, B-10

General information: All anglers must meet Georgia licensing requirements. Standard Georgia fishing regulations apply except for a special creel limit on striped bass and hybrid striped bass; see the *Georgia Sport Fishing Regulations* pamphlet for more information.

The launch ramp is recommended for small boats only. Restrooms, picnic tables, and a children's playground are also available.

The tide (Savannah River Entrance) correction (Hr:Min) for the Coffee Bluff area (still a good distance downstream of Salt Creek) is Low +0:42, High +1:05, and Feet +0.7.

Food, lodging, and supplies are 5 miles away in Savannah.

Nearest camping: The nearest public campground is about 19 miles away at Fort McAllister State Historic Park. The park has 63 campsites each with water, electricity, grill, and a picnic table. Comfort stations have flush toilets and hot showers. Fort McAllister State Historic Park also has a boat ramp and fishing pier.

Directions: From Interstate 95, west of Savannah, take exit 94 and travel east on Georgia Highway 204 for 2.1 miles to U.S. Highway 17. Take US 17 north for 4.1 miles. Park on the left just past the Salt Creek Bridge.

For more information: Contact the Wildlife Resources Division Fisheries Section Office at Demeries Creek. For more information on Fort McAllister State Historic Park, contact the Park Superintendent's Office.

88 Ogeechee River at Kings Ferry See map on page 299

Key species: striped bass, white catfish, channel catfish, red drum, spotted seatrout.

Overview: Although predominantly a freshwater fishery, when the tide comes in the stretch of the Ogeechee River around Kings Ferry offers good fishing for both freshwater and marine species.

Best way to fish: boat, pier.

Best time to fish: year-round, some species seasonal.

Description: With excellent fishing for both freshwater and saltwater species, the Ogeechee River at Kings Ferry is very popular with anglers. The access is also popular with pleasure-boaters and the ramp and parking area can get very crowded in the summer. The conditions at Kings Ferry make it better freshwater fishing than saltwater, but marine species that commonly use the transition areas can be caught at times. When the Ogeechee River is high and flowing strong, the incoming tide may not be able to overcome the rush of freshwater, and this section will be totally a freshwater fishery.

The fishing: White and channel catfish are very abundant in the Kings Ferry area and offer the most consistent year-round angling. Shrimp or liver fished on the bottom should produce bites. In the fall, red drum and spotted seatrout are possible right around the ramp, but the best fishing is downstream below the railroad trestle near the Ford Plantation. Live shrimp fished on a float rig are the best bait for red drum and trout.

If you are purely interested in freshwater fishing, head upriver from Kings Ferry for some good largemouth bass and redbreast sunfish angling. Any of the usual bass lures will work for largemouths, and redbreasts will fall prey to worms, crickets, small spinners, or popping bugs.

Some of the most exciting fishing on the Ogeechee is for striped bass. From February to April, striped bass are stacked up in the river around Kings Ferry. Bridge piers and pilings are the best place to find fish. A 1-ounce Rat-L-Trap fished around the structure is a killer bait, as are big floating/diving stickbaits. Anchor on the upcurrent side and cast past the structure. Retrieve the bait as close as possible to the structure and then stop the retrieve and let the current hold the lure in close to the bridge pier or piling. While the current holds the lure in place, repeatedly pump the rod without taking in line to give the bait an erratic action without pulling it away from the fish-holding structure. The best action is on the turn of the tide. During dead low or high tide, use a depth finder to spot suspended fish near structure and make a vertical presentation of a heavy jig or spoon.

GA~G grid: 55, B-9

General information: The site has one double-lane boat ramp, service dock, and a wheelchair-accessible fishing pier. Other amenities include restrooms, picnic tables, and a playground. Anglers must meet all Georgia licensing requirements. Standard Georgia creel and length limits apply except for special regulations governing the harvest of striped bass and hybrid striped bass; refer to the *Georgia Sport Fishing Regulations* pamphlet for more information.

The tide (Savannah River Entrance) correction (Hr:Min) for the Kings Ferry area is Low +4:25, High +3:19, and Feet -5.4.

Nearest camping: The nearest public campground is 12 miles away at Fort McAllister State Historic Park, the site of the best-preserved earthwork fortification of the Confederacy. The park has 63 campsites each with water, electricity, grill, and a picnic table. Comfort stations have flush toilets and hot showers. Fort McAllister State Historic Park also has a boat ramp and fishing pier.

Directions: From Interstate 95, west of Savannah, take exit 94 and travel east on Georgia Highway 204 for 2.1 miles to U.S. Highway 17. Take US 17 south 2.7 miles to the park on the left just before crossing the Ogeechee River Bridge.

For more information: Contact the Wildlife Resources Division Fisheries Section Office at Demeries Creek. For more information on Fort McAllister State Historic Park, contact the Park Superintendent's Office.

89 Fort Stewart Military Reservation

Key species: largemouth bass, bluegill, redear sunfish, redbreast sunfish, crappie, channel catfish.

Overview: Fort Stewart is not only the home base of the 3D Infantry Division (Mech) "The Rock of the Marne," but is also home to about 20 ponds and lakes totaling more than 1,450 acres available for public fishing. In addition, the Canoochee River flows through the base and is some of the best coastal river fishing in Georgia.

Best way to fish: bank, small boat.

Best time to fish: year-round.

Description: The 279,270 acres of the U.S. Army's Fort Stewart sprawl across five Georgia counties. The military reservation is about 39 miles across east to west, and 19 miles from north to south. Fort Stewart is named for General Daniel Stewart, a native of Liberty County who fought with Francis Marion during the Revolutionary War. The huge base was established during World War II and is the largest military base east of the Mississippi River. Among its other duties during WWII, the facility served as a prisoner-of-war camp for German and Italian soldiers taken prisoner in the North Africa campaigns.

Fort Stewart is the workplace of thousands of America's service men and women who get to take advantage of some of the best small fishing lakes in Georgia. Many Fort Stewart lakes are intensively managed and provide good fishing for largemouth bass, bluegill, redear sunfish, crappie, and catfish. In addition, the Canoochee River, a fine coastal redbreast fishery, flows through the base and there are several landings anglers can use to access the river.

Georgia anglers do not have to enlist to enjoy the good fishing at Fort Stewart. The lakes and river landings are open to the public, although as one might expect, some special regulations are in place regarding access since this is a U.S. military base and serves a more important purpose than just providing good fishing.

Some ponds at Fort Stewart are managed for certain species. A few ponds are managed for catfish anglers, although bream and bass will likely also be present. Some ponds have good bank access, others have virtually none. Boats are allowed on all the ponds, but not every pond has a boat ramp. With one exception, the ponds are limited to electric motors only. A small johnboat or canoe is a good choice for fishing the lakes on the post. A smaller boat can be car-topped or carried in the bed of a pickup truck to the more remote fishing holes.

The Canoochee River diagonally splits Fort Stewart down the middle, and the river's upper and lower sections are open to anglers. The middle section of the Canoochee flows through the artillery impact zone, a section of the base that is always closed. Not only does live fire present a danger, but duds and unexploded ordnance from decades of military training are laying out there waiting to explode. The closed area acts as a refuge for the fish though, and probably explains why the other two sections of the river are so good. The river's upper section above the closed area is small and narrow water with

Fort Stewart Military Reservation

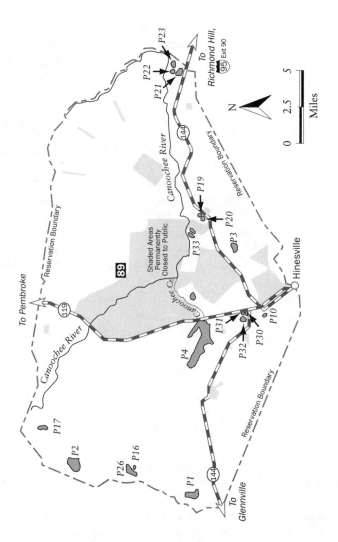

many obstructions, making navigation difficult. Several landings are on this section of the river. However, they are reachable only via tank trails, which are often muddy in wet weather and stay soft even during a dry spell because of the deep, sandy soil. However, as every astute angler knows, the harder it is to get there, the better the fishing. A four-wheel-drive vehicle is a good idea if you plan on trying to reach any of these landings. This section of the fort is heavily used for training and is often closed to the public.

Below the closed impact area, the navigation is easier and the access roads are better. They still can get muddy in wet weather, but these are roads designed for vehicles instead of tanks. This section of the river has several landings, and the area is less frequently closed to the public. Even on the lower section, the Canoochee is best suited to small johnboats or canoes.

When fishing on the Canoochee, keep your catch in a livewell or ice chest. Alligators are abundant in the river and have been known to steal a stringer of fish dangling over the side of the boat. A large gator can capsize your boat by yanking on a stringer of fish.

Before your first trip to Fort Stewart, you should contact the Fort Stewart Pass and Permit Office to find out what is required to fish on the base and if any special regulations apply. This office is also a good source of information on the best pond to try depending on what you want to catch and how you plan to fish.

The fishing: All of the ponds on Fort Stewart are great fishing. A few stand out as consistent producers of trophy largemouth bass. Big Metz (#26) and Dogwood (#28) are two of the best choices for a wallhanger largemouth. All of the lakes on Fort Stewart are shallow and filled with cover. Anything deeper than 10 feet is considered a deep hole, so there is no use in hauling around a selection of deep-diving crankbaits. Topwater plugs, spinnerbaits, and a big plastic worm will easily cover anything you will encounter on the Fort Stewart lakes. For catching big bass, a live golden shiner is hard to beat. Carefully hook the shiner so as not to kill it or impede its swimming, attach a float a few feet above the bait, gently cast it near some good looking cover, and let the shiner do the work for you. When the shiner starts acting nervous, get ready because a big bass is probably cruising the area. When the float goes under, give the fish some line, and then strike hard. Anglers catch some huge bass using this method.

For bream anglers, the two ponds listed above are also good choices. Other ponds that have produced good bream fishing are Pineview (#1), Daisy (#17), Holbrook (#3), and Richmond Hill East (#23). Crickets and worms fished under a float are hard to beat for catching bluegill and redear sunfish. Another fun way to catch bream is a lightweight fly rod and a small popping bug. Twitch the bug slowly along the surface and when a big bream sucks it in, a quick lift of the rod will set the hook and the fight will be on.

Worms, nightcrawlers, a piece of hot dog, or nearly anything else with a scent is good catfish bait. Fish on the bottom and wait until the catfish fully takes the bait before setting the hook hard. Catfish are great nibblers and setting the hook too early will result in missed strikes.

Redbreast fishing on both the upper and lower sections of the Canoochee River is good and the best baits are worms and crickets. Small spinners on ultralight gear are usually just as effective as live bait. For largemouth bass, the lower section of the Canoochee is best and any of the usual bass-fishing tactics should work. Shallow-diving crankbaits, spinnerbaits, topwater plugs, and soft-plastic baits all are effective.

Some huge fish have come from the lakes at Fort Stewart, including several documented bass weighing more than 15 pounds. Stories abound of even bigger fish never officially weighed and reported. Besides big bass, the Canoochee

River is known for producing good numbers of big rooster redbreast weighing upwards of a pound.

GA~G grid: *54, 55*

General information: To fish Fort Stewart, all anglers must meet Georgia licensing requirements and possess a Fort Stewart daily or annual fishing permit. The fishing permits are available from the post Pass and Permit Office. Some ponds are open to fishing for all permit holders, while others are often closed and require a free special access pass whenever they are open to the public. Refer to the appendix on whom to contact for more information about the fishing and rules and regulations that apply to visitors on the base.

All anglers fishing Fort Stewart must check in every visit. Anglers holding an annual fishing permit need not visit the Pass and Permit Office to do this. An automated telephone check-in system is available. The ponds at Fort Stewart are managed under special regulations different from standard Georgia statewide fishing regulations. The regulations vary for different ponds, and the post is heavily patrolled to ensure compliance to game and fish regulations and other rules. Be sure you know the fishing regulations for the pond you are going to fish before you get on the water.

Always keep in mind that Fort Stewart is an active military installation and the rules are there for everyone's safety. Know and follow them and be grateful this fine fishery has been made available for everyone to enjoy.

Food, lodging, and supplies are found in Hinesville on the south side of the post.

Nearest camping: Camping is allowed at the Holbrook Campground (next to Pond 3) on the base. Contact the Fort Stewart Outdoor Recreation Center or Pass and Permit Office for more information.

Directions: To reach the Pass and Permit Office, from Interstate 95, west of Savannah, take Georgia Highway 144 west at exit 90. Travel west for about 20 miles and look for the Game Warden's Office on the right. Take the next paved road on the left. After a mile, you will see a sign reading "Wild Boar Hunting and Fishing Lodge." Turn left here and follow the road to the Pass and Permit Office.

For more information: Contact the Fort Stewart Outdoor Recreation Center or the Pass and Permit Office.

Fort Stewart Fishing Lakes At A Glance

Pond	Surface Acres	Average Depth	Boat Ramp	Constructed	Perimeter Road	Location
1 Pineview Lake	82	8	•	1964	•	GA 144, north of F.R. Rd 2
2 Glisson's Mill Pond	67	8	•	1966		GA 129 (off post), adjacent to Camp Oliver
3 Holbrook Pond	20	6		1966	•	GA 144, south on F.R. Rd 48, east on loop road to Holbrook Campground
4 Canoochee Creek Reservoir	1,070	—	•	—	—	Just east of GA 119 north of the GA 119 and GA 144 intersection
10 Engineer's Pond	4.1	5.3		1975	•	GA 119 south, 0.25 mile from intersection of GA 119 and GA 144
17 Daisy Pond	14.5	6	•	1968	•	GA 119 to F.R. Rd 17 north
19 Evan's Field Ponds	9.6	8		1967	•	GA 144, north of F.R. Rd 102
20 Evan's Field Ponds	5.9	5		1967	•	GA 144, north of F.R. Rd 102
21 Richmond Hill West Pond	15	10	•	1969	•	GA 144, north on F.R. Rd 58
22 Richmond Hill Middle Pond	4.5	5.5		1969	•	GA 144, north on F.R. Rd 58
23 Richmond Hill East Pond	7.5	4.9		1969	•	GA 144, north on F.R. Rd 58
26 Big Metz Lake	53	7	•	1975	•	GA 144, north on F.R. Rd 5, east on F.R. Rd 6, angle north on unnumbered road
16 Little Metz Pond	1.5	4		1975	•	GA 144, north on F.R. Rd 5, east on F.R. Rd 6, angle north on unnumbered road
28 Dogwood Lake	33	6.7	•	1982	•	GA 119, east on F.R. Rd 144, north on F.R. Rd 106
30 Cedar Bay East Pond	7.6	10		1987	•	GA 119, west on F.R. Rd 40A. Near intersection of GA 119 and GA 144
31 Cedar Bay Middle Pond	2.5	8		1988	•	GA 119, west on F.R. Rd 40A. Near intersection of GA 119 and GA 144
32 Cedar Bay West Pond	5.7	8		1996	•	GA 119, west on F.R. Rd 40A. Near intersection GA 119 and GA 144
33 Landing 7 Borrow Pits	36	—	—	—	—	North of GA 144

90 Middle Altamaha River

Key species: flathead catfish, largemouth bass, redbreast sunfish.

Overview: With many twists and turns, the middle Altamaha River has plenty of the channel-bend type of habitat favored by huge flathead catfish. State-record flathead catfish weighing more than 60 pounds have been caught from this stretch of the river.

Best way to fish: boat.

Best time to fish: year-round.

Description: The midsection of the Altamaha River is not much different from its upper reaches (Site 73). The river is wide and meandering as it steadily makes its way to the Atlantic. The additional watershed gained with the influx of a major blackwater tributary, the Ohoopee River, gives the middle Altamaha the feel of a big river.

The riverbanks on this section are sparsely populated, and the river definitely has an Old South ambiance. One fish camp in particular is somewhat of a local historical landmark. Beards Bluff Camp Ground, formerly known as Adamson's Fish Camp, was built in the 1930s. According to local history, people out for a sinful but exciting night made good use of the camp's slot machines, illegal liquor, and women of loose virtue. Those days have long since passed, and the camp is now geared toward family outdoor fun, southern style.

Sloughs, backwaters, and side-channels are abundant in this stretch of the river. The current is surprisingly strong for what looks to be a wide, lazy river, and as always, the current dictates how the fishing will be. High water generally means a poor day, and stable or falling water means your chances of catching fish are good. Since the Altamaha drainage is so large and extends well up into the Piedmont, weather conditions many miles away play a role in what the river is doing. Although the weather is dry in southern Georgia, heavy rains in central Georgia will cause a rise in the river, albeit a delayed one.

Anglers can expect the same from the fish in the middle Altamaha as in the upper section with one exception. As one moves farther downstream, flathead catfish become more abundant. Anglers will find more flathead catfish available in the middle section than the upper Altamaha. Largemouth bass are abundant and will average somewhere around 14 inches. Four-pound fish are common, but anything approaching 10 pounds is going to be an Altamaha River bass of a lifetime.

Like the upper portion, the middle Altamaha does not receive tremendous fishing pressure. Plenty of anglers use the river, but with all the space and fish available, crowding and competition should not be a problem. This section of the river has several good access points and campgrounds, presenting you with several options on where to launch your boat.

The fishing: For the middle Altamaha, use the same tactics recommended for the Upper Altamaha River (Site 73). Hefty-sized live bait fished on the bottom in deep holes is tops for flathead catfish. Largemouth bass can be caught from

Middle Altamaha River

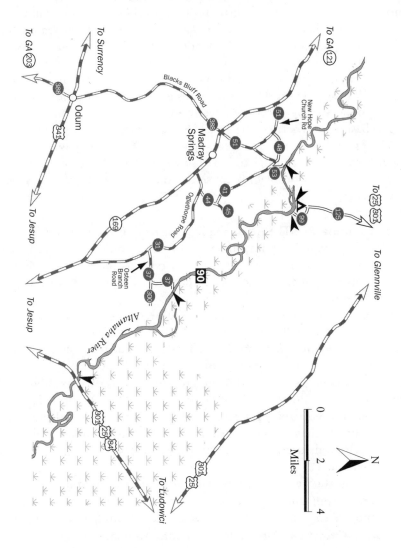

the main channel or the backwaters depending on the time of year and river stage. Spinnerbaits are a local favorite because they cover a lot of water, are virtually snag-free, and just flat out catch fish. Redbreast sunfish will be near cover in the main channel of the river. Worms, crickets, small spinners, and popping bugs are all good choices.

The river is full of good places to fish, but below are some specific locations you may want to try. Upstream from U.S. Highway 84, the big bends in the river have plenty of cover and deep holes. Several large oxbow backwaters are in this stretch too. Just downstream from US 84 and within sight of an old railroad trestle is a truly unique fishing hole. A paddlewheel riverboat met its demise here many years ago, and the upended boat is still visible in the river bend. During high water, the current rounds the bend and runs smack dab into the derelict. The backwash has scoured a deep hole on the upstream side. When the river is down, this hole is a 25-foot deep eddy. Flatheads pushing 60 pounds have been caught here.

The section of the Altamaha downstream of US 25 is known for good crappie fishing. Concentrate on the oxbow lakes and sloughs. Minnows or small jigs fished around woody cover are effective techniques.

The best fishing occurs when the U.S. Geological Survey gauge near Baxley reads 3.5 to 5.5 feet. When the reading is above 6.5, fishing is going to be very tough. Low readings of 0.5 to 2.5 result in good fishing, but navigating the river can become a problem because of sandbars and mudflats, especially in the creeks and cuts.

GA~G grid: 53, 54

General information: The Altamaha River is managed under standard Georgia creel and length limits with one exception regarding the harvest of striped bass, white bass, and hybrid striped bass; refer to the *Georgia Sport Fishing Regulations* pamphlet for more information. All anglers must meet Georgia licensing requirements.

Food, lodging, and supplies are available in the nearby towns of Jesup, Ludowici, or Glennville.The Georgia Wildlife Resources Division publishes a *Guide to Fishing the Altamaha River.* The free guide includes a river map and has information on launch sites, camping, and fishing hints.

Nearest camping: Beards Bluff Campground (also known as Adamson's Fish Camp) is on the north bank of the river north of Madray Springs. The campground offers cabins for rent in addition to the standard campsites. The campground also has modern restrooms, showers, and laundry facilities. Canoe and kayak rentals are available, and there are guided camping trips during cooler weather.

Overnight stays are also allowed at Pat's Baithouse on the river near Jesup.

Directions: From Ludowici, this portion of the river is best reached from US 84 and US 25; from Jesup it can be reached from Georgia Highway 169.

For more information: Although the middle Altamaha River is partly in the Coastal Region, management of the river is carried out by Wildlife Resources Division Fisheries Section Office in Waycross. For information about facilities at any of the fish camps listed, contact the owner (see Appendix for details).

91 Lower Altamaha River

Key species: flathead catfish, largemouth bass, redbreast sunfish.

Overview: The lower Altamaha River is arguably the best fishing of the entire Altamaha Basin. For both flathead catfish and largemouth bass anglers, the lower Altamaha offers tremendous fishing for those who invest the time to learn its secrets.

Lower Altamaha River

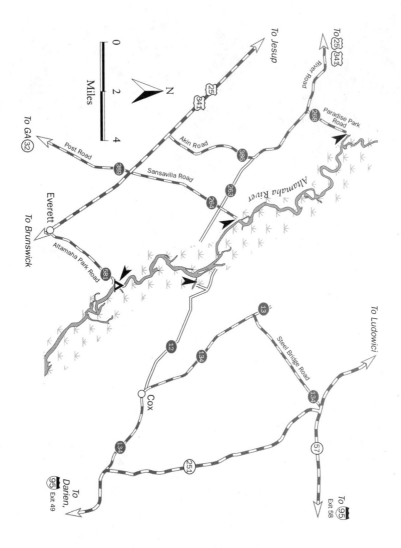

Best way to fish: boat.

Best time to fish: year-round.

Description: To the casual eye, the lower Altamaha River does not look much different from the upper or middle sections of the river. The difference is in what's below the surface—the river is bank to bank fish. Flatheads, largemouth bass, redbreast sunfish, and many other species fill the river and its backwaters. The lower Altamaha is a tremendous fishery that every Georgia angler should experience.

The lower Altamaha River is the most popular with anglers and is a great fishery for flathead catfish, largemouth bass, and other species.

As one might expect, the lower river is the biggest. Also, since the Altamaha is nearing the end of its journey to the ocean, tidal forces begin to come into play. Tidal influences are noticeable nearly up to Altamaha Park near the town of Everett.

The lower portion of the river is the most popular with anglers. Brunswick is nearby and Savannah and Jacksonville, Florida, are an easy drive away. Though you cannot expect to have the river to yourself, especially on weekends, there are still plenty of places to escape the crowds. The lower Altamaha is a popular tournament destination for bass clubs, and even flathead catfish anglers have their own competitive events.

The stage of the river is still important to catching fish and tidal forces introduce even more variables. Stable water is the best fishing, and high water makes things more difficult. More water will flow into the backwaters when the tide is coming in, and when the tide is out, the backwaters will be at their lowest point. The best tide to fish is a matter of personal opinion, but no matter what you find works best, the trick is to make the most of it. For example, anglers preferring water just starting to rise can ride an incoming tide by motoring downstream until they find the conditions they are looking for and then fishing their way back upstream with the tide. On a falling tide, simply reverse the procedure; ride until you find what you are looking for and then follow it downstream.

Although the river is bigger, the fish are still the same. Ten-pound bass are very rare, but there are plenty of 5-pounders, and the river is full of 1- to 2-pound fish. Studies have shown there are more flathead catfish per river mile in the lower Altamaha than anywhere else in the river, although their numbers start to drop off the farther you go into the tidal zone. The great thing about flathead fishing is that you never know for sure what you may catch. There is a very real possibility that a 10-pound fish will be followed up by a 50-pound trophy. There are just so many large fish in the river that a monster catfish could strike at any time.

The fishing: Use the current, whether it is from the river's flow or from the tide, to discern where the fish should be holding in relation to cover, and then make an exact presentation to bring a lure by the fish in a natural manner. For largemouth, spinnerbaits, jigs, and plastic worms are all good choices. Spinnerbaits cover the most water, but sometimes the slower-moving worm or jig is needed for less aggressive fish. Some anglers also do well on crankbaits, but with all the snags in the river, a good lure retriever is a must or a day's fishing may turn into an expensive proposition.

Flathead fishing is simple. Catch a mess of bream (Georgia law requires they must be caught using sport methods) or large shiners (can be caught with commercial gear), find a deep hole, bait up a big strong hook (sizes up to 12/0 are not out of the question here), add enough weight to hold the bait where you want it, and then just hang onto your rod. You stand a good chance of catching the biggest fish of your life this way.

Although the redbreast sunfish population suffered with the illegal introduction of the flatheads back in the 1970s, there are still plenty to be caught. Look for places that have some current, a deep hole, and cover, and you will have found fish. Fish either live bait (worms or crickets are good) or a small spinner in and around the cover.

If catching crappie is your goal, head upriver to some oxbows and sloughs. This type of habitat is perfect for crappie in the early spring and a lot of fish are caught on small jigs or minnows.

GA~G grid: 54, 62, 63

General information: The Altamaha River is managed under standard Georgia creel and length limits with one exception regarding the harvest of striped bass, white bass, and hybrid striped bass; refer to the *Georgia Sport Fishing Regulations* pamphlet for more information. All anglers must meet Georgia licensing requirements.

Food, lodging, and supplies are available in the nearby towns of Jesup, Ludowici, or along the Interstate 95 corridor.

The Georgia Wildlife Resources Division publishes a *Guide to Fishing the Altamaha River*. The free guide includes a river map and contains information on launch sites, camping, and fishing hints.

Nearest camping: Camping is available on this stretch of the river at the Altamaha Fish Camp.

Directions: From Jesup, this portion of the river is best accessed from U.S. Highway 25/341; from Ludowici it can be reached from Georgia Highways 57 and 251.

For more information: Although the lower Altamaha River is in the Coastal Region, management of the river is carried out by the Wildlife Resources Division Fisheries Section Office in Waycross. For information on facilities available at the Altamaha Fish Camp, contact the owner.

92 Darien River at Darien

Key species: spotted seatrout, red drum, croaker, spot.

Overview: The historic Darien waterfront has both a fishing pier and boat ramp.

Best way to fish: boat, pier.

Best time to fish: most species highly seasonal.

Description: Darien is the second-oldest planned town in Georgia. Scottish Highlanders established the community in January 1736 under the direction of James Oglethorpe. Very few buildings in Darien predate June 1863 when raiding Federal troops stationed at nearby Saint Simons Island burned the town. Darien once was one of the busiest timber ports on the Atlantic coast, but the small community's economy is now based on shrimping.

Anglers visiting Darien will find boat launching facilities to serve as a starting point to exploring the Darien River and surrounding waters. Pier anglers

A family spends the morning fishing from the pier on the Darien waterfront.

Darien River at Darien
Champney River at Darien • Brunswick–Overlook Park
Black River at Saint Simons
Little River at Saint Simons
Mackay River at Saint Simons
Saint Simons Island Pier

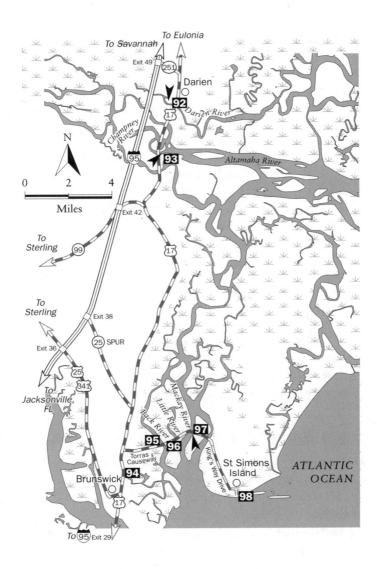

can watch the shrimp fleet come and go while they try their luck for a variety of inshore species.

The fishing: Fishing for most saltwater species is very seasonal. Most species are only found in certain areas for part of the year. Check with local marinas and bait shops to see what is biting and how to catch them. Some favorites with local anglers are spotted seatrout and red drum. Both nearshore species are common on the Georgia coast.

If you just are after anything that will bite, fish a shrimp on bottom with a fish-finder rig. Croaker, spot, yellowtail, flounder, and a host of other species will take a shrimp, and these species are commonly caught using this technique.

GA~G grid: 63, C-7

General information: All anglers must meet Georgia licensing requirements. Standard fishing regulations apply; refer to the *Georgia Sport Fishing Regulations* pamphlet for more information. The launch ramp is single-lane. The Darien waterfront dock is wheelchair-accessible and has handrails. The Darien Welcome Center, found right next to the dock, can provide information on other attractions and local history.

Food, lodging, and supplies are available in Darien.

The tide (Savannah River Entrance) correction (Hr:Min) for the Darien area is Low +1:15, High +1:08, and Feet +0.4.

Nearest camping: There are no developed public campgrounds in the immediate vicinity. Several private campgrounds are available in Darien. Contact the McIntosh County Chamber of Commerce for more information.

Directions: To reach the waterfront dock, from Interstate 95 exit 49, just north of Darien, travel south on Georgia Highway 251 for 1.2 miles to U.S. Highway 17. Turn right (south) on US 17 and travel 1.2 miles to Broad Street (on the left before crossing Darien River Bridge). The waterfront dock is on the river behind the Darien Welcome Center.

To reach the public boat ramp, follow the directions above except turn right before crossing Darien River Bridge. Drive 0.1 mile and take the first left. The boat ramp is at the end of the lane.

For more information: Contact the Coastal Resources Division Office in Brunswick or the McIntosh County Chamber of Commerce.

93 Champney River at Darien

See map on page 323

Key species: spotted seatrout, red drum, flounder, striped bass.

Overview: The Champney River is part of the Altamaha delta and offers good fishing for a variety of species.

Best way to fish: boat, pier.

Best time to fish: highly seasonal depending on species sought.

Description: Boaters will find good access with a paved, double-lane launching ramp and plenty of parking. Shoreline anglers can fish from a catwalk on the

Anglers work a net on the Champney River near Darien.

side of the Champney River bridge. Historic Darien is just a couple of miles down the road.

The fishing: Fishing for saltwater species is highly seasonal. The best tactic for visiting anglers is to stop by a local bait shop to find out what is biting and the best techniques to use.

Fishing for red drum and trout is best in the fall and winter as these species seek the deeper water of the channels. Jigs can outperform live shrimp during this period. Flounder, whiting, spot, croaker, sheepshead, and others can all be found in the area and will fall prey to a shrimp or perhaps a fiddler crab fished on bottom with a fish-finder rig.

GA~G grid: 63, C-7

General information: All anglers must meet Georgia licensing requirements. Standard saltwater fishing regulations apply; refer to the *Georgia Sport Fishing Regulations* pamphlet for more information. The launch ramp is double-lane. The Champney River catwalk is wheelchair-accessible and has handrails. Restrooms are available on site.

Food, lodging, and supplies are available 2 miles away in Darien.

The tide (Savannah River Entrance) correction (Hr:Min) for the Darien area is Low +1:15, High +1:08, and Feet +0.4.

Nearest camping: No developed public campgrounds are in the immediate vicinity. Several private campgrounds are available in Darien. Contact the McIntosh County Chamber of Commerce for more information.

Directions: From Interstate 95 exit 49, just north of Darien, travel south on

Georgia Highway 251 for 1.2 miles to U.S. Highway 17. Turn right (south) and travel 3.3 miles on US 17 to the Champney River Bridge. A parking area is on the left on the south side of the bridge.

For more information: Contact the Coastal Resources Division Office in Brunswick or the McIntosh County Chamber of Commerce.

94 Brunswick–Overlook Park

See map on page 323

Key species: red drum, spotted seatrout, mullet, whiting.

Overview: This roadside park in Brunswick gives shoreline anglers access to tidal creek and salt marsh habitats.

Best way to fish: pier.

Best time to fish: April to October; most species seasonal.

Description: Found alongside U.S. Highway 17, Overlook Park is a pleasant place to gaze out over the salt marsh and tidal flats. A fishing pier is available. At low tide, fishing opportunities are limited since there will be very little water.

The fishing: Try tight-lining a shrimp on the bottom with a fish-finder rig. A jig worked slowly along the bottom can also be productive. To work the mid-depths, use a terminal float rig baited with a shrimp.

GA~G grid: 63, F-7

General information: All anglers must meet Georgia licensing requirements and standard Georgia saltwater creel and length limits apply; refer to the *Georgia Sport Fishing Regulations* pamphlet for more information.

   Picnic facilities are available at the site. The tide (Savannah River Entrance) correction (Hr:Min) for the Mackay River (ICWW) is Low +1:21, High +0:54, and Feet +0.0.

Nearest camping: The nearest public campground is at Glynn County's Blythe Island Regional Park and Campground (not shown on area covered by site map) about 9 miles away. RV, tent, and primitive sites are available. The Jekyll Island Campground is 13 miles away on Jekyll Island. Several private RV parks and campgrounds are also available in the Brunswick area.

Directions: From Interstate 95 exit 38, north of Brunswick, travel south on Georgia Spur 25 (North Golden Isles Expressway) 4.3 miles to U.S. Highway 17. Turn right (south) on US 17 and travel 2.4 miles to the park on the left side of the highway.

For more information: Contact the Coastal Resources Division Office in Brunswick. For camping information, contact the Blythe Island Regional Park and Campground, Jekyll Island Campground, or the Brunswick and the Golden Isles Visitors Bureau.

95 Back River at Saint Simons

See map on page 323

Key species: croaker, flounder, whiting, sheepshead.

Overview: Situated just off the causeway crossing the Intracoastal Waterway to Saint Simons Island, these piers offer good access for the nonboating angler.

Best way to fish: pier.

Best time to fish: most species seasonal.

Description: The Back River fishing piers (one pier on each side of the river) once were part of the old causeway crossing to Saint Simons Island. With the new bridge running overhead, anglers can stand on the old roadway and fish the waters of the Back River.

The fishing: Anglers soaking a shrimp or fiddler crab along the old bridge piers should see action from a variety of inshore species. A bottom rig or fish-finder rig is a good choice for presenting the bait. Autumn is a good time to catch spotted seatrout around the bridges.

GA~G grid: 63, F-7

General information: All anglers must meet Georgia licensing requirements and standard Georgia saltwater creel and length limits apply; refer to the *Georgia Sport Fishing Regulations* pamphlet for more information.

The Back River piers are equipped with handrails and are wheelchair accessible.

The tide (Savannah River Entrance) correction (Hr:Min) for the nearby Mackay River (ICWW) is Low +1:21, High +0:54, and Feet +0.0.

Nearest camping: The nearest public campground is Glynn County's Blythe Island Regional Park and Campground (not shown on area covered by site map), 12 miles away. RV, tent, and primitive sites are available. The Jekyll Island Campground is 15 miles away on Jekyll Island. Several private RV parks and campgrounds are also available in the Brunswick area.

Directions: East Pier: From Interstate 95 exit 38, north of Brunswick, travel south on Georgia Spur 25 (North Golden Isles Expressway) 4.3 miles to U.S. Highway 17. Turn right on US 17 and travel 1.7 miles to the Torras Causeway leading to Saint Simons Island. Turn left (east) on Torras Causeway, travel 2 miles, and cross over Back River bridge. The pier entrance is just across the bridge on the left side of Torras Causeway. For the West Pier, follow the directions above but the entrance to the pier is found on the left before crossing the Back River bridge.

For more information: Contact the Coastal Resources Division Office in Brunswick. For camping information, contact the Blythe Island Regional Park and Campground, Jekyll Island Campground, or the Brunswick and the Golden Isles Visitors Bureau.

96 Little River at Saint Simons

See map on page 323

Key species: croaker, flounder, whiting, sheepshead.

Overview: Located on the causeway crossing the Intracoastal Waterway to Saint Simons Island, a catwalk alongside the Little River bridge provides nonboating anglers access to the river.

Best way to fish: pier.

Best time to fish: most species highly seasonal.

Description: Just a short distance from the Back River fishing piers (site 95) and the Mackay River piers (site 97), the Little River catwalk gives anglers access to the full breadth of Little River. The catwalk runs alongside the highway, but a concrete barrier wall and fencing makes for safe bridge fishing.

The fishing: Anglers should try a fiddler crab or shrimp fished on bottom. Try fishing the bait right beside the bridge piers and pilings for action from several different species. If spotted seatrout are the target, autumn is a good time to catch them around the bridges on the Intracoastal Waterway.

GA~G grid: 63, F-7

General information: All anglers must meet Georgia licensing requirements and standard Georgia saltwater creel and length limits apply; refer to the *Georgia Sport Fishing Regulations* pamphlet for more information.

The Little River catwalk is wheelchair accessible. The tide (Savannah River Entrance) correction (Hr:Min) for the nearby Mackay River (ICWW) is Low +1:21, High +0:54, and Feet +0.0.

Nearest camping: The nearest public campground is Glynn County's Blythe Island Regional Park and Campground (not shown on area covered by site map) 13 miles away. RV, tent, and primitive sites are available. The Jekyll Island Campground is 16 miles away on Jekyll Island. Several private RV parks and campgrounds are also available in the Brunswick area.

Directions: From Interstate 95 exit 38, north of Brunswick, travel south on Georgia Spur 25 (North Golden Isles Expressway) 4.3 miles to U.S. Highway 17. Turn right on US 17 and travel 1.7 miles to the Torras Causeway leading to Saint Simons Island. Turn left (east) on Torras Causeway and travel 2.4 miles to the Little River bridge. Parking area on the right before crossing the bridge.

For more information: Contact the Coastal Resources Division Office in Brunswick. For camping information, contact the Blythe Island Regional Park and Campground, Jekyll Island Campground, or the Brunswick and the Golden Isles Visitors Bureau.

97 Mackay River at Saint Simons

See map on page 323

Key species: croaker, flounder, whiting, sheepshead.

Overview: Located off the causeway crossing the Intracoastal Waterway to Saint Simons Island, the Mackay River access point offers anglers two fishing piers and a boat ramp.

Best way to fish: pier.

Best time to fish: most species highly seasonal.

Description: Just a short distance down the road from the Little River catwalk (Site 96), a paved double-lane boat ramp and two fishing piers give anglers good access to the Mackay River and Saint Simons Sound. The roadbed of the old Saint Simons Island causeway is used to give shoreline anglers easy access to both sides of the river.

The fishing: Anglers fishing from the piers should try a fiddler crab or shrimp for bait. Use a standard fish-finder rig to fish on the bottom, or a float rig to cover the mid-depths. A jig and plastic shrimp tail can also be good. Try fishing the bait right beside the bridge piers and pilings, or cast out and retrieve the bait or lure at different depths until you discover what is effective that day. Spotted seatrout fishing is usually good in the fall and winter in the deeper water of the channels, and a jig is especially effective this time of year.

Although the angling for most species is seasonal, boating anglers can probably find any nearshore species caught along the Georgia coast in the waters of Saint Simons Sound or the tidal rivers and salt marsh.

GA~G grid: 63, F-8

General information: All anglers must meet Georgia licensing requirements and standard Georgia saltwater creel and length limits apply; refer to the *Georgia Sport Fishing Regulations* pamphlet for more information.

The Mackay River piers are wheelchair-accessible. The tide (Savannah River

There is a fishing pier on each side of the Mackay River.

Entrance) correction (Hr:Min) for the Mackay River (ICWW) is Low +1:21, High +0:54, and Feet +0.0.

Nearest camping: The nearest public campground is at Glynn County's Blythe Island Regional Park and Campground (not shown on area covered by site map) 13 miles away. RV, tent, and primitive sites are available. The Jekyll Island Campground is 16 miles away on Jekyll Island. Several private RV parks and campgrounds are also available in the Brunswick area.

Directions: Mackay River East Pier and boat ramp: From Interstate 95 exit 38, north of Brunswick, travel south on Georgia Spur 25 (North Golden Isles Expressway) 4.3 miles to U.S. Highway 17. Turn right on US 17 and travel 1.7 miles to the Torras Causeway leading to Saint Simons Island. Turn left (east) on Torras Causeway and travel 3.7 miles (includes crossing the Mackay River Bridge). The pier and boat ramp access road is 0.3 mile past the Mackay River Bridge on right side of Causeway. Turn right (U-turn) onto access road and drive back toward bridge.

For the Mackay River West Pier, follow the directions listed above but travel 2.8 miles on Torras Causeway to pier entrance on the right just before the Mackay River bridge.

For more information: Contact the Coastal Resources Division Office in Brunswick. For camping information, contact the Blythe Island Regional Park and Campground, Jekyll Island Campground, or the Brunswick and the Golden Isles Visitors Bureau.

98 Saint Simons Island Pier

See map on page 323

Key species: red drum, Spanish mackerel, flounder, shark, croaker, spot, yellowtail, others.

Overview: Found on Saint Simons Island, one of Georgia's fabled "Golden Isles," the pier offers anglers a chance at nearly any nearshore species.

Best way to fish: pier.

Best time to fish: April through October; most species seasonal.

Description: Saint Simons Island was the site of Georgia's first military outpost. Fort Frederica, now a national monument, was established in 1736 by General James Oglethorpe. In 1742, Oglethorpe's troops defeated Spanish invaders in the Battle of Bloody Marsh, fought in Saint Simons' coastal forests.

Rock-hard timber from live oak trees cut and milled on the island was used in many Revolutionary War–era warships, including the USS Constitution, better known to American school children as "Old Ironsides." During the plantation era, cotton was king on Saint Simons Island.

Saint Simons and the Golden Isles are popular Georgia vacation destinations. The island offers a little something for everyone with golf, shopping, beaches, fishing charters, and more.

The fishing: Since the pier is right on the open waters of Saint Simons Sound,

The Saint Simons Island Pier juts out far enough for anglers to catch big fish.

just about any species is liable to be in the area. Sharks, mackerel, whiting, stingrays, red drum, sheepshead, and many others are all available at times.

Pier fishing is a community affair. Talk to pier regulars to find out what is running and the best way to catch them. Shrimp, fiddler crabs, and cut bait are all good choices for bait. Present the bait on the bottom with a fish-finder or bottom rig.

Since the pier is on the big water, big fish are a possibility. Make sure your tackle is up to the task of fighting a big fish without being able to follow it with the boat.

GA~G grid: 63, F-8

General information: All anglers must meet Georgia licensing requirements and standard Georgia saltwater creel and length limits apply; refer to the *Georgia Sport Fishing Regulations* pamphlet for more information.

The Saint Simons Island pier is wheelchair accessible. Bait, fishing gear, ice, and food and drinks are available. Restrooms, a fish cleaning station, picnic tables, and a playground are also present.

The tide (Savannah River Entrance) correction (Hr:Min) for the Saint Simons Light is Low +0:26, High +0:21, and Feet -0.3.

Nearest camping: The nearest public campground is at Glynn County's Blythe Island Regional Park and Campground (not shown on area covered by site map) about 17 miles away. RV, tent, and primitive sites are available. The Jekyll Island Campground is 20 miles away on Jekyll Island. Several private RV parks and campgrounds are also available in the Brunswick area.

Directions: From Interstate 95 exit 38, north of Brunswick, travel south on Georgia Spur 25 (North Golden Isles Expressway) 4.3 miles to U.S. Highway 17. Turn right on US 17 and travel 1.7 miles to the Torras Causeway leading to Saint Simons Island. Turn left (east) and travel 4.4 miles on the Torras Causeway to New Sea Island Drive. Turn right on New Sea Island Drive and travel 0.2 mile to King's Way Drive. Turn left and travel 2.2 miles on Kings Way Drive to Mallory Street. Turn right on Mallory Street and travel 0.2 mile to the pier.

For more information: Contact the Coastal Resources Division Office in Brunswick. For camping information, contact the Blythe Island Regional Park and Campground, Jekyll Island Campground, or the Brunswick and the Golden Isles Visitors Bureau.

99 Jekyll Island

Key species: red drum, spotted seatrout, Spanish mackerel, flounder, shark, croaker, spot, yellowtail, others.

Overview: Jekyll Island is one of Georgia's "Golden Isles." The island offers surf fishing, a drive-up boat launch, and three fishing piers.

Best way to fish: pier, boat, surf.

Best time to fish: most species highly seasonal.

Description: A group of wealthy families purchased Jekyll Island in 1886 for a private winter retreat. By 1900, The Jekyll Island Club membership rolls included the names Rockefeller, Morgan, Crane, Pulitzer, and Gould, and it was said the club's membership controlled one-sixth of the world's wealth. The events of the 1930s eventually led to the Club's closing in 1942, and in 1947 the State of Georgia bought Jekyll Island.

Jekyll Island is a favorite with vacationers. Beaches, tennis, golf, dining, shopping, and other activities all draw visitors to the island.

The fishing: Fishing opportunities include a large fishing pier on Saint Simons Sound, a fishing pier on Jekyll Creek, a drive-up launch ramp on the west side of the island, miles of public beaches, and a footbridge over Clam Creek. Since the main pier is right on the open waters of Saint Simons Sound, just about any species is liable to be in the area. Sharks, mackerel, whiting, stingrays, red drum, sheepshead, and many others are all available at times.

Pier and surf fishing is a community affair. Talk to regulars to find out what is running and the best way to catch them. Shrimp, fiddler crabs, and cut bait are all good choices for bait. Try presenting the bait on the bottom with a fish-finder or bottom rig.

When fishing the surf or an open-water pier, make sure your tackle is ready for anything. Big fish are found in big water, and you never know what may strike next. Several state record fish have been caught from the Jekyll Island pier.

GA~G grid: 63, G-8

General information: All anglers must meet Georgia licensing requirements

Jekyll Island

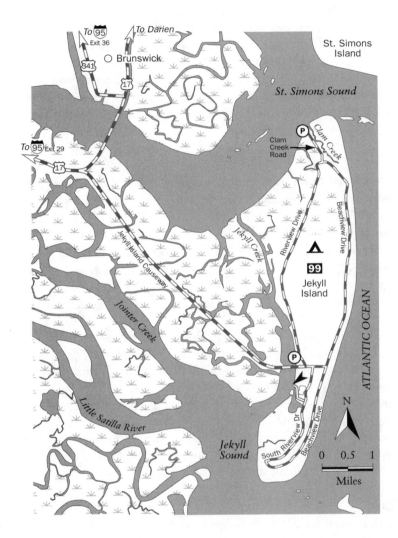

and standard Georgia saltwater creel and length limits apply; refer to the *Georgia Sport Fishing Regulations* pamphlet for more information.

The Jekyll Island pier is wheelchair accessible, the Clam Creek footbridge and Jekyll Creek pier are not. Restrooms and picnic tables are present at the Jekyll Island Pier and Clam Creek footbridge. The public boat ramp on Jekyll Island is a single-lane ramp. Food, lodging, and supplies are available on the island.

The tide (Savannah River Entrance) correction (Hr:Min) for Jekyll Point is Low +0:29, High +0:19, and Feet -0.7.

Nearest camping: Developed camping is available on the island.

Directions: To reach Jekyll Island, from Interstate 95 exit 29, which is south of Brunswick, travel north on U.S. Highway 17 for 5 miles to the Jekyll Island Causeway. Follow the causeway onto the island. Finding your way around the island is not difficult; refer to the site map to reach the area you want to fish.

For more information: Contact the Coastal Resources Division Office in Brunswick. For camping information, contact the Jekyll Island Campground.

100 Crooked River State Park

Key species: red drum, spotted seatrout, flounder, croaker, spot, yellowtail.

Overview: A 500-acre State Park on the south bank of the Crooked River near Cumberland Sound.

Best way to fish: boat, bank.

Best time to fish: April through October; most species seasonal.

Description: This State Park is popular with anglers and other visitors to the Georgia coast. The park contains the ruins of the McIntosh Sugar Works, which was built around 1825. The mill was used as a starch factory during the Civil War.

The area offers some very good fishing for spotted seatrout and red drum. Boating anglers will like the improved launching facilities, and bank anglers have plenty of fishing opportunities also. Cumberland Island is easily reached by boat or sea kayak from Crooked River State Park.

The fishing: A boat or sea kayak is the best way to explore the river and surrounding waters. Red drum, flounder, and spotted seatrout are the most sought-after species, but others are available. Fish a shrimp or mud minnow around shell beds with a float rig for trout and red drum, or worked along the bottom for flounder. A lead-head jig and plastic shrimp tail is sometimes more productive than live bait.

GA~G grid: 71, B-6

General information: All anglers must meet Georgia licensing requirements and standard Georgia saltwater creel and length limits apply; refer to the *Georgia Sport Fishing Regulations* pamphlet for more information.

Restrooms and picnic tables are present. The boat ramp is a double-lane. Food, lodging, and supplies are within 8 miles in Saint Marys or along the Interstate 95 corridor.

The tide (Fernandina Beach Station) correction (Hr:Min) for Crooked River-Harrietts Bluff is Low +1:56, High +1:29.

Nearest camping: The park has 60 campsites and 11 cottages available for rent. Campsites with utilities are available, and the cottages come fully equipped.

Crooked River State Park • Cumberland Island National Seashore

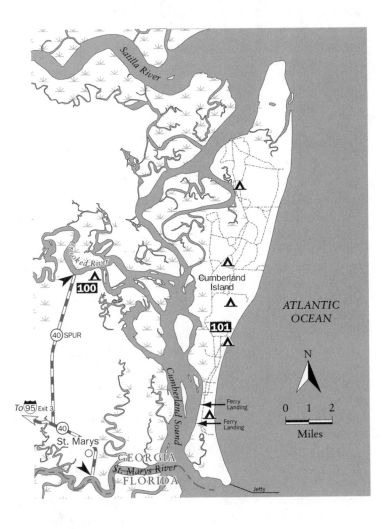

Directions: From Interstate 95 exit 3, just north of the Georgia–Florida border, travel east on Georgia Highway 40 for 3.6 miles to Kings Bay Road. Turn left on Kings Bay Road and travel 2.1 miles to Georgia Spur 40. Turn left and travel 4.2 miles to the boat ramp at the end of Georgia Spur 40.

For more information: For fishing information, contact the Coastal Resources Division Office in Brunswick. For camping information, contact the Crooked River State Park Superintendent's Office.

101 Cumberland Island National Seashore

See map on page 335

Key species: red drum, spotted seatrout, whiting, shark, tarpon.

Overview: Designated a National Seashore in 1972 to preserve the scenic, scientific, and historical value of Georgia's largest and most southerly barrier island, Cumberland Island offers great fishing for a variety of inshore species, especially big red drum.

Best way to fish: wading, surf, boat.

Best time to fish: year-round.

Description: Cumberland Island is 17.5 miles long and 1.5 to 3 miles wide. The island totals 33,900 acres, about half of which are marsh, mudflats, and tidal creeks. The history of the island spans more than 4,000 years and includes Native Americans, Spanish missions, English colonial forts, plantations, Revolutionary War heroes, and wealthy industrialists of the Gilded Age.

Cumberland Island has much to offer besides angling. Wildlife viewing opportunities abound; the island is especially known for its birding and wild horses. Tourists can visit the mansion ruins and the Greyfield Inn, retained by the Carnegie family and operated as an upscale retreat furnished just as it was at the turn of the century. Although a few private holdings still exist, the island is mostly undeveloped and has remained unchanged for the last 100 years. Cumberland Island is one of the best-preserved examples of the complex barrier island ecosystem.

The National Park Service manages the island to allow the public to gain an appreciation of the island while still preserving and protecting its treasures. Angling is well within the scope of the activities allowed, and a week-long angling and sightseeing trip to Cumberland Island would be a great way to escape, get back to nature, and rejuvenate your mind and spirit. The beaches and sounds around Cumberland Island offer great fishing for a variety of species depending on what is in season.

Making this site even more unique, the south end of Cumberland Island anchors a nearly 2.5 mile rock jetty that juts out into the Atlantic. This jetty and its sister on the Florida side of the sound help keep the channel open for nuclear submarines sailing from Kings Bay Submarine Base west of Cumberland Island. The subs usually travel the channel surfaced, and sightings are common.

The list of every species an angler could catch around Cumberland Island would be a long one. The area offers good-sized fish too; several Georgia record fish have been caught from the waters surrounding Cumberland Island.

The fishing: When water temperatures begin to rise in the spring, whiting move into the shallow Atlantic waters along Cumberland Island to spawn. Although whiting average only a couple of pounds, they are plentiful, taste great, and are easy to catch. Using a simple fish-finder rig consisting of an egg sinker, swivel, and 2/0 hook, bait up with a small piece of shrimp and simply toss the bait out and wait for a bite. Slowly dragging the bait along the bottom will sometimes produce more strikes.

May through August is the best time to catch spotted seatrout. The trout move in to spawn during this time, and the peak fishing months are June and July. Trout spawn along the beach and may be running in only 2 or 3 feet of water. A variety of baits will work, but live-bait favorites are live shrimp or mud minnows. Spoons or jigs are among the best artificials. Later in the year, the Cumberland Island jetty is a good spot to try for trout.

A variety of coastal shark species use the shallow waters in front of Cumberland Island as breeding and birthing grounds. So many sharks are in the area during spring and summer that catching one is simply a matter of having bait in the water. Any type of live or dead bait will work but menhaden and mullet are two local favorites. From a boat, drifting with a combination of free-lines and weighted down-lines is a good choice. From the beach, simply bait up, cast out, and wait.

Red drum move into the rivers and creeks behind Cumberland Island in October. A good place to find them is over mud and oyster bars feeding on shrimp, crabs, and mud minnows. During low tide, you can sometimes spot fish in just a foot of water. The best methods for catching red drum are fishing mud minnows or shrimp on the bottom or with a float. For artificial bait, a jig would be an excellent choice. During the rest of the year, especially in June and July, the jetty jutting out from the island's southern tip is a great place to fish with either live bait or jigs for big red drum.

Tarpon begin to arrive around Cumberland Island in July. Tarpon are one of the ocean's greatest sport fish with an awesome combination of leaping ability, strength, endurance, and just pure fight. Tarpon fishing is not for neophyte anglers; success requires some special equipment and tactics and a good knowledge of local waters.

Many other species can be caught from the rich waters around Cumberland Island. Bluefish and Spanish mackerel are common in the spring, flounder and jack crevalle in the summer, and sheepshead in the fall. Around the jetty, one never knows what will strike; nearly anything is possible.

GA~G grid: 71, B-7

General information: Visitation is limited to 300 people per day, and day use and camping fees are in effect. Reservations for camping and day-use trips are accepted up to 6 months in advance. Visitation is highest in March, April, May, and lowest in January. A ferry ride or private boat is required to reach the island. Boat ramps are available in Saint Marys or at nearby Crooked River State Park. The ferry schedule varies by season and reservations are accepted. No supplies are available on Cumberland Island, so you should take everything you need with you. Restrooms and drinking water are available at 4 locations on the island. Foot travel is the best way to explore the island. Bicycles are allowed in some areas, but are restricted from entering the designated-wilderness portion of the island. Visitors may encounter vehicles on the island. Island residents and their guests are permitted to drive vehicles on historic roadways, and park operations also require vehicles.

A visitor center is available on the mainland near the ferry dock in Saint Marys and on the island. Visitors hoping for more than a cursory look at the island should plan on a trip of at least two days.

Anglers fishing the waters around the island must meet Georgia licensing requirements and follow all applicable saltwater fishing regulations. Consult the *Georgia Sport Fishing Regulations* pamphlet for more information.

The tide (Fernandina Beach Station) correction (Hr:Min) for the Saint Marys Entrance (North Jetty) is Low -0:03, High -0:36 and for Saint Marys Low +0:45, High +0:38.

Nearest camping: Camping is allowed on Cumberland Island in designated areas with a reservation. The maximum stay is 7 days. Campers may choose between a developed campground or 4 primitive camping areas. The developed campground has restrooms, cold showers, and drinking water. Each campsite has a grill, fire ring, food cage, and picnic table. No facilities are available at the primitive camping areas and water should be treated; campfires are not allowed in the backcountry.

Directions: From Interstate 95 exit 3, just north of the Georgia–Florida border, travel east 9.3 miles on Georgia Highway 40 until the road ends at the Saint Marys waterfront and the Cumberland Island Visitor Center and ferry dock.

For more information: Contact the Cumberland Island National Seashore Office for reservations and information on island rules and regulations. For more information about Georgia saltwater fishing, contact the Coastal Resources Division.

102 Offshore Atlantic Ocean

Key species: amberjack, barracuda, dolphin, Atlantic sailfish, wahoo, snapper, black sea bass, bluefish, king mackerel, shark.

Overview: The fishing off Georgia's coast is very good. Anglers can find charter opportunities all along the Georgia coast. If you have your own boat, there are plenty of live bottoms, wrecks, and other destinations to explore.

Best way to fish: boat.

Best time to fish: seasonal depending upon target species and weather.

Description: Most offshore fishing is done around structure, natural and man-made. Live bottoms are rocky outcroppings on the ocean's floor that provide a solid footing for the growth of sponges, sea fans, corals, and other marine organisms. These areas are usually ancient shorelines that are now submerged. The reefs are excellent habitat for worms, crabs, and small reef fish. Schools of baitfish also find the reefs to their liking and the combination of food and shelter draws in the larger predatory fish. Live bottoms are scattered off the Georgia coast and most are found well offshore. Black sea bass, grouper, snapper, amberjack, barracuda, and mackerel are common in these areas.

Since most natural live bottoms require a long run to reach them, Georgia has built a number of artificial reefs closer in. Scrap tires, old vessels, and chunk concrete have been sunk to provide the substrate for a reef. Shortly after being placed in the water, a reef begins to form and the fish are drawn to the area. All artificial reefs built by the state are buoyed to aid anglers in locating them.

In 1984, the U.S. Navy placed eight combat aircraft training towers 30 to 40 nautical miles off the Georgia coast. The towers rise up to 150 feet above the ocean's surface and trespassing on them is forbidden. The towers attract baitfish and predators, including bluefish, tuna, amberjack, king mackerel, barracuda, dolphin, wahoo, and sailfish.

Other offshore areas that attract fish include wrecks, jetties, buoys, floating objects, drop-offs, and even changes in water color or tidal nodes and rips. Anything that is different from the surrounding area is going to attract fish.

The fishing: Finding fish in the vast expanses of the open ocean requires specialized knowledge and equipment. First and foremost, you'll need a seaworthy boat. There are plenty of charter boats along the Georgia coast. Unless you are an accomplished offshore angler and have the resources available to fish these areas, chartering a boat is about the only option. Some areas are close enough to shore for an experienced mariner to venture to.

For some species, natural trolling bait or artificials is effective. Fishing with live bait can be done while anchored or drifting using either a weighted rig to hold the bait at the desired depth or no weight at all to let the bait work near the surface. Chumming is commonly used along with this method. Casting natural baits or artificials can be an effective technique as well.Offshore fishing can be very exciting and strenuous. With a large fish on the line, not only is your equipment tested to the max, but also your body. A fight can last hours and finally end when the angler is simply too exhausted to continue. Offshore fishing is something every angler should experience to gain a true feel for the raw power of large ocean-going fish.

GA~G grid: 39,53,63,71

General information: Creel and size limits, seasons, and other regulations are in effect for offshore fish stocks. Some offshore areas may also have special restrictions. Since both state and federal regulations come into play depending on how far out you are fishing, you need to make sure you know the current regulations.

Nearest camping: There are several state parks along the Georgia coast near major ports that offer primitive and developed camping; some also offer cottages for rent.

Directions: Interstate 95 parallels the Georgia coast and allows easy access to any coastal area or port you wish to visit.

For more information: Contact the Coastal Resources Division Office in Brunswick. For camping information contact the Park Superintendent's Office at Skidaway Island, Fort McAllister, and Crooked River State Parks.

The following is a list of artificial reefs off the Georgia coast that should offer good fishing for the offshore angler. The Georgia Coastal Resources Division produces an excellent Georgia Offshore Fishing Guide that has a map and a comprehensive listing of Georgia's reefs and live bottoms.

Artificial Reef	GPS	LORAN
SAV Reef – 6 NM East of Tybee Island		
SAV Reef Buoy	31-55.261'/80-47.209'	45589.7/61305.6
90' Barge	31-54.370'/80-47.207'	45585.5/61310.5
90' Barge/40' Workboat	31-54.299'/80-47.229'	45585.4/61311.1
Concrete Culvert	31-55.042'/80-46.863'	45586.5/61303.6
Concrete Culvert	31-55.196'/80-47.142'	45588.7/61305.6
Concrete	31-55.051'/80-47.182'	45588.8/61306.7
KC Reef - 9.0 NM East of Wassaw Island		
KC Reef Buoy	31-50.810'/80-46.550'	45564.3/61324.2
Barge *Honey*	31-50.944'/80-46.290'	45563.7/61321.1
Sailboat *Jupiter*	31-50.211'/80-46.343'	45560.4/61325.6
Barge *Motherlode*	31-50.699'/80-46.533'	45563.9/61324.6
110' Barge *Olympic*	31-49.904'/80-46.260'	45558.6/61326.6
118' Dump Scow	31-50.502'/80-46.507'	45562.8/61325.5
95' Deck Barge	31-50.775'/80-46.015'	45561.2/61319.6
L Reef - 23 NM East of Ossabaw Island		
L Reef Buoy	31-45.498'/80-36.475'	45480.0/61263.6
M-60 Battle Tanks	31-44.902'/80-35.553'	45472.0/61258.7
M-60 Battle Tanks	31-44.938'/80-35.538'	45472.1/61258.3
M-60 Battle Tanks	31-44.928'/80-35.546'	45472.1/61258.4
M-60 Battle Tanks	31-45.133'/80-35.573'	45473.2/61257.7
M-60 Battle Tanks	31-45.325'/80-35.576'	45474.1/61256.4
M-60 Battle Tanks	31-45.319'/80-35.586'	45474.3/61256.7
M-60 Battle Tanks	31-45.515'/80-35.539'	45475.0/61255.2
M-60 Battle Tanks	31-45.492'/80-35.595'	45475.2/61255.7
Dredge *Henry Bacon*	31-45.385'/80-36.543'	45480.0/61264.7
Latex Barge	31-45.379'/80-36.700'	45480.9/61266.1
Pallet Balls	31-45.492'/80-34.858'	45471.0/61249.1
Pallet Balls	31-45.504'/80-34.942'	45471.5/61249.9
Pallet Balls	31-45.721'/80-34.960'	45472.8/61248.9
Sayler Barge	31-45.200'/80-36.596'	45479.4/61266.1
Tug *Delta Diamond*	31-44.948'/80-36.405'	45477.0/61265.8
Tug *Senasqua*	31-45.030'/80-36.721'	45479.3/61268.3
DUA Reef - 8.0 NM East of Ossabaw Island		
DUA Reef Buoy	31-46.769'/80-54.188'	45589.6/61414.8
Pallet Balls	31-47.442'/80-52.354'	45582.1/61394.7
Pallet Balls	31-47.390'/80-52.616'	45583.3/61397.3
Concrete (boxes/pipe)	31-46.990'/80-53.629'	45587.4/61408.7
Concrete (boxes/pipe)	31-47.104'/80-53.765'	45588.8/61409.3
Concrete (boxes/pipe)	31-47.397'/80-54.000'	45591.1/61409.2

Artificial Reef	GPS	LORAN
Concrete (pipe)	31-46.606'/80-53.178'	45582.8/61406.7
Concrete (pipe)	31-46.597'/80-53.475'	45584.5/61409.5
Concrete (pipe)	31-46.852'/80-53.327'	45584.9/61406.7
Concrete (pipe)	31-46.633'/80-53.753'	45586.4/61411.7
Concrete (pipe)	31-46.785'/80-53.850'	45587.7/61411.8
Concrete (pipe)	31-46.580'/80-54.250'	45589.0/61416.5

CCA Reef - 22 NM East of St. Catherines Island

CCA Reef Buoy	31-43.505'/80-41.144'	45496.7/61315.6
Flat Barge	31-43.180'/80-41.166'	45495.3/61317.8
Flat Barge w/Rubble	31-42.039'/80-41.241'	45489.9/61324.6
Talmadge Bridge debris	31-42.509'/80-41.110'	45491.5/61320.9
Talmadge Bridge debris	31-42.384'/80-41.267'	45491.7/61322.9
Talmadge Bridge debris	31-42.712'/80-41.089'	45492.4/61319.4
Talmadge Bridge debris	31-42.609'/80-41.269'	45492.9/61321.7
Talmadge Bridge debris	31-42.826'/80-41.246'	45493.8/61320.2
Talmadge Bridge debris	31-42.976'/80-41.112'	45493.9/61318.5
Tug *Matt Turecamo*	31-43.200'/80-40.170'	45489.6/61308.8

CAT Reef - 7.0 NM East of St. Catherines Island

CAT Reef Buoy	31-40.080/80-58.555'	45582.3/61489.8
Concrete (boxes/pipe)	31-39.272'/80-57.755'	45573.4/61486.9
Concrete (boxes/pipe)	31-39.490'/80-58.070'	45576.5/61488.7
Concrete (boxes/pipe)	31-39.671'/80-58.063'	45577.3/61487.3
Concrete (boxes/pipe)	31-39.951'/80-58.325'	45580.4/61488.4
Pallet Balls	31-39.425'/80-56.803'	45568.3/61477.6
Pallet Balls		45568.8/61476.5
Pallet Balls	31-39.700'/80-56.928'	45570.6/61477.3
Pallet Balls	31-39.909'/80-57.056'	45572.4/61477.2

J Reef - 17.4 NM East of St. Catherines Island

J Reef Buoy	31-36.110'/80-47.470'	45495.5/61411.7
Buoy Tender *Sagebrush*	31-36.600'/80-47.800'	45500.0/61412.0
Ferry Boat *Janet*	31-36.298'/80-47.575'	45497.1/61411.7
Liberty Ship *A.B. Daniels* (main)	31-36.207'/80-47.750'	45497.8/61413.8
Liberty Ship *A.B. Daniels* (stern)	31-36.260'/80-47.680'	45497.5/61412.8
M-60 Battle Tanks	31-35.990'/80-48.300'	45499.8/61419.9
M-60 Battle Tanks	31-35.993'/80-48.352'	45500.0/61420.2
M-60 Battle Tanks	31-35.924'/80-48.777'	45502.2/61424.3
M-60 Battle Tanks	31-35.987'/80-48.728'	45502.3/61423.6
M-60 Battle Tanks	31-35.989'/80-48.982'	45503.8/61426.0
M-60 Battle Tanks	31-35.987'/80-48.996'	45504.0/61425.9
Tug *Elmira*	31-36.082'/80-47.673'	45496.0/61413.0

KTK Reef - 7.0 NM East of Blackbeard Island

KTK Reef Buoy	31-31.255'/81-01.596'	45555.5/61563.6
Debarking Drums	31-30.718'/81-00.530'	45546.0/61556.8
Debarking Drums	31-31.146'/81-00.863'	45550.4/61557.4
M-60 Battle Tanks	31-30.788'/80-59.643'	45540.7/61548.2

Artificial Reef	GPS	LORAN
M-60 Battle Tanks	31-30.831'/80-59.614'	45541.1/61548.0
Pallet Balls	31-30.109'/81-01.136'	45546.4/61565.1
Pallet Balls	31-29.581'/81-01.194'	45543.8/61568.0
Pallet Balls	31-29.524'/80-59.353'	45544.7/61567.1
Pallet Balls	31-30.688'/81-01.175'	45559.9/61562.3
Concrete Rubble		45550.0/61561.9
Concrete Rubble	31-31.187'/81-01.152'	45552.2/61559.4
Steel Barge *Modena*	31-31.061'/81-00.132'	45545.3/61551.1

DW Reef - 70 NM East of Sapelo Island

Dump Scow *Turecamo*	31-21.500'/79-50.450'	

ALT Reef - 6.0 NM East of Little St. Simons Island

ALT Reef Buoy	31-18.649'/81-09.385'	45536.0/61696.5
40' Crew Boat	31-18.422'/81-09.180'	45533.5/61695.7
Concrete Rubble	31-18.486'/81-09.159'	45533.7/61695.3
Concrete Rubble	31-18.542'/81-09.195'	45534.3/61695.3
Pallet Balls	31-18.467'/81-07.623'	45523.7/61681.6
Pallet Balls	31-18.210'/81-08.120'	45525.4/61687.3

DRH Reef - 15 NM East of Little St. Simons Island

DRH Reef Buoy	31-17.896'/80-58.889'	45465.6/61606.7
Pallet Balls	31-17.422'/80-58.043'	45457.5/61601.6
Pallet Balls	31-17.815'/80-58.060'	45459.8/61599.7
John Bird wreck	31-17.232'/80-58.765'	45461.0/61608.9

F Reef - 9 NM East of St. Simons Island

Reef Buoy	31-05.937'/81-12.808'	45485.4/61787.7
Concrete (rubble)	31-06.281'/81-11.933'	45481.5/61778.2
LCM	31-05.939'/81-12.255'	45481.7/61782.7
LCM	31-05.926'/81-12.483'	45483.0/61784.6
Pallet Balls	31-05.463'/81-12.286'	45479.0/61785.2
Pallet Balls	31-05.445'/81-12.847'	45482.6/61790.2
Small Boat Molds	31-06.223'/81-11.852'	45480.9/61777.8
Small Boat Molds	31-06.255'/81-12.231'	45483.4/61781.1
Small Boat Molds	31-06.242'/81-12.480'	45484.8/61783.4

SFC Reef - 6.0 NM ESE of R2 Buoy

SFC Reef Buoy	31-00.386'/81-02.405'	45384.5/61721.7
M-60 Battle Tanks	31-00.483'/81-02.283'	45384.2/61720.1
M-60 Battle Tanks	31-00.224'/81-02.890'	45386.5/61726.5
M-60 Battle Tanks	31-00.240'/81-02.874'	45386.6/61726.3
Landing Craft	30-59.862'/81-02.298'	45380.6/61723.2
Landing Craft	30-59.928'/81-02.308'	45381.1/61722.9

G Reef - 23 NM East of Cumberland Island

G Reef Buoy	30-58.247'/80-58.804'	45348.4/61700.1
Liberty Ship *E.S. Nettleton*	30-58.704'/80-58.562'	45349.6/61695.7
M-60 Battle Tanks	30-59.215'/80-57.923'	45348.8/61688.2
M-60 Battle Tanks	30-59.224'/80-57.934'	45349.0/61688.1

Artificial Reef	GPS	LORAN
M-60 Battle Tanks	30-59.365'/80-58.583'	45353.8/61693.0
M-60 Battle Tanks	30-59.361'/80-58.603'	45354.0/61693.4
Tug *Recife*	30-58.617'/80-58.034'	45345.9/61691.7
Tug *Tampa*	30-58.203'/80-58.804'	45348.0/61700.3
Utility *Boat*	30-58.198'/80-58.800'	45348.1/61700.3

A Reef - 7.0 NM East of Little Cumberland Island

Artificial Reef	GPS	LORAN
A Reef Buoy	30-55.918'/81-16.175'	45447.0/61862.6
Wharf Rubble	30-55.735'/81-15.205'	45439.3/61854.9
Wharf Rubble	30-55.797'/81-15.212'	45439.8/61854.8
Wharf Rubble	30-55.817'/81-15.999'	45445.1/61861.6
Wharf Rubble	30-55.686'/81-16.130'	45445.3/61863.3
Wharf Rubble	30-55.910'/81-15.987'	45445.7/61861.0
Wharf Rubble	30-55.964'/81-15.998'	45446.1/61860.9

C Reef - 13.5 NM East of Cumberland Island

Artificial Reef	GPS	LORAN
C Reef Buoy	30-50.747'/81-09.848'	45372.5/61829.7
East Concrete	30-50.681'/81-09.663'	45370.6/61828.8
M-60 Battle Tanks	30-51.701'/81-09.846'	45378.6/61825.6
M-60 Battle Tanks	30-51.714'/81-09.864'	45378.8/61825.8
North Concrete	30-50.962'/81-09.831'	45373.8/61828.8
South Concrete	30-50.531'/81-09.784'	45370.8/61830.2
Wreck *Esparta*	30-50.845'/81-10.171'	45375.2/61832.1

MRY Reef - approx. 18.5 NM East of Cumberland Island

Artificial Reef	GPS	LORAN
Pallet Balls	30-46.551'/81-05.759'	45318.6/61813.0
Pallet Balls	30-46.592'/81-06.254'	45322.4/61816.9
Pallet Balls	30-47.104'/81-05.798'	45322.5/61810.7
Pallet Balls	30-46.295'/81-06.757'	45323.6/61822.5
Pallet Balls	30-46.225'/81-07.091'	45325.6/61825.6
Pallet Balls	30-46.310'/81-07.172'	45326.5/61826.0

KBY Reef - 8.0 NM East of Cumberland Island

Artificial Reef	GPS	LORAN
KBY Reef Buoy	30-46.590'/81-17.309'	45395.7/61912.8
USN Wharf Rubble	30-47.092'/81-16.647'	45394.2/61904.9
USN Wharf Rubble	30-46.844'/81-16.874'	45394.4/61908.0
USN Wharf Rubble	30-47.405'/81-16.372'	45394.6/61901.6
USN Wharf Rubble	30-47.197'/81-16.686'	45395.5/61905.0
USN Wharf Rubble	30-47.465'/81-16.461'	45395.6/61901.7
USN Wharf Rubble	30-47.016'/81-16.907'	45396.0/61907.6
USN Wharf Rubble	30-46.829'/81-17.140'	45396.1/61910.4
USN Wharf Rubble	30-47.166'/81-16.846'	45396.3/61906.4
USN Wharf Rubble	30-47.041'/81-17.066'	45397.0/61908.9
USN Wharf Rubble	30-47.273'/81-16.865'	45397.2/61906.2
USN Wharf Rubble	30-47.120'/81-17.042'	45397.3/61908.3

Appendix

Northwest Georgia

Allatoona Lake
P.O. Box 487
Cartersville, GA 30120-0487
770-382-4700
770-386-0549 (lake levels and generation schedules)
www.sam.usace.army.mil/op/rec/allatoon/

Armuchee Ranger District
Chattahoochee National Forest
P.O. Box 465
LaFayette, GA 30728
706-638-1085
www.fs.fed.us/conf/

Arrowhead Campground
770-732-1130

Carters Lake
P.O. Box 96
Oakman, GA 30732-0096
706-334-2248
706-334-2906 (lake levels and generating schedules)
www.sam.usace.army.mil/op/rec/carters/

Cohutta Ranger District
Chattahoochee National Forest
401 Old Ellijay Road
Chatsworth, GA 30705
706-695-6736
www.fs.fed.us/conf/

Fort Mountain State Park
181 Fort Mountain Park Road
Chatsworth, GA 30705
706-695-2621
www.gastateparks.org

Atlanta West Campground
770-948-7302

Lock and Dam Park
181 Lock and Dam Road
Rome, GA 30161
706-234-5001

Wildlife Resources Division
P.O. Box 519
Calhoun, GA 30703-0519
706-629-1259

Rocky Mountain Recreation and Public Fishing Area
706-802-5087

Sweetwater Creek State Conservation Park
P.O. Box 816
Lithia Springs, GA 30122
770-732-5871
www.gastateparks.org

Tennessee Valley Authority
Hiwassee Watershed Team
221 Old Ranger Road
Murphy, NC 28906
828-837-7395
800-238-2264 (lake levels and generation schedules)
www.lakeinfo.tva.gov

Toccoa Ranger District
Chattahoochee National Forest
6050 Appalachian Highway
Blue Ridge, GA 30513
706-632-3031
www.fs.fed.us/conf/

Toccoa Valley Campground
706-838-4317

Northeast Georgia

Brasstown Ranger District
Chattahoochee National Forest
P.O. Box 9
Blairsville, GA 30512
706-745-6928
www.fs.fed.us/conf/

Chattooga Ranger District
Chattahoochee National Forest
200 Highway 197 N
P.O. Box 1960
Clarkesville, GA 30523
706-754-6221
www.fs.fed.us/conf/

Georgia Mountain Fair Campground
706-896-4191

Hart State Park
330 Hart State Park Road
Hartwell, GA 30643
706-376-8756
www.gastateparks.org

Hartwell Lake and Powerplant
Office of the Project Manager
P.O. Box 278
Hartwell, GA 30643-0278
706-856-0300
888-893-0678
www.sas.usace.army.mil/hartwell.htm

Lake Burton Hatchery
Wildlife Resources Division
706-947-3112

Lake Sidney Lanier
Resource Managers Office
P.O. Box 567
Buford, Geogia 30518
770-945-9531
770-945-1466 (water release information)
770-945-1467 (lake information)
www.sam.usace.army.mil/op/rec/lanier/

LaPrade's Marina
706-947-3312

Moccasin Creek State Park
Route 1, Box 1634
Clarkesville, GA 30545
706-947-3194
www.gastateparks.org

North Georgia Land Management Office
Route 1, Box 2556
Lakemont, GA 30552
706-782-4014
www.georgiapower.com/gpclake
888-GPC-LAKE

Wildlife Resources Division
2150 Dawsonville Hwy.
Gainesville, GA 30501
770-535-5498

Smithgall Woods–Dukes Creek
  Conservation Area
61 Tsalaki Trail
Helen, GA 30545
706-878-3087

Tallulah Gorge State Park
P.O. Box 248
Tallulah Falls, GA 30573
706-754-7970
www.gastateparks.org

Tallulah Ranger District
Chattahoochee National Forest
825 Hwy. 441 South
P.O. Box 438
Clayton, GA 30525
706-782-3320
www.fs.fed.us/conf/

Tennessee Valley Authority
Hiwassee Watershed Team
221 Old Ranger Road
Murphy, NC 28906
828-837-7395
800-238-2264 (lake levels and generation
  schedules)
www.lakeinfo.tva.gov

Toccoa Ranger District
Chattahoochee National Forest
6050 Appalachian Highway
Blue Ridge, GA 30513
706-632-3031
www.fs.fed.us/conf/

Towns County Chamber of Commerce
www.towns-county-chamber.org

Tugaloo State Park
1763 Tugaloo State Park Road
Lavonia, GA 30553
706-356-4362
www.gastateparks.org

Unicoi State Park
P.O. Box 997
Helen, GA 30545
706-878-3982
www.gastateparks.org

Vogel State Park
7485 Vogel State Park Road
Blairsville, GA 30512
706-745-2628
www.gastateparks.org

East Central Georgia

Bobby Brown State Park
2509 Bobby Brown State Park Rd.
Elberton, GA 30635
706-213-2046
www.gastateparks.org

Chattahoochee River National Recreation
Area
1978 Island Ford Parkway
Atlanta, Georgia 30350
770-399-8070

Wildlife Resources Division
2123 U.S. Hwy. 278, S.E.
Social Circle, GA 30025
770-918-6418

Elijah Clark State Park
2959 McCormick Highway
Lincolnton, GA 30817
706-359-3458
www.gastateparks.org

Hard Labor Creek State Park
P.O. Box 247
Rutledge, GA 30663
706-557-3001
www.gastateparks.org

J. Strom Thurmond Project
Operations Projects Manager's Office
Rt. 1, Box 12
Clarks Hill, SC 29821-9703
864-333-1100
800-533-3478
www.sas.usace.army.mil/thurmon2.htm

Lake Oconee/Sinclair Land Management
Office
125 Wallace Dam Road
Eatonton, GA 31024
706-485-8704
888-GPC-LAKE
www.georgiapower.com/gpclake

Lake Varner
Newton County Parks and Recreation
Department
770-784-2125

Lawrence Shoals Recreation Area
706-485-5494

McDuffie Public Fishing Area
706-595-1684

Mistletoe State Park
3723 Mistletoe Road
Appling, GA 30802
706-541-0321
www.gastateparks.org

Morgan Falls Dam (water release schedule)
888-660-5890

Oconee National Forest
1199 Madison Road
Eatonton, GA 31024
706-485-7110
www.fs.fed.us/conf/

Old Salem Recreation Area
Georgia Power
706-467-2850

Parks Ferry Recreation Area
Georgia Power
706-453-4308

Richard B. Russell Project Office
4144 Russell Dam Drive
Elberton, GA 30635
706-213-3400
800-944-7207
http://www.sas.usace.army.mil/rbruss.htm

Richard B. Russell State Park
2650 Russell State Park Road
Elberton, GA 30635
706-213-2045
www.gastateparks.org

Stone Mountain Park
P.O. Box 778
Stone Mountain, GA 30086
770-498-5690 (main office)
800-317-2006 (main office)
770-498-5600 (bait shop)
www.stonemountainpark.com

Thomson Office
Fisheries Section
Georgia Wildlife Resources Division
706-595-1619

West Central Georgia

Bartletts Ferry Land Management Office
1516 Bartletts Ferry Road
Fortson, GA 31808
706-322-0228
888-GPC-LAKE
www.georgiapower.com/gpclake

Blanton Creek Park
Georgia Power
706-643-7737

Charlie Elliott Wildlife Center
Wildlife Resources Division
543 Elliott Trail
Mansfield, GA 30055
770-784-3059

Columbus City Marina
706-323-0316

F. D. Roosevelt State Park
2970 Georgia Highway 190
Pine Mountain, GA 31822
706-663-4858
www.gastateparks.org

Flint River Outdoor Center
706-647-2633

Georgia Power Generation Schedules
706-321-3400

Goat Rock Marina
706-322-6076

Indian Springs State Park
678 Lake Clark Road
Flovilla, Georgia 30216
770-504-2277
www.gastateparks.org

Lake Jackson Land Management Office
180 Dam Road
Jackson, Georgia 30233
770-775-4753
888-GPC-LAKE
www.georgiapower.com/gpclake

Lake Oconee/Sinclair Land Management
  Office
125 Wallace Dam Road
Eatonton, GA 31024
706-485-8704
888-GPC-LAKE
www.georgiapower.com/gpclake

Manchester Office
Fisheries Section
Georgia Wildlife Resources Division
706-846-8448

Oconee National Forest
1199 Madison Road
Eatonton, GA 31024
706-485-7110
www.fs.fed.us/conf/

Rocky Creek Recreation Area
Georgia Power
912-453-0022

Sprewell Bluff State Park
740 Sprewell Bluff Road
Thomaston, GA 30286
706-646-6026
www.gastateparks.org

Tobesofkee Recreation Area
6600 Mosely Dixon Road
Macon, GA 31220
912-474-8770

West Point Lake
Project Management Office
706-645-2937
706-645-2929 (lake levels and generation
  schedules)
www.sam.usace.army.mil/op/rec/westpt/

Wildlife Resources Division
1014 Martin Luther King Blvd.
Fort Valley, GA 31030-6246
912-825-6151

Southwest Georgia

Chehaw Park
105 Chehaw Park Road
Albany, GA 31701
912-430-5275
chehaw@surfsouth.com

Georgia Veterans Memorial State Park
2459-A U.S. Highway 280 West
Cordele, GA 31015
912-276-2371
www.georgiastateparks.org

Lake Chehaw
Georgia Power Lake Information
888-GPC-LAKE
www.georgiapower.com/gpclake

Reed Bingham State Park
Box 394 B-1, Route 2
Adel, GA 31620
912-896-3551
www.georgiastateparks.org

Seminole Resource Management Office
P.O. Box 96
Chattahoochee, FL 32324
912-662-2001
912-662-2814 (lake level and generation
    schedule)
www.sam.usace.army.mil/op/rec/seminole/

Seminole State Park
Route 2
Donalsonville, GA 31745
912-861-3137
semipark@surfsouth.com
www.georgiastateparks.org

Wildlife Resources Division
2024 Newton Road
Albany, GA 31701-3576
912-430-4256

Walter F. George Natural Resource Site
    Office
Route 1, Box 176
Fort Gaines, GA 31751-9722
912-768-2516 (office)
912-768-2424 (generation schedule)
www.sam.usace.army.mil/op/rec/wfg

Southeast Georgia

Banks Lake National Wildlife Refuge
c/o Okefenokee National Wildlife Refuge
Route 2 Box 3330
Folkston, GA 31357
912-496-7836
okefenokee.fws.gov

Deen's Campground
912-367-2949

Dodge County Public Fishing Area
912-374-6765

Evans County Public Fishing Area
912-739-1139

Folkston Chamber of Commerce
Folkston, GA 31537
912-496-2536

George L. Smith State Park
P.O. Box 57
Twin City, GA 30471
912-763-2759
www.gastateparks.org

Gordonia–Alatamaha State Park
P.O. Box 1039
Reidsville, GA 30453
912-557-7744
www.gastateparks.org

Laura S. Walker State Park
5653 Laura Walker Road
Waycross, GA 31503
912-287-4900
www.gastateparks.org

Metter Office
Fisheries Section
Georgia Wildlife Resources Division
912-685-6424

Okefenokee National Wildlife Refuge
Route 2 Box 3330
Folkston, GA 31357
912-496-7836
okefenokee.fws.gov

Paradise Public Fishing Area
Route 1 Box 68
Enigma, GA 31749
912-533-4792

Wildlife Resources Division
108 Darling Avenue
Waycross, GA 31501
912-285-6094

Stephen C. Foster State Park
Route 1, Box 131
Fargo, GA 31631
912-637-5274
www.gastateparks.org

Coastal Georgia

Altamaha Fish Camp
912-264-2342

Beards Bluff Camp Ground (formerly
    Adamson's Fish Camp)
912-654-3632

Blythe Island Regional Park & Camp-
    ground
6616 Blythe Island Highway, SR303
Brunswick, GA 31525
912-261-3805
800-343-7855

Brunswick and the Golden Isles Visitors
    Bureau
4 Glynn Avenue
Brunswick, GA 31520
912-265-0620
www.bgivb.com
bgivb@technonet.com

Wildlife Resources Division
22814 Highway 144
Richmond Hill, GA 31324
912-727-2112

Coastal Resources Division
One Conservation Way, Suite 300
Brunswick, GA 31520-8687
912-264-7218

Crooked River State Park
3092 Spur 40
St Marys, GA 31558
912-882-5256
www.gastateparks.org

Cumberland Island N.S.
P. O. Box 806
Saint Marys, GA 31558
912-882-4336 (information)
912-882-4335 (reservations)
cuis_information@nps.gov
www.nps.gov/cuis/

Fort McAllister State Historic Park
3894 Fort McAllister Road
Richmond Hill, GA 31324
912-727-2339
www.gastateparks.org

Fort Stewart Outdoor Recreation Center
912-767-2717

Pass and Permit Office
912-767-5032
912-767-0202 (automated check-in
    number)

Jekyll Island Campground
North Beachview Drive
Jekyll Island, GA 31527
912-635-3021

McIntosh County Chamber of Commerce
912-437-4192

Pat's Baithouse
912-588-9222

River's End Campground and RV Park
P.O. Box 988
Tybee Island, Georgia 31328
912-786-5518
800-786-1016
riversend1@aol.com
www.tybeeisland.com/riversend/index.htm

Skidaway Island State Park
52 Diamond Causeway
Savannah, GA 31411-1102
912-598-2300
www.gastateparks.org

Southeast Region
Wildlife Resources Division
108 Darling Avenue
Waycross, GA 31501
912-285-6094

Tybee Island Information
www.tybeeisland.com

Tybee Island Visitor Center
912-786-5444

Map Sources

Detailed Reservoir Contour Maps

Kingfisher Maps, Inc.
110 Liberty Drive #100
Clemson, SC 29631
800-326-0257

Atlantic Mapping
P.O. Box 7391
Marietta, GA 30065
770-426-5768

TVA Lake Maps (several themes available)

Tennessee Valley Authority
HB1A
1101 Market Street
Chattanooga, TN 37402-2801
615-751-MAPS

Chattahoochee River National Recreation Area

National Park Service
RBR Federal Building
75 Spring Street SW
Atlanta, GA 30303
404-331-3946

Topographic Maps

GA DNR - Geological Survey Branch
Agriculture Building, Room 406A
19 MLK Jr. Drive
Atlanta, GA 30334
404-656-3214

County Maps
(excellent large-scale detailed maps of county road system and other features)

Georgia DOT – County Map Sales
2 Capitol Square
Atlanta, GA 30334
404-656-5336

Georgia GIS Data Clearinghouse (wide variety of on-line maps, including DOT county maps)
gis.state.ga.us/emaps/dotmaps/

Wildlife Resources Division
(a variety of useful maps at no charge; see the *Georgia Sport Fishing Regulations* pamphlet for a listing of what is available)

Department of Natural Resources–
Wildlife Resources Division
    Fisheries Management Section
2070 U.S. Hwy 278 SE
Social Circle, GA 30025
770-918-6418

Corps of Engineers Lakes

Contact the reservoir's Resource Manager's Office for what is available. You will find these listings in the Appendix.

USDA Forest Service Maps
(a variety of excellent maps of National Forest land in Georgia)

USDA Forest Service
1755 Cleveland Highway
Gainesville, GA 30501-3571
www.fs.fed.us/conf/maporder.htm

Index

About the Author

A fisheries biologist by occupation, and a freelance writer by avocation, Kevin Dallmier has published more than 45 magazine articles on fish and fishing in Georgia. Mr. Dallmier is a resident of northwest Georgia, and spends most of his spare time in pursuit of anything with fins.

FALCON GUIDES ® Leading the Way™

www.Falcon.com

Since 1979, Falcon® has brought you the best in outdoor recreational guidebooks. Now you can access that same reliable and accurate information online.

❏ <u>Browse our online catalog</u> for the latest Falcon releases on hiking, climbing, biking, scenic driving, and wildlife viewing as well as our Insiders' travel and relocation guides. Our online catalog is updated weekly.

❏ A <u>Tip of the Week</u> from one of our guidebooks or how-to guides. Each Monday we post a new tip that covers anything from how to cross a rushing stream to reading contour lines on a topo map.

❏ A chance to <u>Meet our Staff</u> with photos and short biographies of Falcon staff.

❏ <u>Outdoor forums</u> where you can exchange ideas and tips with other outdoor enthusiasts.

❏ Also <u>Falcon screensavers and panoramic photos</u> of spectacular destinations.

And much more!

Plan your next outdoor adventure at our web site. Point your browser to www.Falcon.com and get FalconGuided!

FALCON®